THE KALEVALA

THE

COMPILED BY

A Prose Translation with Foreword and Appendices by

CAMBRIDGE, MASSACHUSETTS
AND LONDON, ENGLAND

KALEVALA

or *Poems of the Kaleva District*

ELIAS LÖNNROT

FRANCIS PEABODY MAGOUN, JR.

HARVARD UNIVERSITY PRESS

Library of Congress Catalog Card Number 63-19142

ISBN 0-674-50010-5 (paper)
Printed in the United States of America

Book design by David Ford

CONTENTS

THE KALEVALA

APPENDICES

ILLUSTRATIONS

The device on the title page, the square (or concentric squares) with externally looped corners, is known in Finnish as *hannunvaakuna*, in Swedish as *Sankt Hans vapen* (St. Hans's arms). A favorite decorative motif in Finland today, used also in eastern Karelia and Estonia, it was formerly a common magic and protective sign carved on buildings and objects to safeguard them. In Sweden, too, cattle were protected by it against wizards and ill-disposed persons, and in Norway of old on Christmas Eve it was drawn with pine tar on the doors of houses. The design is found in medieval romanesque carvings, and earlier it occurs on Coptic textiles in Egypt and as far back as the eighth century B.C. on Greek vases.

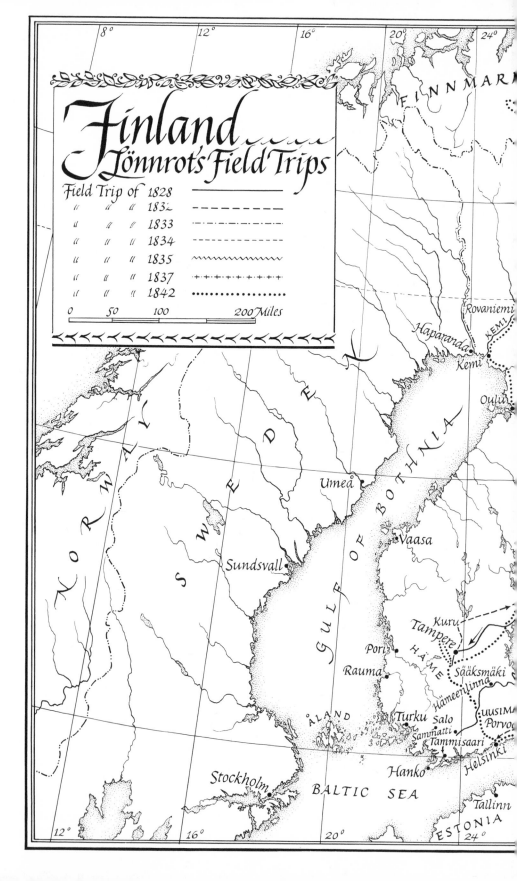

Finland
Lönnrot's Field Trips

Field Trip of	1828	————————
" " "	1832	– – – – – –
" " "	1833	– · – · – · –
" " "	1834	— — — —
" " "	1835	wwwwwwww
" " "	1837	+ + + + + + +
" " "	1842	·············

0   50   100   200 Miles

FINNMARK

NORWAY

SWEDEN

GULF OF BOTHNIA

Rovaniemi
Haparanda
KEMI
Kemi
Oulu

Umeå

Vaasa

Sundsvall

Kuru
Tampere
Pori
HÄME
Rauma
Sääksmäki
Hämeenlinna
ÅLAND
Turku Salo
UUSIMAA
Sammatti   Porvoo
Tammisaari
Hanko   Helsinki

Stockholm   BALTIC SEA

Tallinn

ESTONIA

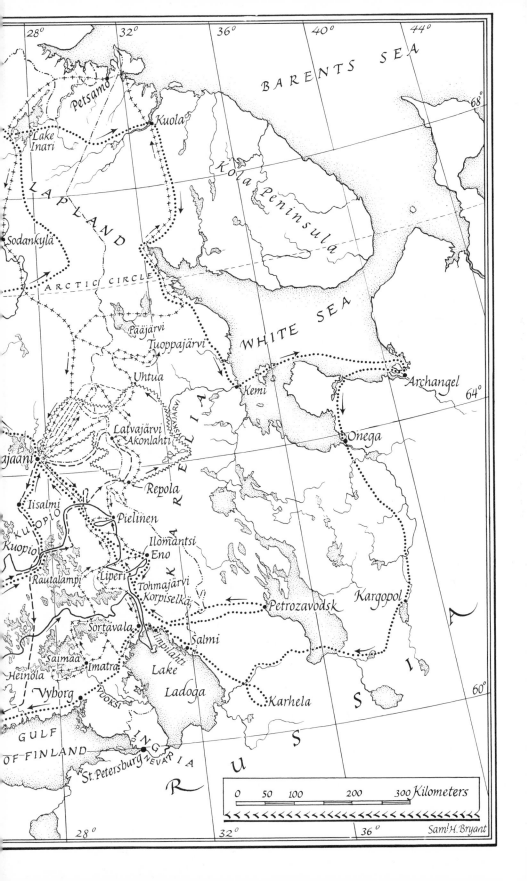

FOREWORD

Again and again the *Kalevala* has been described as the national heroic epic of the Finnish people, a description which, at least outside Finland, has tended to do the work a certain disservice by raising expectations that the reader is not likely to find fulfilled, regardless of what else he may find that is richly rewarding at a poetical, folkloristic, or ethnographic level. Any talk about a national heroic epic is bound to evoke thoughts of the Greek *Iliad* and *Odyssey*, the Old French *Chanson de Roland*, or the Middle High German *Nibelungenlied*, all of which possess a more or less unified and continuously moving plot with actors who are wealthy aristocratic warriors performing deeds of valor and displaying great personal resourcefulness and initiative, often, too, on a rather large stage. The *Kalevala* is really nothing like these. It is essentially a conflation and concatenation of a considerable number and variety of traditional songs, narrative, lyric, and magic, sung by unlettered singers, male and female, living to a great extent in northern Karelia in the general vicinity of Archangel. These songs were collected in the field and ultimately edited into a book by Elias Lönnrot, M.D. (1802–1884), in two stages. The first version appeared in 1835 and is now known as the *Old Kalevala*; it contained about half the material in the 1849 edition here translated. For the many poems added to this 1849 *Kalevala*, now the canonical version, Dr. Lönnrot was indebted to a younger song-collector, David E. D. Europaeus (1820–1884).

Lönnrot's title *Kalevala* is a name rare in the singing tradition; it describes a completely legendary region of no great extent, and is rendered here "the Kaleva District." The personal name Kaleva upon which the local name is based refers to a shadowy background figure of ancient Finnish poetic legend, mentioned in connection with assumed descendants and with a few nature or field names. The action, like that of the Icelandic family sagas, is played on a relatively small stage, centering on the Kaleva District and North Farm (these are discussed in the Glossary). The actors are in effect Finno-Karelian peasants of some indefinite time in the past who rely largely on the practice of magic to carry out their roles. Appearing at a time when there was little or no truly bellelettristic Finnish literature, the *Kalevala* unquestionably—and most understandably —became a source of great satisfaction and pride to the national consciousness then fast developing among the Finns, who had been growing restive under their Russian masters. To some extent the *Kalevala* thus became a rallying point for these feelings, and permitted and in a measure justified such exultant statements as "Finland can [now] say for itself: I, too, have a history!" (*Suomi voi sanoa itselleen: minullakin on historia!*).

Lönnrot's own comments in his prefaces (see Appendix I) make clear that one of his chief aims was to create for Finnish posterity a sort of poetical museum of ancient Finno-Karelian peasant life, with its farmers, huntsmen and fishermen, seafarers and sea-robbers, the latter possibly faint echoes from the Viking Age, also housewives, with social and material patterns looking back no doubt centuries—all reflecting a way of life that was, like the songs themselves, already in Lönnrot's day destined for great changes if not outright extinction. Thus, from Lönnrot's point of view the many sequences of magic charms and wedding lays, at times highly disruptive to the main narrative, are for what they tell of peasant beliefs and domestic life quite as significant as the narrative songs about the Big Three—Väinämöinen, Ilmarinen, and Lemminkäinen.

Owing to the special character of its compilation or concatenation, the *Kalevala* possesses no particular unity of style apart from the general diction of the Karelian singers and the indispensable ubiquitous traditional formulas discussed below. Comprising miscellaneous materials collected over many years from many singers from all over Karelia and some bordering regions, these poems range in style and tone from the lyrically tragical, as in Poem 4, to almost sheer horseplay, as in Poem 3; some are poems of warfare, while a number consist of magic incantations and magic charms. Among the most interesting, though perhaps superficially pedestrian, are the so-called "Wedding Lays" (Poems 21–25), with their keen, detailed observations on the daily life of the Karelian peasant. All call for quite varied styles in any English rendering.

The digests at the beginnings of the poems are Lönnrot's and were written in prose. Lönnrot is also the artless composer of Poem 1, lines 1–110, and Poem 50, lines 513–620; both these passages are pure flights of Lönnrot's fancy, and, despite a semblance of autobiography, bear no relation to the author's life.

On reading the Kalevala. In reading a new poem or a sequence of poems it is normal to begin at the beginning and read straight ahead, but in the case of the *Kalevala* this natural procedure has little to recommend it, since in a general way the present order of the poems is quite arbitrary, differing considerably, for example, from that of Lönnrot's 1835 *Old Kalevala.* Instead of starting with Poem 1 and reading through to the end, the reader is likely to derive greater satisfaction by beginning with some single story cycle—say, the Lemminkäinen stories (Poem 11 and following); though not in sequence, these can easily be picked out from the table of contents. One might then pass on to the Ilmarinen stories and to those dealing with Kullervo. The Väinämöinen poems form a somewhat miscellaneous group, and Väinämöinen keeps appearing here and there in a large number of poems dealing primarily with the other principals.

The many magic charms, inserted here and there, can usually be skipped on a first reading of the poem or poems in which they occur, though some of the shorter are entirely appropriate in their contexts and do not appreciably obstruct the flow of the narrative. Some of the more extensive charms and series of charms—for example, the Milk and Cattle Charms of Poem 32 and the Bear Charms of Poem 46—can be enjoyed when read out of context. In the table of contents the presence of charms in the poems is always indicated. For the translation of many additional Finnish magic charms (*loitsurunot*) the reader is referred to John Abercrombie, *The Pre- and Proto-historic Finns* . . . , II (London, 1898), 65–389.

There are surely many possible approaches to a first reading of the *Kalevala,* and the remarks in the preceding paragraphs should be taken only as the suggestion of one person, proffered in the hope of making a first acquaintance with this remarkable work a greater pleasure and more meaningful than the head-on approach. I shall now turn to certain matters characteristic of the style and structure of *Kalevala* verse, matters which also have considerable bearing on the manner of translation.

The style adopted here. Most translators of the *Kalevala* have imposed on themselves a heavy burden by attempting to reproduce or recapture something of the spirit of the original meter. In a strict sense of the word the "meter" cannot be reproduced in English, since Finnish is quantitative and English is a nonquantitative language; nevertheless a trochaic, four-beat, mainly eight-syllable line can be reproduced, though inevitably with the incredibly monotonous effect familiar to the many children who have read Longfellow's *Song of Hiawatha* (1855), itself considerably influenced by a German verse translation of the *Kalevala*. More unfortunate than this rhythmical monotony is the highly restrictive nature of the measure, which allows a translator almost no latitude for rendering adequately or fully many verses of the original. And if the translator, as is often the case, also makes use of alliteration, so characteristic of the original, though often artificial in its effect, he finds himself even more restricted in his rendering or in his choice of words.

In the present prose translation, which aims to render the original as literally as possible within the limits of idiomatic English, the translator is freed of all such restraints, and is in a position to render the verses as exactly and completely as his competence allows. There can be no excuse for any significant departure from the original text, and such departures as may occur can only be put down to a lack of comprehension on the translator's part. Once prose has been settled on as the medium of translation, many questions arise concerning the kind of prose to be used, the tone to be adopted. Here a simple, straightforward, and dignified language seems to be in order, with a minimal use of bookish words or exalted language and without slang, though in many dialogues a thoroughly colloquial idiom seems appropriate. In many respects the translation style used here recalls that used by the late A. H. Krappe and myself in translating the *German Folk Tales* (*Kinder-und Hausmärchen*) collected and edited by Jakob and Wilhelm

Grimm (Carbondale, Ill., 1960), and a similar style would also be suitable in translating the Icelandic family sagas. It is hoped that this approach to the present task, insofar as it has been fulfilled, will permit the reader to enjoy the *Kalevala* in a more natural atmosphere than seems possible in a versified rendering.

The oral poetry of unlettered singers. That all but some very small per cent of the verses in the *Kalevala* are the spontaneous product of native singers, mostly from Russian Karelia and to a considerable extent from the country around Archangel, nearly a century and a half ago, is apparent from a reading of Lönnrot's prefaces and from the encyclopedia articles in Appendix I. The songs were commonly recited to the accompaniment of a small harplike instrument, usually of five strings but sometimes more, called the *kantele,* here rendered "harp." The singers were of both sexes, old men predominating in the north around Archangel, young women in the south, in Ingria and the Karelian Isthmus. The *Kalevala* is, then, in essence the work of unlettered singers and belongs to the large category of so-called oral poetry.

The traditional, oral poetry of many peoples past and present has been amply studied, and the techniques which make possible spontaneous, improvised, and usually rapid composition of isochronous verse is well understood. The techniques of the Finno-Karelian singers differ no more from those of their Indo-European fellow-singers than do the latter among one another.[1]

The formula. The sole known device by which it is possible spontaneously to compose isochronous verse is the formula, which may be defined as a word or group of words, forming a just measure of verse, regularly employed under the same metrical conditions to express a given essential idea. Any use of formulas except for such occasional rhetorical purposes as a refrain is unknown among lettered poets, whether Aeschylus or T. S. Eliot, and the presence of any appreciable number of formulas consequently identifies

[1] For some basic bibliography touching on Homeric Greek and Serbo-Croatian oral poetry see my paper "The Oral-Formulaic Character of Anglo-Saxon Poetry," *Speculum,* XXVIII (1953), 446–464, and on Serbo-Croatian poetry Albert B. Lord, *The Singer of Tales* (Cambridge, Mass., 1960). On the possible Germanic (Old Swedish) influence on the development of the oldest traditional Finnish poetry see my paper "Conceptions and Images Common to Anglo-Saxon Poetry and the *Kalevala,*" *Britannica: Festschrift für Hermann M. Flasdieck* (Heidelberg, 1960), p. 181.

poetry as oral. All oral poetry, then, is made up of formulas; *siitä* 'then,' so commonly used as the first measure of a Karelo-Finnish verse, is a formula, though small and inconspicuous. Equally a formula is *sanan virkkoi, noin nimesi* 'uttered a word, spoke thus,' but large (a whole verse) and quite conspicuous. For a translator to keep track of all the small, inconspicuous formulas and always render them in the same way would be a Herculean task and would require the preparation of a vast indexing apparatus. It is feasible, however, to take note of the more conspicuous formulas and render them by the same English words on each occasion; and this I have tried to do.[2]

The traditional or stock epithet. A striking feature that Finnish traditional poetry shares with the Homeric and Serbo-Croatian poems, a feature not in, say, Anglo-Saxon oral poetry, is the traditional or stock epithet for a person or even a place or thing.[3] The use of the traditional epithet is highly developed in the Karelo-Finnish singing tradition and is amply represented in the *Kalevala.* The most famous epithet is, no doubt, "steadfast old" (*vaka vanha*), used of Väinämöinen; Väinämöinen is also often an "eternal sage" (*tietäjä iänikuinen*). Lemminkäinen is apt to be "reckless," as I have rendered the obsolete word *lieto,* Ilmarinen a "craftsman" (*seppo Ilmarinen*), also an "eternal smith" (*takoja iänikuinen*). Among place names, North Farm (*Pohjola*) tends to be "gloomy" (*pimeä*). Here and elsewhere it is clear that the demands of alliteration have influenced the singer's or the tradition's choice of epithets. In the Glossary of Proper Names I have tried to include with the names any epithets used with them, but an adequate treatment of the subject would require a special monograph or paper.

[2] Here I derived much help from August Engelbrekt Ahlqvist's *Sanasto* [Verbal Index], which though not quite complete nor 100 per cent accurate was often invaluable in following a formula through the text. I used the convenient reprint included in Väinö Kaukonen's *Elias Lönnrotin Kalevalan toinen painos* (Helsinki, 1956), esp. pp. 511–625 (including the proper names).

[3] For a very full discussion of such epithets, Parry's *epithètes fixes*, see Milman Parry, *L'Epithète traditionelle dans Homère* (Paris, 1928). In Anglo-Saxon poetry the nearest thing to this is the formula-phrase *mære théoden* 'illustrious prince' used with reference to a number of persons in the *Beowulf* songs. In imitation of Homer Virgil makes some use of the stock epithet, as Parry points out; and in imitation of the *Kalevala* Longfellow in *The Song of Hiawatha* uses such epithets as "Iagoo, the great boaster" and "Gitchie Manito, the mighty."

Parallelism and repetition. As used here, "parallelism," answering to the "variation" in Old Germanic verse, describes the device of repeating or substantially repeating the same idea or the same object in different terms in successive verses. In the *Kalevala* this device is pervasive, and is illustrated, for example, at the opening of Poem 33:

> 5   He uttered a word as he went along,
> kept saying while walking:
> "Woe is me, poor lad,
> woe the unfortunate lad.
> Now I have got into something,
> 10   got into the futile occupation
> of being the herdsman of a steer's tail,
> a tender of calves . . ."

Here it will be noticed that every second line to all intents and purposes repeats the thought of the line before. This device is common in Anglo-Saxon poetry, though to no such extent as in the Finnish tradition, which here, as in other compositional matters, may have been influenced by Germanic, perhaps specifically Old Swedish, singing.

Far less common than parallelism is outright repetition, as in Poem 33, lines 99–100, 220–221:

> "With what shall I now pay back the woman's mockery,
> 100   the woman's mockery, the girl's derision?"

Here the end of line 99 is repeated as the beginning of line 100, itself finished off by parallelism in its second half. Similarly:

> In this way Kullervo, son of Kalervo,
> 220   took vengeance on the girl's ridicule,
> the girl's ridicule, the woman's derision,
> paid the bad wife her wages.

Here one sees a criss-cross arrangement of parallelism and repetition, where the first part of line 221 repeats the last part of line 220, the last part of line 221 parallels the first part of the same line, and line 222 parallels line 220. Where there is repetition in the text I have aways repeated in the translation, just as in instances of variation I have sought for variation in the translation.

To print the short lines that correspond to the verses of the original in a single column would be uneconomical of space and would make for an unattractive type-page. Consequently, and partly in imitation of the scheme first used to my knowledge in the Centenary Commemorative Edition, *Kalevala—Uuden Kalevalan satavuotismuistopainos—1949* (Helsinki, 1949), and followed by Björn Collinder in his selective Swedish translation, *Kalevala: svensk Tolkning* (Helsinki, 1950), the lines have been printed in pairs, with line 2 following line 1, line 4 following line 3, and so on, but—as opposed to those texts—with a slight space as a break between the verses of the original:

5 He uttered a word as he went along,   kept saying while walking:
   "Woe is me, poor lad,   woe the unfortunate lad.
   Now I have got into something,   got into the futile occupation
11 of being the herdsman of a steer's tail,   a tender of calves . . ."

This arrangement tends, furthermore, graphically to emphasize parallelisms and repetitions where these occur.

The historical present. The historical present tense is, if not to quite the same extent as in the Old Icelandic sagas,[4] favored by the traditional singers, and it often alternates in a lively fashion with preterite forms, as, for example, in lines 151–152 and 277–278 of Poem 1:

She *keeps* weeping softly and continuously,   *uttered* a word, *spoke* thus

She *forms* little islands in the sea,   *produced* hidden reefs

As in translating the Icelandic sagas, one may at times feel tempted to level out these presents in favor of preterites; but the temptation is to be resisted as somewhat willfully doing away with a feature of the style that was surely felt by the singers, as by the Icelandic saga men, to add a pleasing vividness and variety.

Hypocorisms. Hypocorisms—that is, short names, nicknames, or pet names based on longer names, such as Nicky for Nicholas, Bill for William—are as common in Finnish as in English and are conspicuous in the *Kalevala.* Thus along with Lemminkäinen's epithet-name *Kaukomieli* 'man with a far-roving mind' there is a

---

[4] See Andreas Heusler, *Altisländisches Elementarbuch,* 3d ed. (Heidelberg, 1932), p. 128, § 412; cf. p. 129, § 416.

commonly used hypocorism *Kauko* 'far' formed by abbreviatory truncation. Here and in other similar cases I have only used the full form, since to retain short forms alongside of full forms could easily lead to confusion of identity—as would the Ted, Ned, and Eddie of an English original, all referring to one and the same Edward, if kept in a German translation and read by a German who knew no English nor anything about the makeup of English names.

Nonsense words. As in the Old Icelandic and Serbo-Croatian singing traditions, Finno-Karelian makes some use of nonsense words to fill out the meter. The favorite is a pleonastic or expletive measure-filling *on,* formally identical with *on* 'is,' but without meaning and of course never to be translated; this suggests a similar use of *um,* formally 'around,' and *of* 'from' by the Old Icelandic singers of verse of the Edda type.[5] Two other words seem often to be used very much like the pleonastic *on,* especially in the first measure of a verse, namely *itse* 'self' and *tuopa, tuop'on* (pleonastic) 'that (indeed),' and are but rarely translated. Of a quite different order is the coining of new non-words for the sake of maintaining rhythm in a verse or of producing a jingling effect. Such words are often modeled on the real word to which they are parallel. In the original these are striking and constitute a minor but definite feature, and these I have tried to imitate in translation. For example, one may note in Poem 47, lines 259, 279, 299, the repeated verse (and formula) *uiskenteli, kuiskenteli,* where *uiskennella* is a normal verb meaning "to swim about," but there is no word *kuiskennella.* Accordingly I have translated *kuiskenteli* by an English non-word, "wam about," and so in other such cases. In Poem 11, line 56, mention is made of Ingria (Finnish *Inkeri*), immediately echoed by the non-words *Penkeri, Pänkeri;* these are rendered by "Pengria, Pangria."

Pronunciation. While it is hardly feasible to give anything approaching a complete or precise account of the Finnish pronunciation of the proper names in the *Kalevala,* enough can perhaps be said or suggested to let the non-Finnish reader achieve a reasonable approximation of what a Finn might say. Syllable division is here marked by a hyphen.

[5] See Heusler, *Altisländisches Elementarbuch,* p. 41, § 41, § 125 and note.

The main stress, shown by an acute accent, is always on the first syllable, with a slighter, secondary stress, shown by a grave accent, on the third; these stresses are less strong than in the Germanic languages, including English.

The consonants are in the main like their English equivalents, though to an English-speaker's ear the unaspirated Finnish *k*'s, *p*'s, *t*'s sound somewhat weak and as if slightly approaching *g*, *b*, *d*. Double consonants are, as in Italian, pronounced twice, with a distinct if short pause between the two, as *Úk-ko*; cf. Italian *bóc-ca* 'mouth.' Initial *h-* (*Hä-me*) is as in English, but at the end of a syllable, as in *Áh-ti*, *h* has about the value of *ch* in Scottish *loch* or German *ach!*; spelled in German fashion this would appear as *Achti*.

The vowels have the so-called Continental or Latin values: *i* is tense as in *machine*, not lax as in *hit*, *is*; *y* has the value of French *u* in *lu*, *vu*, or German *ü* as in *für*; *ö* has the value of German *ö* in *schön* or French *e* in *ce*, *le*; *ä* is a very fronted sound but approximates the *a* of British and sometimes American English *at*, *sat*, and may be compared with the *a* of the French negative *pas*. A long vowel, written double, is pronounced or held about twice as long as a short vowel, written single, as *Túu-ri* vs. *Túr-so*; there is, of course, no absolute length, and the relation of a long vowel to a short one may be compared to that of a quarter to an eighth note or a Morse dash to a dot.

Finnish is rich in diphthongs, that is, in pairs of vowels spoken within the compass or confines of one syllable and in writing never hyphenated, though each vowel tends to retain its full identity. Thus, in *Lóu-hi* one hears both the *o* and the *u* with an effect suggesting that in British and sometimes in American English of *low*, *row* (a boat); so in *Kúip-pa-nà* and *Vúok-si*, again, both vowels are clearly heard though quickly spoken, and so in *Káup-pi*, where *u* is something of an offglide. In diphthongs in *-i*, as *ai* in *Ái-no* and *äi* and *öi* in *Väi-nä-möi-nen*, the *i* is a palatal offglide and *ai* is about equivalent to English *I* or the *y* in *my*. In the case of the long but ubiquitous name *Väinämöinen* the reader may perhaps come off best by letting it go at *Vý-na-mòi-nen!*

Lexical aids. I have made use of the ordinary lexical aids, including especially Elias Lönnrot, *Finskt-Svenskt Lexikon—Suomalais-ruotsalainen sanakirja*, 2 vols. (Helsinki, 1874–1880), with *Sup-*

plementhäfte—Lisäwihko, ed. A. H. Kallio (Helsinki, 1886); this great work contains many words and short passages from the *Kalevala* with Lönnrot's rendering; *Nykysuomen sanakirja* [Dictionary of Contemporary Finnish], 6 vols. (Helsinki, 1951–1961), like Lönnrot's work above, includes and interprets many specifically *Kalevala* words; Aimo Turunen's *Kalevalan sanakirja* [*Kalevala* Dictionary] (Helsinki, 1949) is encyclopedic and helpfully illustrated, and though incomplete was an invaluable adjunct to this task. For a wealth of terms covering the flora and fauna of the *Kalevala* poems, *Metsäsanakirja* . . . *Forest Dictionary* by many editors (Helsinki, 1944) was of great use, as, with their many helpful suggestions, were Eemil A. Saarimaa's *Kalevalan selityksiä kouluja varten* [A *Kalevala* Commentary for Schools] (Helsinki, 1946), and Toivo Vuorela's *Kansatieteen sanasto* [Archaeological Dictionary] (Helsinki, 1958). Only very occasionally have I derived any significant help from previous translators, for our procedures have been basically too different to make mutual assistance even *a priori* likely.

Personal acknowledgments. The key lexical aids mentioned above and certain other smaller publications aside, my obligations to various friends are considerable. At an early stage I received substantial help from Mr. Toivo J. Heiskanen of *Helsingin Sanomat,* my coauthor of Graded Finnish Readers Nos. 1–3 (Helsinki, 1957); from Dr. Daniel V. Thompson of Beverly Farms, Massachusetts, for the proper technical rendering of certain verbs connected with spinning and weaving; and from Dr. Richard E. Schultes of Harvard University for certain botanical terms not covered by *Metsäsanakirja.* I would here also express my gratitude to Dr. Aimo Turunen of Helsinki for his kindness in reading an early draft of the Glossary of Proper Names and for some other happy suggestions, and to Mr. Aimo A. Seppänen of Helsinki for help in some very crabbed passages in Lönnrot's Preface to the *Old Kalevala* of 1835, composed in the just emergent literary-scholarly Finnish. Dr. Jorma V. Vallinkoski, Director of the Helsinki University Library, likewise most kindly helped me with several matters of bibliographical detail, while a 1955–56 fellowship of the John Simon Guggenheim Memorial Foundation of New York City may be said to have launched me on this project. For many conferences over the interpretation of specific passages and for much enlightening discussion of matters concerning the material things or *realia* of Finnish peasant life I am exceedingly grateful to Mr. Aarne T. K. Lahtinen of Helsinki. To Professor Tauno F. Mustanoja of Helsinki University I would express my profoundest appreciation and gratitude for his almost unbelievable kindness in reading in the course of a busy life considerable portions of my translation against the original, and for countless other favors. Finally, I want to thank the Syndics of Harvard University Press for undertaking the publication of the book, and the editorial staff for the patience and skill with which they have carried out the work.

F.P.M., Jr.

Cambridge, Massachusetts
March 1963

THE KALEVALA

POEM 1

The poem begins (1–102).
A virgin of the air comes down to the sea, where,
tossed by wind and water, she becomes the mother of the water (103–176).
A goldeneye makes its nest and lays its eggs on the knee
of the mother of the water (177–212). The eggs roll out of the nest,
break to bits, and the bits are formed into the earth,
the heavens, the sun, the moon, and the clouds (213–244).
The mother of the water creates headlands, bays, and various shores,
deep and shoal places in the sea (245–280). Väinämöinen is born
of the mother of the water and drifts about on the waves for a long time
until at last he comes to a stop on the shore (281–344).

It is my desire,   it is my wish
to set out to sing,   to begin to recite,
to let a song of our clan glide on,   to sing a family lay.
The words are melting in my mouth,   utterances dropping out,
coming to my tongue,   being scattered about on my teeth.

Beloved friend, my boon companion,   my fair boyhood comrade,
start now to sing with me,   begin to recite together
now that we have come together,   have come from two directions.
Seldom do we come together,   meet one another
on these wretched marches,   these poor northern parts.
Let us clasp hand in hand,   fingers in fingers,
so that we may sing fine things,   give voice to the best things
for those dear ones to hear,   for those desiring to know them
among the rising younger generation,   among the people which is growing
    up,
those songs got about,   those lays inspired by
old Väinämöinen's belt,   the depths of Ilmarinen's forge,
the point of the sword of [Lemminkäinen,] a man with a far-roving mind,
    the range of Joukahainen's crossbow,
the remote corners of North Farm's fields,   the heaths of the Kaleva District.
These my father formerly sang   while carving an ax handle,
these my mother taught me   while turning her spindle,
me a child rolling on the floor   in front of her knee,
miserable milkbeard,   little clabbermouth.
There was no lack of songs in the Sampo   nor did Louhi lack magic charms.
In the songs the Sampo grew old,   in the charms Louhi disappeared,
in the lays Vipunen died,   Lemminkäinen in his frolics.

There are still other songs, magic words learned of,
plucked from the wayside, broken off from the heather,
torn from thickets, dragged from saplings,
rubbed off the top of hay, ripped from lanes
when I was going about as a herdsman, as a child in cow pastures,
on honeyed hillocks, on lovely knolls,
following dusky Blackie, going along with spotted Frisky.
The cold recited me a lay, the rain kept bringing me songs.
The winds brought another song, the waves of the sea drove some to me.
The birds added songs, the treetops magic sayings.
These I wound up in a ball, arranged in a clew.
I thrust the ball into my sled, the clew into my sleigh;
I pulled it home on my sled, on my sleigh to the threshing barn,
put it up in the storehouse loft in a round copper box.

For a long time my lays have been in the cold, housed in darkness.
Shall I pull the lays out of the cold, draw the songs out of the frost,
bring my box into the house to the end of the long bench
under the fine ridgepole, under the lovely roof?
Shall I open my chest of words, unlock my song box,
clip the end off the ball, undo the knot in the clew?
Thus I will sing a really fine lay, intone a beautiful one
out of rye bread, barley beer.
If no one happens to bring any beer, serves no table beer,
I will sing from a leaner mouth, intone on water
to gladden this evening of ours, to honor this memorable day
or to delight the morrow, to begin a new morn.

Thus I heard a song being sung, knew a lay to be composed:
in loneliness do the nights come upon us, in loneliness do the days shine
     bright upon us;
in loneliness Väinämöinen was born, the eternal singer emerged
from the maiden who bore him, from his Air Spirit mother.

There was a virgin, maiden of the air, lovely woman, a spirit of nature.
Long she kept her purity, ever her virginity
in the spacious farmyards, on the smooth fields of the air.
In time she got bored, her life seemed strange
in always being alone, living as a virgin
in the spacious farmyards, in the vast wastes of the air.
Now indeed she comes lower down, settled down on the billows,
on the broad expanse of the sea, on the wide open sea.
There came a great blast of wind, severe weather from the east;
it raised the sea up into foam, splashed it into billows.

4

The wind kept rocking the girl,   a wave kept driving the virgin
around about on the blue sea,   on the whitecapped billows.
The wind blew her pregnant,   the sea made her thick through.
She carried a hard womb,   a stiff bellyful
for seven hundred years,   for nine ages of man.
Nothing is born,   the self-begotten fetus does not come free.

As mother of the water the virgin went hither and yon.   She swims east,
    swims west,
swims northwest, south,   swims along the whole horizon
in the agonies of her burning gestation,   with severe labor pains.
Nothing is born,   the self-begotten fetus does not come free.

She keeps weeping softly and unceasingly,   uttered a word, spoke thus:
"Woe are my days, poor me,   woe is my wandering, wretched child!
Now I have got into trouble: ever to be under the sky,
to be rocked by the wind,   to be driven by the waves
on these extensive waters, boundless billows! It would have been better   to
    live as a virgin of the air
than it is nowadays   to keep floating about as the mother of the water.
It is cold for me to be here,   painful for me to be adrift,
to dwell in the waves,   to be going hither and yon in the water.
O Ukko, god on high,   supporter of the whole sky!
Come here, since there is need,   come here, since you are summoned.
Deliver the maiden from her predicament,   the woman from her labor pains!
Come soon, get here without delay;   you are needed without any delay at all."

A little time passed,   a little bit passed quickly.
A goldeneye came, a straight-flying bird;   it fluttered about
seeking a place for its nest,   considering a place to live.
It flew east, it flew west,   flew northwest, south.
It does not find such a place,   not even the poorest kind of place,
in which it might build its nest,   take up its dwelling place.
It flits about, soars about,   it ponders, it reflects:
"Shall I build my house in the wind,   my dwelling place on the waves?
The wind will tip the house over,   a wave will carry off my dwelling place."

So then the mother of the water,   mother of the water, virgin of the air,
raised her knee from the sea,   her shoulder blade from a billow,
for the goldeneye as a place for a nest,   as an agreeable dwelling place.
That goldeneye, graceful bird,   flits about, soars about.
She discovered the knee of the mother of the water   on the bluish open sea;
she thought it a grass-grown tussock,   fresh turf.
She soars about, flits about,   settles down on the knee.

On it she builds her nest,   laid her golden eggs,
six golden eggs,   the seventh an iron egg.
She began to brood the eggs,   to warm the top of the knee.
She brooded one day, brooded a second,   then brooded a third, too.

Now because of that the mother of the water,   mother of the water, virgin of
  the air,
feels burning hot,   her skin scorched;
she thought her knee was burning,   all her sinews melting.
Suddenly she twitched her knee,   made her limbs tremble;
the eggs tumbled into the water,   are sent into the waves of the sea;
the eggs cracked to pieces,   broke to bits.
The eggs do not get into the ooze,   the bits not get mixed up with the water.
The bits were turned into fine things,   the pieces into beautiful things:
the lower half of one egg   into the earth beneath,
the top half of another egg   into the heavens above.
The top half of one yolk   gets to glow like the sun,
the top half of one white   gets to gleam palely as the moon;
any mottled things on an egg,   those become stars in heaven,
anything black on an egg,   those indeed become clouds in the sky.

The ages go on,   the years go by still longer
while the new sun is glowing,   the new moon gleaming palely.
The mother of the water, the mother of the water,   virgin of the air, keeps
  on swimming
on those gentle waters,   on the misty billows,
before her the flowing water,   behind her the clear heavens.

Now in the ninth year,   in the tenth summer
she raised her head from the sea,   lifts up the crown of her head.
She began to perform her acts of creation,   to accomplish her works
on the wide expanse of the sea,   on the wide open sea.
Where she swung her hand,   there she arranged headlands;
where she touched bottom with her foot,   she hollowed out deep spots for
  fish;
where, moreover, bubbles came up,   there she deepened deep places.
She turned her side against the land;   there she made the coasts smooth;
she turned her feet against the land;   there she formed places to seine for
  salmon;
she came with her head against the land;   there she fashioned bays.
Then she swam farther out from land,   lingered on the open sea.
She forms little islands in the sea,   produced hidden reefs
for a ship to run aground on,   to destroy seamen.
Now the islands were arranged,   little islands created in the sea,

6

the pillars of the sky erected,   lands and continents sung into being,
patterns marbled in rocks,   designs drawn on crags.
Väinämöinen is not yet born,   the eternal singer has not appeared.

Steadfast old Väinämöinen   went about in his mother's womb
for thirty summers,   the same number of winters, too,
on those gentle waters,   on the misty billows.
He ponders, he reflects   how to exist, how to live
in his dark hiding place,   in the cramped dwelling
where he never saw the moon   nor spied the sun.
He speaks these words,   made this utterance:
"Moon, free me; sun, release me;   Great Bear, ever guide
the man out of the strange doors,   the alien gates,
from this little nest,   the cramped dwellings.
Escort the traveler to land,   the child of man to the outer air,
to look at the moon in the sky,   to admire the sun,
to inspect the Great Bear,   to scan the stars."

When the moon did not free him   nor the sun release him,
he thought his time strange,   became impatient with his life;
he moved the gate of the fort   with his ring finger,
suddenly turned the bony lock   with his left toe;
with his nails he got outside the threshold,   with his knees out from the door
    of the entrance.
Then he plunged straight into the sea,   rolled right into the billows;
the man remains on the sea,   the person among the waves.
There he lay outstretched for five years,   both five years and six,
seven years, eight.   At last he came to a stop on the surface,
by a nameless headland,   a treeless land.
With his knees he struggled up from the ground,   with his arms he turned
    himself over.
He got up to look at the moon,   to admire the sun,
to observe the Great Bear,   to scan the stars.

That was the birth of Väinämöinen,   the ancestry of the stouthearted singer,
out of the maiden who bore him,   from his Air Spirit mother.

POEM 2

Väinämöinen comes up onto the treeless land
and gets Sampsa, Spirit of Arable, to sow trees (1–42).
At first no oak sprouts, but later one comes up
and spreads out over the whole land and with its leafy branches
keeps both the moon and the sun out of sight (43–110).
The little man comes up out of the sea and fells the oak;
the moon and sun again come into view (111–224). The birds sing
in the trees; grass, flowers, and berries grow on the ground;
only no growth of barley is yet found (225–236).
Väinämöinen finds a few grains of barley in the sand of the shore,
fells a clearing, and leaves one birch growing
for birds to perch on (237–264). An eagle, pleased that a tree
has been left standing for it to perch on, strikes for Väinämöinen fire
with which he can burn over his clearing (265–286).
Väinämöinen sows the barley, prays for successful growth,
and hopes for prosperity in times to come (287–378).

Then Väinämöinen got up   with his two feet onto a heath,
onto an island in the open sea,   onto a treeless land.
He remained there many years,   kept living along
on the silent uninhabited land,   the treeless land.
He ponders, he reflects   long with head on hand:
"Who is to sow the lands,   sow crops thickly?"

The Spirit of Arable, lad of the field,   Sampsa, tiny lad,
he indeed will sow the lands,   sow crops thickly.
He sowed the land at an easy pace,   sowed lands, sowed fens,
sowed loose-soiled clearings,   has stony soil sown.
He sowed the hills with pine groves,   sowed the knolls with stands of fir,
the heaths with a growth of heather,   the dells with young undergrowth.
He sowed birches in swales,   alders on light-soiled lands;
chokecherries he sowed in moist spots,   sallows in wet lands,
rowans in holy places,   willows on flooded lands,
junipers on barren lands,   oaks by the sides of a stream.
Trees began to tower aloft,   young saplings to rise up.
The firs grew with red cones on their crowns,   the pines spread their bushy
    tops.
Birch trees grew up in the swales,   alders on light-soiled lands,
chokecherries on moist spots,   junipers on barren lands,
a lovely berry on the juniper,   good fruit on the chokecherry.

8

Steadfast old Väinämöinen   went to look at that land
seeded by Sampsa,   the places sown by the Spirit of Arable.
He saw that trees have towered aloft,   young saplings risen up;
only the oak has not sprouted,   God's tree not struck root.
He left the wretched thing to its own devices, . to its present fortunes.
He waited three more nights,   the same number of days, too.
Then at the very end of the week   he went to look:
the oak had not grown,   God's tree not struck root.

Then he sees four girls,   five brides of the water.
They were mowing grass,   cutting coarse grass
at the tip of a misty headland,   on the end of a foggy island;
what they mowed, they raked,   gathered it all into windrows.
Tursas came out of the sea,   the man rose up from the waves.
He thrust the hay into a fire,   into the power of a glowing fire.
It all burned to ashes,   was reduced to fluffy ashes.

There resulted a pile of ashes,   a heap of dry ashes.
Into it went a lovely leaf,   a lovely leaf, the fruit of an oak
from which grew a fair shoot,   from which a green shoot rose up;
it went up from the ground like a strawberry plant,   grew two-forked.
It stretched out its boughs,   spread its leafy branches.
The crown extended to the heavens,   the foliage spread up to the sky;
it stopped the clouds from scudding,   the cloud patches from drifting;
it hid the sun so that it did not glow,   the moon so that it did not gleam
   palely.

Then old Väinämöinen   ponders, reflects
whether there would be someone to break up the oak,   to fell the fine tree.
It is unpleasant for a human being to exist,   dreadful for fish to swim
with no sun shining,   no moon gleaming palely.
There was not a single person   or brave man
who could fell the oak,   bring down the luxuriantly crowned tree.

Then old Väinämöinen   utters these words:
"Maiden mother, you who bore me,   Nature Spirit, my upbringer!
Order indeed some water spirit   —in the water are many spirits—
to break up this oak,   to cause this bad tree to vanish
from in front of the blazing sun,   out of the way of the palely gleaming
   moon."
A man came up from the sea,   a person rose from the waves.
That man was neither very big   nor really very small;
he was as tall as a man's thumb,   as high as a woman's span.
On his shoulders was a copper helmet,   copper boots on his feet,

9

copper mittens on his hands,   copper embroidery on the mittens,
a copper belt girded around his waist,   a copper ax in his belt;
the shaft was a thumb's length,   the blade the height of a thumbnail.

Steadfast old Väinämöinen   ponders, reflects;
he is one of the strangest men he has seen,   one of the oddest persons he has
     laid eyes on,
tall as an upright thumb,   high as a steer's hoof.
Then he uttered these words,   gave utterance, spoke thus:
"What manner of man are you,   what kind of a person, wretch?
Little better than a dead man,   little handsomer than one deceased."
The little person from the sea spoke,   the man of the waves answered:
"I am this sort of a man,   a little person, a water spirit.
I came to fell the oak,   to crumble the fragile tree."
Steadfast old Väinämöinen   uttered these words:
"You are hardly created,   neither created nor suited,
to fell the big oak,   to drop the dreadful tree."

He had scarcely spoken;   he again took a look;
he saw that the man was changed,   the person made over.
His feet are dancing about on the ground,   his head is supporting the clouds;
in front his beard reaches to his knees,   behind his hair to his heels.
It was a fathom between his eyes,   his trousers were a fathom wide at the
     bottom,
one and a half at the knee,   two at the waist.
He is whetting his ax,   was sharpening the bit
on six whetstones,   on seven stones.
He swings along,   walks lightly
in his wide-bottomed trousers,   in his full pants.
With one step he swung along with head thrown back   to the fine sand of
     the beach,
with the second he leapt   onto the liver-colored soil,
with the third he took a long stride   to the foot of the huge oak.
He struck the tree with his ax,   dealt a smart blow with the bit.
He struck once, he struck twice,   he immediately took a third try;
fire flashed from the ax,   flame spurted from the oak,
the oak was on the point of listing,   the great tree on the point of breaking
     off.
Thus on the third time   he was able to fell the oak,
to shatter the great tree,   to bring down the luxuriantly crowned one.
He shoved the butt to the east,   let the crown down to the northwest,
the leafy twigs toward the south,   the branches due north.

Whoever took a branch from it   took everlasting good fortune;
whoever broke a top branch off it   broke off everlasting wizardry;

whoever cut off a leafy twig   cut off everlasting love.
Whatever chips had flown about,   whatever splinters had blown out
to the broad expanse of the sea,   to the boundless billows,
them the wind rocked,   the surge of the sea rolled
like boats on the surface of the water,   like ships on the billows.

The wind carried them to North Farm.   The little maid of North Farm
is rinsing out her kerchiefs,   is washing her clothes
on a rock in the water by the shore   at the end of a long headland.
She saw a chip on the billows,   she put it away in her rucksack,
carried it home in the rucksack,   in the rucksack with a long strap
to the farmyard for a wizard to make his arrows,   for a magician-bowman to
   make his weapons of.

When the oak had been brought down,   the dreadful tree felled,
the sun got free to shine,   the moon to gleam palely,
the clouds to race along,   the rainbow to arch over
the tip of the misty headland,   the end of the foggy island.
Then the wilderness began to get beautiful,   woods to grow as one would
   desire,
with foliage on the trees, grass on the ground;   the birds began to sing in a
   tree,
thrushes to rejoice,   the cuckoo to call on high.
Berrystalks grew on the ground,   lovely flowers in the field;
all sorts of herbs grew,   many kinds were brought forth.
Barley alone has not sprung up,   the precious crop not grown.

Then old Väinämöinen   walks about, reflects
on the shore of the blue sea,   on the coasts of the mighty water he reflects.
He found six grains,   seven seeds
on the seashore,   on the fine sand of the beach;
he hid them in a pine marten's skin,   in the leg of a squirrel caught in
   summer.
He set out to sow the land,   to scatter seed
by the Kaleva spring,   by the edge of the Osmo field.
From a tree a tomtit twittered: "The Osmo barley will certainly not come up,
the Kaleva oats not grow   unless the land is tamed,
a clearing cut down,   and burned over by fire."

Steadfast old Väinämöinen   had a sharp ax made;
then he cut down a big clearing,   cleared a huge tract.
He felled all the pretty trees,   he left one birch
as a resting place for birds,   as a tree for a cuckoo to call in.
An eagle flew through the heavens,   a bird across the sky.
It came to look at that.   "Why indeed has that birch

been left unfelled,   the pretty tree not cut down?"
Old Väinämöinen said: "This is why that one has been left;
it was left for birds to rest in,   just for an eagle to perch on."
The eagle said, bird of the air: "You indeed did very well!
You left the birch growing,   the pretty tree standing
for birds to rest in,   for myself to perch on."
The bird of the air struck fire,   caused flame to flash.
The north wind burned the clearing,   the northeast wind blew hard,
burned all the trees to ashes,   reduced them to fluffy ashes.
Then old Väinämöinen   took the six grains,
the seven seeds   from the skin of the pine marten,
from the leg of the squirrel caught in summer,   from a summer weasel's paw.
He set out to sow the land,   to scatter the seed.
He uttered these words:

A SOWER'S CHARM, LINES 296-330

"With back bent I am sowing
between the Creator's fingers,   through the hand of the Almighty
onto this flourishing land,   this growing clearing.

"Woman living under the earth,   old ruler of the soil, mistress of the earth!
Now make the turf grow,   the rich soil force up grass.
The land will not lack vital strength   never, never at all
so long as there may be favor from those who gave it,   permission from the
daughters of Nature.

"Rise, land, from slumbering,   Creator's grass, from sleeping!
Let stems grow stems,   and stalks grow stalks.
Send up shoots by the thousand,   spread sprouts by the hundred
as a result of my plowing, my sowing,   especially of my toil.

"O Ukko, god on high   or heavenly father,
holder of power in the clouds,   ruler of the cloud patches!
Hold folk assemblies in the clouds,   open meetings in the upper stories of
the sky.
Make a cloud spring up in the east,   raise up a cloudbank in the northwest,
send others from the west,   drive others from the south.
Shed rain gently from the heavens,   sprinkle honey from the clouds
on the sprouting shoots,   on the murmuring crops."

That Ukko, god on high,   ruling father of the heavens,
held folk assemblies in the clouds,   open meetings in the upper stories of
the sky.
He made a cloud spring up in the east,   raised a cloudbank in the northwest,

sent another from the west,   drove one from the south.
He pushed them right together,   banged them against one another.
He shed rain gently from the heavens,   sprinkled honey from the clouds
on the sprouting shoots,   on the murmuring crops.
A many-branched shoot sprang up indeed,   a crop moss-green like a tree
stump
rose from the soft soil of the field   as a result of Väinämöinen's toil.

Now indeed the next day after that,   after two, three nights,
after a week at the latest,   steadfast old Väinämöinen
took a walk to look   at what he had plowed, at what he had sown,
at the result of his toil.   The barley was growing to his heart's desire,
the ears with six ranks,   the stalks with three joints.
Then old Väinämöinen   glances about, turns around.
Then a spring cuckoo came,   saw the birch growing:
"Why indeed has that birch   been left unfelled?"
Old Väinämöinen said: "This is why the birch
has been left growing: as a tree for you to call in.
Call there, cuckoo!   Warble, sandy-breast!
Cry out, you with a silvery voice,   you with a ringing voice, warble away!
Call out evenings, call out mornings,   once at midday, too,
for the delightfulness of my skies,   for the pleasantness of my untilled lands,
for the prosperity of my shores,   for the fertility of my districts."

POEM 3

Väinämöinen grows in knowledge and becomes famous (1–20).
Joukahainen sets out to defeat him in a contest of wisdom and,
when he does not win, challenges him to duel with him with swords.
At this Väinämöinen gets angry
and sings Joukahainen down into a fen (21–330).
In the fen Joukahainen gets sorely distressed
and finally promises Väinämöinen his sister as a spouse.
Väinämöinen is appeased by this and releases him from the fen (331–476).
In distress of mind Joukahainen sets out for home and reports
to his mother how unfortunately his trip has turned out (477–524).
His mother is delighted when she hears
that she is getting Väinämöinen as her son-in-law
but the daughter becomes distressed and begins to weep and weep (525–580).

Steadfast old Väinämöinen   lives his days
on those clearings of Väinämöinen's district,   on the heaths of the Kaleva
    District.
He keeps singing his songs,   keeps singing, goes on practicing his art.
Day after day he sang,   night after night he recited
recollections of ancient times,   those profound origin songs
which not all children sing,   not even men understand
in this dreadful time,   in this fleeting final age.
Far away the news is heard,   the tidings spread quickly
of Väinämöinen's singing,   of the man's skill.
The tidings spread quickly to the south,   the news reached the north country.

Joukahainen was young,   a scrawny Lappish lad.
Once he was gadding about;   he heard that remarkable charms,
magic songs were being rattled off,   better ones intoned
on those burned-over tracts of Väinämöinen's district,   on the heaths of the
    Kaleva District,
better than what he himself knew,   had learned from his father.
That he took greatly amiss,   constantly envied
Väinämöinen's being a singer   better than himself.

Now he came to his mother,   to his esteemed parent.
He vowed to set out,   promised to go
to those dwellings in Väinämöinen's district   for a contest with Väinämöinen.
The father forbade his son,   the father forbade, the mother objected
to his setting out for Väinämöinen's district   for a contest with Väinä-
    möinen:

"There they will bewitch you,   bewitch, exorcise you
right into the snow, straight into new-fallen snow,   right into the bitter cold
    air
so that you will not be able to turn your hands   or move your feet."
Young Joukahainen said: "Good indeed is my father's knowledge,
my mother's even better,   but my own knowledge is supreme.
If I wish to rival,   to be the equal of men,
I will sing down my rival singers,   enchant my enchanters.
I will sing the best singer   into the worst singer,
sing shoes of stone onto his feet,   wooden pants onto his hips,
a stone weight onto his chest,   a chunk of rock onto his shoulders,
stone mittens onto his hands,   onto his head a high-peaked hat of rock."

Then he set out, did not obey.   He took his own gelding
whose muzzle snorted fire,   whose shanks struck out sparks;
he harnessed the fiery gelding   to a lovely sleigh.
He sits down in the sled,   settles down in his sleigh;
he struck the spirited steed with a whip,   hit it with a beaded lash.
The spirited steed gets going,   the horse trots along.
He whizzes along.   He drove one day, drove a second,
drove ahead the third, too.   Now on the third day
he reached the clearings in Väinämöinen's district,   the heaths of the Kaleva
    District.

Steadfast old Väinämöinen,   eternal sage,
was driving on his way,   covering ground
on those clearings of Väinämöinen's district,   the heaths of the Kaleva
    District.
Young Joukahainen came along,   he was driving on the road in the opposite
    direction.
Shaft caught in shaft,   trace got tangled in trace,
hames became fast in hames,   shaft-bow in butt of shaft-bow.
Therefore they then stop,   stop, deliberate;
water poured from shaft-bow,   vapor steamed from the shafts.

Old Väinämöinen asked: "Of what clan are you
to come along foolishly,   recklessly onward?
You break the bent-wood hames,   the sapling shaft-bows;
you splinter my sleigh to pieces,   my poor sleigh to bits."
Then young Joukahainen   uttered a word, spoke thus:
"I am young Joukahainen.   But name your own clan;
of what clan are you,   of what crew, miserable creature?"
Then steadfast old Väinämöinen   now told his name.
Then he managed to say: "If you are young Joukahainen,
pull over a little to the side.   You are younger than I."

Then young Joukahainen   uttered a word, spoke thus:
"A man's youth is a small matter,   his youth, his age.
Whichever of two men is the better in knowledge,   the stronger in memory,
let him indeed stay on the road,   let the other get off the road.
If you are old Väinämöinen,   eternal singer,
let us begin to sing,   start to recite magic,
one man to test the other,   one to defeat the other."
Steadfast old Väinämöinen   uttered a word, spoke thus:
"What can I really do   as a singer, as an expert!
I have always lived my life   just on these clearings,
on the edges of the home field,   again and again have listened to the cuckoo
    by the house.
But be this as it may,   speak so that I may hear with my ears:
what do you know most about,   understand beyond other people?"

Young Joukahainen said: "I indeed know something!
This I know clearly,   understand precisely:

[JOUKAHAINEN'S MAXIMS]

"A smoke hole is near a ceiling;   a flame is near a fireplace.
It is pleasant for a seal to live,   for a pike, dog of the water, to roll about;
it eats the salmon around it,   the whitefish beside it.
A whitefish has smooth fields,   a salmon a level ceiling.
A pike spawns in the chill of night,   the slobberer in bitter cold weather.
Autumns the timid, obstinate perch   swims deep,
summers it spawns on dry land,   flaps about on shores.

"If this may not be enough,   I have still another bit of knowledge,
understand a certain thing:
                "The North plows with a reindeer,
the South with a mare,   remotest Lapland with an elk.
I know the trees of Pisa's Hill,   the tall evergreens on Goblin's Crag;
tall are the trees on Pisa's Hill,   the evergreens on Goblin's Crag.
There are three strong rapids,   three great lakes,
three high mountains   under the vault of this sky.
In Häme is Hällä-whirlpool,   in Karelia Loon Rapids;
none exceed the Vuoksi rapids,   surpass those of Imatra."

Old Väinämöinen said: "A child's knowledge, a woman's power of memory!
It is neither that of a bearded man   nor indeed of a married man.
Speak of profound origins,   of unique matters."

Young Joukahainen   uttered a word, spoke thus:
"I know the origin of the tomtit,   I know the tomtit is a bird,
the hissing adder a snake,   the roach a fish of the water.

16

I know iron is brittle,   black soil sour,
boiling-hot water painful,   being burned by fire bad.
Water is the oldest of ointments,   foam of a rapids oldest of magic nostrums,
the Creator himself the oldest of magicians,   God the oldest of healers.
The source of water is from a mountain,   the source of fire from the heavens;
the origin of iron is from rust,   the basis of copper is a crag.
A wet tussock is the oldest land,   the willow the first tree,
the foot of a tall evergreen the first habitation,   a flat stone the first wretched
   cooking vessel."

Steadfast old Väinämöinen   uttered these words:
"Do you remember anything more   or has your foolish talk now come to an
   end?"

Young Joukahainen spoke: "I remember a little more,
I remember indeed that time   when I was plowing the sea,
hoeing out the hollows of the sea   digging deep spots for fish,
deepening the deep places in the water,   putting the lily ponds in place,
overturning hills,   heaping up blocks of stone.
I was already the sixth man,   seventh person,
when they were creating this earth,   fashioning the sky,
erecting the pillars of the sky,   bringing the rainbow,
guiding the moon,   helping the sun,
arranging the Great Bear,   studding the heavens with stars."

Old Väinämöinen said: "You are certainly lying about this.
No one saw you   when they were plowing the sea,
hoeing out the hollows of the sea,   digging deep spots for fish,
deepening the deep places in the water,   putting lily ponds in place,
overturning hills,   heaping up blocks of stone.
Nor were you probably seen,   probably neither seen nor heard,
when the earth was being created,   the sky fashioned,
the pillars of the sky erected,   the rainbow brought,
the moon guided,   the sun helped,
the Great Bear arranged,   the heavens studded with stars."

Young Joukahainen   then uttered these words:
"If I do not happen to have intelligence,   I will ask for intelligence from my
   sword.
O old Väinämöinen,   big-mouthed singer!
Proceed to measure off our swords,   set out to fight a duel!"
Old Väinämöinen said: "I do not think I am much afraid
of those swords of yours, your intelligence,   your ice picks, your thoughts.
But be that as it may,   I will not proceed to measure swords
with you, wretch,   with you, miserable fellow."

17

Then young Joukahainen   screwed up his mouth, twisted his head around,
clawed at his black beard.   He uttered these words:
"Whoever does not proceed to measure swords,   nor set out to fight a duel,
him I will sing into a swine,   change into a pig with lowered snout.
Such men I enchant,   one thus, the other so,
strike dead onto a dunghill,   jam into the corner of a cattle shed."

Old Väinämöinen then got angry,   then got angry and felt shamed.
He began to sing,   got to reciting;
the magic songs are not children's songs,   not children's songs, women's
    jokes;
they are a bearded man's   which not all children sing
nor half the boys indeed,   not one bachelor in three
in this dreadful time,   in this fleeting final age.
Old Väinämöinen sang.   Lakes splashed over, the earth shook,
copper mountains trembled,   solid slabs of rock split,
the crags flew apart,   stones on the shore cracked.

He bewitched young Joukahainen.   He sang sprouts onto his shaft-bow,
a willow bush onto his hames,   sallows onto the end of his traces.
He bewitched the lovely basket sleigh;   he sang it into a pond as fallen trees.
He sang the whip with a beaded lash   into shore reed of the sea,
he sang the horse with a blaze   to the bank of a rapid as a rock.
He sang the gold-hilted sword   to the sky as flashes of lightning;
then he sang the ornamented shaft of the crossbow   into a rainbow over the
    waters,
then his feathered arrows   into speeding hawks,
then the dog with an undershot jaw,   it he sang onto the ground as rocks.
He sang the cap off the man's head   into the peak of a cloudbank,
he sang the mittens off his hands   into pond lilies,
then his blue broadcloth coat   to the heavens as a cloud patch,
the soft woolen belt from his waist   into stars throughout the heavens.
He bewitched Joukahainen himself,   sang him into a fen up to the loins,
into a grassy meadow up to the groin,   into a heath up to the armpits.

Now young Joukahainen   indeed knew and realized:
he knew that he had got on the way,   got on the route to a contest,
a contest in magic singing   with old Väinämöinen.
He keeps trying to get a foot free;   he could not lift his foot.
However, he tried the other;   here his shoe was of stone.
Then young Joukahainen   indeed becomes anguished,
gets into a more precarious situation.   He uttered a word, spoke thus:
"O wise Väinämöinen,   eternal sage!
Reverse your magic charm,   revoke your enchantment.
Free me from this predicament,   get me out of this situation.

I will indeed make the best payment,   pay the most substantial ransom."
Old Väinämöinen said: "Well, what will you give me
if I reverse my magic charm,   revoke my enchantment,
free you from this predicament,   get you out of this situation?"

Young Joukahainen said: "I have indeed two bows,
two splendid crossbows: one is swift in striking,
the other accurate for shooting.   Take either of these."
Old Väinämöinen said: "I do not care, rash fellow, about your crossbows,
not, wretch, about your bows.   Those I, too, have,
with every wall stacked,   every peg loaded;
they go hunting without men,   do outdoor work without people."
He bewitched young Joukahainen,   bewitched him still deeper in.

Young Joukahainen spoke: "I have two vessels,
two lovely boats;   one is swift in a race,
the other transports much.   Take either of these."
Old Väinämöinen spoke: "I really do not care about your vessels.
I will not select any of your boats.   Those I, too, have,
with every roller hauled up,   every cove piled full,
one steady in a high wind,   the other that goes into a headwind."
He bewitched young Joukahainen,   bewitched him still deeper in.

Young Joukahainen said: "I have two stallions,
two lovely steeds;   one is better for racing,
the other lively in the traces.   Take either of these."
Old Väinämöinen said: "I do not care about your horses,
do not bother about your white-fetlocked horses!   Those I, too, have,
with every stall hitched full,   every stable full,
with fat as clear as water on their backbones,   a pond of fat on their crup-
    pers."
He bewitched young Joukahainen,   bewitched him still deeper in.

Young Joukahainen said: "O old Väinämöinen!
Reverse your magic words,   revoke your enchantment.
I will give a high-peaked hat full of gold pieces,   a felt hat full of silver pieces
got by my father in war,   brought from battle."
Old Väinämöinen said: "I care nothing about your silver pieces,
I have no need, wretch, for your gold pieces.   Those I, too, have,
with every storehouse crammed,   every little box fully stocked;
they are gold pieces as old as the moon,   silver pieces the age of the sun."
He bewitched young Joukahainen,   bewitched him still deeper in.

Young Joukahainen said: "O old Väinämöinen!
Free me from this predicament,   release me from this situation.

19

I will give you my windrows back home, surrender my fields of sandy soil
to free my own head, to ransom myself."
Old Väinämöinen spoke: "I do not want your windrows,
useless person, not your fields of sandy soil. Those I, too, have,
fields in every direction, windrows in every clearing.
My own are better fields, my own windrows finer."
He bewitched young Joukahainen, kept bewitching him further down.

Then young Joukahainen at last, however, grew desperate
when he was up to his chin in the mud, up to his beard in a bad place,
up to his mouth in the fen, in mossy places, up to his teeth behind a rotten
  tree trunk.
Young Joukahainen said: "O wise Väinämöinen,
eternal sage! Now sing your song backward,
grant me yet my feeble life, set me free from here.
The current is already dragging at my feet, the sand scratching my eyes.
If you will reverse your magic words, leave off your magic spell,
I will give my sister Aino, give my mother's child
to wash the cabin for you, to sweep the floor,
to rinse out the wooden firkins, to wash the blankets,
to weave fine stuff, to bake sweet bread."

Then old Väinämöinen was exceedingly delighted
when he got Joukahainen's girl to provide for his old age.
He sits down on a song stone, seats himself on a song rock.
He sang once, he sang twice, sang a third time, too.
He revoked his magic words, took back his spell completely.
Young Joukahainen got free, got his chin free of the mud,
his beard from the bad place, his horse from being a rock in the rapids,
his sleigh on the shore from being a rotten tree trunk in the water, his whip
  from being a shore reed.
he climbed slowly into his basket sleigh, flung himself limply into his sled.
He set out in a sorry state of mind, with heavy heart
to his dear mother's, to his esteemed parents.

He thunders along. He drove home strangely,
wrecked his sled against the threshing barn with the shafts across the outer
  stairs.
The mother began to speak her mind, the father says a word:
"You wrecked your sled on purpose, you smashed the shafts deliberately.
Why indeed are you driving oddly, coming home foolishly?"

At this young Joukahainen shed tears
downcast, low in mind, high-peaked hat all askew,
with white lips, down in the mouth.

His mother managed to ask,   she who had experienced pain got to inquiring:
"What are you weeping about, my boy,   what are you bewailing, you born
     of me as a young woman?
Your lips are white,   you are down in the mouth."
Young Joukahainen said: "Oh mother mine, you who bore me,
now there has been a reason,   magic has taken place,
cause enough for me to weep,   for me to bewail the magic.
That I will always bewail,   will grieve about throughout my life:
I gave away my sister Aino,   pledged my mother's child
to provide for Väinämöinen,   to be a spouse for the singer,
a defense for a dodderer,   a protection for an old stick-in-the-corner."
The mother rubbed   her two hands together,
uttered a word, spoke thus: "Do not weep, my boy.
There is nothing to weep about,   nothing to grieve greatly about.
I have longed for that always,   throughout my life wanted
the great man in my clan,   the brave one in my tribe,
wanted Väinämöinen as my son-in-law,   the singer as my relative."

Weeping, young Joukahainen's sister   got distressed and started to cry.
She wept one day, wept a second   prone across the outer stairs;
she wept from great grief,   from a dejected state of mind.
The mother began to speak: "What are you bewailing, Aino,
when you will be going to the home of a distinguished bridegroom,
     man of high estate,
to sit by the windows,   to prattle away on the wall benches?"
The daughter uttered these words: "Oh mother mine, you who bore me!
I am indeed bewailing something.   I bewail the beauty of my braids,
the thickness of my young tresses,   the fineness of my hair,
if they are to be covered with a coif while I am young,   be hidden while I
     am growing up.
That indeed I will always bewail: that sweetness of the sun,
the loveliness of the splendid moon,   the charms of the whole sky,
if while young I must give these up,   if while a child I must forget them
and leave them in my brother's workshop,   by my father's window."

The mother says to the daughter,   the aged woman spoke to her child:
"Begone, crazy girl, along with your anxieties!   Begone, good-for-nothing,
     along with your weeping.
There is no reason to get gloomy,   no cause to get dejected.
God's sun shines   elsewhere in the world,
not just on your father's window,   at the entrance to your brother's gate.
Likewise there will be berries on the hill,   strawberries on the cleared land
for poor you to pick   farther off in the world,
not just on your father's clearings,   on your brother's burned-over heaths."

POEM 4

*Väinämöinen meets Joukahainen's sister as she is breaking off
twigs for bath whisks and asks her to be his spouse (1–30).
The daughter runs home weeping and tells her mother (31–116).
The mother forbids her to grieve and orders her
rather to rejoice and to go about in fine clothes (117–188).
The daughter weeps and weeps
and says she does not want to marry the terribly old man (189–254).
Walking along in her distress she strays into the backwoods,
reaches a strange seashore, starts to wash herself,
and drowns in the water (255–370).
The mother weeps night and day over her drowned daughter (371–518).*

Aino, the young maiden, young Joukahainen's sister,
set out to get a twig broom from a grove, bath whisks from a thicket.
She broke off a whisk for her father, broke off another for her mother,
gathered a third, too, for her ruddy-cheeked brother.

She was now stepping along toward home, walking lightly through an alder
  grove.
Old Väinämöinen came along; he saw the maiden in the grove,
the girl with a finely woven dress in the glade. He uttered a word, spoke thus:
"Not indeed for others, young girl! only for me, young girl,
wear the bead necklace, wear the cross on your breast,
do your hair only for me, tie up your hair with silk ribbons."
The girl uttered these words: "Neither for you nor for others
will I wear a cross on my breast, tie up my hair with silk ribbons.
I do not care about imported cloth nor lament a lack of slices of wheaten
  bread.
I will live in poor clothes, grow up on crusts of bread
at my good father's, with my beloved mother."

She tore the cross from her breast, the rings from her finger,
shook the beads off her neck, the red ribbons from her head;
she left them on the ground for the ground, in the grove for the grove.
She went home weeping, bawling to the farmstead.

Her father was sitting at the window, he is ornamenting an ax-shaft:
"What are you weeping about, poor girl, poor girl, young maiden?"
"There is indeed reason for me to weep, to complain about my troubles.
This, father mine, I am weeping about: the ornament dropped from my belt,
the silver cross from my breast, the copper filigree from off my belt."

At the entrance of the gate her brother   is carving away at a shaft-bow:
"What are you weeping about, poor sister,   poor sister, young maiden?"
"There is indeed reason for me to weep,   to complain about my troubles.
This, poor brother, I am weeping about,   this I am weeping and complaining about:
the ring fell from my finger,   the beads dropped from my neck,
the gold ring from my finger,   the silver beads from my neck."

At the threshold her sister   is weaving a golden belt:
"What are you weeping about, poor sister,   poor sister, young maiden?"
"There is indeed reason for me to weep,   to shed tears over my troubles.
This, poor sister, I am weeping about,   this I am weeping and complaining about:
the gold ornaments fell from my brow,   the silver ones from my tresses,
blue silk ribbons from my face,   red ribbons from my head."

On the steps of the storehouse her mother   is skimming cream:
"What are you weeping about, poor girl,   poor girl, young maiden?"
"Oh mother, you who bore me,   oh mother, you who suckled me!
There are indeed reasons for my gloominess,   for my very great state of dejection.
This, poor mother, I am weeping about,   this, mother mine, I am complaining about:
I went to get a twig broom in the grove,   bath whisks from the thicket.
I broke off a whisk for my father,   I broke a second for my mother,
I plucked a third, too,   for my ruddy-cheeked brother.
I started to step along toward home,   I was indeed stepping along a clearing.
An Osmo descendant spoke from the hollow,   a Kaleva descendant from the clearing:
'Not indeed for others, poor girl,   only for me, poor girl,
wear the bead necklace,   wear the cross on your breast;
do your hair only for me,   tie up your hair with silk ribbons.'
I tore the cross off my breast,   shook the beads from my neck,
the blue ribbons from my face,   the red ribbons from my hair;
I threw them on the ground for the ground,   into the grove for the grove.
I uttered these words: 'Neither for you nor for others
will I wear a cross on my breast,   tie up my hair with silk ribbons.
I do not care about imported cloth   nor lament a lack of slices of wheaten bread;
I will live in poor clothes,   grow up on crusts of bread
at my good father's,   with my beloved mother.'"

Her mother said these words,   the parent remarked to her child:
"Do not weep, my daughter, do not lament,   begotten by me when young.
For one year eat sweet butter: you will get plumper than others;

for a second year eat pork: you will get handsomer than others;
for a third year eat cream pasties: you will get to be lovelier than others.
Step to the storehouse out there,   open the best chest.
There chest is on chest,   box on box.
Open the best chest,   fling open the lid of many colors;
in it are six gold belts,   seven blue dresses;
those were woven by Moon Spirit,   finished off by Sun Spirit.

"Formerly when I was a girl,   when I was living as a virgin,
I set out to the woods for berries,   for raspberries at the foot of a hill.
I heard Moon Spirit weaving,   Sun Spirit spinning
on the edge of the hazy blue wilderness,   at the side of a lovely grove.
I drew near,   I went near.
I began to entreat them,   I uttered this and said:
'Moon Spirit, give some of your gold,   Sun Spirit, some of your silver
to this desolate girl,   to the child who is entreating you.'
Moon Spirit gave me some of her gold,   Sun Spirit some of her silver.
There I was with gold ornaments on my brow,   with fine silver ones on my
     head!
I came like a flower into the house,   as a joy into my father's farmyard.
I wore them one day, wore them a second.   Already on the third day
I pulled the gold ornaments from my brow,   the good silver ones from my
     head.
I brought them to the storehouse out there,   put them under the lid of the
     chest;
they have been there since then,   the whole time without being looked at.
Now tie the silk ribbons on your face,   put the gold ones up on your brow,
the bright beads on your neck,   the gold crosses on your breast.
Put on a linen shirt,   don one of sheer linen.
Put on a fine wool dress,   on it, indeed, a silk belt,
fine silk stockings,   beautiful shoes with ornamented uppers.
Do up your hair in ribbons,   tie the braids with silk ribbons,
with gold rings on your fingers,   gold bracelets on your hands.
Thus you will come from out there into the house,   step in from the store-
     house
as the delight of your clan,   as something charming for the whole family.
You will walk on the pathways like a flower,   will wander about like a rasp-
     berry,
lovelier than you were before,   better than you were in days gone by."
These words the mother uttered,   this she said to her child.

The daughter did not obey that,   did not listen to the mother's words;
she went weeping to the farmyard,   grieving to the yard.
She says these words,   made this remark:

"What is the state of mind of the lucky,   the thoughts of the fortunate?
Indeed the state of mind of the lucky,   the thoughts of the fortunate
are as billowing water   or a wave in a trough.
What indeed is the state of mind of the unlucky,   what are the thoughts of
    old squaws?
Indeed the state of mind of the unlucky,   indeed the thoughts of old sqaws
are like crusted snow at the foot of a ridge,   like water in a deep well.
Often now the thoughts of melancholy me,   often those of the melancholy
    child
walk about in the withered grass,   crawl about in a thicket,
creep about in the grass,   tumble about in bushes.
My state of mind is no better than wood tar,   my heart no brighter than
    charcoal.
It would have been better for me,   would have been better
not to have been born, not to have grown up,   not to have got big
in these evil days,   in this joyless world.
Had I died when six days old,   vanished when eight days old,
I would not have needed much: a span's length of linen,
a tiny bit of unplowed field,   a little weeping by the mother,
still less indeed by the father,   not even a little by the brother."

She wept one day, wept a second.   Her mother got to asking:
"What are you weeping about, poor girl?   What are you, miserable one
    complaining about?"
"This I, poor girl, am bewailing,   am complaining of all the time,
because you gave wretched me,   pledged your own child,
ordered me to provide for an old man,   to be a source of joy for an aged one,
a refuge for a dodderer,   a shelter for an old stick-in-the-corner.
You might better have ordered me   under the deep waves,
to be a sister to the whitefish,   a brother to the fishes of the water!
Better to be in the sea,   to live beneath the waves
as a sister to the whitefish,   a brother to the fishes of the water
than it is to provide for an old man,   to be a refuge for a dodderer,
for a man who stumbles on his stocking,   falls over a dry pine branch."

Then she walked to the storehouse out there,   stepped inside the storehouse.
She opened the best chest,   flung open the lid of many colors,
found the six gold belts,   the seven blue dresses;
she clothes herself in these,   garbs her figure.
She puts the gold ornaments on her brow,   the silver ones in her hair,
blue silk ribbons on her face,   red ribbons on her head.
Then she set out to walk   across one clearing, along the next;
she proceeded over fens, proceeded over fields,   proceeded through gloomy
    wildernesses.

She sang as she went, spoke while walking along:
"It pains my heart, it makes my head ache.
It will indeed not pain more painfully, ache more achingly
if I, wretched one, should really die, really be cut off, miserable one,
from these great sorrows, from dejected states of mind.
Now would be the time for me to part from this world,
time for me to go to the Abode of the Dead, time to come to Death's Domain.
My father will not weep for me, my mother not feel grieved,
my sister's face not get wet, my brother's eyes not shed tears
even if I should go into the water, fall into the sea with its fish
under the deep waves onto the black ooze."
She walked one day, walked a second; on the third day indeed
she soon got to where the sea was ahead, a reed-grown shore in front of her;
there night overtakes her, darkness stops her.
There the virgin wept that evening, lamented all night
on a rock in the water by the shore at the head of a big bay.
Very early in the morning she looked yonder toward the end of a headland.
There were three maidens on the end of the headland; they were bathing
  in the sea
with the maiden Aino as a fourth, a slip of a girl as a fifth.

She threw her shirt on a willow, her dress on an aspen,
her stockings on the sandy shore, her shoes on a rock in the water,
the beads on the pleasant shore, the rings on the gravelly beach.
There was a marbled rock in the water, a boulder gleaming like gold;
she tried to swim to the rock, wanted to flee to the boulder.
Then when she got there, she stops to sit down
on the marbled rock, on the gleaming flat boulder;
the stone went clunk into the water, the boulder to the bottom.
the maiden along with the rock, Aino beside the flat boulder.
There indeed the chick vanished, there the poor virgin died.
Once as she was dying she spoke, said while she was still going down:
"I went to the sea to bathe, I got to swimming in the water;
there I, a chick, vanished, died, bird, an unnatural death.
May my father never, never, never at all
pull fish of the water out of this great sea!
I set out to the shore to wash, I went to the sea to bathe;
there I, a chick, vanished, died, bird, an unnatural death.
May my mother never, never, never at all
put water in her dough from the big bay near home!
I set out to the shore to wash, I went to the sea to bathe;
there I, a chick, vanished, died, bird, an unnatural death.
May my brother never, never, never at all
water his horse by the shore of the sea.

I set out to the shore to wash,   I went to the sea to bathe;
there I, a chick, vanished,   died, bird, an unnatural death.
May my sister never,   never, never at all
wash her face   on the pier on our bay.
As the waters of the sea,   so my blood;
as the fish of the sea,   so my flesh;
what dead branches are on the shore,   those are the ribs of wretched me;
what shore grass there is   has been rubbed from my hair."
That was the death of the young maiden,   the end of the beautiful chick.

Who now is to bring the word,   report the news by word of mouth
to the maiden's fine home,   to the beautiful farmstead?
Let a bear bring the word,   report the news by word of mouth.
The bear does not bring the word;   it disappeared in among a herd of cows.
Who is to bring the word,   report the news by word of mouth
to the maiden's fine home,   to the beautiful farmstead?
Let a wolf bring the word,   report the news by word of mouth.
The wolf does not bring the word;   it disappeared in among a flock of sheep.
Who is to bring the word,   report the news by word of mouth
to the maiden's fine home,   to the beautiful farmstead?
Let a fox bring the word,   report the news by word of mouth.
The fox does not bring the word;   it disappeared in among a flock of geese.
Who is to bring the word,   report the news by word of mouth
to the maiden's fine home,   to the beautiful farmstead?
Let a hare bring the word,   report the news by word of mouth.
The hare gave a definite answer: "The word will not disappear in among
   men."

The hare set out to run,   long-ears to go at top speed,
bandy-legs to run,   hare-lip to fly along
to the maiden's fine home,   to the beautiful farmstead.
It ran to the threshold of the sauna,   crouched on the threshold.
The sauna is full of girls   who, whisks in hand, receive him:
"Did you come, squint-eyes, to be boiled,   round-eyes, to be roasted
as supper for the master,   as breakfast for the mistress,
as snacks for the daughter,   as a midday meal for the son?"
The hare was able to speak,   round-eyes to talk big:
"Perhaps, indeed, the devil set out   to be boiled in the stew-pots!
I set out to bring the word,   to report the news by word of mouth:
'The beautiful girl has now been killed,   she with a tin cross on her breast
   has pined away,
she with a silver brooch has perished,   she with a copper belt has suddenly
   drowned,
departed into the surging sea,   under the deep open sea
to become a sister to the whitefish,   a brother to the fish of the water.'"

At that the mother began to weep,   the tearful one to cry.
Then she began to speak,   the anguished one to lament:
"Do not, wretched mothers,   ever, ever at all
lull your daughters,   rock your children
into a marriage against their will   as I, wretched mother,
lulled my girls,   brought up my chicks."
The mother wept, a tear flowed,   her copious tears flowed
from her blue eyes   onto her sad cheeks.
One tear flowed, another flowed,   copious tears flowed
from the top of her sad cheeks   onto her ample breasts.
One tear flowed, another flowed,   copious tears flowed
from her ample breasts   onto her fine skirt.
One tear flowed, another flowed,   copious tears flowed
from her fine skirt   onto her red-topped stockings.
One tear flowed, another flowed,   copious tears flowed
from her red-topped stockings   onto the fine uppers of the lovely shoes.
One tear flowed, another flowed,   copious tears flowed
from the fine uppers of the lovely shoes   to the ground under her feet;
they flowed into the ground for the ground,   into the water for the water.

After the tears had got into the ground,   they began to flow like a river.
Three rivers grew indeed   from the tears shed by her,
tears coming through her head,   going from under her brow.
In each river there grew   three swift rapids,
in the foam of each rapid   three little islands rose up,
on the shore of each little island   a golden knoll rose up,
on the top of each knoll   grew three birches,
on each birch   three golden cuckoos.
[ESTONIAN CUCKOO-SONG]
The cuckoos began to call.   One called: "Dear love, dear love!"
The second called: "Suitor, suitor!"   The third called: "Joy, joy!"
The one that called "Dear love, dear love!"   it called for three months
to the loveless girl   lying in the sea.
The one that called "Suitor, suitor!"   it called for six months
to the joyless suitor,   to the man sitting in his distress.
The one that called "Joy, joy!"   it called its life long
to the joyless mother   who was ever weeping.

As the mother listened to the cuckoo,   she spoke thus:
"Let no distressed mother   listen long to a cuckoo!
When a cuckoo calls out,   then the heart pounds,
tears come to the eyes,   tears stream down the cheek
plumper than peas,   fatter than beans.
By the moment my life is passing,   by the minute my body aging,
my whole body collapsing   after hearing the spring cuckoo."

POEM 5

Väinämöinen sets out to catch Joukahainen's sister in the sea
and gets her onto his hook, changed into a peculiar fish (1–58).
He tries to cut it into pieces but the fish flips out of his hands
into the sea and from there announces who it is (59–133).
Väinämöinen tries in vain both with words and with fishing gear
to get the fish again (134–163).
He proceeds home in a depressed state of mind
and by his deceased mother is advised
to set out to woo the daughter of North Farm (164–241).

The news had already been received,   the message carried farther off
about the young maiden's passing away,   about the beautiful girl's dying.

Steadfast old Väinämöinen,   that he took badly.
He wept evenings, he wept mornings,   most of all he wept nights
because the beautiful girl had met her death,   the maiden passed away,
departed into the billowing sea,   under the deep waves.
Grieving and sighing he walked   with heavy heart
to the shore of the blue sea.   He uttered a word, spoke thus:
"Tell now, Untamo, your dream,   your vision when stretched out on
    ground,
tell where Ahto's realm is,   where Vellamo's maidens are lolling about."
Untamo indeed told his dream,   his vision when stretched out on the ground:
"Ahto's realm is yonder,   Vellamo's maidens are lolling
at the tip of a misty headland,   at the end of a foggy island,
under the deep waves   on the black ooze.
Ahto's realm is there,   there Vellamo's maidens are lolling about
in a little cabin,   in a confined chamber,
in the side of a marbled rock,   in the recess of a big boulder."

Thence old Väinämöinen   withdrew to where the boats were.
He eyes his lines,   looks at his hooks;
he put a hook in his pouch,   an iron barb in his wallet.
He paddles along,   gets to the end of an island,
to the tip of a misty headland,   to the end of a foggy island.
There he busied himself with his hook,   was ever active with his line,
was turning his landing net about.   He lowered a gorge into the sea,
he angled, he moved his net about;   the copper pole shivered,
the silver line whistled,   the golden cord sang.
Now after a few days,   after many mornings

a fish took his angle,   a sea trout his baited hook.
He pulled it into his boat,   hauled it onto his floorboards.

He looks at it, turns it over and over;   he uttered a word, spoke thus:
"That fish is a fish   I really do not know.
It is rather smooth for a whitefish,   lightish colored for a lake trout,
lightish for a pike,   finless for a female fish,
remarkable for a male fish, too;   lacking a fillet it is no maiden,
lacking a belt no water girl,   lacking ears no chick,
most fitly a salmon,   a deepwater perch."
Väinämöinen's knife is in his belt,   the silver hilt in the sheath.
He drew the knife from his side,   the silver hilt from its sheath
in order to slice up the fish,   cut up the salmon
for morning meals,   for midmorning snacks,
for salmon dinners,   big evening meals.
He began to cut up the salmon,   to slice the fish with his knife.
Like a flash the salmon bounced into the sea,   the beautiful fish flipped
out of the bottom of the red craft,   out of Väinämöinen's boat.
Then it raised its head,   its right shoulder
where the fifth gust blew,   on the sixth high wave;
it raised its right hand,   showed its left foot
on the seventh sea,   on the ninth wave.
From there it said these words,   remarked and spoke thus:
"O you old Väinämöinen!   I did not come
for you to cut up a salmon,   for you to slice up the fish
for morning meals,   for midmorning snacks,
for salmon dinners,   big evening meals."

Old Väinämöinen said: "Why did you come?"

"I came indeed   to be a chick by your side,
to stay forever,   to be a lifelong spouse,
to open your bed,   to fix your pillow,
to wash up the little cabin,   to sweep the floor,
to bring fire into the house,   to strike a flame,
to bake a plump loaf,   to bake honey bread,
to carry a beer-jug,   to prepare a meal.
I was not a salmon,   not a deep-sea perch;
I was a girl, a young maiden,   young Joukahainen's sister
for whom you were ever searching,   looking for all your life.
O you, you wretched old man,   stupid Väinämöinen
when you did not understand how to keep   Vellamo's maiden out of the
     waters,
Ahto's favorite child."

Old Väinämöinen spoke
downcast, low in mind: "O sister of Joukahainen,
please do come again!"   Indeed she did not come again,
never, never again.   She now went away, slipped away,
vanished from the surface of the water   to inside a marbled rock,
into a chink in a liver-colored stone.

Steadfast old Väinämöinen
reflects on that,   on how to exist, how to live.
Now he wove a silken net,   dragged the water this way and that
along the sound, a second time crosswise;   he dragged the gentle waters,
the spaces between the little salmon islands,   those waters of Väinämöinen's
    district,
the isthmuses of the Kaleva District,   the gloomy depths,
the great expanses of the deep,   the river waters of Joukahainen's farm,
the shore of the cove of Lapland.   He got plenty of other fishes,
of all water fishes;   he was not able to fish up
the one his heart desires,   Vellamo's maiden of the waters,
Ahto's favorite child.

Then old Väinämöinen
downcast, low in mind,   high-peaked hat all askew,
uttered these words: "Alas, madman, crazy me,
alas my craziness, my manly power!   I used indeed to have some sense,
was endowed with some power of thought,   was allotted a generous heart,
had such of yore.   But indeed nowadays
in this dreadful time,   in a wretched generation
my whole wit is only so-so,   my thoughts not worth much,
all mental power elsewhere.   The one I waited for all my life,
for whom I waited half my life,   Vellamo's maiden of the waters,
youngest daughter of the water,   to be an everlasting friend,
a lifelong spouse,   she it was who took my hook,
rolled into my boat.   I did not understand how to keep her
nor how to take her off home;   I let her go back into the billows,
to under the deep waves."

He went a bit of a way,
walked grieving and sighing;   he proceeds toward home.
He uttered a word, spoke thus: "My cuckoos of old used to call,
my joyous cuckoos of yore;   formerly they called evenings, mornings,
and once at midday, too.   What now suppressed the great voice,
destroyed the beautiful voice?   Grief suppressed the great voice,
anxiety reduced the precious thing;   therefore it is not heard crying out,
singing at sunset   to delight my evening with music,

to ease my morning.   Now I do not indeed know
how to exist, how to live,   to dwell in this world,
to travel about in these lands.   If only my mother were alive,
my parent awake,   she would certainly be able to say
how to bear up,   how not to be crushed by anxieties,
not lapse into distress   in these evil days,
in my dejected state of mind."

                                        The mother awoke in her grave,
answered from beneath the waves: "Your mother is still alive,
your parent awake,   she who is able to say
how to be all right,   how not to be crushed by anxieties,
not to lapse into distress   in these evil days,
in your dejected state of mind.   Go to the daughters of North Farm!
There there are prettier daughters,   maidens twice as beautiful,
five, six times more spirited,   not Joukahainen's loutish girls,
churlish children of Lapland.   From there, my son, marry
the best of the daughters of North Farm,   one who is attractive as to her
    eyes,
beautiful as to her looks,   always fleet of foot
and nimble of movement."

POEM 6

Joukahainen nurses a grudge against Väinämöinen
and watches out for him on the journey to North Farm (1–78).
He sees him riding across a river and shoots at him
but only hits the horse (79–182).
Väinämöinen falls into the water; a strong wind floats him
out to the open sea and Joukahainen is delighted, for he thinks
that Väinämöinen has now sung his last magic song (183–234).

Steadfast old Väinämöinen   vowed to set out
for the cold settlement yonder,   to gloomy North Farm.
He took his straw stallion,   his peastalk horse,
he thrust a gold bit into its mouth,   put its head into a silver bridle;
he himself sits on its back,   settled his thighs quickly astride.
He rides along easily,   measures off the distance
on his straw stallion,   on his peastalk horse.
He rode over the clearings of Väinämöinen's district,   the heaths of the
    Kaleva District.
The horse ran, the journey advanced;   his home is left behind, the road grew
    short.
Now he was riding on the surface of the sea,   on the open expanse of the sea
without a hoof getting wet,   without a hock sinking in.

There to be sure was young Joukahainen,   scrawny Lappish lad.
He nursed an enduring grudge,   extremely long-lasting ill will
against old Väinämöinen   against the eternal singer.

He makes a hard-hitting crossbow,   ornaments the splendid bow.
He made the bow of iron,   casts the back from copper,
adorned those with gold,   ornamented them with silver.
Where does he get a bow string for it,   where find a tendon?
From the sinews of the Demon's elk,   from the Devil's flaxen cord.
He got the bow into good shape,   the crossbow really ready.
The bow was splendid looking,   the crossbow cost a little something!
A horse was standing on the back,   a colt running along the stock,
a young woman lying outstretched on the bow,   a hare where the trigger was.
He whittled a pile of arrows,   a heap of arrows with three feathers;
the shafts he turns from oak,   the heads he makes of resinous wood.
Whatever he gets ready,   he then feathers it
with little swallow feathers,   with a sparrow's tailfeathers.
He hardened his arrows in fire,   sharpened the tips

in a reptile's dark venom, in the poisonous blood of a snake.
He got the blunt-headed bolts ready, the crossbow drawn.

Then he waited for Väinämöinen, for the man of Slack Water Farm to set
out;
he waited evenings, waited mornings, waited once at midday.
He waited for Väinämöinen for a long time, waited a long time, did not get
tired
sitting by windows, watching on the top landing of the outer stairs,
listening behind a lane, lurking in fields
with a quiver of arrows on his back, the good bow under his arm.
He kept waiting farther off, on the far side of another farm,
on the tip of a very big headland, in the bend in a narrow cape,
beside a fierce rapids, on the banks of a sacred stream.

So on a certain day, on a certain morning,
he cast his gaze to the northwest, turned his head to the south;
he spied a dark spot on the sea, a blue spot on the billows.
"Is that a cloud in the east, daybreak in the northeast?"
It was not a cloud in the east, not daybreak in the northeast;
it was old Väinämöinen, the eternal singer,
traveling to North Farm, proceeding to Gloomy Farm
on his straw stallion, his peastalk horse.
Young Joukahainen, scrawny Lappish lad,
quickly got his hard-hitting crossbow ready, snatched up his most splendid
bow
in readiness for Väinämöinen's head, to kill the man of Slack Water Farm.

His mother had time to ask, his parent to inquire:
"At whom are you bending the crossbow, suddenly shooting the iron bow?"
Young Joukahainen uttered a word, spoke thus:
"I am bending my crossbow suddenly at that, shooting the iron bow
at Väinämöinen's head to kill the man of Slack Water Farm.
I will shoot old Väinämöinen, lay low the eternal singer
through the heart, through the liver, through the shoulder muscles."
The mother forbade him to shoot, the mother forbade and said not to:
"Do not shoot Väinämöinen, do not kill the man of the Kalevala District.
Väinämöinen is of a great clan, the son of my brother-in-law's sister.
If you were to shoot Väinämöinen, lay low the man of the Kaleva District,
joyous music would vanish from the world, singing disappear from on earth.
Joyous music is better in the world, singing is more fitting on earth
than it is in the lands of the Abode of the Dead, in those dwellings of
Death's Domain."

34

Now young Joukahainen   reflects a little,
holds back a little;   one hand gave the order to shoot,
one hand said yes, the other said no;   his sinewy fingers insisted.
At last he said these words,   remarked, spoke thus:
"Let vanish even if twice over   all our worldly joys,
let all songs disappear!   I will certainly shoot, I am not likely to hold back."
He bent his hard-hitting crossbow,   pulled the copper roller
against his left knee,   holding down the bow with his right foot.
He drew a bolt from his quiver,   a feathered arrow from a quiver of three
    shankskins.
He took the swiftest arrow,   selected the best shaft;
he laid it in the groove,   put it up to the flaxen bowstring.
He lined the hard-hitting crossbow   up to his right shoulder,
got ready to shoot,   to shoot Väinämöinen.

He uttered these words: "Hit now, curved birchwood branch,
smite, pinewood bow!   Strike hard, flaxen string!
By as much as my hand goes down,   by so much let the arrow go up;
by as much as my hand goes up,   by so much let the arrow go down."
He moved the trigger,   shot the first arrow;
it went straight up,   right ahead to the sky,
to the scudding clouds,   to the whirling cloud patches.
He shot; it did not obey;   he shot his second arrow;
it went straight down,   into Mother Earth below;
the earth was on the point of death,   the sandy ridge about to split open.
He immediately shot a third, too;   the third time it went straight,
into the withers of the blue elk   under old Väinämöinen;
it shot the straw stallion,   the peastalk horse
through the shoulder muscles,   just behind the left foreleg.

Then old Väinämöinen   plunged straight into the water,
tipped over right into the billows,   went right into the breakers
from the back of the blue elk,   of the peastalk horse.
Then a great wind arose,   a heavy surf on the sea;
it carried old Väinämöinen along,   floated him farther out from land
onto those extensive waters,   the wide open sea.

Then young Joukahainen   boasted with his tongue:
"You will never, old Väinämöinen,   never more alive,
never, never at all,   not while the moon shines gold-bright,
tread the clearings of Väinämöinen's district,   the heaths of the Kaleva Dis-
    trict.
Now bob up and down there for six years,   drift for seven summers,

splash along for eight years   on those extensive waters,
on the boundless billows,   for six years as a fir tree,
for seven as a pine tree,   for eight like the butt end of a stump."

Then he betook himself indoors.   His mother managed to ask:
"Have you already shot Väinämöinen,   laid low the Kaleva descendant?"
Young Joukahainen   says a word in reply:
"I have now already shot Väinämöinen   and laid low the man of the Kaleva
     District;
I threw him in to comb the sea,   to sweep the billows.
The old man tumbled straight   into that restless sea,
tipped over   right among the waves;
then he fell over onto his side,   stayed on his back
to ride the billows of the sea,   to float along on the swell of the sea."
The mother uttered these words: "You did wrong, you wretch,
when you shot Väinämöinen,   laid low the man of the Kaleva District,
the great man of Slack Water Farm,   the handsomest in the Kaleva District."

POEM 7

Väinämöinen floats for several days on the open sea;
he meets the eagle who, still pleased because Väinämöinen,
while making clearings, had left a birch growing for him,
takes him on his back, and carries him to the shore of North Farm,
where the mistress of North Farm
escorts him to her home and treats him well (1–274).
Väinämöinen, however, longs for his own lands
and the mistress of North Farm promises not only to get him there
but also to give him her daughter as a spouse
if he will forge a Sampo at North Farm (275–322).
Väinämöinen promises, once he gets home, to send craftsman Ilmarinen
to forge a Sampo, and receives from the mistress of North Farm
a sleigh and horse with which to set out for his homeland (323–368).

Steadfast old Väinämöinen   swims the deep waves;
he goes along like a rotten fir log,   like a rotten pine stump
for six summer days,   six nights in succession,
before him the flowing water,   behind him the clear sky.
He swims indeed two nights more,   two very long days.
So on the ninth night,   at the end of the eighth day
he begins however to suffer,   starts to ache
because there is no nail on his toes,   no joint in his fingers.

Then old Väinämöinen   said these words:
"Woe is me, wretched fellow,   woe is the miserable fellow
for setting out from my own lands,   from former dwelling places,
to be forever under the sky,   ever on the move,
to be rocked by the wind,   driven by the waves
on these extensive waters,   on the wide open seas.
I am cold here,   it is painful for me to linger here,
ever to live in the waves,   to frequent the surface of the water.
Indeed I do not know   how to exist, how to live
in this dreadful time,   in this fleeting final age.
Shall I build my house in the wind,   make a cabin in the water?
If I build my house in the wind,   it will be no refuge in the wind;
if I make my cabin in the water,   the water will carry my handiwork away."

A bird flew from Lapland,   an eagle from the northeast.
The eagle is not very big   nor is the eagle very small;

one wing grazed the water,   the other swept the heavens,
the tail stroked the sea,   the bill brushed the little islands.
It flies about, it glides about,   it looks about, it wheels about.
It saw old Väinämöinen   on the surface of the blue sea:
"Why are you in the sea, man,   why, fellow, among the waves?"

Steadfast old Väinämöinen   uttered a word, spoke thus:
"This is why I, a man, am in the sea,   a fellow in the custody of the waves:
I set out for a girl at North Farm,   a virgin at Gloomy Farm.
I was speeding   over the restless sea.
Thus after several days,   many mornings,
I came to the bay of Luotola,   to the river water of Joukahainen's farm.
My horse was shot from under me;   it was myself they were after.
Then I rolled into the water,   fell straight into the billows
to be rocked by the wind,   to be driven by the waves.
A wind indeed came from the northwest,   a big gust from the east;
it carried me far,   it floated me farther out from land.
For many days I have been driven,   many nights been swimming along
on these extensive waters,   on the wide open sea.
Indeed I do not know at all,   not appreciate, not understand
which of the two will be the death of me,   which will come first:
exhaustion from hunger   or sinking into the water."

The eagle spoke, bird of the air: "Do not be upset by that!
Stand on my back,   get onto the tips of my wings.
I will carry you from the sea   to where you wish.
I still remember another day, too,   appreciate a better time
when you were cutting down the Kaleva clearing,   felling the wilderness of
    the Osmo District.
You left a birch growing,   a lovely tree standing
as a resting place for birds,   as a place for myself to perch on."

Then old Väinämöinen   raises his head;
the man rises from the sea,   the fellow gets out of the waves,
takes his place on the wings,   on the tip of the eagle's wing.
The eagle, indeed, bird of the air,   carried old Väinämöinen,
takes him along the path of the wind,   along the track of the cold spring
    wind
to the extensive back part of North Farm,   to dark Sedgy Farm.
There it left Väinämöinen,   itself rose into the air.
Then Väinämöinen wept,   then wept and lamented
on the seashore,   on an unknown headland
with a hundred wounds in his side,   a thousand lashes from the wind;

his beard, too, was badly disordered,   his hair tangled.
He wept two nights, three,   the same number of days, too;
he did not indeed know what way to go,   a stranger, not know the route
to get back home,   to go to familiar lands,
to the places of his birth,   to his former dwelling places.

The little maid of North Farm,   a woman of fair complexion,
made a pact with the sun,   with the sun, with the moon,
to get up at the same time   and to wake up together at the same time as
    they.
She got ahead of them,   before the moon, before the sun,
without the cock's raucous crowing   or the chicken's singing.
She clipped five fleeces,   sheared the wool of six sheep,
she made the fleeces into coarse cloth,   fulled them all into homespun
before the sun rose,   the sun came up.
Then she washed the long tables,   swept the spacious floors
with a twig broom,   with a leafy besom.
She gathered up her rubbish   in a copper box,
took it out past the door,   to the field past the farmyard,
to the end of the back field,   to the opening in the fence farther down.
She stood on the rubbish heap,   listened and turned about;
she hears weeping from the sea,   lamentation across the river.
She gets back on the run,   goes quickly into the cabin;
she spoke after she got there,   announced earnestly after she had come:
"I heard weeping from the sea,   lamentation across the river."

Louhi, mistress of North Farm,   gat-toothed dame of North Farm,
at once betook herself to the farmyard,   proceeded to the opening of the gate.
There she listens hard;   she uttered a word, spoke thus:
The weeping is no child's weeping   no women's lamentation;
it is the weeping of a bearded man,   the lamentation of someone with a
    beard."
She pushed a boat into the water,   a three-planked craft onto the billows;
she began to row.   She both rowed and hurried on,
rowed to Väinämöinen,   to the weeping man.
There Väinämöinen was weeping,   the suitor from Slack Water Farm wailing
by a miserable willow-banked brook,   by a stand of bushy chokecherries.
His mouth was working, his beard was shaking   but his chin did not tremble.

The mistress of North Farm spoke,   said, remarked:
"Oh you! miserable old man,   now you are in a strange land!"
Steadfast old Väinämöinen   raises his head,
uttered a word, spoke thus: "I already know that myself!

I am in a strange land, in one completely unknown.
In my country I was better off, in my home more highly esteemed."

Louhi, mistress of North Farm, uttered a word, spoke thus:
"Might I say, would I have leave to ask
what manner of man you are and what kind of a person?"
Steadfast old Väinämöinen uttered a word, spoke thus:
"People used to talk about me, in my time I was esteemed
as a jolly fellow of an evening, as a singer in every dell,
on those clearings in Väinämöinen's district, on the heaths of the Kaleva
District.
Now I am downcast, I hardly know even myself."

Louhi, mistress of North Farm, uttered a word, spoke thus:
"Rise now, man, from the swale, fellow, to enter on a new course,
to speak of your grief, to tell what befell you."
She got the man to stop weeping, the fellow to stop wailing;
then she escorted him into the craft, seated him in the stern of the boat.
She took her place at the oars, applied herself to the oars,
rowed across to North Farm, brings the stranger into the house.
She fed the famished man, dried the drenched person,
then for a long time rubs him down, rubs him down, bathes him with warm
water.
She made the man well, the fellow better.
She questioned, she remarked, she uttered a word, spoke thus:
"Why were you weeping, Väinämöinen, why wailing, man of Slack Water
Farm,
in that wretched spot, on the shore by the sea?"

Steadfast old Väinämöinen uttered a word, spoke thus:
"There is reason indeed for me to weep, to bewail my sufferings.
I have long been swimming the seas, shoveling the billows
in those extensive waters, in the wide open sea.
Always bewailing that I was ever grieving
because I was swimming away from my own lands, going from familiar parts
to these unfamiliar doors, to strange gates.
Here all the trees bite me, all the evergreens hew at me,
every birch strikes mè, every alder cuts me;
only the wind is familiar to me, the sun something I have seen before
in these strange lands, at these quite unfamiliar doors."

Louhi, mistress of North Farm, then put this into words:
"Do not weep, Väinämöinen, not moan, man of Slack Water Farm.

It is fine for you to be here,   delightful that you linger on
to eat salmon from a dish,   pork beside it."

Then old Väinämöinen   said these words:
" 'Eating with strangers is to no purpose,   even among nice strangers;
in his own country a man is better off,   at home more highly esteemed.'
Would merciful God,   the dear Creator, indeed grant
that I might reach my own country,   my former dwelling places!
'Better in one's own country   is even water from out of a birchbark shoe
than is in a foreign country   mead from a golden bowl.' "

Louhi, mistress of North Farm,   uttered a word, spoke thus:
"Well, what will you give me   if I get you to your own lands,
right to your own field,   to the vicinity of your own sauna?"
Väinämöinen said: "What indeed do you ask of me
to get me to my own lands,   right to my own fields,
to the cries of my own cuckoo,   to the songs of my own bird?
Will you accept a high-peaked hat full of gold pieces,   a hatful of silver
    pieces?"

Louhi, mistress of North Farm,   uttered a word, spoke thus:
"O wise Väinämöinen,   eternal sage!
I am not asking for your gold pieces,   I do not desire your silver pieces;
gold pieces are children's playthings,   silver pieces a horse's jingling bells.
If you have the skill to forge a Sampo,   to beat out a lid of many colors
from the tip of the shaft of a swan's feather,   from the milk of a farrow cow,
from a single barleycorn,   from the fleece of one sheep,
then I will give you my girl,   will put up the maiden as your reward,
get you home to your own lands,   to the songs of your own bird,
to where you will hear your cuckoo,   right to your own field.

Steadfast old Väinämöinen   uttered a word, spoke thus:
"I have not the skill to forge a Sampo,   to decorate a lid of many colors.
Get me to my own lands;   then I will dispatch craftsman Ilmarinen
who will forge your Sampo,   beat out a lid of many colors,
appease your maiden,   satisfy your daughter.
He is that kind of craftsman,   an exceedingly skilled smith
who forged the heavens,   beat out the firmament.
No trace of a hammer is visible   nor of where his tongs gripped it."

Louhi, mistress of North Farm,   uttered a word, spoke thus:
"I will dispatch my daughter,   will pledge my child to him
who forges a Sampo,   decorates the lid of many colors

from the tip of the shaft of a swan's feather,   from the milk of a farrow cow,
from a single barleycorn,   from the fleece of one sheep."
She put a colt into harness,   a brown one in front of a sleigh;
she escorted old Väinämöinen to it,   seated him in the stallion's sled.
Then she said these words,   remarked, spoke thus:
"Do not raise your head   nor lift up your pate
unless the stallion by chance gets tired   or evening overtakes you.
If indeed you raise your head   or lift up your pate,
then disaster will certainly come,   an evil day beset you."

Then old Väinämöinen   whipped up the horse into a run,
the flaxen-maned one into getting going.   He rattles along
from gloomy North Farm,   from dark Sedgy Farm.

POEM 8

On his journey Väinämöinen sees the charmingly dressed maid
of North Farm and asks her to be his spouse (1–50).
The girl finally promises to accept Väinämöinen if he will fashion
a boat from a bit of a distaff and get the boat into the water
without touching it in any way whatever (51–132).
Väinämöinen starts to make it, with his ax inflicts a big wound in his knee,
and is unable to stanch the flow of blood (133–204).
He sets out to search for an expert in stanching blood and finds an old man
who says that by threats he will stanch the blood (205–282).

Fair was the maid of North Farm,   famed on land, renowned on sea.
She was sitting on a shaft-bow of the sky,   was resplendent on a rainbow
in clean clothes,   in white garments.
She is weaving cloth of gold,   carefully preparing cloth of silver
off a gold shuttle   against a silver batten.
The shuttle sang under her hands,   the bobbin flew between her hands;
the copper heddles rattled,   the silver batten creaked
as the girl wove the cloth,   prepared cloth of silver.

Steadfast old Väinämöinen   is rattling along
from gloomy North Farm,   from dark Sedgy Farm.
He drove a bit of a way,   went on a little.
He heard the whir of the shuttle   high above his head.
At this he raised his head,   glanced up to the heavens.
There is a beautiful rainbow in the heavens,   a maiden on the edge of the
    rainbow
is weaving cloth of gold,   with easy motions is weaving cloth of silver.
Steadfast old Väinämöinen   at once stopped the horse.
Then he said these words,   remarked, spoke thus:
"Come, maiden, into my sleigh;   get down into my sled."
The girl said these words,   remarked and asks:
"Why should a maiden get into your sleigh,   a girl into your sled?"
Steadfast old Väinämöinen   replied to this:
"This is why a maiden should get into my sleigh,   a girl get into my sled:
to bake honey bread,   to brew beer skillfully,
to sing on every bench,   to bring joyous music to the window
on those farms of Väinämöinen's district,   in the farmsteads of the Kaleva
    District."

The maiden said these words,   remarked and spoke:

"When I was walking on the land grown with yellow madder,   moving
   lightly on the yellow heath
yesterday late in the afternoon   as the sun was setting,
a bird was singing in a grove,   a fieldfare warbling.
It was singing of maidens' desires   and sang of a daughter-in-law's desire.
I got to speaking,   to questioning the bird:
'Oh you fieldfare,   sing so that I may hear with my ears
which of the two it is better to be,   which is the more esteemed:
a girl in her father's house   or a daughter-in-law in a husband's house?'
The tomtit indeed gave me the information,   the fieldfare warbled:
'Bright a summer's day,   brighter the time of maidenhood;
cold is iron in a cold spell,   colder is being a daughter-in-law.
A maiden in her father's house   is like a berry on good soil;
a daughter-in-law in a husband's house   is like a dog in chains.
Seldom does a slave get affection,   a daughter-in-law never at all.' "

Steadfast old Väinämöinen   said these words:
"Vapid the songs of a fieldfare,   the warblings of a thrush.
'At home a daughter is a child,   only after she has married, a woman.'
Come, maiden, into my sleigh,   get down into my sled.
I am no insignificant man,   a no less enterprising person than others."

The girl answered warily,   uttered a word, spoke thus:
"I would call you a man,   would esteem you as something of a person
if indeed you should cleave a swan   with a knife without a point,
knot an egg   with an invisible knot."
Steadfast old Väinämöinen   cleaves a swan
with a knife without a point,   quite without a point at all;
he knots an egg   with an invisible knot.
He ordered the maiden into his sleigh,   the girl into his sled.
The maiden answered warily: "Perhaps indeed I will come to you
if you pull birchbark off a stone,   break off poles from a piece of ice
without a bit splitting off,   without a chip flying off."
Steadfast old Väinämöinen   does not make any great business of that:
he pulled birchbark off a stone,   broke off a pole from a piece of ice
without a bit splitting off,   without a chip flying off.
He invited the maiden into the sleigh,   the girl into his sled.

The maiden answers warily,   speaks these words:
"I would go to that person   who would fashion a boat
from bits of my distaff,   from pieces of my flax scraper,
who would push the boat into the water,   the new ship onto the billows
without a knee pushing it,   without a hand touching it,
an arm turning it,   a shoulder directing it."
Then old Väinämöinen   uttered these words:

44

"There is probably not on earth, not in the world, not under the whole firmament
a shipbuilder the like of me, shipwright my equal."
He took bits of the distaff, of the stock of the spindle;
he set out to a steel mountain, to an iron crag
to fashion a boat, to prepare a ship with a hundred planks.
He shaped the ship out of bravado, made the wooden vessel arrogantly.
He fashioned one day, fashioned a second, fashioned a third in succession, too;
the ax does not touch the rock, the corner of the bit does not strike the crag.
Then on the third day the Demon turned the ax handle,
the Devil jerked the bit, the Evil One made the shaft slip.
The ax hit the stone, the corner of the bit struck the crag,
the ax slid off the stone, the bit slid into the flesh,
into the knee of the capable fellow, into Väinämöinen's toe.
The Devil joined it to the flesh, the Demon fitted it into the veins;
blood started to stream, gore to spurt.

Steadfast old Väinämöinen eternal sage,
then said these words, remarked and spoke thus:
"O you ax with a stub-nosed blade, you straight-bladed battle-ax!
Did you think you had cut a tree, struck a tall evergreen,
hit a pine tree, struck a birch,
when you slipped into my flesh, slid into my veins?"
Then he began to exorcize, began to speak magic words.
He recited origin charms in the right way, magic words in proper order
but he does not remember certain important iron charms
from which one might get a bolt, might fetch a substantial lock
for those rents made by the iron, gashes made by the steel-blue mouth.
Already the blood was running like a river, the gore rushing like a rapids.
It covered the berrystalks on the ground, the heather blooms on the heath.
There was not a single tussock that was not flooded
by those excesses of blood, by gore streaming
from the knee of the earnest fellow, from Väinämöinen's toe.
Steadfast old Väinämöinen stripped lichens from a stone,
took mosses from a fen, tore a tussock from the ground
as a plug for the fearful hole, as a stopper for the bad floodgate.
It does not restrain it in the slightest, check it the least little bit.

He indeed becomes anguished, gets more distressed.
Steadfast old Väinämöinen burst into tears.
He put the colt into harness, the brown one in front of the sleigh;
then he flings himself into the sled, settles down in his basket sleigh.
He struck the spirited steed with the whip, made a ringing sound with the beaded lash.

The spirited steed ran, the journey was coming to an end,   the sled went on,
   the way grew short.
Now soon there comes a settlement;   three roads meet.

Steadfast old Väinämöinen   drives along the lowest road
to the lowest-lying house.   Over the threshold he asks:
"Would there be in this house   a healer of a wound inflicted by iron,
an expert in the matter of a man's anguish,   a mitigator of injuries?"
There was a child on the floor,   a little boy on the stove-bench.
He is the one who answers that: "There is not in this house here
a healer of a wound inflicted by iron,   no expert in the matter of a man's
   anguish,
no one to seize hold of pain,   no magic treater of injuries.
There is in the next house;   drive to the next house."

Steadfast old Väinämöinen   struck the spirited steed with the whip,
whizzes along.   He drove a bit of a way
along the middle road   to the middle house.
From outside the threshold he asked,   from beneath a window he entreated:
"Would there be in this house   a healer of a wound inflicted by iron,
a bolt for the downpour of blood,   a stopper for the rapids flowing from my
   veins?"
There was an old woman there wearing a cloak,   a chatterbox on the hearth
   bench.
The old woman answered up,   she with three teeth snarled:
"There is not in this house here   a healer of a wound inflicted by iron,
an expert in the origin of blood,   no one to seize hold of pain.
There is one in the next house;   drive to the next house."

Steadfast old Väinämöinen   struck the spirited steed with the whip,
whizzes along.   He drove a bit of a way
along the uppermost road   to the uppermost house.
Over the threshold he asks,   said from behind an upright in the entryway:
"Would there be in this house   a healer of a wound inflicted by iron,
a plug for this blood,   a stopper for this dark blood?"
An old man was by the stove,   a graybeard under the ridgepole.
The old man growled from the stove,   the graybeard shouted:
"Even bigger things have been closed,   larger ones vanquished
by three words of the Creator,   by the decree of the Profound Birth:
rivers at their mouths, lakes at their heads,   fierce rapids at their falls,
bays at the tips of their headlands,   isthmuses at their narrowest parts."

POEM 9

Väinämöinen tells the old man of the origin of iron (1–266).
The old man reviles iron and recites blood-stanching charms;
the blood is checked (267–418).
The old man has his son make an ointment, and anoints and binds the wound.
Väinämöinen recovers and thanks God for providing help (419–586).

Then old Väinämöinen got up from the sleigh,
rose from the sled without being lifted, stood up without being raised.
Thence he comes into the cabin, betakes himself under the roof.
A silver stoup is brought, a golden jug is carried in;
they do not carry even a little bit, not hold even a small amount
of old Väinämöinen's blood, of the great man's gore.
The old man growled from the stove, the graybeard shouted:
"What manner of man may you be and what kind of person?
Seven boatfuls, eight buckets of blood,
have, you poor wretch, been discharged from your knee to the floor.
I might remember other charms but I am not acquainted with the beginning,
with where iron originated, with what wretched bog ore grew from."
Then old Väinämöinen uttered a word, spoke thus:
"I know the origin of iron, I am acquainted with the beginning of steel.

ORIGIN CHARMS OF IRON, LINES 29–258
[THE CREATION OF IRON, LINES 29–104]

Air is its first of mothers, water the eldest of brothers,
iron the youngest of brothers, fire in turn the middle one.
Ukko, creator on high, god of the skies,
separated the water from the air, made the mainland into land from the
   water.
Wretched iron is not born, not born, not grown up.
Ukko, heavenly god, rubbed his two hands,
pressed both on his left knee.
From that three maidens were born, all three Nature Spirits
to be the mothers of iron ore, begetters of a steel-blue mouth.
The maidens walked along with a springy gait, the virgins stepped along the
   edge of a cloud
with full breasts, with aching nipples.
They milked their milk onto the ground, let their breasts spurt;
they milked onto the ground, milked onto fens, milked onto gentle waters.
One, the very oldest of the maidens, milked out black milk;
the second, the middle one of the maidens, spilled white milk;

47

the third, the youngest of the maidens,   spurted red milk.
From the one who milked out black milk   bar-iron was born,
from the one who spilled white milk   steel was made,
from the one who spurted red milk   iron ore was got.
A little time passed.   Iron wanted to meet
its elder brother,   to go to make the acquaintance of fire.
Fire began to get bad,   got quite horrible;
it was just about to burn the wretch,   miserable iron, its brother.

Iron was able to hide,   to hide, to save itself
from the hands of that fierce fire,   from the mouth of the bright angry one.
Then iron hid from it,   both hid and was saved
in a shifting quagmire,   in a plashing spring,
on the very big surface of a fen,   on the top of a rough bald hill
where swans lay their eggs,   where the goose broods its young.
Iron lies sprawling in a fen,   stretches out in watery places;
it hid for one year, hid a second,   forthwith hid a third, too,
between two stumps,   at the foot of three birches.
But it did not escape by flight   from the grim hands of fire;
it had to come a second time,   set out to fire's dwellings
to be made into a weapon,   be forged into a sword.

A wolf ran along the fen,   a bear wandered in from the heath;
the fen stirred where the wolf stepped,   the heath where the bear set its paws;
there bog-iron ore came to the surface   and a steel ingot grew
in the prints of the wolf's claws,   in the marks of the bear's heel.

[ILMARINEN DISCOVERS BOG IRON, LINES 105–156]

Craftsman Ilmarinen was born,   both was born and grew up.
He was born on a charred hill,   grew up on a charred heath
with a copper hammer in his hand,   a little tongs in his grip.
Ilmarinen was born at night,   the next day he made a smithy.
He looked for a spot for his smithy,   an open place for his bellows.
He saw a narrow strip of fen,   a bit of wet ground;
he set out to look at that,   to examine it closely from near at hand;
in that he thrust his bellows,   in that he put his forge.

Now he reached the wolf's tracks,   the bear's heelmarks.
He saw sprouts of iron,   lumps of steel
in the wolf's big tracks,   in the prints of the bear's paw.
He speaks these words: "Woe is you, wretched iron,
for you are in a miserable situation,   in a lowly position,
in a wolf's clawmarks in a fen,   right in a bear's footprints."
He ponders, he reflects: "What would become of that indeed

48

if I should thrust it into the fire,   put it into the forge?"
Wretched iron took fright,   took fright, got terrified
when it heard fire's messages,   fire's grim utterances.
Craftsman Ilmarinen said: "Do not be upset by that!
Fire will not burn you once it has made your acquaintance,   will not abuse
   its kin.
When you come to fire's dwellings,   to the bright one's barricade,
there you will become beautiful,   rise up to be magnificent
as men's fine swords,   as the tips of women's laces."
By the end of that day   bog-iron ore had been got loose from the fen,
got separated from the miry place,   been brought to the craftsman's smithy.

[IRON IS FORGED, LINES 157–200]

That the craftsman thrust into the fire,   forced it into the depths of his forge.
He blew his bellows once, blew twice,   blew a third time, too.
The iron gets liquid like gruel,   heaves like slag,
stretches like wheat paste,   like rye dough,
in the craftsman's great fires,   in the power of the glowing flame.
Then wretched Iron howled: "Oh craftsman Ilmarinen,
take me away from here,   from the agonies of red fire!"
Craftsman Ilmarinen spoke: "If I take you out of the fire,
perhaps you will grow to be terrible,   will start raging exceedingly,
cut your brother even further,   carve up your mother's child."
Then wretched iron swore,   swore a solemn oath
by the forge, by the anvil,   by the hammers, by the sledges;
it says these words,   made this utterance:
"There is indeed wood for me to bite,   heart of stone for me to eat
so that I will not cut my brother,   carve up my mother's child.
It is better for me to exist,   nicer for me to live
by going about as a comrade,   going about as a work tool
than to eat my own clan,   abuse my tribe."
Then craftsman Ilmarinen,   eternal smith,
pulled iron out of the fire,   put it on the anvil;
he works it soft,   makes it into edged tools,
spears, axes,   all kinds of tools.

[THE MISSING TEMPERING AGENT, LINES 201–258]

A little something was still lacking,   wretched iron needed something.
Iron's tongue is not boiling,   steel's mouth is not born,
iron will not get tempered   without being wet in a liquid.
Then craftsman Ilmarinen   ponders that.
He prepared a little lye,   dissolved the leach
as a steel-tempering venom,   as an iron-tempering liquid.
The craftsman tested it with his tongue;   he tasted it all he wanted.

He uttered these words: "These are no good for me
as bitter steel-tempering liquids,   as preparations for making iron."

A bee rose from the ground,   a blue-wings from a tussock.
It flies about, it keeps moving   around the craftsman's smithy.
The craftsman spoke thus: "Bee, lively fellow,
bring honey on your wings,   carry honey on your tongue
from the tips of six flowers,   from seven sheaths of grass,
for steel objects to be made,   for iron objects to be prepared."

A wasp, the Demon's bird,   looks about, listens,
looked from the eaves of the roof,   stared from under the birchbark roof,
at the iron objects to be prepared,   at the steel objects to be made.
Humming it flies along,   it hurled abroad the Demon's terrors,
carried the poisons of a snake,   the black venoms of a reptile,
the poisonous acids of an ant,   the secret poisons of a toad
to be poisonous venoms for steel-tempering,   iron-tempering liquid.
Craftsman Ilmarinen,   eternal smith,
thinks, reflects   that the bee has come,
that the latter has brought honey,   carried honey.
He uttered a word, spoke thus: "Just look at those things good for me
as steel-tempering liquids,   things for preparing iron!"
He grabbed the steel and put it in this,   wet the wretched iron in it
after he had brought it from the fire,   taken it from the forge.

Steel then got bad,   iron got raging,
the wretch violated its oath,   trifled like a dog with its honor;
it cut its brother, the wretch,   took hold of its relatives with its mouth,
let blood loose to flow,   gore to stream."

The old man growled from the stove,   the graybeard sang; his head shook:
"Now I know the origin of iron,   understand the ways of steel."

CHARMS AGAINST ABUSES BY IRON, LINES 271–342

"O you wretched iron,   wretched iron, miserable bog iron,
bewitched steel!   Was this what you were begotten from,
from this that you got horrible,   grew very big?
At that time you were not big,   neither big nor small;
you were not very tall   or particularly fierce
when you were lying stretched out as milk,   lying as sweet milk
in the nipples of a young maiden,   developing under the armpit of a virgin
on the edge of a long cloud   under the smooth heavens.
At that time you were not big,   you were neither big nor small
when you were resting as ooze,   standing as clear water

on the very big surface of a fen,   on the top of a rough bald hill,
when you were changed there to earthy muck,   began to become rusty soil.
At that time you were not big,   you were neither big nor small
when the elks trampled you on the fen,   when the wild reindeer lashed you
   on the heath,
a wolf trod on you with its claws,   a bear with its paws.
At that time you were not big,   you were neither big nor small
when you were worked up out of the fen,   softened up out of earthy muck,
were brought to the craftsman's smithy,   put into Ilmarinen's forge.
At that time you were not big,   you were neither big nor small
when as slag you murmured,   splashed like warm water
on grim heaths,   when you swore a solemn oath
by the forge, by the anvil,   by the hammers, by sledges,
by the smith's station,   by the forging place.

"Have you now grown big,   got very angry,
violated, wretch, your oath,   trifled like a dog with your honor
in mangling your clan,   in seizing your relatives with your mouth?
Who ordered you to do the evil work?   Who urged you on to the vile deed?
Your father or your mother   or the eldest of your brothers
or the youngest of your sisters   or some other mighty member of your clan?
Neither your father nor your mother   nor the eldest of your brothers
nor the youngest of your sisters   nor other mighty member of your clan!
You yourself did the evil deed,   you struck the mortal blow.
Come now to recognize your deed,   to make amends for your evil
before I tell your mother,   complain to your parent.
'A mother has more distress,   a parent great anguish
when a son acts badly,   a child does malicious damage.' "

CHARMS FOR STANCHING BLOOD, LINES 343–416

"Restrain yourself, blood, from flowing,   gore, from gushing,
from spattering on me,   from spurting on my chest.
Blood, stand fast like a wall;   stay there, gore, like a fence,
stand like a blade of sedge in the sea,   like sedge grass in moss;
like a boulder on the edge of a field,   a stone by a mighty rapids.
But if you want   to move about more quickly,
then move about in flesh   and glide about in bones.
It is better for you inside,   nicer under the skin,
rippling in the veins   and gliding in the bones
than in flowing onto the ground,   dripping onto the dust.

"You will not, milk, go onto the ground,   onto the grass, innocent blood,
adornment of men, onto a hayfield,   onto a knoll, people's treasure.
Your place is in the heart,   your cellar under the lungs;

move there without delay,   run there fast!
You are not a river to flow   nor a pond to stream,
not a quagmire in a fen to ripple   nor a boat to leak.
Stop now, precious stuff, from trickling,   red stuff, from dripping.
If you do not stop, dry up just the same.   Formerly the rapids of Tyrjä were
   stopped,
the river of Death's Domain dried up,   the sea grew dry, the heavens grew dry
during that great drought year,   the wretched year of forest fires.

"If you do not obey that indeed,   still other charms will be recalled,
new devices discovered.   I will shout for a pot from the Demon's,
in which blood is boiled,   gore heated up
without a drop dripping,   without the red stuff dropping,
with no blood flowing onto the ground,   no gore gushing.

"But if I am perhaps not the man,   if the lad is not Ukko's fellow
to check this flood,   to subdue this cataract from the veins,
there is indeed a heavenly father,   a god above the clouds
who among men has the competence,   who among people is able
to close blood's outlet,   to check the flood.

"O Ukko, creator on high,   heavenly god!
Come here when needed,   come here when summoned!
Press your fat hand,   push your thick thumb
as a stopper of the grim hole,   as a plug for the evil floodgate!
Draw a lovely leaf over it,   pull a beautiful water lily quickly across it
as a dam to the blood's course,   as a plug for the flood,
so that it does not splash on my beard,   run onto my poor clothes."

Then he closed the outlet of the blood,   blocked the course of the gore.

AN OINTMENT CHARM, LINES 419-500

He sent his son to the smithy   to make ointments
from those sheaves of grass,   from the florets of yarrow,
from plants which let honey flow onto the ground,   which drip honeydew.

The boy went to the smithy,   set about making an ointment.
He came upon an oak;   he questioned the oak:
"Is there honey on your branches,   honeydew under your bark?"
The oak answers knowingly: "Yesterday indeed
honeydew was dripping on my branches,   honey sprinkling onto my top
   branches
from the gently dripping clouds,   from cloud patches that were breaking up."
He took some chips from the oak,   bits of the fragile tree,

took some good grasses,   herbs of diverse appearance
which in these parts one does not see   growing everywhere.
He puts a pot on the fire,   gets ready to boil the brew
full of bits of oak bark,   lovely looking grasses.
The pot boiled noisily   for three whole nights,
for three spring days.   Then he looked at the ointments
to see whether the ointments were reliable,   the magic nostrums effective.
The ointments are not reliable,   the magic nostrums not effective.
He put in more grasses,   herbs of diverse appearance
which had been brought from elsewhere,   from a hundred days' journey away,
from nine magicians,   from eight seers.
He boiled them three more nights,   nine nights in all.
He lifts the pot from the fire,   looks at the ointments
to see whether the ointments are reliable,   the magic nostrums effective.

There was a many-branched aspen,   it was growing on the edge of a field.
That the base fellow broke off,   split right in two;
he anointed it with these ointments,   treated it with these magic nostrums.
He uttered these words: "If there is in these ointments
something fit to be put on an injury,   to be poured on wounds,
get whole, aspen,   finer than before!"
The aspen got whole,   finer than before,
grew fair above,   got quite well below.
Then he tested the ointments,   looks at the magic nostrums,
tested them in the cracks of a stone,   in the crevices of boulders.
Already stones were gripping stones,   boulders seizing boulders.

The boy came from the smithy   from making the ointments,
from preparing the unguents;   he thrust them into the old man's hand:
"Here are reliable ointments,   effective nostrums,
though you were even to anoint mountains,   to join all crags together."
The old man tried it with his tongue,   tasted it with his lovely mouth;
he recognized that the magic nostrums were good,   the ointments reliable.

Then he anointed Väinämöinen,   healed the one who had fared badly;
he anointed him below, anointed him above,   once gave his middle a quick
   rub.
He speaks these words,   made this remark:

PROTECTIVE CHARMS, LINES 507–516

"I am not moving by virtue of my own muscles,   I am moving by virtue of
   my Creator's muscles;
I am not moving quickly by my own powers,   I am moving quickly by the
   Almighty's power;

I am not speaking with my own mouth,   I am speaking with God's mouth.
If I have a lovely mouth,   God's mouth is lovelier;
if my hand is fair,   the Creator's hand is fairer."

When the ointment had been put on,   those reliable magic nostrums,
it made him partly swoon,   made Väinämöinen writhe;
he flung himself this way, flung himself that   but he found no rest.

In this way the old man exorcized the pains,   thrust away those agonies
into the middle of Pain Hill,   into the ridge of Pain Mountain,
to break stones,   to crush boulders.
He seized a piece of silk,   cut it into wide strips,
tore it to pieces,   made it into bandages.
With those pieces of silk he bound,   with the lovely silk he bandages
the splendid fellow's knee,   Väinämöinen's toes.
He speaks these words,   made this remark:

A BANDAGE CHARM, LINES 539–546

"Let the Creator's silk be a bandage,   the Creator's cloak be a covering
for this good knee,   for the innocent toes.
Look now, gracious God,   keep us, steadfast Creator,
from being drawn to evil,   snatched into sin."

Then old Väinämöinen   already felt a real relief.
He soon got well,   his flesh grew fair,
altogether well below,   his middle became painless,
his sides perfect,   no scar above,
healthier than before,   finer than in the past.
Now the leg was already strong enough to walk on,   the knee able to stamp;
he does not complain to speak of,   not groan in the very least.

Then old Väinämöinen   raised his eyes upward,
glances courteously   up to the heavens.
He says these words,   made this remark:
"From yonder indeed gracious things ever come,   merciful safeguards come
from heaven above,   from the almighty Creator.
Thanks now, God!   alone be praised, Creator,
for having granted me relief,   mercifully brought protection
in these violent pains,   in the wounds of sharp iron."
Then old Väinämöinen   further uttered these words:
"Do not, people of the future,   people just growing up,
make a boat out of bravado,   a boat rib arrogantly.
'God starts the race,   the Creator determines the finish,
not the skill of a human being,   by no means the power of a strong man.' "

POEM 10

Väinämöinen comes home and urges Ilmarinen to set out to woo
the maid of North Farm whom he would get by forging a Sampo (1–100).
Ilmarinen will never promise to set out for North Farm,
for which reason Väinämöinen must by other means set him on his way
against his will (101–200). Ilmarinen comes to North Farm,
is well received, and is set to forging the Sampo (201–280).
Ilmarinen forges the Sampo and the mistress of North Farm
takes it into North Farm's hill of rock (281–432).
Ilmarinen asks for the girl in payment for his work;
the girl makes difficulties and says she cannot yet leave home (433–462).
Ilmarinen gets a vessel, returns to his home and tells Väinämöinen
that he has already forged the Sampo for North Farm (463–510).

Steadfast old Väinämöinen   took the brown stallion,
put the colt into harness,   the brown one in front of the sleigh;
he flings himself into the sled,   settles down in his sleigh.
He struck the spirited steed with the whip,   made a ringing sound with the
    beaded lash.
The spirited steed ran, the journey was coming to an end;   the sled went on,
    the way grew short,
the birchwood runners clattered along,   the ashwood shaft-bow creaked.
He drives along easily,   drove over fens, drove across country,
drove over extensive clearings.   He proceeded one day, proceeded a second,
then on the third day   he came to a long corduroy causeway,
to the heath of the Kaleva District,   to the edge of the Osmo field.

Then he uttered these words,   spoke and talked:
"Wolf, eat the wizard;   disease, kill the Lapp.
He said I would never get home   never, never alive,
never, never   while the moon shines gold-bright,
to these clearings in Väinämöinen's district,   to the heaths of the Kaleva
    District."
Then old Väinämöinen   sings away magically, practices his art.
He sang up a bushy-crowned fir,   bushy-crowned with golden leaves;
it thrust its crown to the heavens,   rose up through the clouds;
the foliage extended to the skies,   spread in all directions through the heavens.
He sings away magically, practices his art;   he sang a moon to gleam palely
in the golden-crowned fir,   sang a Great Bear onto the branches.

He clatters along   to the lovely dwellings

downcast, low in mind,   high-peaked hat all askew,
because he had pledged craftsman Ilmarinen,   eternal smith,
as a ransom,   as a pledge for his own head,
to gloomy North Farm,   to dark Sedgy Farm.
Now the stallion stopped   at the head of the newly cleared Osmo field.
Then old Väinämöinen   raised his head from the sleigh;
he hears a noise from the smithy,   a din from the charcoal shed.
Steadfast old Väinämöinen   pressed on into the smithy.

Craftsman Ilmarinen is there   he is hammering away.
Craftsman Ilmarinen said: "O you old Väinämöinen!
Where have you been staying so long,   living all this while?"
Steadfast old Väinämöinen   uttered these words:
"I stayed yonder a long time,   was living all the time
at gloomy North Farm,   at dark Sedgy Farm,
skied about on Lappish skis   in the magicians' districts."

Then craftsman Ilmarinen   uttered a word, spoke thus:
"O you old Väinämöinen,   eternal sage!
What have you to say about your travels   now that you have come to the
   dwellings here at home?"
Old Väinämöinen spoke: "I have many things to say.
There is a maiden at North Farm,   a virgin in the cold settlement,
who does not yield to suitors,   does not fancy nice men.
Half the north land praises her,   for she is very comely.
It was as if the moon were shining on her brow,   the sun gleaming on her
   breasts,
the Great Bear on her shoulders,   the Pleiades on her back.
You, craftsman Ilmarinen,   eternal smith,
set out to fetch the maiden,   to look at her luxuriant hair.
If you can forge a Sampo,   decorate a lid of many colors,
then you will get the maiden as your payment,   the lovely girl for your work."

Cratfsman Ilmarinen said: "O old Väinämöinen!
Have you already promised me   to gloomy North Farm
as a pledge for your own head,   as a ransom for yourself?
I will never at all   not while the moon shines gold-bright,
set out for the dwellings of North Farm,   for the log buildings of Sedgy Farm,
for places where men are devoured,   people destroyed."
Then old Väinämöinen   uttered these words:
"There is yet another marvelous marvel;   there is a bushy-crowned fir,
bushy-crowned with golden leaves   on the edge of the Osmo field.
The moon was gleaming palely in the crown,   the Great Bear was standing
   still on the branches."

Craftsman Ilmarinen said: "I will not believe that that is true
unless I go and look, see with these eyes of mine."
Old Väinämöinen said: "If you do not really believe it,
let us go look and see whether this is the truth or a lie."
They set out to look at the bushy-topped fir,
old Väinämöinen the one, craftsman Ilmarinen the other.
Then when they got there to the edge of the Osmo field,
the craftsman stands still right by it, marvels at the new fir,
for on its branches was the Great Bear, the moon in the crown of the fir.
Then old Väinämöinen uttered these words:
"Now you craftsman, my boon companion, go up and fetch the moon,
get the Great Bear from the golden-crowned fir."
Then craftsman Ilmarinen went high up the tree,
way up to the heavens, went up to fetch the moon,
to take the Great Bear from the golden-crowned fir.
The bushy-crowned fir spoke, the broad-crowned pine gave utterance:
"Woe is a foolish man, a quite inexperienced person!
You went up, funny fellow, onto my branches, childish you, to my crown
to fetch the feigned moon, for a false star."

Then old Väinämöinen sings in a low voice.
He sang the wind into a gale, worked the weather into a fury.
He speaks these words, makes this magic utterance:
"Take him, wind, into your vessel, get him, cold spring wind,
into your boat to transport him to gloomy North Farm."
The wind rose to a gale, the weather got into a fury.
It took craftsman Ilmarinen and sped him
to gloomy North Farm, to dark Sedgy Farm.

Then craftsman Ilmarinen now went on until he got there.
He went on along the path of the wind, along the course of the cold spring
   wind
over the moon, along under the sun, along the shoulder of the Great Bear.
He ended up in the yard at North Farm, on the path to the sauna at Sedgy
   Farm.
Neither did the dogs hear him nor the barkers notice him.

Louhi, mistress of North Farm, gat-toothed dame of North Farm,
she comes to the yard. She managed to speak:
"What manner of man are you and what kind of a fellow?
You came here on the path of the wind, on the sled course of the cold
   spring wind.
And the dogs are not barking, the bushytails not uttering a sound!"
Craftsman Ilmarinen said: "I by no means came here

57

to be torn by the dogs of the settlement,   to be attacked by bushytails,
at these strange doors,   at these alien gates."
Then the mistress of North Farm   inquired of the newcomer:
"Have you come to make the acquaintance of,   to hear about, to know about
that craftsman Ilmarinen,   the highly skilled smith?
We have now long been waiting   and long been wanting him
to make a new Sampo   for these wilderness districts of North Farm."
Craftsman Ilmarinen   uttered a word, spoke thus:
"I have probably got to know   that craftsman Ilmarinen
since I myself am Ilmarinen,   myself the skilled smith."

Louhi, mistress of North Farm,   gat-toothed dame of North Farm,
made her way quickly into the house.   She speaks these words:
"My girl younger than I,   my very steady-going child,
now put your best things on your head,   the most charming things on your
     body,
the most shining on your bosom,   the most splendid on your breast,
on your neck the most beautiful,   the loveliest on your brow
to make your cheeks rosy,   to set off your face.
Craftsman Ilmarinen,   eternal smith,
has now come to make a Sampo,   to decorate a lid of many colors."
That fair girl of North Farm,   famed by land, renowned by sea,
took choice garments,   the most beautiful of her dresses,
clothes herself, garbs herself,   dons head ornaments,
puts on copper belts,   makes herself uncommonly fine in gold belts.
She came from the storehouse into the house,   walking with springy step
     from the farmyard,
her eyes radiant,   her forehead high,
her face beautiful,   her cheeks rosy.
Gold objects hung on her breast,   silver ones shone on her head.

The mistress of North Farm   led craftsman Ilmarinen
into those dwellings of North Farm,   into the log buildings of Sedgy Farm;
there she gave him food to eat,   gave the man drink to drink,
entertained him very well.   Then she began to speak:
"O craftsman Ilmarinen,   eternal smith!
If you are able to forge a Sampo,   to decorate a lid of many colors
from the tip of the shaft of a swan's feather,   from the milk of a farrow cow,
from a tiny ear of barley,   from the fleece of a summer ewe,
then you will get the maiden as your payment,   the lovely girl for your work."

Then craftsman Ilmarinen   uttered these words:
"I will probably be able to forge a Sampo,   to decorate a lid of many colors
from the tip of the shaft of a swan's feather,   from the milk of a farrow cow,

from a tiny ear of barley,   from the fleece of a summer ewe
just as I forged the heavens,   tapped out the firmament
without any ground plan,   without benefit of a piece of string."
He started the construction of the Sampo,   the decoration of the lid of many
    colors.
He asked for a forge there,   he lacked a smith's tools;
there was no forge there,   no forge, no bellows,
no smithy, no anvil,   no hammer, no handle.
Then craftsman Ilmarinen   uttered these words, spoke thus:
"Let women be irresolute,   poor wretches leave a task half done
but not a really rather inferior man,   a really less enterprising person."

He searched for a base for a forge,   an open place for a bellows
in those parts, in those regions   behind the fields of North Farm.
He searched one day, searched a second.   Then on the third day
he came upon a marbled stone,   a big block of rock.
There the craftsman stopped,   the smith built a fire;
one day he made a bellows,   the next he set up the forge.
Then craftsman Ilmarinen,   eternal smith,
thrust the things into the fire,   his work down to the bottom of the forge;
he employed slaves to blow,   serfs to pump the bellows.
The slaves blew and fanned the flames,   the serfs pumped the bellows
for three summer days,   three summer nights.
The stones grew into their heels,   boulders into where their toes were.
Thus on the first day   craftsman Ilmarinen
bent down to look   at the bottom of his forge
to see what might be coming out of the fire,   emerging from the blaze.
A crossbow poked up out of the fire,   a golden bow out of the glow,
a golden bow, a silver tip,   a shaft ornamented with copper.
The crossbow is fine-looking   but is not well-mannered:
every day it demands a head,   on a really good day two heads.

Craftsman Ilmarinen   is not greatly delighted with this;
he broke the bow in two,   then thrusts it into the fire.
He set slaves to blowing,   the serfs to pumping the bellows.
Now indeed the day after   craftsman Ilmarinen
bent down to look   at the bottom of his forge:
a boat pokes up out of the fire,   a red craft out of the glow,
bow and stern adorned with gold,   tholepins cast of copper.
The boat is fine-looking   but is not well-mannered:
for no reason it would set out to war,   needlessly go to battle.

Craftsman Ilmarinen   is not delighted with that at all;
he smashed the boat to pieces,   thrusts it into the hearth.

He set the slaves to blowing,   the serfs to pumping the bellows.
Now on the third day   craftsman Ilmarinen
bent down to look   at the bottom of his forge:
a heifer pokes up out of the fire,   a golden horned one out of the glow;
on its shoulder is the constellation of the Great Bear,   on its head the sun's
   disk.
The heifer is fine-looking   but is not well-mannered:
in the forest it keeps lying down,   keeps spilling milk on the ground.

Craftsman Ilmarinen   is not delighted with that at all;
he broke the cow to bits,   then thrusts them into the fire.
He sets the slaves to blowing,   the serfs to pumping the bellows.
Now on the fourth day   craftsman Ilmarinen
bent down to look   at the bottom of his forge:
a plow pokes up out of the fire,   the blade of gold out of the glow,
blade of gold, shaft of copper,   silver on the hilt.
The plow is fine-looking   but is not well-mannered:
it plows up the community fields,   furrows cultivated lands.

Craftsman Ilmarinen   is not delighted with that at all;
he broke the plow in two,   thrusts it into the depths of the forge.
He set the winds to blowing,   strong gusts to pumping the bellows.
The winds blew and fanned the flames,   the east wind blew, the west wind
   blew,
the south wind blew still more,   the north wind roared loud.
It blew one day, blew a second,   forthwith it blew a third day, too;
fire swirled out of the opening,   sparks flashed from the fire door,
ashes rose to heaven,   the smoke gets dense up to the clouds.
At the end of the third day   craftsman Ilmarinen
bent down to look   at the bottom of his forge;
he saw that a Sampo was being born,   a lid of many colors forming.
Then craftsman Ilmarinen,   eternal smith,
taps away fast,   pounds away spiritedly.
He forged the Sampo skillfully: on one side a grain mill,
on the second side a salt mill,   on the third a money mill.
Then the new Sampo ground away,   the lid of many colors went round and
   round;
it ground a binful in the dawn,   one binful of things to eat;
it ground a second of things to sell,   a third of household supplies.

Thus the dame of North Farm was delighted.   Then she took the big Sampo
to North Farm's hill of rock,   to inside the copper mountain
behind nine locks.   There it struck root
to the depth of nine fathoms;   it put one root down into solid ground,
a second into the water's edge,   the third into the rise near the house.

Then craftsman Ilmarinen   went to sue for the girl.
He uttered these words, spoke thus: "Is the girl now mine
since the Sampo has been finished,   your lid of many colors made a thing of
   beauty?"
That beautiful girl of North Farm   spoke these words thus:
"Who indeed here next year,   who indeed three summers from now
would make cuckoos call,   birds sing,
if I should go elsewhere,   I, a berry, get to other lands?
If this chick should vanish,   this gosling disappear,
the mother's offspring get lost,   the red whortleberry go away,
all the cuckoos would indeed vanish,   the birds of joyous music move away
from the heights of this region,   from the crests of this ridge.
Besides, I have no time at all,   cannot get away from my days of maidenhood,
from those tasks that must be performed,   from summer's pressing tasks,
with the berries on the ground unpicked,   the shores of the bay not sung to,
the meadows untrod by me,   the groves not sported in by me."

Then craftsman Ilmarinen,   eternal smith,
downcast, low in mind,   high-peaked hat all askew,
now reflects on this,   long holds his head on his hand,
reflecting on how to go home,   how to reach familiar lands
from gloomy North Farm,   from dark Sedgy Farm.

The mistress of North Farm said: "O craftsman Ilmarinen,
why are you low in mind,   your high-peaked hat all askew?
Would you like to go   to your former dwelling places?"
Craftsman Ilmarinen said: "I should like to go there
to my home to die,   to my country quietly to pine away."
Then the mistress of North Farm   fed the man, gave the man drink,
seated him in the stern of a craft   provided with a copper paddle.
She told the wind to blow,   the north wind to blow a gale.
Then craftsman Ilmarinen,   eternal smith,
journeyed to his own lands   over the blue sea.
He went for one day, went a second;   on the third day, indeed,
the craftsman now got home   to the place of his birth.

Old Väinämöinen inquired   of craftsman Ilmarinen:
"Boon companion, craftsman Ilmarinen,   eternal smith!
Have you already made a new Sampo,   decorated a lid of many colors?"
Craftsman Ilmarinen said,   the maker himself spoke:
"The new Sampo was already grinding away,   the lid of many colors going
   round and round;
it was grinding a binful in the dawn,   one binful of things to eat,
it ground a second of things to sell,   a third of household supplies."

POEM 11

Lemminkäinen sets out to woo the high-born maid of the Island (1–110).
The maidens of the Island at first ridicule him
but they soon become all too well acquainted with him (111–156).
The one, Kyllikki, for whom he set out,
he does not get to agree voluntarily,
for which reason he finally abducts her forcibly,
throws her into the sleigh and sets out on the journey (157–222).
Kyllikki weeps and in particular
condemns Lemminkäinen's warlike proclivities.
Lemminkäinen promises never to set out to war
if Kyllikki will promise never to gad about, and both indeed swear
they will stay home (223–314). Lemminkäinen's mother
is delighted with her young daughter-in-law (315–402).

It is time to speak of Ahti,   to go on about the rascal.

Ahti, lad of the Island,   that reckless son of Lempi,
grew up in a grand home   at his dear mother's
at the head of a very large bay,   in a cove in Faraway Headland.
There the man with a far-roving mind grew up on fish,   Ahti grew tall on
    perch.
He got to be the very finest man,   the ruddy-cheeked fellow flourished;
he has a good head on him,   for his part he is competent.
But he went a little astray,   got into trouble because of his ways:
he was always around the women,   visiting all night
to the delight of those virgins,   dancing with girls with luxuriant hair.

Kyllikki was a maiden of the Island,   maiden of the Island, flower of the
    Island.
She grew up in a grand home,   grew up to be very lovely,
sitting in her father's cottages,   on the curves of the highbacked bench.
Long she flourished, was famed far and wide.   Suitors came from afar
to the maiden's fine home,   to the lovely farmstead.
Sun proposed for his son;   she did not go to Sun's abode
to roast at Sun's   during the summer's pressing tasks.
Moon proposed for his son;   she did not go to Moon's abode
to gleam palely at Moon's,   to circle domains of the sky.
Star proposed for his son;   she did not go to Star's abode
to twinkle through the nights   in the wintry heavens.
Suitors come from Estonia,   others from yonder in Ingria.

The girl certainly did not go there.   In reply she answered:
"Your gold is going for nothing,   your silver is getting less and less.
Nor will I set out for Estonia,   will not set out, not pledge myself
to row Estonian waters,   to punt away from the people of the Island
to eat Estonian fish,   gulp down Estonian broth.
I will not set out to Ingria,   Pengria, Pangria.
There is dearth there, dearth of everything,   dearth of wood, dearth of splints,
dearth of water, dearth of wheat,   dearth of rye bread."

Reckless Lemminkäinen,   the handsome man with a far-roving mind,
vowed to set out   to woo the flower of the Island,
that fine bride-to-be,   beautiful creature with luxuriant hair.
His mother tried to forbid it,   the old woman kept warning him:
"Do not go, my son,   to people better than yourself.
You may not be tolerated   in the great clan of the Island."
Reckless Lemminkäinen spoke,   the handsome man with a far-roving mind
   said:
"If I am not elegant as to my house,   not very great as to my clan,
I will prevail by my figure,   take her by other ways of mine."
His mother keeps forbidding   Lemminkäinen to set out
to the great clan of the Island,   to the large family:
"There the maidens will ridicule you,   the women laugh at you."
What did Lemminkäinen care!   He said these words:
"I will certainly stop the women's laughter,   the daughters' peals of laughter;
I will knock a boy into their wombs,   a baby into their embrace.
There is an end to even good ridicule,   to even the best insult!"
Then his mother spoke these words: "Woe is me, wretched me!
Should you seduce the women of the Island,   ravish the pure maidens,
then strife would come of it,   a great war arise.
All the suitors of the Island,   a hundred men with their swords
would attack you, poor wretch,   beset the solitary man."

What did Lemminkäinen care   about his mother's warnings!
He takes a good stallion,   harnessed a choice colt;
he clatters along   to the famed settlement of the Island
to woo the flower of the Island,   the Island's fine bride-to-be.

The women laughed at Lemminkäinen,   the maidens showed their scorn
when he drove up the lane oddly,   strangely to the farmstead.
He tipped his basket sleigh over,   rolled into the gate.
Then Lemminkäinen screwed up his mouth,   twisted his head around,
clawed at his black beard.   He uttered these words:
"I have not seen that before,   not previously seen or heard
a woman laughing at me,   have not tolerated a maiden's scorn."

What did Lemminkäinen care!   He uttered a word, spoke thus:
"Is there a place on the Island,   land on the mainland of the Island,
for me to sport in,   a field for me to dance on
as a delight to the maidens of the Island,   dancing with the girls with
    luxuriant hair?"
The virgins of the Island,   the maidens of the headland answer:
"Indeed there is a place on the Island,   land on the mainland of the Island
for you to sport on,   a field for you to dance on
as a herdsman on burned-over lands,   as a herder on a burned-over clearing.
'On the lands of the Island children are scrawny,   colts fat.' "

What did Lemminkäinen care!   He hired out as a herdsman,
by day went about his herding,   by night the delight of the virgins,
sport for those maidens,   dancing with the girls with luxuriant hair.
Then reckless Lemminkäinen,   the handsome man with a far-roving mind,
now indeed stopped woman's laughter,   restrained maiden's ridicule.
There was not a single daughter,   not the very purest maiden
whom he did not touch,   by whose side he did not stretch out.

There was one virgin among them all   in the great clan of the Island
who had not given in to suitors,   not taken a fancy to nice men:
that was elegant Kyllikki,   gracious flower of the Island.
Reckless Lemminkäinen,   handsome man with a far-roving mind,
wore out a hundred boots,   rowed a hundred oars to pieces
while getting that girl,   while catching Kyllikki.
Kyllikki, elegant girl,   she indeed uttered these words:
"Why, wretched fellow, do you keep roving about?   Why, whimpering shore
    bird, are you driving about,
asking for girls from here,   inquiring about girls with tin-adorned belts?
I will not have time for this   until I grind my quern stone to rubbish,
pound my pestle to a mere stub,   stamp the mortar to bits.
I will not marry frivolous men,   frivolous men, insignificant persons;
I want a sturdy body   for my sturdy body,
I want a rather finer figure   for my fine figure,
also a most handsome face   for my handsome face."
It was a short time,   barely half a month elapsed.
Now on a certain day,   on a certain evening,
the maidens were sporting,   the fair ones dancing
secretly on the land side of the Island,   on a lovely heath,
Kyllikki supreme over the others,   most famous flower of the Island.
The ruddy-cheeked rascal came along,   reckless Lemminkäinen drove
his own stallion,   his choice colt
to the middle of the playing field,   of the fair ones' dance.
He snatched Kyllikki into the sleigh,   dragged the maiden into his sled,

put her on his fur rug,   tied her to the slatted bottom of his sleigh.
He struck the horse with the whip,   cracked the lash,
then started sliding along.   As he was setting out, he says:
"Do not, virgins,   ever let on,
that I came here,   that I abducted the maiden from here.
If you do not obey this,   then evil will befall you:
I will sing your suitors away to war,   the young men laid low by a sword,
so that you will never hear them,   never see them
walking in the cattle runs,   driving on the meadows."

Kyllikki of course complained,   the flower of the Island kept lamenting:
"Release me now,   let the child go free
to proceed to her home,   to her weeping mother.
If you do not grant me leave   to proceed home,
there are still my five brothers,   seven children of my father's brother
to follow the hare's trail,   to claim the girl's head."
Since, however, she was by no means set free,   she burst out crying.
She uttered a word, spoke thus: "In vain was I born, wretched me,
born in vain, grew up in vain,   lived my life in vain;
now I have got into the hands   of a worthless, insignificant man,
into the protection of a wager of war,   of an ever fierce fighter."

Reckless Lemminkäinen spoke,   the handsome man with a far-roving mind
    said:
"Kyllikki, my dear heart,   my sweet little berry!
Do not be upset by this.   I will probably not treat you badly;
you will be in my embrace while I am eating,   holding my hands when I am
    going about,
at my side when I am standing still,   beside me when I am stretched out.
What indeed are you grieving over,   what are you anxiously sighing about?
Are you grieving over that,   anxiously sighing about that,
over a lack of cows, lack of bread,   and over a shortage of all provisions?
Do not be upset by that.   I have many cows,
many givers of milk;   the one on the fen is Blackie,
a second on the hill is Strawberry,   a third in the clearing is Whortleberry.
They are lovely yet do no eating,   beautiful yet not looked after;
evenings there is no tying them up,   nor mornings any turning them loose,
no throwing them fodder,   salt, no bother about mash.
Or were you grieving over,   anxiously sighing about
my family not being great,   my house not very elegant?
If I am not of a great family   and my house is not elegant,
I have a flashing sword,   a glittering blade.
That indeed is of a big clan,   of a large family:
it was sharpened at the Demon's,   polished at the gods'.

65

With that I will enlarge my clan,   extend my whole family,
with the tempered sword,   the flashing blade."

The poor girl grieved,   uttered these words:
"O Ahti, son of Lempi!   If you want a girl like me
as an eternal spouse,   as a chick by your side,
swear eternal oaths   that you will not go to war
from any craving for gold,   desire for silver, either."
Then reckless Lemminkäinen   uttered these words:
"I swear eternal oaths   that I will not go to war
from any craving for gold,   desire for silver, either.
You yourself swear an oath   that you will not gad about
from a desire for a good dance,   from a craving to go dancing."
Then they swore their oaths,   made their eternal vows
in the presence of illustrious God,   humbly looking up at the face of the
   Almighty:
Ahti will not go to war,   Kyllikki not gad about.

Then reckless Lemminkäinen   whipped up the spirited steed with the switch,
struck the stallion with the reins.   He uttered these words:
"Farewell, grasslands of the Island,   fir-tree roots, resinous stumps
which I have walked over summers,   trod on every winter,
hiding on cloudy nights,   fleeing in bad weather
while I was hunting hazel grouse,   ever pursuing old squaws."
He drives along easily;   his home now soon appears.
The girl utters these words,   spoke and said thus:
"A house is looming up yonder,   it looks like a hunger-haunted ruin.
Whose house indeed is it,   what good-for-nothing's home is it?"
Reckless Lemminkäinen   uttered a word, spoke thus:
"Do not grieve over the houses,   do not sigh over the buildings.
We will make other houses,   put up better ones
from huge stands of timber,   from the best stands of slender trees."

Then reckless Lemminkäinen   now gets home
to his dear mother's,   to his own parent's.
The mother uttered these words,   remarked, spoke thus:
"You stayed a long time, my son,   a long time in strange lands."
Reckless Lemminkäinen said,   uttered a word, spoke thus:
"I seduced the women for me to laugh at,   took vengeance on the virtuous
   maidens,
put a stop to the protracted ridicule,   to their mocking of me.
I got the best one into my basket sleigh,   put her on my fur rug,
tied her to the slatted bottom of my sleigh,   rolled her under the woolen robe.
Thus I paid off the women's laughter,   the girls' fun.

66

O mother mine, you who bore me, my mother who brought me up!
What I set out for, that indeed I obtained; what I asked for, that I got.
Now lay out the best bedding, the softest pillows
for me to lie down on in my own land with my young maiden."

The mother uttered these words, spoke and talked:
"Now thanks be, God, glory be, Creator, especially
because you gave me a daughter-in-law, brought a girl good at blowing up
  the fire,
an excellent weaver of cloth, a very capable spinner,
a fine washer of laundry, bleacher of clothes.
Thank your good luck! You got a good thing, you met a good thing,
your Creator granted you a good thing, the Gracious One gave you a good
  thing.
A snow bunting on the snow is pure, purer the one at your side;
white is the foam on the sea, whiter she who is in your power;
graceful is a mallard on the sea, more graceful she who is in your protection;
bright is a star in heaven, brighter the one wedded to you.
Now build broad floors, get bigger windows,
set up new walls, make the whole house better,
with thresholds before the house, new doors on the thresholds,
now that you have got the young maiden, have picked a beautiful one,
better than yourself, greater than your clan."

POEM 12

Kyllikki forgets her oath and starts to gad about,
at which Lemminkäinen gets very angry and decides then and there
to cast her off and to set out to woo the maiden of North Farm (1–128).
His mother tries in every way to stop her son from setting out
and says that he will meet his death there.
Lemminkäinen, while brushing his hair,
out of spite flings the brush from his hand and then and there
demands that blood flow from the brush as if from himself (129–212).
He gets ready, sets out on his journey, comes to North Farm,
and enchants every man out of the house at North Farm.
Just one, a loathsome cattle herder [Soppy Hat],
he leaves unenchanted (213–504).

Then Ahti Lemminkäinen,   that handsome man from Faraway Farm,
spent all his time   with the young maiden;
he himself did not go to the wars   nor did Kyllikki gad about.

So on a certain day,   on a certain morning
Ahti Lemminkäinen   sets out for fish-roe;
he did not come home in the evening,   did not get there the next night.
Kyllikki now went gadding about,   went to the sport of those maidens.
Who indeed brings the news,   who indeed relays the gossip?
Ahti has a sister Ainikki;   she is the one who brings the news,
she is the one who relays the gossip: "My dear brother Ahti,
Kyllikki has already been gadding about,   going to the gates of outsiders,
sporting with the neighborhood maidens,   dancing with the girls with lux-
    uriant hair."
The lad Ahti, beloved lad,   reckless Lemminkäinen,
got angry at that, got irked at that,   was furious at that for a long time.
He uttered these words: "O my mother, aged woman!
If only you would wash my shirt   in the poisons of a black snake,
if you would dry it quickly   so that I may war
on the home fires of the lads of North Farm,   on the fields of the children of
    Lapland!
Kyllikki has now been gadding about,   going to the gates of outsiders,
sporting with those maidens,   dancing with the girls with luxuriant hair."

Of course Kyllikki says,   the woman first hastens to say:
"O my dear Ahti,   do not set out to war!
I had a dream while I was lying down,   while I was stretched out sound
    asleep:

68

fire belched forth as from a forge, fire blazed
right along under the window,   along the embankment by the back wall;
from there it surged into the house,   roared like a rapids
from the floorboards to the ceiling,   from window to window."
Then reckless Lemminkäinen   uttered these words:
"I do not believe in women's dreams   or in wives' oaths.
O my mother, you who bore me,   bring my war gear here,
fetch my battle dress.   It is my desire
to drink the beer of war,   taste the mead of war."
The mother uttered these words.   "O Ahti my son,
do not set out to war.   We have in the house beer
in alderwood kegs   behind an oak spigot,
enough for you to drink   even if you drank all day."
Reckless Lemminkäinen said: "I do not care for homemade beer;
I prefer to drink river water   from the blade of the tarred paddle;
I find it sweeter to drink   than all the homemade table beers.
Bring my war gear here,   fetch my battle dress.
I am setting out for the houses of North Farm,   for the fields of the children
   of Lapland
to ask for gold pieces,   to demand silver pieces."
Lemminkäinen's mother said: "O Ahti my son,
there are indeed gold pieces in the house,   silver pieces in our storehouse.
Only yesterday   very early in the morning
a slave was plowing an adder-ridden field,   was turning over one infested by
   snakes.
The plough lifted up the lid of a chest,   the tongue of the plough brought
   up money.
In it were locked hundreds of coins,   thousands heaped up.
I took the chest to the storehouse,   put it up in the storehouse loft."
Reckless Lemminkäinen said: "I do not care for household stores.
If I happen to get a mark piece in battle,   I regard that as better
than all the gold pieces at home,   silver pieces brought up by a plough.
Bring my war gear here,   fetch my battle dress.
I am setting out to war against North Farm,   to fight the children of Lapland.
It is my desire   and it is my wish
to hear with my own ears,   see with these eyes of mine,
whether there is a maiden at North Farm,   a girl at Gloomy Farm,
who has not given in to suitors,   not taken a fancy to nice men."

Lemminkäinen's mother said: "O Ahti my son,
you have Kyllikki in the house,   a rather highborn housewife.
Two women are dreadful   in one man's bed!"

Reckless Lemminkäinen said: "Kyllikki is a gadabout.
Let her hop in every dance,   let her lie down in every cottage

where the neighborhood virgins are having fun, the girls with luxuriant hair
    dancing."
The mother tried to forbid it, the old woman warned him again and again:
"Just do not go, my son, to the houses of North Farm
without knowledge of magic, without competence in magic skill,
not to the houses of the lads of North Farm, to the fields of the children of
    Lapland.
There a Lapp will likely enchant you, a Finnmark Lapp thrust you
right into the ashes, straight into the clay, right into fluffy ashes,
directly into hot ashes, into red-hot boulders."

Lemminkäinen speaks thus: "Already wizards have bewitched me,
wizards bewitched, the snakes-in-the-grass cursed me. One summer evening
three Laplanders tried it on me lying naked on a solid boulder
without a belt, without clothes, not wrapped in a shred of clothing.
This much they got out of me, this much they got, the wretches:
what an ax gets from a stone, an auger from a crag,
a block of wood from slippery ice, Death from an empty house.
They threatened one way, it indeed turned out another.
They wanted to put me, they threatened to sink me
as a corduroy road into fens, as planks into dirty wet places,
to put me into the mire up to my chin, into a bad place up to my beard.
But being the man I am, I did not greatly worry about that.
I began to practice magic myself, got to singing magic songs.
I sang the wizards with their arrows, the magic bowmen with their weapons,
those magicians with their knife blades, the seers with their steel weapons,
into Death's fierce rapids, into the dreadful maelstrom
under the highest cataract, under the worst whirlpool.
May the wizards sleep there, the ill-disposed sorcerers lie there
until grass grows through their heads, through their high-peaked hats,
through a wizard's shoulders, through the shoulder muscles
of the wizard lying there, the sleeping sorcerer!"

The mother kept disapproving of Lemminkäinen's setting out,
the mother forbade her son, the wife disapproved of her husband:
"Just do not go there at all to the cold settlement,
to gloomy North Farm. Ruin will surely come,
the ruin of a splendid youth, disaster for reckless Lemminkäinen.
Even if you say it a hundred times over, I just do not believe it at all.
You are no singer compared to the lads of North Farm
nor do you understand the speech of Finnmark, not know how to sing magic
    in Lappish."
Then reckless Lemminkäinen, the handsome man with a far-roving mind,
groomed his head, brushed his hair.

He dashed the brush against the wall, flung it against the corner post of the
  stove,
uttered a word, spoke thus, spoke and said:
"It will be the disaster of Lemminkäinen, the ruin of the splendid youth,
when the brush is streaming with blood, the brush flowing with gore."
Reckless Lemminkäinen set out for gloomy North Farm
in the face of his mother's no, his parent's warning.
He girds himself, he dirds himself, puts on his iron shirts,
wraps himself in steel belts. He uttered these words:
"A man is more secure in a byrnie, better in an iron shirt,
more powerful in a steel belt among those wizards,
so that he does not worry about the poorer ones, not bother about the really
  good ones."
He took his own sword, seized his flashing blade
which had been sharpened at the Demon's, polished at the gods';
he girds it to his side, thrust it into the lined sheath.

Where shall the man arm himself by incantations, the bold fellow protect
  himself?
Now he is arming himself somewhat, the bold one protecting himself
yonder under the lintel at the opening of the door, by the doorjamb of the
  cabin,
in the yard at the entrance to the lane, at the farthest gates.
There the man is arming himself against womenfolk.
Those measures are not effective nor are the places of shelter dependable,
so he takes further precautions against menfolk
where two roads cross, on top of a blue stone,
by shifting quagmires, by plashing springs,
by the mighty falls of a rapid, in the bend of a mighty stream.

PROTECTIVE CHARMS, LINES 255-296

There reckless Lemminkäinen uttered words and spoke magic:
"Up from the earth, swordsmen, men as old as the earth,
from wells, swordsmen, from rivers, crossbowmen!
Rise up, forest, with your men, the whole backwoods with your people,
old man of the mountain with your forces, water demon with your terrors,
mistress of the water with your spirits, oldest woman of the water with your
  powers,
maidens from every swale, fine ladies from quagmires,
to aid a solitary man, as comrades for a famous lad,
so that a wizard's arrows will not cut, neither a seer's steel weapons
nor an ill-disposed sorcerer's knife-blades nor the weapons of magic marks-
  men.
If this is not enough, I recall still another means, too.

I will sigh deeply looking higher up to that Ukko of the sky
who rules the clouds, governs the cloud patches:
'O Ukko, god on high, ancient heavenly father
who speaks through the clouds, talks through the sky!
Bring me a flaming sword inside a flaming sheath
with which I will sunder obstacles, with which I will undo destructive magic,
kill the earthly sorcerers, defeat the water wizards
in the air in front of me, back of me,
above me, beside me, on either flank—
I will fell the wizards with their arrows, the sorcerers with their knifeblades,
the seers with their steel weapons, the bad men with their swords.' "

Then reckless Lemminkäinen, that handsome man with a far-roving mind,
whistled a colt in from a copse, a golden-maned horse from off last year's
grass;
he put the colt into harness, the fiery-red one into the shafts.
He sat down in the sleigh, flung himself into his basket sleigh,
struck the spirited steed with the whip, urged it on with the lash.
The spirited steed ran, the journey proceeded, the sleigh went on, the way
grew short,
the silver sand sang, the lovely heath re-echoes.
He went on one day, went a second, soon went on a third, too.
On the third day indeed he comes upon the settlement.
Then reckless Lemminkäinen clatters along
a very remote road to a very remote house.
Over the threshold he asks, spoke from behind an upright in the entryway:
"Would there be anyone in this house to undo my breast strap,
to let down my shafts, to dismount the shaft-bow?"
A child on the floor spoke up, a boy at the top of the outer stairs:
"There is nobody in this house to undo your breast strap,
to let down your shafts, to dismount the shaft-bow."

What did Lemminkäinen care! He struck the spirited steed with the whip,
rang out with the beaded lash; he clatters along
the middle road to the middle house.
Over the threshold he asks, speaks from outside the entryway:
"Would there be anybody in this house to take the reins,
to undo the breast strap, pull off the traces?"
A woman spoke crossly from the stove stone, a chatterbox from the stove
bench:
"In this house you will certainly get someone to take your reins,
to undo your breast strap, to let down your shafts.
There are indeed tens, you can have, if you wish, hundreds
who will get you a conveyance, give you a driving horse

to go, loathsome person, to your home,   to flee, bad man, to your land,
to your father's dwelling place,   to your mother's doorsteps,
to the opening of your brother's gate,   to the top of your sister's stairs
before the close of day,   the setting of the sun."

What did Lemminkäinen care!   He uttered a word, spoke thus:
"The old woman ought to be shot,   she with an underhung jaw shot with
   an arrow."
He struck the spirited steed to get it going;   he whizzes along
the uppermost road   to the uppermost house.
Then as he was nearing the house   reckless Lemminkäinen
speaks these words,   made this remark:

A DOG CHARM [TO PREVENT BARKING], LINES 373–378

"Close, Demon, the barking dog's mouth,   Devil, the dog's jaw;
make a lock in front of its mouth,   a bolt between its teeth
so that it will not let out a sound   before the man has gone by."
Accordingly, when he came to the farmyard,   he struck the ground with his
   whip:
a fine haze rose from the track of his whip,   a little man appeared in the haze;
he was the one who undid the breast straps,   he the one who let down the
   shafts.
Then reckless Lemminkäinen   listened closely
without anybody discovering him,   anybody noticing him.
From outside he heard songs,   words between the moss-caulked logs,
musicians through the wall,   magic singers through the window-hatch.
From there he took a look into the house,   peeked surreptitiously.
The house was full of experts,   the benches full of magician singers,
the side walls lined with musicians,   the opening of the door full of experts,
the high bench full of seers,   the inglenooks full of magicians.
They were singing Lappish songs,   loudly singing the Demon's lays.

Then reckless Lemminkäinen   ventured to change himself into someone
   different,
made bold to change himself into something else.   He went from his corner
   into the house,
from his nook he got inside.   He uttered these words:
"Good is song when ended,   beautiful a song when short;
it is better to stop voluntarily   than to be cut off in the middle."

The mistress of North Farm was moving about   where the floorboards meet,
shuffling around on the middle of the floor.   She uttered a word, spoke thus:
"A dog was here just now,   an iron-colored cur,
an eater of flesh, a biter of bone,   a drawer of fresh blood.

73

What may you be among your men, who may you be among your people
in coming into this house, in getting inside the log building
without the dog hearing you, the barker noticing?"
Reckless Lemminkäinen said: "I by no means came here
without my skills, without my magic art, without my powers, without my
    competence,
without my father's magic power, my parent's equipment
to be devoured by your dogs, chewed to pieces by the barkers.
My mother used to wash me, wash me as a slip of a lad
three times of a summer night, nine times of an autumn night
to make me a seer for every place, make me competent for every land,
a magic singer in my home, an expert abroad."

Then reckless Lemminkäinen, that handsome man with a far-roving mind,
now indeed began to perform magic, burst out into magic song;
the hems of his fur coat spurted fire, his eyes shot out flame
as Lemminkäinen sang, sang, uttered magic.
He sang the best singers into being the worst singers;
he pushed stones straight into their mouths, stacked rocks on the flat side
for the best singers, for those most proficient in song.
Thus he sang such men— one hither, one thither—
off to treeless clearings, fallow fields,
to fishless ponds, ponds quite without perch,
to strong rapids of Finnmark, to a raging whirlpool,
sang them under the current into foam, into rocks in the middle of the
    rapids,
to burn like fire, to flash like sparks.
Thither reckless Lemminkäinen bewitched the men with their swords,
the people with their weapons; he bewitched the young, bewitched the old,
in turn bewitched the middle-aged.

                One he left unbewitched,
an evil cattle herder, a blind old man.
Cattle herder Soppy Hat uttered these words:
"Oh you reckless son of Lempi! You bewitched the young, bewitched the
    old,
in turn bewitched the middle-aged, so why do you not bewitch me?"
Reckless Lemminkäinen said: "This is why I am not touching you,
because you are wretched to look at, miserable without my touching you.
When still a rather young man, when an evil cattle herder,
you seduced your mother's child, slept with your sister;
you used to violate all the horses, abuse fillies,
on the expanses of the fen, on the farthest parts of the world, on places
    washed by silty water."

74

Cattle herder Soppy Hat   took offense at this and got angry.
He went out past the door,   along the farmyard to a field;
he ran to the river of Death's Domain,   to the whirlpool of the sacred stream.
There he watched for the man with a far-roving mind,   waits for
   Lemminkäinen
to go back from North Farm,   to proceed to his home.

POEM 13

Lemminkäinen asks the dame of North Farm for her daughter;
the former assigns him as a first task to ski down the Demon's elk (1–30).
Boasting arrogantly, Lemminkäinen sets out in pursuit of the elk,
but to his discomfiture he soon comes to see
that he cannot possibly get the elk by bravado (31–270).

Then reckless Lemminkäinen   said to the dame of North Farm:
"Now, dame, give me your maidens,   bring your girls here,
the best one of the bevy for me,   the tallest of your band of maidens."
The mistress of North Farm   uttered a word, spoke thus:
"I will not give you my maidens   nor thrust my girls forward,
not the best, not the worst,   not the tallest, not the shortest.
You already have a wedded wife,   already an established mistress."
Reckless Lemminkäinen said: "I will tie Kyllikki up at a stranger's,
at a stranger's thresholds,   at strangers' gates;
I will get a better woman here.   Now bring your daughter here,
the loveliest of the bevy of virgins,   the fairest of those with luxuriant hair."
The mistress of North Farm said: "I am certainly not giving my girl
to good-for-nothing men,   to do-nothing fellows.
Only sue for my girls,   inquire about the ones with flowers in their hair
after you have skied down the Demon's elk   beyond the Demon's fields."

Then reckless Lemminkäinen   tipped his spears,
strung his crossbows,   fixed up his bolts.
He uttered these words: "Now though the spear is tipped,
all the bolts in order,   the crossbow strung,
there is no left ski for pushing with,   no right ski to stamp the heel on."
Then reckless Lemminkäinen   ponders, reflects
where indeed he might get right-hand skis,   where get skis at all.
He went to Kauppi's farmstead,   got to Lyylikki's workshop:
"Oh wise man of northern parts,   handsome Kauppi of Lapland!
Make me nice skis,   shape me fine right-hand skis
with which I will ski down the Demon's elk   beyond the Demon's fields."
Lyylikki speaks a word,   Kauppi hastens to say:
"To no purpose, Lemminkäinen,   are you setting out   to pursue the Demon's
    elk;
you will get a piece of rotten wood   and that with a lot of misery."

What did Lemminkäinen care!   He uttered these words:
"Make a left ski for pushing with,   a right ski for shoving with.

I am setting out to ski down an elk   beyond the Demon's fields."
Lyylikki, a shaper of left skis,   Kauppi, maker of right skis
fashioned the left ski during the autumn,   shaped the right ski during the
    winter;
one day he carved a ski pole,   the next he carved a disk.
He made the left ski for pushing,   the right ski for stamping the heel on.
He got the shafts of the ski poles ready,   the disks fitted.
The shaft of the pole cost an otterskin,   the disk a reddish foxskin.
He greases the skis with fat,   greased them thickly with reindeer fat.
Then he ponders,   says these words:
"Is there in this younger group,   among the people growing up,
someone to push my left ski,   to kick the right one with his heel?"

Reckless Lemminkäinen said,   the ruddy-cheeked rascal spoke:
"Indeed there is in this younger group,   among the people growing up,
someone to push that left ski of yours,   to kick the right one with his heel."
He fastened the quiver on his back,   the new crossbow on his shoulders,
grasped the pole in his hand;   he started to push the left ski,
to kick the right one with his heel.   He uttered these words:
"In God's sky,   under the vault of heaven
there is not to be found in the forest   anything running on four legs
which will not be overtaken by these,   not caught up with easily
by right skis of the Kaleva descendant,   by Lemminkäinen's skiing."

The demons got to hear of this,   the evil creatures to looking into this.
The demons constructed an elk,   the evil creatures made a reindeer.
They make the head from a rotten stump,   the horns from a forked sallow,
the legs from shore saplings,   the shanks from fence poles in a fen,
the back from a fence rail,   the sinews from last year's dry grass,
the eyes from yellow water lilies,   the ears from white pond lilies,
the skin from fir bark,   the rest of the flesh from a rotten tree.
The Demon counseled his elk,   spoke to his reindeer:
"Now, you, elk of the demons,   race your legs, you noble reindeer,
to the reindeers' calving grounds,   to the fields of the children of Lapland.
Ski a man into a sweat,   especially Lemminkäinen!"

Then the demons' elk ran,   the reindeer sped along
below the storehouses of North Farm,   along the meadows of the children of
    Lapland.
It kicked a bucket out of a Lappish tent,   upset the kettles on the fire,
dirtied pieces of meat in the ashes,   spilled the soup in the fireplace.
A great uproar arose   on the fields of the children of Lapland;
the Lappish dogs started barking,   the Lappish children crying,
the Lappish women laughing,   other people grumbling.

Reckless Lemminkäinen   kept on skiing after the elk.
He skied over fens, skied over the countryside,   skied over open clearings.
Fire spurted from the skis,   smoke from the tips of the poles,
but he did not see his elk,   neither saw nor heard it.
He glided over hills, glided over dills,   he glided over the regions beyond the sea;
he skied over all the Demon's backwoods,   all the Grave Spirit's heaths, too,
skied along in front of the jaws of Death,   behind the Grave Spirit's farmstead.
Now Death opens his jaws,   the Grave Spirit raises his head
to capture the man,   to swallow Lemminkäinen;
Death did not really get him,   did not have time to at all.
A little stretch was still not glided over,   a corner of the backwoods untouched
in the great back country of North Farm,   in the open region of Lapland.
He set out to glide over it, too,   to touch that corner of the backwoods.

Thus as he was reaching his destination,   he heard a considerable uproar
from the great back country of North Farm,   from the fields of the children of Lapland.
He heard the dogs barking,   the Lappish children crying,
Lappish women laughing,   another Lapp grumbling.
Then reckless Lemminkäinen   at once started to ski there,
to where the dogs were barking,   to the fields of the children of Lapland.
After he got there he said,   after he arrived he inquired:
"What were the women laughing about here,   the women laughing about, the children crying about,
the old people moaning about?   Who were the grey dogs barking at?"
"This the women here were laughing about,   the women laughing about, the children crying about,
the old people moaning about,   this the grey dogs were barking at:
the demons' elk ran away from here,   the long-legged creature was galloping;
it kicked a bucket out of a Lappish tent,   upset the kettles on the fire,
knocked over the stews,   spilled the soup in the fireplace."
Then the ruddy-cheeked rascal,   that reckless Lemminkäinen,
pushed his left ski on the snow   like an adder in last year's withered grass,
shoved the bog-pine ski along   like a live snake.
As he was going along, he said,   spoke equipped with the ski pole:
"As many men as there may be in Lapland,   let them all be put to carrying the elk;
as many women as there may be in Lapland,   let them all be put to washing a kettle;
as many children as there may be in Lapland,   let them all be put to gathering kindling;
as many kettles as the Lapps have,   let them all be put to boiling the elk."

He exerted himself, strained himself,   he gave a kick, made an effort.
The first time he kicked himself   farther than eye can see,
the second time he pawed himself   farther than ear can hear,
the third time he picked up speed   and reached the flanks of the demons' elk.
He took a maple tethering stake,   grabbed a birch withe
with which he fastened the demons' elk   inside an oakwood pen:
"Stand there, demons' elk,   keep prancing, reindeer!"
He keeps stroking its back,   patting its coat:
"I should like to be over there,   it would suit me to lie down
with a young girl,   with a chick who was growing up."
Then the Demon's elk got angry,   the reindeer began to kick,
spoke these words, says this: "May the devil arrange for you
to lie down with young maidens,   to go about with daughters!"
It exerted itself, it strained itself,   it tore the birch withe,
broke the maple tethering stake,   kicked the oakwood pen to bits.
Then it began to race along,   the elk to set out to speed along
toward the fens, toward open country,   toward a scrub-grown hill
farther than eye can see,   farther than ear can hear.
Then the ruddy-cheeked rascal   now indeed grew angry and lost his temper,
got very angry and mad.   He skied after the elk;
but when he once gives a kick,   the left ski cracked at the strap,
the ski broke by the footplate,   the right ski broke off at the heel,
the spearlike pole broke off at the spike,   the ski pole at the disk.
The Demon's elk ran   so that there was no sign of its head at all.
Then reckless Lemminkäinen   downcast, low in mind,
looks at his gear.   He uttered these words:
"Never, never at all   let another of our men go
arrogantly to hunt a forest animal,   ski after the Demon's elk
as I went, poor wretch.   I have spoiled good skis,
lost a fine pole,   the most eager of my spearlike poles."

POEM 14

Entreating nicely with the usual huntsmen's charms and prayers
Lemminkäinen finally gets the elk and takes it to North Farm (1–270).
As a second task he is assigned to bridle the Demon's fire-breathing gelding,
which he bridles and drives to North Farm (271–372).
As a third assignment he is put to shooting a swan
in the river of Death's Domain.
Lemminkäinen comes to the river of Death's Domain;
there the despised cattle herder [Soppy Hat] is on the lookout for him,
kills him, and throws him into Death's rapids.
In the bargain Death's son cuts the body to pieces (373–460).

Then reckless Lemminkäinen   pondered, reflected
along what path he should make his way,   what trail he should go down,
whether he should give up the Demon's elks,   go home
or keep on trying further,   should ski in leisurely fashion
as a pleasure for the mistress of the forest,   as a joy to the virgins of the
    wilderness.
He speaks these words,   made this remark:
"O Ukko, god on high   or heavenly father!
Make me now reliable skis,   light skis
with which I will ski easily   across fens, across the countryside,
ski to the Demon's lands,   over the heaths of North Farm,
to the trails of the Demon's elk,   to the tracks of the reindeer.

    A HUNTSMAN'S CHARMS, LINES 23–78, 105–230
"I am setting out now for the forest away from men,   for work in the open
    away from people,
along the trail of Tapio's domain,   through Tapio's farms.
Hail, mountains, hail, hills,   hail, echoing fir groves,
hail, groves of light-green alders,   hail the one who is hailing you!
Woods, be favoring; accede, backwoods;   be gracious, beloved Tapio!
Bring the man to a dry spot in the fen,   bring him to that knoll
where the quarry is to be got,   the game to be obtained.

"Nyyrikki, son of Tapio,   fair man with a red high-peaked hat!
Cut blazes through the countryside,   make guide signs leading to the hills,
so that I, simple fellow, will see how to go,   I, quite ignorant, will know the
    way
while I am searching for the quarry,   seeking out the game.

"Darling, mistress of the forest,   fair lady, fair-featured one!
Command the gold to proceed,   the silver to go
in front of the man in search of it,   in the seeker's way.
Take the golden keys   from the ring on your thigh,
open Tapio's storehouse,   remove the forest's fort
on my hunting days,   while I am in search of game.
If indeed you yourself may not be ashamed,   then urge your maids,
oblige your hired girls,   order those who listen to your orders.
Perhaps you are not the mistress   if you cannot control the serving maid,
control a hundred serving maids,   a thousand obeyers of your orders,
tenders of all your cattle,   keepers of all the game.

"Little maid of the forest,   Tapio's honey-mouthed girl!
Play your honeyed pipe,   pipe on your sweet pipe
into the ear of your fine mistress,   charming mistress of the forest,
that she may quickly hear,   may get up from lying down
since she is not hearing at all,   does not wake up even at times,
though I am imploring with fair words,   pleading with tongue of gold."

Then reckless Lemminkäinen,   the whole time without prey,
skied the fens, skied the countryside,   skied the rugged backwoods,
over God's hill with charred trees,   over the Demon's charred heaths.
He skied one day, skied a second,   Now on the third day
he went to a big hill,   got up on a big rock,
cast his eyes to the northwest,   to the north across the fens.
Tapio's dwellings appeared,   the golden doors loomed up
from across the fen, from the north,   from the foot of a hill, from a scrub
    growth.
Reckless Lemminkäinen   at once approached,
went right near it   to under Tapio's window.
He stooped to look   through the sixth window:
there the dispensers of the game were living   and the old women of the
    game lolling
in altogether workday clothes,   in dirty ragged clothes.

[CHARMS CONTINUED, LINES 105-230]

Reckless Lemminkäinen said: "Why, mistress of the forest,
are you in workday clothes,   wallowing filthily in threshing rags,
very black in your appearance,   dreadful to look at,
with loathsome breasts,   with a nasty looking body?
When formerly I was going about in the forest   there were three forts in the
    forest,
one of wood, the second of bone,   your third a stone fort.
There were six gold windows   on the side of each fort.

81

I took a look inside at them   while I was standing beneath the wall.
I saw the master of Tapio's house,   the mistress of Tapio's house,
Tellervo, Tapio's maid,   Tapio's other folk there, too,
all loaded with gold,   heaped with silver.
Gold bracelets were on the hands   of the mistress of the forest herself,
of the gracious mistress of the forest,   gold rings on her fingers,
gold ornaments on her head,   her hair in golden ringlets,
gold earrings in her ears,   lovely beads on her neck.

"O gracious mistress of the forest,   sweet lady of Woodland!
Cast aside your hay-stuffed shoes,   shake off your birchbark shoes,
take off your threshing rags,   take off your workday blouse.
Dress yourself in propitious garments,   put on booty-yielding blouses
on my hunting days,   while I am in search of game.
An empty feeling,   a lack of game all the time
will become tedious to me,   will get to be tedious
if at least you do not give,   once in a while hand me something.
'Tedious is a joyless evening,   long a day without quarry.'

"Gray-bearded old man of the forest   with fir-sprig hat, furry coat of lichens!
Clothe now the forests in linen cloth,   dress the wilderness in fine woolen
    cloth,
all the aspens in grey broadcloth,   the alders in lovely clothes.
Deck out the tall evergreens in silver,   the firs in gold,
the tall old evergreens in copper belts,   the firs in silver belts,
the birches in golden dandelions,   the stumps in golden jingling things.
Clothe things as indeed they were of old,   as in your better days;
the fir-branches used to shine like the moon,   the tops of pines like the sun;
the forest smelled of mead,   the hazy blue wilderness of honey,
the borders of the clearings of sweetwort,   the edges of the fens of soft butter.

"Girl of the forest, lovely maid,   Wind Spirit, Tapio's daughter!
Drive the game to the sides of the way,   to the most extensive clearings.
Should it be stubborn in running   or sluggish in galloping,
take a switch from a thicket,   a birch switch from a dell in the wilderness
with which you will smack its flank   and poke it between the legs.
Make it run fast,   dash swiftly
in front of the man in search of it,   in the way of the man always on the go.
When the game gets on to the course,   drive it along the course.
Put your two hands   on both sides as a railing
that the game may not swerve   nor veer suddenly to the wayside.
If indeed the game swerves,   veers suddenly to the wayside,
lead it on to the trail by the ears,   get it on to course by the horns.

"A rotten tree trunk is across the way,   shove it aside;
there are trees on the ground on the course,   break them in two.
A fence gets in the way,   topple the fence over
at five-post intervals,   every seven posts.
A river gets in front,   a brook across the track,
pull silk across it as a bridge,   red cloth as a stairs.
Escort the game across the sound, too;   drag it across the waters,
across the river of North Farm,   over the foamy patches in the rapids.

"Master of Tapio's house,   mistress of Tapio's house,
grey-bearded old man of the forest,   fair king of the forest!
Mimerkki, mistress of the forest,   gracious gamekeeper of the forest,
blue-mantled old woman of the grove,   red-stockinged mistress of the fen!
Come now to the exchange of gold,   to change silver.
My gold pieces are as old as the moon,   my silver ones the age of the sun,
fetched specially from war,   at a risk from combat;
they will languish in my purse,   tarnish in my tinder pouch
if there is no exchanger of gold,   no changer of silver."

Thus reckless Lemminkäinen   skied undaunted a long time;
on the edge of a grove he sang lays,   three in a bend in the backwoods.
He pleased the mistress of the forest,   the master of the forest himself, too,
delighted all the virgins,   persuaded Tapio's maidens.
They made it run,   drove the Demon's elk from its hiding place
behind Tapio's fell,   from the side of the Demon's fort
to in front of the man in search of it,   to where the magic singer will get it.
Reckless Lemminkäinen   now indeed sent his lasso
onto the shoulders of the Demon's elk,   onto the neck of the camel's colt,
so that it did not kick viciously   while he was stroking its back.

A RANSOM CHARM, LINES 253–264

Then reckless Lemminkäinen   uttered these words:
"Lord of the wilderness, master of the land,   fair heath-dweller!
Darling, mistress of the forest,   gracious gamekeeper of the forest!
Come now to take the gold pieces,   to choose the silver pieces!
Put your linen sheet on the ground,   spread out your lovely linen
under the palely gleaming gold,   under the glistening silver,
without spilling it on the ground,   soiling it in the dust."

Then he set out for North Farm;   when he got there he said:
"Now I have already skied down the Demon's elk   beyond the Demon's fields.
Give me, dame, your girl,   the young bride-to-be."
To that Louhi, mistress of North Farm,   said in reply:

"I will give you my daughter   and the young bride-to-be
only if you bridle the big gelding,   the Demon's brown horse,
the Demon's foamy-jawed colt   beyond the Demon's meadows."

Then reckless Lemminkäinen   took his golden reins,
the silver halter;   he sets out to fetch the horse,
in search of the golden-maned steed   beyond the Demon's meadows.
He steps along quickly,   walks lightly
to the green field,   to the edge of the sacred field.
There he looks for the horse,   searches for the flaxen-maned steed,
with the yearling's bridle in his belt,   the colt's harness on his shoulder.
He looked one day, looked a second,   then on the third day
he went up on a big hill,   climbed to the top of a rock.
He cast his eyes to the east,   turned his head to the south.
He saw the horse on the sand,   golden-mane in a fir grove.
Its coat, indeed, is blazing fire,   its mane giving off smoke.

Lemminkäinen speaks thus: "O Ukko, god on high,
Ukko, controller of the clouds,   ruler of cloud patches!
Open wide the heavens,   make windows in the whole sky!
Bring iron hailstones,   let icy hail descend
on the mane of the good horse,   on the flanks of the Demon's horse with a
    blaze."
Ukko, creator on high,   a god above the clouds,
tore the sky to shreds,   the vault of heaven in two.
Down came sleet, down came ice,   down came iron hail
smaller than a horse's head,   bigger than a man's head,
onto the mane of the good horse,   on the flanks of the Demon's horse with a
    blaze.

Then reckless Lemminkäinen   went from there to look,
to observe from near at hand.   He uttered these words:
"Good horse of the Demon's Domain,   foamy-jawed colt of the mountain!
Present now your golden mouth,   thrust your silver head
into the golden ring-adorned bridle,   into the silver bells.
I am not likely to treat you badly,   probably will not drive you very hard.
I will drive a bit of a way,   a very slight distance
there to the dwellings of North Farm,   to the home of the stern mother-in-
    law.
Whatever I lash with a thong   or drive on with a switch,
that I will lash with silk,   drive on with a strip of broadcloth."
The Demon's brown horse,   the Demon's foamy-jawed colt
pressed its golden mouth,   thrust its silver head

into the golden ring-adorned bridle,   into the silver bells.
Thus indeed reckless Lemminkäinen   now bridled the big gelding,
thrust the bit into the golden mouth,   the silver head into the bridle;
he jumped onto the good animal's back,   onto the flanks of the Demon's
   horse with a blaze.

He drove the spirited steed with a switch,   struck it with a willow shoot.
He drove a short distance,   trotted lightly over some treeless mountains
to the north side of a hill,   of the ridge of a snowy mountain.
He came to the dwellings of North Farm.   From the farmyard he went into
   the cabin,
said after he arrived there,   after he had got to North Farm:
"I have already bridled the big gelding,   harnessed the Demon's colt
in the green field,   on the edge of the sacred field,
and I skied down the Demon's elk   beyond the Demon's fields.
Now give me, dame, your girl,   the young bride-to-be."

Louhi, mistress of North Farm,   she indeed uttered these words:
"I will give you my daughter   and the young bride-to-be
only when you shoot the swan in the river,   the splendid bird in the stream,
on Death's dark river,   in the whirlpool of the sacred stream
with one shot,   after picking up just one arrow."
Then reckless Lemminkäinen,   that handsome man with a far-roving mind,
set out to where the swan was gabbling,   in search of the long-necked bird
on Death's dark river,   in the lower parts of the Abode of the Dead.
He swings along,   walks briskly
there to the river of Death's Domain,   to the whirlpool of the sacred stream,
with a fine crossbow on his shoulder,   a quiver of arrows on his back.

Soppy Hat the cattle herder,   blind old man of North Farm,
is by the river of Death's Domain,   by the whirlpool of the sacred stream;
he is looking about, turning about   for Lemminkäinen to come.
Now on a certain day   he saw reckless Lemminkäinen
coming, approaching   the river of Death's Domain over there,
the margin of the green rapids,   the whirlpool of the sacred stream.
From the water he conjured up a water dragon,   a cowbane-poisoned tube
   from the billows,
hurled it through the man's heart,   through Lemminkäinen's liver,
through his left armpit,   into his right shoulder.
Now indeed reckless Lemminkäinen   felt himself sorely hurt.
He uttered a word, spoke thus: "I did the worst thing
when I did not remember to ask   my mother, her who bore me
at least two charms,   tremendous ones, maybe three.

how to exist, how to live   in these evil days.
I do not know how to counter the injuries of a water dragon,   the stabbing
  pains of a cowbane-poisoned dart.
O my mother, you who bore me,   who tended me and endured suffering!
If you knew, if you were acquainted   with where your wretched son is,
you would surely come in haste,   would find time to help him;
you would spare the wretched lad   from dying on this trail,
from passing on while young,   from dropping dead when ruddy-cheeked."

Then Soppy Hat,   blind cattle herder of North Farm,
rushed on reckless Lemminkäinen,   hurled the Kaleva descendant
into Death's dark river,   into the most terrible whirlpool.
Reckless Lemminkäinen went,   went bumping along in the rapids,
like a flash downstream   there to the dwellings of Death's Domain.
The blood-stained son of Death   struck the man with his sword,
gave him a quick blow with his short sword.   Like a flash
he cut the man into five pieces,   into eight bits.
He threw them into the river of Death's Domain,   into the backwaters of the
  Abode of the Dead:
"Lie there forever   with your crossbow, with your arrows!
Shoot the swans on the river,   the waterfowl on the banks!"

That was the end of Lemminkäinen,   the death of the brave suitor,
in Death's dark river,   in the lower reaches below the Abode of the Dead.

POEM 15

One day in Lemminkäinen's home blood begins to ooze from his brush,
from which his mother at once suspects that death has already
overtaken her son, hastens to North Farm, and asks the mistress
of North Farm where she had dispatched Lemminkäinen (1–62).
The mistress of North Farm finally says, however, to what tasks
she had put him, and the sun gives quite precise information
about Lemminkäinen's death (63–194).
A long rake in hand, Lemminkäinen's mother sets out to below Death's rapids,
rakes the water until she assembles all the pieces of her son's body,
fits them together, and out of them, with the help of charms and ointments,
makes Lemminkäinen as he was before (195–554).
After he has been restored, Lemminkäinen tells how he was killed
in the river of Death's Domain and sets out home with his mother (555–650).

At home reckless Lemminkäinen's mother   keeps reflecting:
"Where has Lemminkäinen got to,   where has my boy with a far-roving mind
     disappeared
since no one hears him coming now   from his journey out in the world?"
The poor mother does not know,   not the wretched woman who bore him,
where her flesh and blood is moving about,   her own flesh and blood floating
     about,
does not know whether he was walking on a hill grown with evergreens,   on a
     heather-grown heath,
or whether he took to the open sea,   to the foam-capped billows
or to a big war,   to some dreadful feud
where blood will be over his shins,   red blood up to his knees.

Kyllikki, elegant woman,   looks about, turns around
in reckless Lemminkäinen's home,   in the farmstead of the man with a far-
     roving mind.
In the evening she used to look at the brush,   in the morning at his brush.
So on a certain day,   on a certain morning
blood indeed was now flowing from the brush,   gore trickling from the brush.
Kyllikki, elegant woman,   uttered a word, spoke thus:
"Now my husband has already departed from me,   the handsome man with
     a far-roving mind vanished
on uninhabited ways,   on unknown paths;
blood is now flowing from the brush,   gore trickling from the brush."

Then Lemminkäinen's mother   herself looks at the brush,
got distressed and started to weep: "Woe is the day, wretched me,

woe my time, unlucky me!   Now my boy, unhappy one,
now indeed the hapless one, my child,   has fallen on evil days.
It is the ruin of the splendid boy,   the destruction of reckless Lemminkäinen;
now the brush is running with blood,   gore trickling from the brush."
She caught up her skirt in her hand,   her clothes in her arm.
She quickly ran a little distance,   both ran and hurried.
The hills resounded as she went,   the swales rose, the mountains sank,
the highlands went down,   the lowlands rose up.
She came to the dwellings of North Farm.   She kept inquiring for her son,
inquiring, speaking: "O you mistress of North Farm,
where did you dispatch Lemminkäinen,   where did you do away with my son?"
Louhi, mistress of North Farm,   replied to this:
"I really do not know about your son,   where he went and disappeared to.
I seated him in the stallion's sleigh,   in the very spirited steed's basket sled.
Would he have sunk into the slush,   got frozen stiff in sea ice
or got into a wolf's mouth,   into the jaws of a dreadful bear?"

Lemminkäinen's mother said: "Now you just plain lied.
No wolf will eat one of my clan,   no bear destroy Lemminkäinen;
he crushes wolves with his fingers,   lays bears low with his hands.
If, indeed, you will not tell   where you dispatched Lemminkäinen,
I will smash the door of the new threshing barn,   break the hinges of the Sampo."
The mistress of North Farm said: "I gave the man food to eat,
gave the man drink to drink;   I gave him drink till his head nodded,
I seated him in the stern of a boat,   got him ready to go down the rapids.
I do not indeed know   where the poor wretch got to,
whether into the surging rapids   or the swirling currents."

Lemminkäinen's mother said: "Now you just plain lied.
Tell the exact truth,   your last lies!
Tell me where you dispatched Lemminkäinen,   did away with the man of the Kaleva District
else death will befall you,   death come upon you."
The mistress of North Farm said: "Perhaps I will now tell the truth!
I set him to skiing after elks,   to skinning choice reindeer,
to bridling big geldings,   harnessing colts.
I got him ready for the quest of the swan,   ready to catch the sacred bird.
Now I do not know at all   how he came to grief,
managed to get delayed   since one does not hear him coming now
to ask for his bride-to-be,   to sue for the girl."

The mother searches for the lost one,   digs about for the man who has vanished.
She ran about the vast fens as a wolf,   waded rapids as a bear,
roved the waters as an otter,   walked over the countryside as a badger,

over the shores of headlands as a hedgehog,   along the banks of rivers as a
   hare.
She tipped stones on their sides,   toppled over stumps,
shifted brush to the roadside,   kicked fallen branches into landing stages.
Long she searched for the lost one,   long she searched, just does not find him.
She asked the trees about her son,   she dug about for her vanished one.
A tree spoke, a tall evergreen sighed,   an oak answered shrewdly:
"I have worries of my own   without worrying about your son,
for I have been created for hardships,   made for evil days,
to be split into kindling wood,   to be chopped up into cord wood,
to waste away as wood for burning in a threshing barn,   to topple over as trees
   in a clearing."

Long she searched for the lost one,   long she searched, just does not find him.
She comes upon a road,   so she bows to the road:
"O road, God's creation,   have you not seen my son,
my golden apple,   my silver staff?"
The road answered shrewdly   both spoke and talked:
"I have worries of my own   without worrying about your son,
for I have been created for hardships,   made for evil days,
to be run upon by every dog,   ridden on by a horseback rider,
walked on by a heavy boot,   crushed by a heel."

Long she searched for the lost one,   long she searched, just does not find him.
She comes upon the moon,   so she bows to the moon:
"Lovely moon, God's creation,   have you not seen my son,
my golden apple,   my silver staff?"
The moon, God's creation,   indeed answered shrewdly:
"I have worries of my own   without worrying about your son,
for I have been created for hardships,   made for evil days,
to go about alone nights,   to shine in the cold,
winters to be on watch attentively,   to vanish for the summer."

Long she searched for the lost one,   long she searched, just does not find him.
She comes upon the sun,   so she bows to the sun:
"O sun, God's creation,   have you not seen my boy,
my golden apple,   my silver staff?"
Now indeed the sun knew something,   the sun expressed an opinion:
"Your son, poor wretch,   has already vanished, died
in Death's dark river,   in the eternal waters of the Abode of the Dead,
gone bumping along the rapids,   whizzing downstream
to the back parts of Death's Domain,   to the lower parts of the Abode of the
   Dead."

Then Lemminkäinen's mother   burst out crying.

She went to the craftsman's forge: "O you craftsman Ilmarinen,
you forged before, you forged yesterday; forge something today, too.
Fit a copper rake with a handle, fit it with iron teeth,
forge teeth a hundred fathoms long, prepare a handle five hundred long."
Craftsman Ilmarinen, eternal smith,
put a handle on a copper rake, fitted it with iron teeth;
he forged teeth a hundred fathoms long, prepared a handle five hundred long.

Lemminkäinen's mother gets the iron rake,
sped to the river of Death's Domain. She implores the sun:
"O sun, God's creation, our bright creation of the Creator,
shine hot for one hour, faintly for a second and make people sweat,
shine a third hour at full strength. Put the inhospitable folk to sleep,
exhaust the people of the Abode of the Dead, make Death's forces sleep deep."
That sun, God's creation, flew to the knee of a birch branch,
winged its way to the bend in an alder branch.
It shone hot for one hour, faintly for a second and made people sweat,
shone a third at full strength. It put the inhospitable folk to sleep,
exhausted the people of the Abode of the Dead, young men with their swords,
old ones leaning on their staffs, the middle-aged on their spears.
Then it flew languidly up to the smooth heavens,
to its former seat, to its dwelling of yore.

Then Lemminkäinen's mother took the iron rake;
she rakes for her son in the roaring rapids
in the flashing current. She rakes and does not find him.
Then she moved lower down, went along into the sea,
into the water up to her garters, into the water up to her waist.
She rakes for her son along the river of Death's Domain,
keeps dragging against the stream. She dragged it once, dragged it twice;
she gets her son's shirt, to her distress of mind the shirt.
She dragged once again; she got his stockings, came upon his hat,
his stockings, in a great state of grief, his hat, in anxiety of mind.

Then she stepped further downstream to the lower parts of the Abode of the Dead.
She dragged once with the current, a second time across the current,
a third time aslant. The third time indeed
she got a sheaf of grain in the iron rake.
It was not a sheaf of grain, it was really reckless Lemminkäinen,
the handsome man with a far-roving mind caught fast in the teeth of the rake

by his ring finger,   his left toe.
Reckless Lemminkäinen rose up,   the Kaleva descendant came up
in the copper rake   to the surface of the clear waters.
But a little something was lacking,   one hand, half his head,
a lot of other bits and pieces,   his life to boot.

The mother reflects on this,   weeping she says:
"Might this still become a man,   might a new person be contrived?"
A raven came to listen;   in reply to that it says:
"There is no man in the departed one,   not really in the vanished one.
A whitefish has already eaten out the eyes,   a pike split the shoulders in two.
Drop the man into the water,   push him into the river of Death's Domain.
Perhaps he might become a cod,   grow up to be a whale."
Lemminkäinen's mother   does not indeed push her son in.
She drags once more   with the copper rake
along the river of Death's Domain,   both longways and crossways.
She gets a hand, gets the head,   gets half the backbone,
the other half of the ribs,   many other bits and pieces.
Out of these she constructed the son,   made reckless Lemminkäinen.
She joined muscles to muscles,   fitted bones to bones,
members to members,   veins to breaks in veins.
She tied up the veins,   bound up the ends of the veins,
spoke magic over the small blood vessels,   saying these words:

VEIN CHARMS, LINES 315–376

"Pretty woman of veins,   Vein Spirit, pretty woman,
nice spinner of veins   with a pretty distaff,
with a copper spindle,   an iron wharve!
Come here when you are needed,   come here when you are summoned,
with a package of veins in your arms,   a bundle of wound-up membrane
    under your arm
to tie up veins,   to bind up the ends of veins
in the gaping wounds,   in gaps split open.

"If that is not enough,   there is indeed a virgin up in the sky
in a copper boat,   in a red-prowed vessel.
Come, virgin, down from the sky,   maiden from the heavenly pole.
Row a boat made of veins,   move one made of limbs;
row along the breaks in the bones,   along the cracks in the members.
Put the veins in their place,   set them in position,
the big veins opening to opening,   main veins facing each other,
fine veins with the ends doubled over,   little veins tip to tip.
Then take a fine needle   with a silk thread in the needle;
sew up the veins with fine needles,   stitch them with tin needles;
bind up the ends of the veins,   tie them with silk bands.

"If that is not enough,   heavenly god,
harness your colts,   get your steeds ready.
Drive with your decorated sleigh   through a bone, through a member,
through displaced tissues,   through slippery veins.
Join bone to tissue,   vein to tip of vein
to the gap in the silver bone,   to the rupture in a golden vein.
Where a membrane has broken,   make a membrane grow there;
where a vein has ruptured,   there bind up the vein;
where blood has dripped,   pour blood in there.
Where a bone has been crushed,   fit a bone in there.
Where tissue has shifted,   add tissue there,
put it in its place with a blessing,   put it in its proper position:
bone to bone, tissue to tissue,   members to members."

Then Lemminkäinen's mother   fashioned the man, shaped the fellow
into his former state,   to his form of old.
She got the veins magically mended,   the ends of the veins tied,
did not get the man to talking,   her child to speaking.
Then she uttered these words,   remarked, spoke thus:
"Where may a salve now be got,   where a drop of honey brought from,
with which to anoint the weary man,   mend the man who has fared ill,
so that the man may get to speaking,   break out into speech?

BEE CHARMS, LINES 393-534 PASSIM

"Bee, our bird,   king of the forest flowers!
Set out now to fetch honey,   to try to get honey
from pleasant Woodland,   from the keen-eyed folk of Tapio's Domain,
from the cup of many a flower,   from the sheath of many grasses,
as an ointment for sick men,   as remedies for those in a bad way."
The bee, fleet bird,   now indeed swung gently along
to pleasant Woodland,   to the keen-eyed people of Tapio's Domain.
With its bill it seized flowers in a meadow,   with its tongue boiled the honey
from the tips of six flowers,   from the sheaths of a hundred herbs.
Then it comes slowly,   comes circling,
with all its wings covered with honey,   its plumage wet with liquid honey.
Lemminkäinen's mother   took those salves,
anointed the weary man with them,   mended the man who had got into a
    bad way.
No help came from those,   none gave the man speech.

Then she uttered these words: "Bee, my little bird!
Fly yonder to somewhere else,   over nine seas
to an island in the open water,   to a land of honey,
to Tuuri's new house,   to the worshipful one's roofless home.

There is lovely honey there, fine salve there
which is suitable for veins, effective for members.
Bring indeed these salves, carry these magic nostrums
for me to put on a blemish, for me to pour on injuries."
The bee, nimble fellow, again soared off
over nine seas, half way over the tenth sea.
It flew one day, it flew a second, it soon flew a third, too,
without sitting down on a reed, without resting on a leaf,
to an island in the open water, a land of honey
by a rushing rapids, to the whirlpool of a sacred stream.
There honey was being boiled, salves being prepared
in little clay pots, in lovely kettles
with room for a thumb, fitting a fingertip.
The bee, nimble fellow, got these salves.
A little time elapses, a short time passes quickly.
Now it comes buzzing along, bustling along,
with six bowls on its flanks, seven behind on its back;
these are full of salves, full of good ointments.
Lemminkäinen's mother anointed him with those ointments,
with nine ointments, eight nostrums.
Still no help is got, none indeed is found in that.

Then she said these words, made this remark:
"Bee, bird of the air, fly yonder a third time
up to the heavens, to the ninth heaven.
There there is honey aplenty, honey there to one's heart's desire,
on which the Creator formerly spoke a charm, on which the pure God
    breathed,
with which the Creator anointed injuries inflicted on his children by an evil
    power.
Wet your wings in the honey, your plumage in the liquid honey,
bring the honey on your wings, carry the honey in your cloak
as salves for sick men, as something to pour on injuries."
The bee, good bird, it indeed uttered these words:
"How now will I get there, I, weak little fellow?"
"It will be pleasant for you to get there, lovely for you to flit there
over the moon, along under the sun, along among the stars of heaven.
You will flutter along for one day to the brows of a constellation,
then on the second you will whisk away to the shoulders of the Great Bear,
on the third you will rise up to the back of the Pleiades.
Then it is only a bit of a journey, a short stretch
to Holy God, to the dwelling-places of the Blissful One."

The bee rose from the ground, honey-wings from a tussock.

Now indeed it fluttered along,   whisked along with its little wings.
It flew along the ring around the moon,   it wandered by the edge of the sun,
past the shoulders of the Great Bear,   past the back of the Pleiades.
It flew into the Creator's cellars,   then up to the Almighty's upper chambers.
There salves were being made,   ointments being prepared
in silver pots,   in golden kettles;
honey was boiling in the middle,   liquid butter on the sides,
honey in the south,   salves in the north.
The bee, bird of the air,   got plenty of honey from that,
honey to its heart's desire.   A little time passed.
Now it comes quickly,   comes circling
with a hundred hornsful in its arms,   a thousand other bundles;
in this one honey, in that one water,   in another one the best salve.

Then Lemminkäinen's mother   took those in her own mouth,
tried them with her tongue,   in her opinion it tasted good:
"These are the salves,   the nostrums of the Almighty
with which indeed God anointed,   the Creator poured on injuries."
Then she anointed the weary man,   mended the man who had fared ill.
She anointed along the breaks in the bones,   along the cracks in the members,
anointed him below, anointed him above,   once gave his middle a quick rub.
Then she uttered these words,   remarked and talked:
"Get up from lying down,   arise from dreaming,
from these evil places,   from your bed of hard luck."
The man got up from lying down,   woke up from dreaming.
Now indeed he is able to talk,   to speak with his tongue:
"For a long time I, wretched one, was sleeping,   long, useless me, was lying
   down;
I lay in a sweet sleep,   sleeping deeply."
Lemminkäinen's mother said,   spoke and talked:
"You would have lain there longer, too,   stretched out longer
but for your unhappy mother,   the wretched one who bore you.
Say now, my miserable son,   tell so that I may hear with my ears,
who took you to the Abode of the Dead,   pushed you into the river of Death's
   Domain."

Reckless Lemminkäinen said,   answered his mother:
"The cattle herder Soppy Hat,   the blind man from Untamo's farm;
he took me to the Abode of the Dead,   pushed me into the river of Death's
   Domain.
He conjured up a water dragon from the water,   a winged dragon from the
   billows
for wretched me;   that I did not know at all,
did not know the wrath of a water dragon,   the stabbing pains of a cowbane-
   poisoned dart."

Lemminkäinen's mother said: "Woe is the foolish man!
You boasted that you would bewitch the wizards, outsing the Lapps,
yet you do not know the wrath of a water dragon, the stabbing pains of a
cowbane-poisoned dart."

THE ORIGIN OF THE WATER DRAGON, LINES 591–602

"A water dragon is born of the water, a cowbane-poisoned dart of the billows
from an old squaw's good brains, from inside the head of a tern.
The Ogress spat into the water, let a blob of spittle drop into the waves;
the water spread it way out, the sun shone on it until it was soft.
Then the wind rocked it, the spirit of the water swayed it about,
the waves carried it ashore, the surf brought it to land."

Then Lemminkäinen's mother rocked her dear one
back to his former state, to his form of old,
so that he was a little better, sounder than before.
Then she asked her son if there was anything lacking.
Reckless Lemminkäinen said: "I still lack a great deal.
My heart is there indeed, there my desire, too, remains
with those maidens of North Farm, with the beautiful girls with luxuriant
hair.
The woman of North Farm with moldy ears will not indeed give over her
girl
unless an old squaw is shot, a swan hit
on the river of Death's Domain, in the whirlpool of the sacred stream."
Lemminkäinen's mother said, spoke and talked:
"Leave your wretched swans alone, let the old squaws stay
in Death's dark river, in the fiery whirlpool.
You set out toward home with your wretched mother.
Still thank your good luck, praise your God,
since He granted you true help, roused you, furthermore, to life
from Death's certain path, from behind the cottage of the Abode of the
Dead.
I could do nothing, nothing at all by myself,
nothing without the grace of God, without the direction of the true Creator."
Then reckless Lemminkäinen set out toward home
with his dear mother, with his esteemed parent.

Now I will drop my man with the far-roving mind, drop reckless Lemminkäinen
from my lay for quite a long time. Meanwhile I will turn my lay about,
get the song going on another tack, push it into a new channel.

POEM 16

Väinämöinen has Sampsa, the Spirit of Arable, look for ship's timbers,
from these shapes a boat and lacks three charms (1–118).
When he does not get the charms elsewhere, he sets out for Death's Domain,
where they want to keep him (119–362).
By his magic powers, however, Väinämöinen gets away from Death's Domain;
after he returns he warns against going there of one's own accord
and relates in what a very gloomy and frightful state
the bad people there are living (363–412).

Steadfast old Väinämöinen, eternal sage,
was shaping a boat, was busy with a new vessel
on the tip of a misty headland, at the end of a foggy island.
The shipwright lacked timbers, the boatbuilder lacked planks.
Who indeed is to look for a tree, to try to get an oak
for a boat for Väinämöinen, for a keel for the singer?

The Spirit of Arable, son of the field the little fellow Sampsa,
he indeed is the one to look for a tree, to try and get an oak
for a boat for Väinämöinen, a keel for the singer.
He walks along a road, steps along in a northeast direction.
He went up one hill, goes up a second, proceeded toward a third, too,
with a golden ax on his shoulder, a copper shaft to his ax.

He comes upon an aspen three fathoms high.
He wanted to touch the aspen, to chop down the tree with his ax.
Speaking the aspen says, chatters with its tongue:
"What, man, do you want of me? Whatever do you desire?"
The lad Sampsa, Spirit of Arable, he, indeed, uttered these words:
"That indeed I want of you, that I am looking for and desire:
a boat for Väinämöinen, ship's timber for the singer."
The aspen spoke rather oddly, the hundred-branched tree was able to say:
"A leaky boat will come of me and a sinking sort of vessel.
I am hollow in the lower part of my trunk; three times this summer
a grub ate my heart, a maggot ravished my root."

The lad Sampsa, Spirit of Arable, then goes farther on,
steps along thoughtfully in a northerly direction.
He came upon a tall evergreen six fathoms high.
He struck the tree with his ax, dealt it a blow with his mattock;
he inquired, he spoke: "Would you be the one, evergreen,

to be a boat for Väinämöinen,   ship's timber for the singer?"
The evergreen made a quick answer,   snarled out:
"No vessel is likely to come from me,   no bearer of six ribs.
I am knotty evergreen.   Three times this summer
a raven rocked on my crown,   a crow swayed on my branches."

The lad Sampsa, Spirit of Arable,   keeps going farther on,
steps along thoughtfully   in a southerly direction.
He came upon an oak   nine fathoms around.
He inquired, he spoke: "Would the keel of a man-of-war
come from you, oak,   the keel of a warship?"
The oak answered shrewdly,   the fine tree knew what to say:
"In me there is only wood   for the keel of one boat;
I am not indeed a knotty pine   nor am I hollow inside.
Three times this summer,   this lovely summer,
the sun circled my middle,   the moon gleamed palely on my crown,
the cuckoos called on my branches,   the birds rested on my twigs."
The lad Sampsa, Spirit of Arable,   took the ax from his shoulder,
struck the tree with the ax,   the oak with the bit.
He was soon able to topple the oak,   to fell the graceful tree.
First he lopped off the crown,   split up every bit of the lower trunk.
Then he shaped keels,   an uncountable number of planks
as shipbuilding materials for the singer,   as a boat for Väinämöinen.

Then old Väinämöinen,   eternal sage,
made a boat skillfully,   by magic singing fashioned a vessel
from the shattered remains of a single oak,   from the fragments of the fragile
   tree.
He sang a charm, made fast the bottom;   he sang a second, joined the planks;
soon he sang a third charm, too,   while he was cutting tholepins,
finishing off the ends of the ribs,   bringing together the overlapping planks.
After he had furnished the boat with ribs,   joined the side planks,
three charms were lacking   for placing the gunwales,
for mounting the bow and stern posts,   for finishing off the end of the stern.
Steadfast old Väinämöinen,   eternal sage,
uttered a word, spoke thus: "Woe is my day, poor me!
The boat has not got into the water,   the new ship not onto the billows."

He ponders, reflects   where he might get magic words,
find precious charms: "Would it be from the pates of swallows,
from the line of flight of a flock of swans   or from the shoulders of a skein
   of geese?"
He set out to get the magic words.   He destroyed a flock of swans,
killed off a skein of geese,   swallows in countless numbers.

97

He did not get a charm at all, not a charm, not half a charm.
He ponders, he reflects: "There might be a hundred charms
under the tongue of a reindeer in its summer vigor, in the mouth of a white
squirrel."
He sets out to get charms, to get magic words.
He cut open a whole pastureful of reindeer, a big branchful of squirrels;
from this he got a lot of charms, all of no help.

He ponders, he reflects: "I will get a hundred charms yonder,
yonder from a home in Death's Domain, from an age-old cottage in the
Abode of the Dead."
He set out for charms from Death's Domain, magic wisdom from the
Abode of the Dead.
He steps along quietly; he walked a week through a stand of saplings,
a second week through a stand of chokecherries, a third through a stand of
junipers.
Now the island of the Abode of the Dead appeared, Death's knoll looms up.

Steadfast old Väinämöinen now cried out loudly
by the river of Death's Domain, by the lower parts of the Abode of the
Dead:
"Bring a boat, daughter of Death, a raft, child of the Abode of the Dead,
for me to get over the sound, for me to get off across the river."

Death's stumpy daughter, short maiden of the Abode of the Dead,
she was washing laundry, battling clothes
in Death's dark river, in the still waters of the Abode of the Dead.
She uttered a word, spoke thus, declared and talked:
"Maybe someone will bring a boat from here if the reason is told
what brought you to the Abode of the Dead without disease killing you,
without a natural death taking you off, without some other death crushing
you."
Steadfast old Väinämöinen uttered a word, spoke thus:
"Death brought me here, the man of the Abode of the Dead dragged me
from my lands."

Death's stumpy daughter, short maiden of the Abode of the Dead,
uttered these words: "Now indeed I detect a liar!
If Death really brought you here, had the man of the Abode of the Dead
transported you from your lands,
Death would have brought you as he came, the man of the Abode of the
Dead brought you as he journeyed
with Death's hat reaching to your shoulders, with the mittens of the man
of the Abode of the Dead on your hands.

Tell the truth, Väinämöinen!   What brought you to the Abode of the Dead?"
Steadfast old Väinämöinen   thereupon uttered these words:
"Iron brought me to the Abode of the Dead,   steel snatched me off to Death's
Domain."

Death's stumpy daughter,   short maiden of the Abode of the Dead,
uttered a word, spoke thus: "From this I recognize a liar!
If iron had got you to the Abode of the Dead,   had steel brought you to
Death's Domain,
your clothes would be dripping blood,   fiercely streaming gore.
Tell the truth, Väinämöinen,   tell the truth this second time."
Steadfast old Väinämöinen   gave utterance, spoke thus:
"Water brought me to the Abode of the Dead,   a wave brought me to Death's
Domain."

Death's stumpy daughter,   short maiden of the Abode of the Dead,
uttered a word, spoke thus: "I am aware of a liar!
Had water got you to the Abode of the Dead,   a wave brought you to Death's
Domain,
your clothes would be dripping water,   the hem of your coat ever trickling
water.
Tell the exact truth: what brought you to the Abode of the Dead?"
Then old Väinämöinen   lied once again:
"Fire brought me to Death's Domain,   flame transported me to the Abode
of the Dead."

Death's stumpy daughter,   short maiden of the Abode of the Dead,
she indeed uttered these words: "I size up a liar!
Had fire brought you to the Abode of the Dead,   flame to Death's Domain,
your locks would be singed,   your beard, too, badly burned.
O you old Väinämöinen!   If you want a boat from here,
speak the exact truth,   tell your last lies,
say how you came to the Abode of the Dead   without a disease killing you,
without a natural death taking you off,   without some other death crushing
you."

Old Väinämöinen said: "Even if I did lie a little,
spoke false the second time,   I will, however, really speak the truth.
I was making a boat skillfully,   fashioning a vessel by magic singing.
I sang one day, I sang a second,   then on the third
the course of my song was broken off,   the flow of my magic utterance was
interrupted.
I set out for an awl from Death's Domain,   for an auger from the Abode of
the Dead,

in order to construct the sled, to fashion the magically created sleigh.
Bring now indeed a boat here, prepare your raft for me,
for me to get over the sound, for me to get off across the river."

Death's daughter indeed scolds, the maiden of the Abode of the Dead
shrills:
"O fool, your folly! Man, your lack of sense!
You come without cause to Death's Domain, without disease to the cottages
of the Abode of the Dead.
It would be better for you to return to your own lands:
many have come here, not many returned."
Old Väinämöinen said: "Let a woman change her course
but not indeed even a really rather inferior man, a really less enterprising
person.
Bring a boat, daughter of Death, a raft, child of the Abode of the Dead."
Death's daughter brought a boat; with it she gets old Väinämöinen
over the sound, lets him off across the river.
She utters these words: "Woe is you, Väinämöinen!
Without dying you set out for the Abode of the Dead, for Death's Domain
without death."

Death's consort, good mistress, she of the Abode of the Dead, aged woman,
brought beer in a stoup, carried it in a two-eared vessel:
she uttered these words: "Drink, old Väinämöinen!"
Steadfast old Väinämöinen looked long at his stoup;
frogs were spawning inside, reptiles crawling on the sides.
Then he uttered these words: "I have not come here at all
to drink from the cups of the Abode of the Dead, to lap from Death's
stoups;
'drinkers of beer get drunk, drainers of the jug vanish.' "

The mistress of Death's Domain said: "O old Väinämöinen,
why did you come to the Abode of the Dead? Why to the houses of Death's
Domain
without Death's wishing it, without an invitation from the regions of the
Abode of the Dead?"
Old Väinämöinen said: "While I was shaping a boat,
was busy about a new vessel, I lacked three charms
as I was finishing off the stern, mounting the bow.
When I did not get those at all, did not find them on earth, in the heavens,
it was necessary to come to Death's Domain, to set out to the cottages of
the Abode of the Dead
to get those charms, to learn about the magic words."

The mistress of Death's Domain   uttered a word, spoke thus:
"Death does not give away charms,   the man of the Abode of the Dead not
distribute magic powers.
You will probably never get away from here,   never, never at all,
to proceed to your home,   to crawl back to your lands."
She lulled the man to sleep,   got the traveler stretched out
on Death's bed of skins.   Then the man stretches out,
the fellow takes a nap;   the man slept, the clothes kept watch.

There was a woman in Death's Domain,   an old woman with a little pointed
chin,
a spinner of iron thread,   a caster of copper wire.
She spun a seine a hundred fathoms long,   wound one up a thousand
fathoms long
in one summer's night   on a rock out in the water.
There was an old man in Death's Domain,   an old man with three fingers,
a weaver of iron nets,   the maker of a copper seine.
He wove a seine a hundred fathoms long,   wound one up a thousand
fathoms long
in the same summer's night   on the same rock out in the water.
Death's son with gnarled fingers,   with gnarled fingers, with iron fingertips,
drew the seine a hundred fathoms long   across the river of Death's Domain,
both crosswise and longwise   and aslant, too,
so that it will not release Väinämöinen,   not set free the man of Slack Water
Farm,
never, never at all,   not while the moon shines gold-bright,
from the homes of Death there,   from the eternal cottages of the Abode of
the Dead.

Steadfast old Väinämöinen   uttered a word, spoke thus:
"Has my ruin perhaps already come?   the day of distress come
in these houses of Death's Domain,   in these wretched dwellings of the
Abode of the Dead?"
He soon changed himself into something different   quickly became something else,
went in the form of something black into the sea,   as an otter into a sedgy
place.
He crept in the form of an iron reptile,   went as a poisonous snake
across the river of Death's Domain,   through Death's nets.
Death's son with gnarled fingers,   with gnarled fingers, with iron fingertips,
went very early in the morning   to look at his nets.
He gets a hundred sea trout,   a thousand young fry;
he did not get Väinämöinen,   the old man of Slack Water Farm.

After old Väinämöinen　had come from Death's Domain,
he spoke these words,　made this utterance:
"May good God not,　may He not tolerate that person,
one who of his own accord has gone to the Abode of the Dead,　forced his
　way into Death's Domain!
Many have got there,　few have come back from there,
from that home in Death's Domain,　from the eternal cottages of the Abode
　of the Dead."
He further uttered these words,　made this utterance, spoke thus
to the rising generation,　to the people growing up:
"Do not, children of men,　ever, ever at all
do wrong to an innocent person,　harm to a guiltless one.
They pay bad wages　there in the home of Death's Domain;
there there is place for the guilty,　beds for sinners,
a bedstead of hot stones,　of burning boulders,
a coverlet of adders, of snakes,　woven out of Death's reptiles."

POEM 17

Väinämöinen sets out to get charms from Antero Vipunen
and awakens Vipunen from his long sleep under the ground (1–98).
Vipunen swallows Väinämöinen
and Väinämöinen begins to torture him severely in the belly (99–146).
Now Vipunen thinks an attack of illness—he does not know what—
has got into his belly, tries to get rid of it
by many charms, enchantments, imprecations, and menaces,
but Väinämöinen threatens not to leave before he gets from Vipunen
his missing shipbuilding charms (147–526).
Vipunen sings forth all his knowledge for Väinämöinen,
who now sets forth up from his belly,
returns to his shipbuilding, and finishes his work on the ship (527–628).

When steadfast old Väinämöinen   did not get any charms
from the homes in Death's Domain yonder,   from the eternal cottages of
    the Abode of the Dead,
he still keeps pondering,   for a long time props his head on his hand,
wondering where he might get the charms,   find the precious magic words.
He comes upon a herdsman;   he is the one who uttered these words:
"You will get a hundred charms from over yonder,   a thousand odds and
    ends of verse
from the mouth of Antero Vipunen,   from the belly of the man richly
    stocked with them.
One must, however, get there,   the path must be trodden.
It is not a pleasant journey   nor by any means quite the worst;
the first stage is for you to run   on the points of women's needles,
the second for you then to walk   on the points of men's swords,
the third for you to stride   over the blades of a man's battle-ax."

Steadfast old Väinämöinen   nevertheless planned to go.
He hurries into the craftsman's smithy,   speaks these words:
"O craftsman Ilmarinen!   forge iron footwear,
forge iron gauntlets,   make an iron byrnie.
Make an iron cowlstaff,   make one of steel for pay.
Put steel in the core,   draw tough iron over it.
I am setting out to get charms,   to take magic words
from the belly of a man of great resources,   from the mouth of Antero
    Vipunen."
Craftsman Ilmarinen   uttered a word, spoke thus:
"Vipunen is long since dead,   Antero has long not been seen

setting out his snares, filling his trap line with traps.
You will probably get no charm there, no charm from that quarter at all."

Steadfast old Väinämöinen, however, set out, paid no attention.
He walked along lightly for one day on the points of women's needles,
lightheartedly walked a second on the points of men's swords,
a third with long strides on the blades of a man's battle-ax.
Vipunen rich in songs, an old man of great resources,
he is lying stretched out with his lays, sprawled out with his charms.
An aspen was growing on his shoulders, a birch rising from his brows,
an alder on the tip of his jaw, a willow on the end of his beard,
on his forehead a fir, the haunt of squirrels, a tall evergreen on his teeth.

Now Väinämöinen comes along. He drew his sword, snatched his blade
from the leather sheath, from the bast-lined belt;
he toppled over the aspen from the shoulders, the birches he brought down
off the brows,
from the jaws the spreading alders, the willows from the beard,
the firs, the haunts of squirrels, from the forehead, the tall evergreens from
the teeth.
He drove the iron cowlstaff into Antero Vipunen's mouth,
into the grinning gums, the rattling jaws.
He uttered a word, spoke thus: "Slave of mankind, get up
from lying under the ground, from sleeping a long time."
Vipunen rich in songs at once left off sleeping.
He felt someone touching him roughly, hurting him sorely;
he bit the iron cowlstaff, bit the tip of tough iron;
he could not bite the steel nor eat the iron core.

There while standing by his mouth old Väinämöinen's
right foot slipped, the left foot slid
into Antero Vipunen's mouth, suddenly slipped onto his jaw.
Immediately Vipunen rich in songs opened his mouth wider,
spread open his jaws; he swallowed the man along with his sword,
gulped down that old Väinämöinen into his throat.
Then Vipunen skilled in song uttered these words:
"I have already eaten something, eaten a ewe, eaten a goat,
eaten a farrow cow, eaten a wild boar;
I have not yet eaten the like of this, nothing tasting like this morsel."

Old Väinämöinen, he was the one to say these words:
"Now my ruin might come about, my day of distress come unexpectedly
in this demon's stall, in this Grave Spirit's cattle shed."
He ponders, he reflects how to get along, how to live.
A knife is in Väinämöinen's belt, a curly-grained haft to his knife;

of that he built a boat,   built a boat artfully.
He rows, he glides lightly   from end of gut to end of gut,
rowed through every narrow space,   wound his way through every nook.
Old Vipunen rich in songs   did not intend to pay attention to this.
Then old Väinämöinen   made himself into a blacksmith,
prepared to be an ironsmith.   Of his shirt he made a smithy,
of the shirt-sleeves a bellows,   of his fur coat blowers,
of his pants he made a bellows tube,   of his stockings the mouthpiece of
   the bellows tube,
of his knee an anvil,   of his funnybone a hammer.
He taps away,   forges deliberately and powerfully;
he forged for a night without resting,   for a day without stopping for breath
in the belly of the man of great resources,   in the bosom of the man of
   great magic knowledge.

Then Vipunen rich in songs   said these words:
"What are you among your men   and who are you among your people?
I have already eaten a hundred people,   destroyed a thousand men
and I do not seem to have eaten such a one;   hot coals are coming into my
   mouth,
firebrands onto my tongue,   iron slag into my throat."

AN EXPULSION CHARM, LINES 157-166

"Set out now, strange creature, to go,   bad creature of the earth, to take flight
before I search out your mother,   look for your esteemed parent.
If I tell the mother,   say, declare it to the parent,
it will be a trial for the mother,   a great anguish for the parent
that the son is acting badly,   the child behaving roughly."

ORIGIN CHARMS AGAINST UNCERTAIN INJURIES, LINES 167-244
[VARIOUS SOURCES OF DISEASE, LINES 167-178]

"I do not now understand that   nor do I know
whence you, demon, have fastened onto me,   whence, ruination, you have
   come here
to bite, to gnaw,   to eat, to chew.
Are you a disease created by the Creator,   a death brought by God?
Or are you a deed done,   one brought by another, created by another,
brought here for a price,   done for money?"

A PROTECTIVE CHARM AGAINST NATURAL DISEASES, LINES 179-184

"If you chance to be a disease created by the Creator,   a death brought by
   God,
then indeed I seek protection in my Creator,   fall back on my God.

The Lord does not cast a good person aside, the Creator does not reject a worthy person."

AN ORIGIN CHARM AGAINST A DISEASE OR MISADVENTURE INDUCED BY MAGIC OR BY ANOTHER PERSON, LINES 185–244

"If you chance to be a deed done, an injury caused by another,
I will certainly get to know your clan, discover your birthplace.
From there the injuries came previously, from there harm caused by magic occurred,
from sorcerers' districts, from magic singers' pastures,
from scoundrels' homesites, from wizards' fields,
from Grave Spirit's heaths, from land within the world below,
from a dead man's home, from the farmstead of one departed,
from spongy soil, from crumbly earth,
from rattling gravel, from tinkling sands,
from boggy swales, from mossless fens,
from heaving quagmires, from plashing springs,
from a cave in the Demon's wood, from five mountain crevices,
from the summit of a copper mountain, from the ridge of a copper one,
from murmuring firs, soughing evergreens,
from the crown of a rotten pine, from pines with rotted crowns,
from places where foxes bark, from the trails where one skis after an elk,
from a brown bear's lair in a rock, from a bear's den in the rock,
from the extensive back parts of North Farm, from Lapland's vast regions,
from clearings without underbrush, unplowed lands,
from great battlefields, fields where men are slaughtered,
from rustling grass, from reeking gore,
from the great expanses of the sea, from the wide open sea,
from the black ooze of the sea, from the depth of a thousand fathoms,
from murmuring currents, from flashing whirlpools,
from the strong rapids of Finnmark, from the eddy of a mighty water,
from the farther side of the heavens, from behind fine-weather clouds,
from the path of the cold spring wind, from the cradle of the wind.
Have you, too, come from there, did you, magic infection, come from there
into a guiltless heart, an innocent belly,
to eat, to gnaw, to bite, to quarry?"

A CHARM TO RESTRAIN INJURIES, LINES 245–256

"Fade away now, Demon's hound, tractable one, cur from the Abode of the Dead;
set out from my womb, wretched being, from my liver, horrible creature of the earth,
stop eating the core of my heart, tearing my spleen,
making my belly writhe, twisting my lungs,

gnawing my navel,   tearing my groin,
stripping my backbone of flesh,   drilling my sides."

CHARMS SUMMONING HELP, LINES 257–308

"If I may not be the man,   then I will sing up men better than I
to cast out this disease,   to cause this horrible thing to vanish.
From the earth I will raise up female earth spirits,   male earth spirits from
   the field,
all swordsmen from the earth,   all horsemen from the sand
as my powers, as my strength,   as my support, as my protection
in this toilsome trouble,   in this severe agony.

"If it will not obey even that,   not yield even a little,
rise up, forest, with your men,   juniper grove with your people,
pine grove with your family,   landlocked fen with your children,
a hundred sword-girt men,   a thousand ironclad warriors,
to erase this demon,   to crush the evil creature.

"If it will not obey even that,   not yield even a little,
rise from the water, mistress of the water,   blue-cap from the billows,
you with a fine kirtle from a quagmire,   beautiful one from the ooze
to be the little fellow's power,   the little man's strength,
so that no one will eat me without reason   or kill me except by a disease.

"If it will not obey even that,   not yield even a little,
splendid old woman, maiden of Nature,   resplendent lovely creature,
you who are the oldest of women,   the very first female being,
go now to identify the agonies,   to banish the days of distress,
to remove this distress,   do away with the disease.

"And if it will not obey this,   not yield even a little,
Ukko of the heavenly pole,   haloed by a thundercloud,
come when you are needed,   set out when you are summoned
to do away with painful labors,   to remove ailments
by your sharp sword,   your flashing blade."

A CHARM FOR SENDING SOMEONE HOME, LINES 309–316

"Set out now, strange monster, to go,   evil of the earth, to take flight.
There is no place for you here   even if you need a place.
Move your cottage to somewhere else,   your dwelling place farther off,
to your master's dwellings,   to your mistress' haunts."

REVENGE CHARMS, LINES 317–346

"Then after you have come there,   have got to the end of your journey,
to the districts of him who made you,   to your creator's pastures,

give a signal when you have come, a secret sign when you have got there,
rumble like a thunderclap, crash like a flash of lightning.
From the farmyard give the door a kick, let down the hatch from the
window,
then go inside, fly like a blizzard into the house.
Take firmly by the heel, by the narrowest part of the heel,
masters from out of their back corners, mistresses from their corners by the
door.
Gouge out the master's eye, smash the mistress' head,
twist the fingers, twist the heads crooked.

"If little should come of that, fly to the lane in the form of a cock,
to the farmyard as a chicken straight to the rubbish heap.
Drive the horse from the stall, horned cattle from the cowshed;
push their horns into the dung, their tails down to the floor,
turn their eyes around, break their necks suddenly."

[EXORCISM CHARMS, LINES 347–396]

"Whether you are a disease brought by the wind, brought by the wind,
driven by the flood,
given by the cold spring wind or escorted by chill air,
go along the path of the wind, along the sled track of the cold spring wind
without sitting down on a tree, without resting on an alder,
to the summit of a copper mountain, to the ridge of a copper one
for the wind to rock you there, for the cold spring wind to take care of you.

"If you have come from the heavens, from behind fair-weather clouds,
go up again to the heavens, ascend there into the sky,
to the gently dripping clouds, to the twinkling stars
to burn like fire, to glitter like sparks
on the track of the sun, on the course of the disk of the moon.

"If, gentle one, you have been dragged by the water, driven by the waves of
the sea,
then, gentle one, go into the water, betake yourself under the waves,
beside a stronghold in the ooze, onto the crests of the billows,
for the waves there to drive you on, for the dreary water to rock you.

"If you have come from the Grave Spirit's heath, from the cottages of one
forever departed,
nevertheless try to get home, to those farmsteads of the Grave Spirit,
to spongy soil, to crumbly earth,
into which a people has vanished, a staunch folk sunk down.

"If, bad creature, you came from there,   from a cave in the demon's wood,
from piny nests,   from evergreen rooms,
then I will exorcise you there   to the cave in the demon's wood,
to the evergreen rooms,   to piny nests,
for you to be there   till the floors rot,
the wall studding gets overgrown with mold,   the ceiling collapses from
    above."

GENERAL EXORCISM CHARMS, LINES 397–432

"And I will exorcise you thither,   urge the wretched creature thither,
to the home of an old male bear,   to the farmstead of an old female bear,
to those low-lying swales,   frozen fens,
heaving quagmires,   quaggy springs,
ponds without fish,   quite without perch.

"If perchance you do not get a place there,   then I will exorcise you yonder
to the extensive back parts of North Farm,   to Lapland's vast regions,
to clearings without underbrush,   to unplowed lands
where there is no moon, no sun,   nor dawn in the east.
It will be lucky for you to be there,   lovely for you to move about easily;
elk have been hung in the trees,   big wild reindeer slaughtered
for a hungry man to eat,   for a greedy man to take a bite of.

"And I will exorcise you thither,   will order and urge you thither
into the strong rapids of Finnmark,   into the burning whirlpool
where trees fall right in,   pines roll about roots up,
big evergreens plunging with their butts,   bushy-topped pines with their
    crowns.
Swim there, evil pagan,   in the violent surgings of the rapids,
go round and round in open waters,   dwell on in confined waters."

AN IMPRISONMENT CHARM, LINES 433–446

"If you perchance do not get a place there,   then I will exorcise you yonder
into Death's dark river,   into the eternal stream of the Abode of the Dead
from which you will not get free,   never, never at all,
unless I happen to free you,   have time to release you
by means of nine castrated rams,   the offspring of one ewe,
nine calves,   the calves of one cow,
along with nine male foals,   the get of one mare."

A CONVEYANCE CHARM, LINES 447–460

"If indeed you perchance ask for a conveyance,   plead for a carriage horse,
I will certainly make you a conveyance   and give you a carriage horse.

There is a good horse at the Demon's,   a brown mane on a bald mountain
whose mouth sprays fire,   whose nostrils indeed flash;
all its hoofs are of iron,   its pawing hoofs of steel;
these are able to go up a hill,   ascend the slope of a gully
under a good horseman,   a hard rider."

[A CHARM FOR MAGIC SKI EQUIPMENT, LINES 461–474]

"If this is not enough,   get the Demon's ski equipment,
the Devil's alderwood right skis,   the Evil One's thick ski pole,
with which you will ski over the Demon's lands,   rove the Devil's copses,
proceeding quickly over the Demon's lands,   gliding over the lands of the
   Evil One.
A stone lies straight across the way,   smash it to pieces;
a fir branch is lying longwise on the road,   break it in two;
a man is standing up in the road,   he is the one to dispatch to the side."

A CHARM FOR GETTING UNDER WAY, LINES 475–484

"Set out now, useless one, to get moving,   bad man, to take flight
before sunrise,   before the Dawn God's dawning,
the rising of the sun,   before hearing the cock's voice.
Now it is time for the useless man to get going   and for the evil one to take
   flight,
for you, walker in the moonlight, to move on,   you, moonlit one, to stroll off."

AN INTIMIDATION CHARM, LINES 485–494

"If perchance you do not give way quickly,   not get out, motherless cur,
I will get talons from an eagle,   teeth from a bloodsucker,
claws from a bird of prey,   talons from a hawk
with which I will squeeze loathsome creatures hard,   stop bad ones forever
from moving their heads,   from drawing a breath."

A CHARM FOR A TIME OF TROUBLE, LINES 495–504

"Of yore the real devil took himself off,   one born of a mother, too, indeed
   got lost
when God's hour [of dawn] came,   when the Creator's help was revealed.
Motherless one, will you not get lost,   not depart, unnatural monster,
not vanish, ownerless dog,   not clear out, motherless cur,
at the end of this hour [before dawn],   on the waning of this moon?"

[NARRATIVE RESUMED FROM LINE 156]

Steadfast old Väinämöinen   then uttered these words:
"It is nice for me to be here,   lovely for me to linger on.
Your liver does for bread,   the fat of your belly for a relish;
your lungs do for stew,   your fat for good food.

I will set my anvil   deeper in the flesh of your heart,
press my sledge hammer more firmly   on the more painful spots, too,
so that you will never get free,   never, never at all
unless I get to hear charms,   take along propitious spells,
hear enough charms,   thousands of magic formulas.
The charms will not get into a hiding place   nor the spells into a cranny;
the mighty power will not get buried   though the mighty ones depart."

Then Vipunen rich in songs,   that old man of great resources,
in whose mouth was great knowledge,   unlimited magic power in his bosom,
opened his chest of words,   exposed his box of lays
for him to sing good things,   sing the best things,
those profound origin charms,   age-old sacrificial spells
which all children do not sing,   some men not understand
in this dreadful time,   in this fleeting final age.
He sang the origin charms in the proper way,   the spells correctly,
how by leave of its Creator,   at the Almighty's demand,
the sky was created of itself,   how water separated from the heavens,
how solid land was formed into earth apart from the water,   how on solid
   ground all growing things sprang up.
He sang of the forming of the moon,   the establishing of the sun,
of the erecting of the pillars of heaven,   the studding of the heavens with
   stars.

Then Vipunen rich in songs   indeed sang and well knew how to.
A better singer   was not heard or seen,
never, never at all   a more accurate seer;
that mouth threw out magic words,   the tongue dropped charms flowingly
as a two-year-old colt does its legs,   a riding horse its fine limbs.
He sang day after day,   he sang night after night.
The sun stopped to hear,   the lovely moon to look;
the waves stood still in the sea,   the billows at the head of the bay;
the streams stopped flowing,   the rapids of Finnmark stopped foaming,
the rapids of the Vuoksi stopped flowing,   the river Jourtan came to a stop.

Then old Väinämöinen,   when he had heard the songs,
had received charms aplenty,   found his propitious spells,
started to set out   from Antero Vipunen's mouth,
from the belly of the man of great resources,   from the bosom of the man of
   great magic knowledge.
Old Väinämöinen said: "O you Antero Vipunen,
if you would open your mouth wider,   spread open your jaws,
I would get out of your belly onto the ground   in order to proceed to my
   home."

Then Vipunen rich in songs   uttered these words:
"Many things have I eaten, drunk many things,   destroyed thousands and
    thousands of things;
I have never yet eaten such a one   before I ate old Väinämöinen.
You did well when you came,   you are doing better now that you are going!"
Then Antero Vipunen   bared his teeth,
opened his mouth wider,   spread open his jaws.
Old Väinämöinen   set out from the mouth of the man of great learning,
from the belly of the man of great resources,   from the bosom of the man of
    great magic knowledge.
Suddenly he slips out of the mouth,   jumps onto the heath
like a golden squirrel   or a golden-breasted marten.

Thence he set out to walk;   he came to his craftsman's smithy.
Craftsman Ilmarinen said: "Were you now able to hear magic words,
find the propitious charms,   hear how one sets a ship's side in place,
joins a stern plank,   mounts the bow and stern posts?"
Steadfast old Väinämöinen   uttered these words:
"Now I have already got a hundred charms,   thousands of magic formulas;
I got the charms from a hiding place,   magic words from a cranny."
Then he went to his boat,   rich in charms to his workshop.
He got the boat ready,   the side planks fastened,
the stern finished,   the bow structure mounted.
The boat was produced without using a tool,   the ship without removing a
    chip.

POEM 18

Väinämöinen sails with his new boat to woo the maid of North Farm (1–40).
Ilmarinen's sister sees him and speaks to him from the shore,
obtains knowledge of his journey, and hurries to inform her brother
that his bride-to-be, earned of yore at North Farm, is now in jeopardy (41–266).
Ilmarinen gets ready and he, too, hurries with his horse
along the shore to North Farm (267–470).
When the mistress of North Farm sees the suitors coming,
she advises her daughter to marry Väinämöinen (471–634).
The daughter herself vows to marry Ilmarinen, forger of the Sampo,
and to Väinämöinen, who has now entered the house,
replies that she will not be bothered with him (635–706).

Steadfast old Väinämöinen   ponders, reflects
about going to woo the girl,   to look at the one with luxuriant hair
at gloomy North Farm,   dark Sedgy Farm,
famed daughter of North Farm,   such a bride-to-be at North Farm.
He put a blue broadcloth coat on the boat,   a red one on the vessel;
the bow and stern posts he decorated with gold,   overlaid them with silver.
So on a certain day   very early in the morning
he pushed the boat into the water,   the vessel with a hundred planks into
    the billows
from the rollers stripped of bark,   from the pinewood chocks.
He stepped the mast,   hoisted the sails onto the mast,
hauled up one red sail,   a second blue sail;
he got down into the ship,   steps into the craft.
He set out to sail the sea,   to speed over the blue.

A CHARM FOR SETTING OUT ON THE WATER, LINES 29–40
Then he uttered these words,   spoke and talked:
"Come now, God, into the vessel,   into the craft, Gracious One,
as a little fellow's power,   as a little man's strength
on those extensive waters,   on the boundless billows.
Wind, rock the vessel;   wave, drive the ship
without rowing with fingers,   without disturbing the water's gleaming surface,
on the broad expanses of the sea,   on the wide open sea."

Annikki of fair name,   a girl working at dusk, working at dawn
worker in the early morning watch,   early on watch at dawn,
was doing laundry,   washing the clothes
at the end of a red landing stage,   the top of a big pier
at a tip of the misty headland,   on the end of a foggy island.

She looks about, turns her head   around the lovely sky
toward the heavens above,   along the shore of the sea.
The sun was shining aloft,   the waves were glistening below.
Her eyes lit upon the surface of the sea,   she turned her head to the south
along the mouth of the river of Suomela,   along the waters of Väinämöinen's
   district;
she detected something dark on the sea,   something blue on the billows.
She uttered a word, spoke thus,   spoke and talked:
"What are you, black thing on the sea?   Who are you, blue thing on the
   billows?
If you are a skein of geese   or a lovely flock of old squaws,
then rush off in flight   to the heavens above.
If you are an island, the haunt of salmon,   or or some other school of fish,
then go splash and swim,   betake yourselves under the water.
Were you a stony island   or a rotten stump in the water,
a wave would break on you,   water would splash on you."

The boat comes nearer,   the new vessel sails
along the tip of the misty headland,   along the end of the foggy island.
Annikki of fair name   now knew that a boat was coming,
a ship of a hundred planks tacking along.   She uttered a word, spoke thus:
"If you happen to be my brother's boat   or my father's vessel,
then try to make straight for home,   turn straight toward your own lands
with bow toward these landing places,   stern toward other landing places.
If you happen to be a totally strange vessel,   drift farther out
toward other landing places   with your stern toward these landing places."
It was neither a boat from home   nor a totally strange vessel;
it was actually Väinämöinen's vessel,   the eternal singer's ship.
Now he was approaching there,   was speeding on for a talk,
to utter one word, to produce a second,   to speak a third distinctly.
Annikki of fair name,   a girl working at dusk, working at dawn,
began to inquire about the vessel: "Where were you setting out for,
   Väinämöinen,
getting along to, suitor from Slack Water Farm,   preparing to go, best man
   in the world?"

Old Väinämöinen   speaks from his vessel:
"I was setting out to catch a salmon,   to catch a spawning lake trout
in Death's dark river,   in the deep stream of Sedgy Farm."
Annikki of fair name,   she indeed was the one to say these words:
"Do not tell empty lies!   I know about spawning, too.
Differently indeed did my father in the past,   differently indeed did my
   esteemed parent
set out to catch a salmon,   to try to catch a sea trout.
The boat was full of seines,   full of the ship's drag-nets,

here seines, there lines,   here beating poles on the side,
fish spears under the rowing bench,   long punting poles in the stern.
Where were you setting out for, Väinämöinen,   heading out for, man of
    Slack Water Farm?"

Old Väinämöinen said: "I set out in quest of geese,
to the playground of the mottled wings,   to hunt the wranglers
on the deep sounds of Germany,   on the open expanses of the sea."
Annikki of fair name   uttered a word, spoke thus:
"I recognize a speaker of the truth,   also I detect a liar.
Differently indeed did my father in the past,   differently did my esteemed
    parent
set out to hunt geese,   to search for the red-beaked ones.
The big crossbow was strung,   the fine bow drawn,
the black dog on a leash,   the leash tied to a rib;
a cur ran along the shore road,   a pup sped over the stones.
Tell the truth, Väinämöinen!   Where were you really intending to go?"

Old Väinämöinen said: "What if I should be going
to those great wars,   evenly matched combats
where there will be blood over the shins,   red blood up to the knees?"
Annikki says,   she with a tin ornament on her breast, snaps:
"I recognize going to war, too.   When in the past my father set out
for those great wars,   evenly matched combats,
a hundred men were rowing,   a thousand seated besides,
tipped crossbows in the bow,   bladed swords on the rowers' benches.
Now tell the real truth,   unvarnished, trustworthy.
Where were you setting out for, Väinämöinen,   making for, man of Slack
    Water Farm?"

Then old Väinämöinen   uttered a word, spoke thus:
"Come, girl, into my vessel,   maiden, into my boat;
then I will tell the real truth,   unvarnished, trustworthy."
Annikki says a word,   she with a tin ornament on her breast snapped:
"May the wind blow on your vessel,   the cold spring wind on your boat!
I will turn your vessel upside down,   tip your bow under
if I cannot hear the truth,   hear where you were intending to set out for,
hear the exact truth,   the last of your lies."
Then old Väinämöinen   uttered a word, spoke thus:
"Well, I will really tell the truth   even if I did lie a little.
I set out to woo a maiden,   to sue for a virgin
at gloomy North Farm,   at dark Sedgy Farm,
a place where a man is devoured,   a person destroyed."

Annikki of fair name,   a girl working at dusk, working at dawn,
when she recognized the real truth,   unvarnished, trustworthy,

she left her kerchiefs unrinsed,   her clothes unwashed
at the top of the big pier,   at the end of the red landing stage.
She grasped her clothes with her hand,   gathered up her skirt in her grip;
then she got to walking,   at once managed to run.
She comes to the craftsman's home,   steps into the smithy.
Craftsman Ilmarinen,   eternal smith,
was forging a long iron bench,   was carefully making one of silver,
with a yard of fluffy ashes on his head,   a fathom of charcoal dust on his
   shoulders.
Annikki stepped to the door,   uttered a word, spoke thus:
"Brother, craftsman Ilmarinen,   eternal smith!
Forge me a shuttle,   forge pretty rings,
two or three pairs of earrings,   five or six belt chains;
then I will tell the real truth,   unvarnished, trustworthy."
Craftsman Ilmarinen said: "If you tell me good news
I will forge you a shuttle,   will forge pretty rings,
will forge a cross for your breast,   mend your clasp.
If you tell me bad news,   I will break up the old ornaments,
thrust them from your head into the fire,   thrust them into the bottom of my
   forge."

Annikki of fair name,   she was the one who uttered these words:
"O craftsman Ilmarinen,   so that is how you remember to marry
the one whom long ago you engaged to marry,   whom you reserved as your
   wife!
You still keep on forging,   you keep pounding all the time!
In the summer you shoe the horse,   in the winter you make horseshoes;
at night you repair your sleds,   by day you make traveling sleighs
for you to go courting in,   for you to reach North Farm.
Now already slyer men are going there,   more eminent men are finding time
   to go;
they will take away your very own,   seize your beloved
eyed by you for two years,   wooed by you for three years.
Now Väinämöinen is going along   on the surface of the blue sea
in a boat with a lovely bow,   with a copper steering oar
to gloomy North Farm,   to dark Sedgy Farm."

Anguish oppressed the craftsman,   heaviness of heart the smith;
the tongs dropped from his grasp,   the hammer fell from his hand.
Craftsman Ilmarinen said: "Annikki my sister,
I will forge a shuttle for you,   will forge pretty finger rings,
two or three pairs of earrings,   five or six belt chains.
Warm up a delicious bath,   smoke up a sweet sauna
with small sticks,   with little splints.

Prepare a little soft soap, quickly dissolve lye
with which I may wash my head, whiten my body,
ridding it of the autumn soot, the winter's smithyings."

Annikki of fair name secretly warmed up the sauna
with sticks broken off by the wind, evidently knocked off by Ukko.
She collected stones from a rapids, produced dry steam
with water got from a lovely spring, from a spongy quagmire.
She broke off a bath whisk from a thicket, a lovely whisk from a grove,
softened the sweet whisk on the top of a sweet stone.
She prepared tacky soft soap, marrowy soap,
soap sparkling, sparkling, lathery,
as soap for the suitor's head, as a rinse for his body.

Craftsman Ilmarinen, eternal smith,
forged what the maiden required, repaired her clasps
while she was preparing the bath, getting the sauna ready;
these he thrust into the girl's hand. The girl uttered these words:
"I have now smoked up the sauna, warmed up the vapory bath,
softened the whisks just right, prepared passion-inducing whisks.
Bathe, brother, as much as you want; throw water as you like,
wash your head till the hair is like flax, your face till it is like a snowflake."
Then craftsman Ilmarinen went to bathe
and bathed as much as he wanted, washed himself white;
he washed his face till it was bright, his temples till they were fine,
his neck till it was white as a hen's egg, the whole trunk white.
He came from the sauna into the house, came unrecognized,
his face very handsome, his cheeks bright red.
Then he uttered these words: "Annikki my sister,
now bring my linen shirt, fetch the suitable clothes
in which I garb my body when getting ready to go courting."

Annikki of fair name brought the linen shirt
for the skin free of sweat, for the bare skin,
then form-fitting trousers, those sewed by his mother,
for the flanks free of soot with no bones visible.
Then she brought sheer stockings woven by his mother when a virgin
for the shanks free of lather, for the plump calves,
then good shoes, the best German boots
over his fine stockings stitched by his mother as a maiden.
She fetched a blue broadcloth jacket, liver-colored below,
on top of the linen shirt, the pure linen one;
on that a long homespun topcoat edged with four stripes,
on top of the blue broadcloth jacket, a brand new one

with thousands of buttons of new fur,   decorated with hundreds of loops,
on top of the long homespun topcoat,   the latter edged with broadcloth;
further still a belt for his waist,   a long belt with gold ornaments,
woven by his mother as a virgin,   thumped off the loom when a girl with
 luxuriant hair;
then ornamented mittens,   gloves with gold-adorned edges
woven by Lapland's children   for his handsome hands;
then a high-peaked hat   for his fine locks,
purchased by his father,   got when a suitor.

Then craftsman Ilmarinen   dresses himself, gets himself ready,
clothes himself, decks himself out.   Then he said to his slave:
"Now harness the splendid colt   in front of the decorated sleigh
for me to set out driving,   for me to go to North Farm."
The slave uttered these words: "We have six stallions,
a steed fed on oats.   Which of these should I harness?"
Craftsman Ilmarinen said: "Take the best stallion,
put the colt into the harness,   the brown one in front of the sleigh.
Put six cuckooing bells,   seven bells with the voice of those bluish birds
to sing mournfully on the shaft-bow,   to give out low tones on the traces,
so that the fair ones might take a look,   the virgins be delighted.
Bring there a bearskin   for me to sit upon,
bring a second, a water monster's skin   to cover the decorated basket sleigh."
That perpetual slave,   a servant bought with money,
put the colt in the harness,   the brown one in front of the sleigh.
He put six cuckooing bells,   seven bells with the voice of those bluish birds
to call mournfully on the shaft-bow,   to give out low tones on the traces.
He brought a bear skin there   for his master to sit on,
brought a second, a water monster's skin,   to cover the decorated basket
 sleigh.

Craftsman Ilmarinen,   eternal smith,
prays Ukko,   humbly beseeches the Thunderer:
"Send down fresh snow, Ukko,   throw down new powder snow,
snow for the sleigh to slip along on,   new-fallen snow for the sled to speed
 along on."
Ukko did send down new snow,   threw down new powder snow;
it covered the stalks of the heather,   covered the berry stalks on the ground.
Then craftsman Ilmarinen   sits down in the sled with steel runners;
he speaks these words,   made this remark:
"Set out now, Good Luck, on my reins!   Set out, God, in my sleigh!
Good Luck will not break the reins,   God not smash up the sleigh."
He took the reins in one hand,   in the other he grasped the whip;
he struck the horse with the whip,   uttered these words:
"Set out, horse with a blaze, to speed along,   flaxen mane, to get under way."

He drives easily along   the sandy dunes by the sea,
along the side of sounds with pastured shores,   along the crests of alder-
   grown ridges.
He rattled along the shores,   clattered over the sands of the shore.
Gravel stung his eyes,   sea spray struck his chest.

He drove one day, drove a second,   soon he drives a third;
already on the third day   he overtakes Väinämöinen.
He uttered a word, spoke thus,   remarked and talked:
"O old Väinämöinen,   let us make a friendly agreement
if we happen to be wooing in rivalry,   be going to pay court in rivalry:
not to drag the girl away by force,   against her will to a husband's home."
Old Väinämöinen says: "I will make a friendly agreement:
not to drag the girl away by force,   against her will to a husband's home.
A girl ought to be given to him   whom she desires
without anyone's feeling long-lasting jealousy,   without being angry for long."

They drove on from there,   each indeed his own way.
The vessel ran along, the shore resounded;   the stallion ran, the earth
   rumbled.
A little while passed,   a short time went quickly by.
Already the dog was barking,   the watchdog of the fine house baying,
at gloomy North Farm,   at great Sedgy Farm.
At first it gave rather low growls,   uttered low growls once in a while,
striking its behind on the edge of a field,   wagging its tail on the ground.

The master of North Farm said: "Go, girl, and see
what the grey dog is barking at,   what flop-ears keeps yapping at."
The girl answered shrewdly: "I have no time, my dear master;
the big cattle shed must be cleaned,   the big herd inspected,
the heavy quern stone turned,   fine meal bolted.
The quern stone is heavy, the meal fine,   weak the turner of the quern."
The demon of the fine house uttered low barks,   the grey dog growled once
   in a while.

The master of North Farm said: "Go, dame, and see
what the grey dog is barking at,   what flop-ears of the fine house is yapping
   at."
The dame uttered these words: "I have no time, do not intend to at all;
the big family must be fed,   the morning meal prepared,
a thick loaf baked,   dough kneaded.
The loaf is thick, the meal fine,   weak the baker."

The master of North Farm said: "Women are, to be sure, always in a hurry,
daughters always have work   while toasting themselves on the stove bench,

stretching out on a bed, too. Go, son, and see."
The son uttered these words: "I have no time to look;
the dull ax must be ground,   a heavy log of wood chopped,
a big pile of wood split,   small firewood stacked.
The pile is big, the firewood small,   weak the hewer."
The hound of the fine house kept barking,   the watchdog of the fine house
kept baying,
the fierce whelp kept barking loudly,   the island watchdog kept complaining,
striking its behind on the field,   curling up its tail.

The master of North Farm said: "The grey dog is not barking for nothing,
the old fellow not speaking idly,   not just mumbling at the evergreens."
He himself went to look.   He walks across the farmyard
to the field farthest back,   to the cattle yard most in the rear.
He sighted along the dog's muzzle,   took a close sight along the bridge of
its nose,
along the crest of a wind-swept ridge,   along the shoulder of an alder-grown
ridge.
Now he saw the real truth,   what the grey dog was barking at,
what the pride of the land was complaining about,   what bushy-tail was
giving tongue to.
A red boat was sailing along   the surface of Lovers' Bay;
a decorated sleigh was moving swiftly   over the land side of Honey-fragrant
Island.

The master of North Farm   goes quickly into the house,
betakes himself under the roof,   uttered a word, spoke thus:
"Now strangers are coming   on the surface of the blue sea;
someone is driving a decorated basket sleigh   on this side of Honey-fragrant
Island;
someone is landing with a big ship   on this side of Lovers' Bay."

The mistress of North Farm said: "Where may an omen be got
about the strangers who are arriving?   O my little girl,
put rowan sticks in the fire,   choice wood into the flame.
If perchance blood streams,   then war is coming;
if perchance water streams,   we will continue to live in peace."
The little hired girl of North Farm,   humble maiden, the servant,
thrust rowan sticks into the fire,   choice wood into the flame.
No blood streams at all,   neither blood nor water;
honey started to stream,   honey to ooze.
From her corner Suovakko spoke,   an old woman under a rough blanket:
"When wood streams honey,   oozes honey,
then whatever strangers may be coming,   they will be a suitor and his big
retinuc."

Then the mistress of North Farm, dame of North Farm, girl of North Farm,
soon made her way to the farmyard, bounded into the yard,
casting her eyes toward the sea, turning her head south.
From there she saw it coming, a new vessel sailing along,
a ship with a hundred planks tacking along the water of Lovers' Bay.
The ship was gleaming in a blue coat, the vessel in a red one;
a handsome man was in the stern of the vessel with a copper steering oar.
She saw a stallion running, a red sled going along,
a decorated basket sleigh speeding along the land side of Honey-fragrant
Island
with six gold cuckoos calling on the shaft-bow,
with seven of those bluish birds calling on the traces;
a sturdy man is in the back of the sleigh, a gallant fellow holding the reins.

The mistress of North Farm spoke, gave utterance, spoke thus:
"To which of the two do you want to go when they come to seek you
as a lifelong friend, as a chick by their side?
The one who is coming in the ship, proceeding with the red boat
along the surface of Lovers' Bay, that is old Väinämöinen.
He is bringing goods in his ship, treasures in his craft.
The one who is driving in the sleigh, speeding on in the decorated basket
sleigh
along the land side of Honey-fragrant Island, that is craftsman Ilmarinen.
He is bringing an empty illusion, a sleighful of magic spells.
When, indeed, they come into the house, bring mead in stoups,
carry it in two-eared mugs; thrust the stoup into the hand of him
whom you wish to marry. Give it to the old man of Väinämöinen's district
who is bringing goods in his ship, treasures in his craft!"
The handsome maid of North Farm, she managed to speak thus:
"O mother, you who bore me, O mother, you who reared me!
I will not marry the power of wealth or a man's intelligence;
I will marry the goodness of his forehead, the handsomeness of his whole
body.
No maiden has ever before been sold for riches.
The maid must be given for nothing to craftsman Ilmarinen
who forged the Sampo, tapped out the lid of many colors."
The mistress of North Farm said: "O lamb of a child!
So you are marrying craftsman Ilmarinen to provide for a sweaty forehead,
to rinse out the craftsman's sheets, to wash the craftsman's head!"
To this the girl replied, uttered a word, spoke thus:
"I am not marrying the old man of Väinämöinen's district to provide for
the awfully old man;
misery would come from the old man, boredom from the aged person."

Then old Väinämöinen got there ahead.

He sailed his red vessel,   brought his craft with its broadcloth coat
to the steel rollers,   to the copper rollers;
he makes his way into the house,   betakes himself under the roof.
Then he spoke from the floor,   at the opening of the door, under the lintel
speaks these words,   made this remark:
"Will you come to me, maiden,   as an eternal friend,
as a lifelong consort,   as a chick by my side?"
The beautiful girl of North Farm   managed to say:
"Will you now shape a boat,   make a big ship now
from the fragments of my spindle,   from bits of my flax scraper?"
Old Väinämöinen said,   spoke and talked:
"Now I will make a good ship indeed,   I will shape a substantial boat,
which is steady in the wind   and stable in a headwind
to drive through the waves,   to float along the surface of the water.
It will raise itself up like bubbles,   will glide along like water lilies
across the waters of North Farm,   the whitecapped billows."
The fair girl of North Farm   uttered a word, spoke thus:
"I do not commend a seafaring man,   a person who sets out on the waves;
at sea the wind distorts the mind,   the cold spring wind harms the brain.
I cannot possibly come,   I will not come to you
as an eternal friend,   as a chick by your side,
to lay out your bed,   to arrange your pillow."

POEM 19

Ilmarinen enters the house at North Farm,
asks for the daughter, and is assigned dangerous tasks (1–32).
By the advice of the maiden of North Farm he gets the tasks successfully completed:
first, he plows a snake-infested field;
second, he gets Death's bear and the wolf of the Abode of the Dead;
third, he catches the great terrible pike in the river of Death's Domain (33–344).
The mistress of North Farm
promises and betroths her daughter to Ilmarinen (345–498).
In a sorry state of mind Väinämöinen returns from North Farm
and forbids anyone else to set out
as a rival in courtship with one younger than himself (499–518).

Then craftsman Ilmarinen,   eternal smith,
makes his way into the house,   gets in under the roof.
A stoup of mead was brought,   a pot of mead carried
to craftsman Ilmarinen's hand.   The craftsman uttered these words:
"Never, never at all,   not while the moon shines gold-bright
will I drink these drinks   before I can see my very own,
see whether the one I longed for is ready,   ready she for whom I had to
   wait."

The mistress of North Farm   uttered a word, spoke thus:
"The one longed for is in great trouble,   the one you had to wait for is in
   trouble:
one foot is half shod,   the other even less so.
The one you longed for will be ready,   the one you wailed for ready,
just as soon as you plow an adder-infested field,   turn over a snake-ridden
   field
without the plow proceeding,   the plowshare shaking.
That is the one the demon plowed of yore,   the Devil indeed furrowed
with a copper plowshare,   with a very sharp plow;
my own wretched son   left it less than half plowed."

[THE FIRST TASK: PLOWING A SNAKE-INFESTED FIELD,
LINES 33–74]

Then craftsman Ilmarinen   went into his maiden's room.
He said these words: "Girl working at dusk, working at dawn,
do you remember that time   when I was decorating the new Sampo,
was tapping out the lid of many colors?   You vowed your eternal oath
in the presence of illustrious God,   looking up at the face of the Almighty,

vowed that you would come   to me, a good man,
as an eternal friend,   as a chick by my side.
Now your mother will not grant you,   not proffer me her girl
unless I plow an adder-infested field,   turn over a snake-ridden one."
The bride-to-be gave assistance,   the girl proffered suggestions:
"O craftsman Ilmarinen,   eternal smith,
fashion a golden plough,   decorate one of silver;
with that you will plow the adder-infested field,   turn over the snake-ridden
    one."

Craftsman Ilmarinen   put gold in the forge,
his silver in the hearth;   from that he forges a plow.
He forged iron footwear,   steel leggings,
dresses himself in these,   fixes them on his legs;
he puts on an iron byrnie,   girds himself with steel belts,
took his iron gauntlets,   fetched stone mittens.
Then he got a fiery gelding,   harnessed the good horse,
set out to plow the field,   to furrow the meadow.

A CHARM TO WARD OFF SNAKES, LINES 75–90

He saw the writhing heads,   the rattling skulls.
He says these words: "Alas, reptile, creation of God!
Who raised your head up,   who indeed ordered and urged you
to hold your head erect,   the pillar of your neck stiff?
Now get out of the way,   thrust yourself, wretch, into last year's withered
    grass,
weave your way down into the underbrush,   swing around into a grassy place.
If indeed you lift your head from there,   Ukko will harm your head
with steel-tipped arrows,   with iron hailstones."

Then he plowed the adder-infested field,   furrowed the viper-ridden ground,
lifted the adders up on the freshly plowed field,   the snakes to the top of the
    furrows.
When he came back he said: "Now I have plowed the adder-infested field,
furrowed the viper-ridden ground,   turned over the snake-ridden earth.
Will the girl now be proferred me,   my beloved granted to me?"

[THE SECOND TASK: CATCHING DEATH'S BEAR AND BRIDLING THE WOLF OF THE ABODE OF THE DEAD, LINES 101–150]

The mistress of North Farm   uttered a word, spoke thus:
"The maiden will be granted,   the girl from here proffered
just as soon as you bring Death's bear,   bridle the wolf of the Abode of the
    Dead

in the wilderness of Death's Domain,   behind the cottages of the Abode of
  the Dead.
A hundred have gone to bridle it,   not a single one has come back."

Then craftsman Ilmarinen   went into his maiden's room.
He uttered a word, spoke thus: "I have been assigned the task
of bridling the wolves of the Abode of the Dead,   of fetching Death's bears
yonder from the wilderness of Death's Domain   from behind the cottages of
  the Abode of the Dead."
The bride-to-be gave assistance,   the girl proffered suggestions:
"O craftsman Ilmarinen,   eternal smith,
make the bits out of steel,   make the bridles out of iron
on a certain stone out in the water,   in the foaming waters of three rapids.
With these you will get Death's bears,   bridle the wolves of the Abode of
  the Dead."

Then craftsman Ilmarinen,   eternal smith,
prepared the bits out of steel,   made the bridles out of iron
on a certain stone out in the water,   in the foaming waters of three rapids.
Then he went to do the bridling.

[A HUNTSMAN'S CHARM, LINES 135-142]
                              He uttered these words, spoke thus:
"Girl, Fog Spirit,   sift out mist with your sieve,
sprinkle some fog   on the haunts of the forest game
so that it will not hear to move off   nor flee from before me."
He got the bit into the wolf's mouth,   the iron shackles onto the bear
there on Death's heath,   inside the hazy blue wilderness.
When he came back from there he said: "Grant, dame, your daughter!
Now I have brought Death's bear,   bridled the wolf of the Abode of the
  Dead."

[THE THIRD TASK: CATCHING THE PIKE IN THE RIVER
      OF DEATH'S DOMAIN, LINES 151-312]
The mistress of North Farm   uttered a word, spoke thus:
"The old squaw will be granted,   the blue goldeneye will be provided
just as soon as you catch the big scaly pike,   the active fat fish
in the river of Death's Domain,   in the lower parts of the Abode of the Dead,
without lifting a net,   without turning a landing net.
A hundred have gone to catch it,   not a single one has come back."

Now indeed he becomes anguished,   gets into a more precarious situation.
He went into his maiden's room,   uttered these words:
"I have been assigned a task,   always better than the one before:

to get a big scaly pike,   an active fat fish
from Death's dark river,   from the eternal stream of the Abode of the Dead,
without a seine, without a net,   without anything else to catch it with."
The bride-to-be gave assistance,   the girl proffered suggestions:
"O craftsman Ilmarinen,   do not be upset by that!
Forge a fiery eagle,   a flaming griffin.
With that you will get the big pike,   the active fat fish
from Death's dark river,   from the lower parts of the Abode of the Dead."

Craftsman Ilmarinen,   eternal smith,
forges a fiery eagle,   a flaming griffin;
he fashioned the talons out of iron,   the claws out of steel,
the sides of a boat into the wings.   He mounted the wings,
took his place on its back,   on the tip of the eagle's wing.
Then he counseled his eagle,   cautioned the griffin:
"My eagle, my bird,   go fly where I order you,
fly to Death's dark river,   to the lower parts of the Abode of the Dead;
strike the big scaly pike,   the active fat fish."
That eagle, fine bird,   flaps along;
it flew to catch the pike,   to seek out the one with dreadful teeth
there in the river of Death's Domain,   in the lower parts of the Abode of
    the Dead.
One wing grazed the water,   the other touched the heavens;
the talons scratched the sea,   the bill brushed the little islands.

Then craftsman Ilmarinen   sets out to drag
that river of Death's Domain   with the eagle close by to keep watch.
A water demon rose up from the water;   it seized Ilmarinen.
The eagle dived onto the nape of its neck,   twisted the water demon's head,
pushed its head nearer the bottom   toward the black ooze.
Now Death's pike comes,   the dog of the water moves forward slightly.
It was not a very small pike   nor really a very big one;
the tongue was two ax handles long,   the teeth a rake handle long,
the jaw equal to three rapids,   its back as long as seven boats.
It wanted to seize the craftsman,   to eat craftsman Ilmarinen.
The eagle came like a beast of prey,   the bird of the air striking.
It was not a very small eagle   nor really a very big one;
its mouth was a hundred fathoms long,   the jaws the size of five rapids,
the tongue five spear shafts long,   its talons five scythe lengths.

It discovered the big scaly pike,   the active fat fish;
it strikes that fish,   tore the scales.
Then the big scaly pike,   the active fat fish
presses the eagle's talon   down under the clear waters.
Then the eagle lifts itself up,   rises up into the air;

it brought black ooze   up to the surface of the clear waters.
It moves about, it stirs about,   then rises a second time.
It struck one of its talons   into the shoulders of the dreadful pike,
into the arched back of the dog of the water;   it struck the other talon
into a steel mountain,   into an iron crag.
Its talon slipped off the stone,   slid off the crag.
Now the pike dived,   the clumsy lout of the water pulled itself away
from the talons of the eagle's foot,   from the toes of the bird of prey;
there are talon marks on the rib bones,   rips in the shoulders.

Then the iron-taloned eagle   once again exerted itself violently;
the wings flashed like flame,   the eyes like bright fire;
it got the pike in its talons,   the dog of the water in its grip.
It lifted the big scaly pike,   pulled the clumsy lout of the water
up from under the deep waves   to the surface of the clear waters.
Thus the iron-taloned eagle   on its third try indeed
gets Death's pike,   the active fat fish
from that river of Death's Domain,   from the lower parts of the Abode of
    the Dead.
The water did not feel like water   because of the scales of the big pike,
the air did not smell like air   because of the big eagle's feathers.

Then the iron-taloned eagle   carried the big scaly pike
to the branch of an oak with lots of acorns,   to the top of a bushy-crowned
    pine.
Then it tasted the stomach,   slashed through the pike's belly,
tore the breast,   struck the head clear off.
Craftsman Ilmarinen said: "O you, wretched eagle!
What sort of a bird may you be?   What sort of a beast may you be
now that you have tasted the stomach,   slashed through the pike's belly,
also torn the breast,   struck the head clear off?"
The iron-taloned eagle   then flew away in anger.
It rose up in the air   to the edge of a long cloud.
The clouds moved about, the heavens wailed,   the vault of heaven bent
    down;
Ukko's bow broke,   the pointed horns of the moon.

Then craftsman Ilmarinen   carried the fish's head
to his future mother-in-law as a gift.   He uttered a word, spoke thus:
"Here are the makings of an everlasting chair   for the house of good North
    Farm."
Then he uttered these words,   remarked and talked:
"Now I have plowed the adder-infested fields,   furrowed the viper-ridden
    grounds,
bridled the wolves of the Abode of the Dead,   shackled Death's bears;

I got the big scaly pike,   the active fat fish
from that river of Death's Domain,   from the lower parts of the Abode of
   the Dead.
Will you now grant me the maiden,   proffer the girl here?"
The mistress of North Farm said: "You really did badly indeed
when you struck the head clear off,   slashed through the pike's stomach,
further tore the breast,   also tasted the stomach."
Then craftsman Ilmarinen   uttered these words:
"One does not get game undamaged   from even better places;
this was got from the river of Death's Domain,   from the lower parts of the
   Abode of the Dead.
Is the one I longed for now ready,   the one I had to wait for ready?"

The mistress of North Farm spoke,   remarked and said:
"Now the one you longed for is ready,   the one you had to wait for is ready.
My old squaw must now be granted,   my mallard provided
for craftsman Ilmarinen   as a lifelong companion,
as an everlasting comfort,   as a chick by his side."

A HANDSHAKE LAY
[TO CONFIRM A BETROTHAL],
LINES 357-497

There was a baby on the floor.   The baby was singing on the floor:
"A bird came into this house,   a useless bird into our fine house.
An eagle flew from the northeast,   a hawk through the heavens:
one wing hit the edge of the sky,   the other swept the billows:
the tail brushed the sea lightly,   the head touched the heavens.
It looks about, it turns about,   it moves about, noves about;
it lit upon the men's fine house,   it keeps rapping with its beak.
The men's stronghold had an iron roof,   it did not get inside that!
It looks about, it turns about,   it moves about, it noves about.
It lit upon the women's stronghold,   it keeps rapping with its beak;
the women's stronghold had a copper roof;   it did not get inside that!
It looks about, it turns about,   it noves about, it moves about.
It lit upon the maidens' stronghold,   it keeps rapping with its beak;
the maidens' stronghold had a flaxen roof,   now it got inside that!
It lit upon the chimney flue of the fine house,   then it settled down on the
   roof;
it moved the shutter of the stronghold,   it sat on the window ledge of the
   stronghold,
the bird with green plumage in a recess in the wall,   the hundred-pinioned
   bird where the butt ends of the logs meet.
It looks at the girls with luxuriant hair,   it tested the heads of hair

of the best bevy of maidens,   of the most beautiful of those with luxuriant hair,
of the lustrous heads adorned with beads,   of the famed flower-decked heads.
Then the eagle grasps her,   the bird of the pine forest seizes hold of her;
it struck the best one of the bevy,   the prettiest of the flock of mallards,
the fairest, most charming,   pinkest-cheeked, with the most brilliant coloring.
She was the one the bird of the air struck,   her its long claws carried off,
the one who held her head erect   and was sought after, too, for her figure,
who was softest as to feathers,   finest as to plumage."

Then the mistress of North Farm   uttered a word, spoke thus:
"Where did you get to know, lucky man,   where did you hear, golden apple,
that this girl was growing up,   her flaxen hair waving?
Did the maiden's silver ornaments gleam,   the maiden's gold ones become famed yonder?
Did our suns blaze over there,   our moons gleam palely?"

The baby spoke up from the floor,   the growing child just sang:
"This is how the lucky man knew,   the lucky fellow found the way
to the maiden's splendid home,   to the beautiful farmstead:
her father's reputation was good   for steering a big ship,
the mother's even better   for baking a thick loaf,
for baking a wheaten loaf,   for feeding a guest.
This is how the lucky one knew,   the total stranger became aware
that the young girl had shot up,   the virgin grown tall:
one time when he was walking by the farmyard,   walking down below the storehouses
very early one morning,   right in the very early morning,
smoke was rising straight up,   dense smoke was escaping
from the maiden's splendid home,   from the farmstead of the growing girl.
The maiden herself was grinding grain,   was swaying easily on the quern staff;
the quern staff was calling out like a cuckoo,   the hole for the staff like a wild goose,
the disk in the hole like a bunting,   the stone jingling like a string of beads.
Then he took a walk a second time,   stepped along the edge of a field.
The girl was gathering yellow bedstraw,   was moving nimbly on the yellow heath;
she was preparing pots of red dye,   was boiling kettles of yellow dye.
Then he took a walk a third time   along under the maiden's window;
he heard the maiden weaving,   the batten thumping in her hand.
The shuttle was slipping along   like a weasel in the crevice in a rock,
the blades of the reed made a clicking sound   like a woodpecker on the side of a tree;

the warp beam was turning around quickly   like a squirrel in the branches of
   a tree."

Then the mistress of North Farm   uttered a word, spoke thus:
"There, there, my girl!   Have I not always said:
'Do not cuckoo out among the firs,   do not sing in the valleys,
do not display the arch of your neck,   the whiteness of your arm,
the fullness of your young breast,   the loveliness of your other features.'
All autumn I kept saying,   sang on during this summer,
even during the swift-passing spring,   even during the next sowing season:
'Let us build a secret cabin   with little secret windows
for a maiden to weave cloth in,   to make a fretting sound with the four
   heddles
so that Finnish suitors may not hear,   Finnish suitors, the suitors of the
   countryside.' "

The baby on the floor sang,   the two-week-old child cried out:
"It is easy to hide a horse,   to conceal a shaggy coat;
it is hard to hide a maiden,   to conceal long tresses.
Even if you built a stone fort   in the middle of the sea
to keep maidens there,   to rear your chicks in,
the maidens will not be hidden there,   the virgins indeed not grow up
without important suitors getting in,   suitors of the countryside,
men with high-peaked hats,   horses with shod hoofs."

Old Väinämöinen, downcast, low in mind,
as he proceeded home,   uttered a word, spoke thus:
"Woe is me, decrepit man,   that I did not know enough
to marry at a youthful age,   to go a-wooing at an age of youthful vigor.
'A man regrets everything he has done,   everybody regrets his youthful
   marriage,
his begetting a child when a mere child,   becoming a family man when
   young.' "
Then Väinämöinen forbade,   the man of Slack Water Farm banned
an old man's going to get a young girl,   planning to woo a beautiful girl.
He forbade swimming in competition,   rowing on the water on a bet,
wooing a maiden in rivalry   with another, younger man.

POEM 20

At North Farm a terribly big steer is slaughtered for the wedding (1–118).
Beer is brewed and food prepared (119–516).
Messengers are dispatched to invite people to the wedding;
Lemminkäinen alone is left uninvited (517–614).

What sort of thing shall we sing about now?   What kind of a song shall we
    rattle off?
We will sing that kind,   will rattle off that song:
that feast at North Farm,   the drinking bout of the Devout Ones.

The wedding was long arranging,   supplies being got ready
in those dwellings at North Farm,   in those log cabins at Sedgy Farm.
What was brought there   and what was fetched
for the big feast at North Farm,   for the drinking bout of the big crowd,
for catering to the country people,   for feeding the big crowd?

A steer grew up in Karelia,   a bullock grew fat in Finland.
It was neither big nor small;   it was a really proper calf!
Its tail swung to and fro in Häme,   its head swayed to and fro on the Kemi
    river,
its long horns were a hundred fathoms long,   its fat muzzle a hundred and
    fifty.
A weasel took a week to round   the site of one stanchion,
a swallow a day to fly   between the steer's horns,
to reach its destination in all haste   without resting in between.
A summer-born squirrel ran for a month   from its neck to its tail
and did not get there,   not reach its goal in the first month.
That prodigious calf,   huge Finnish bullock,
was led from Karelia   to the edge of a field at North Farm.
A hundred men were holding it by the horns,   a thousand by the muzzle
as they escorted the steer,   brought it to North Farm.
The steer went swaying along   at the mouth of the bay of Sedgy Farm,
it eats grass by a spring;   its back grazes the clouds.

There was no knocker,   no feller in the dreadful country
among the lads of North Farm,   in the whole big clan,
among the rising generation   nor indeed among the old people.
An old foreigner came,   Virokannas a Karelian;

he uttered these words: "Easy, easy, poor steer,
until I come with a club, until I bang you on the skull
with my stick, you wretched creature. Then another summer you will not
turn your snout much, sway your muzzle around clumsily
on the edge of this field, at the mouth of the bay of Sedgy Farm."
The old man began to knock it, Virokannas to strike it,
the Worshipful One to deal with it. The steer swung its head to and fro,
its black eyes glared; the old man suddenly jumped up into a fir,
Virokannas into a grove, the Worshipful One into a willow.

They looked for a knocker, a feller of the big steer
from lovely Karelia, from the biggest farms of Finland,
from the quiet land of Russia, from the brave land of Sweden,
from the spacious back parts of Lapland, from the mighty region of Finnmark.
They searched in Death's Domain, in the Abode of the Dead, under the
earth, too.
They searched but did not find one; they sent to get one, none was
discovered.
They searched for a knocker, looked for a feller
on the broad expanse of the sea, on the boundless billows.

A black man rose from the sea, someone from the gentle swell,
right out of the clear water, from the extensive open sea.
The latter was not among the biggest nor among the smallest;
he could lie down under a wooden bowl, stand up under a flour sieve.
He was an iron-fisted old man with iron-grey hair to judge from his looks;
on his head was a high-peaked hat of rock, on his feet shoes of stone,
a gold knife in his hand, the handle ornamented with copper.
Then it got its knocker, met indeed its slayer,
the Finnish bullock its tamer, the dreadful creature of the land its feller.
As soon as he saw his quarry, he all at once struck its neck,
brought the bullock to its knees, flattened its flank to the ground.
Did they get much in the way of spoils? They didn't get much in the way
of spoils!
A hundred tubs of meat, a hundred fathoms of sausage,
seven boatloads of blood, six kegs of suet
for that feast at North Farm, for that banquet at Sedgy Farm.

A house was built at North Farm, a large house, a big one-room cabin;
it was nine fathoms across, seven from end to end.
When a cock crowed in the ceiling, its voice was not heard on the ground;
a dog's bark at the back of the room is not heard as far as the door.
The mistress of North Farm moved quickly to where the floorboards meet,

moved briskly along down the middle of the floor.   She ponders, she reflects:
"Where indeed will we get beer,   skillfully brew table beers
for the wedding which is being arranged for,   for the splendid banquet
    which is to be given?
I do not know about the preparation of table beer   nor the origin of beer."

A BEER LAY, LINES 137–414

There was an old man on the stove;   the old man spoke from the top of the
    stove:
"The origin of beer is barley,   of the superior drink the hop plant,
though that is not produced without water   or a good hot fire.
The hop, son of Remunen,   was stuck into the ground when little,
was plowed into the ground like a serpent,   was thrown away like a stinging
    nettle
to the side of a Kaleva spring,   to the edge of an Osmo field.
Then the young seedling came up,   a slender green shoot rose up;
it went up into a little tree,   climbed to the crown.
The father of good fortune sowed barley   at the end of the newly cultivated
    Osmo field;
the barley grew beautifully,   rose up finely
at the end of the newly cultivated Osmo field,   on the clearing of a Kaleva
    descendant.
A little time passed.   Now the hop vine cried out from the tree,
the barley spoke from the end of the field,   the water from the Kaleva spring:
'When will we be joined together,   when to one another?
Life alone is dreary;   it is nicer with two or three.'

"An Osmo descendant, a brewer of beer,   a maiden, maker of table beers,
took some grains of barley,   six grains of barley,
seven hop pods,   eight dippers of water;
then she put a pot on the fire,   brought the liquor to a boil.
She boiled barley beer   in a swift-passing summer's day
on the tip of a misty headland,   at the end of a foggy island,
put it in a new wooden tub,   inside a birchwood keg.
She got the beer boiled,   she could not get it fermented.
She ponders, reflects,   uttered a word, spoke thus:
'What may one put into that   and what should one look for
as a barm for the beer,   as a leaven for the table beer?'

"The Kaleva descendant, fair maiden,   one graceful with her fingers,
nimble of movement,   always light in her shoes,
moved quickly to where the floorboards meet,   moved briskly along down
    the middle of the floor
arranging one thing and another   between two kettles.

She saw a splinter on the floor,   picked the splinter up off the floor.
She looks about, she turns about: 'What would come of this
in the hands of a fair young girl,   in the fingertips of a good virgin,
if I put it in a young girl's hand,   in the fingertips of a good virgin?'
The young girl rubbed it   with her two palms, with both hands,
with both her thighs: a white squirrel was produced.

"In this way she counseled her son,   instructed her squirrel:
'Squirrel, lovely gold,   lovely cuckoo, delight of the earth!
Run where I order,   where I order and exhort,
to pleasant Woodland,   to the keen-eyed people of Tapio's Domain.
Go up a little tree,   cleverly into a broad-crowned tree
so that no eagle may seize you   nor bird of the air strike you.
Bring some cones from a fir,   some scales from a pine cone;
put them into the young girl's hand,   into the beer of the Osmo descendant.'
The squirrel knew how to run.   bushy-tail to circle about,
to run a long way quickly,   to rove quickly over the distance in between,
across one wilderness, along another,   a little aslant a third
to pleasant Woodland,   to the keen-eyed people of Tapio's Domain.
It saw three tall firs,   four small pines;
it went up a fir in a swale,   up a pine on a heath.
No eagle seized it,   no bird of the air struck it.
It looked for cones in the fir,   tips of a leafy twig in the pine;
it hid the cones in its claws,   wrapped them in its paws;
it carried them to the young girl's hand,   to the good fingertips.
The young girl stuck them in her table beer,   the Osmo descendant into her beer;
the beer does not get to fermenting,   the young drink to bubbling.

"The Osmo descendant, brewer of beer,   the young girl, maker of table beers,
to say the least reflects: 'What may one perhaps put into this
as a barm for the beer,   as a leaven for the table beer?'
The Kaleva descendant, fair maiden,   graceful with her fingers,
always nimble of movement,   always light in her shoes,
moved quickly to where the floorboards meet,   moved briskly along down the middle of the floor
arranging one thing and another   between two kettles.
She saw a chip on the floor,   picked the chip up off the floor.
She looks about, she turns about: 'What would perhaps come of this
in the hands of a fair young girl,   in the fingertips of a good virgin
if I put it in a maiden's hand,   in the fingertips of a good virgin?'
She did put it in a maiden's hand,   in the fingertips of a good virgin.
The young girl rubbed it   with her two palms, with both hands,
with both her thighs: a golden-breasted marten was produced.

"In this way she counseled her marten,   instructed her orphan child:
'My marten, my bird,   my beauty with a valuable pelt!
Go where I order,   where I order and exhort,
to bruin's lair in a rock,   to the forest bear's homestead
where bears fight,   brown bears lead a hard life.
With your fist collect some leaven,   with your hands make some frothy spittle flow;
put it in the maiden's hand,   bring it to the shoulder of the Osmo descendant.'
Now indeed the marten knew how to run,   golden-breast how to go whisking
along.
It soon ran a long way,   quickly roved over the intervening distance,
across one river, along another,   a little aslant a third
to bruin's lair in a rock,   to the bear's cave in a pile of rocks.
There bears were fighting,   brown bears leading a hard life
in an iron crag,   in a steel mountain.
The frothy spittle was flowing from a bear's mouth,   some dreadful leaven
from its jaws;
with its hands it made some frothy spittle flow,   with its fist collected some
leaven.
It put it in the young girl's hand,   on the fingertips of the good virgin.
The Osmo descendant poured it into her beer,   the young girl into her table
beer.
The beer did not get to fermenting,   the elixir of men to humming.

"The Osmo descendant, brewer of beer,   young girl, maker of table beer,
to say the least reflects: 'What may one perhaps put into this
as a barm for the beer,   as a leaven for the table beer?'
The Kaleva descendant, fair maiden,   graceful with her fingers
always nimble of movement,   always light in her shoes,
moved quickly to where the floorboards meet,   moved briskly along down the
middle of the floor
arranging one thing and another   between two kettles.
She saw a yellow mustard plant on the ground,   she picked it up off the
ground.
She looks about, turns about: 'What would come of this, too,
in the hands of a beautiful young girl,   on the fingertips of a good virgin
if I put it in a young girl's hand,   in the fingertips of a good virgin?'
She put it in a young girl's hand,   in the fingertips of a good virgin.
The young girl rubbed it   with her two palms, with both hands,
with both her thighs: a bee was produced from it.

"In this way she counseled her bird,   instructed her bee:

135

A BEE CHARM, LINES 345–380

'Bee, smooth-flying bird,   king of the blossoms of the meadow!
Fly to where I order you,   where I order and exhort,
to an island in the open sea,   to a little island in the ocean.
There a maiden has gone to sleep,   her copper belt has dropped down,
at her side is honeyed hay,   honeyed grass on the hem of her skirt.
Bring some honey on your wing,   carry some honey in your mantle
from the bright-colored tip of a grass-stalk,   from the cup of a lovely bloom.
Carry that to the young girl's hand,   bring it to the shoulder of the Osmo
   descendant.'
The bee, smooth-flying bird   flew until it got there.
It soon flew a long distance,   quickly it shortened the distance in between,
across one sea, along another,   a little aslant a third
to an island in the open sea,   to a little island in the ocean.
It saw the maiden asleep,   her with a tin ornament lying exhausted
on an uninhabited meadow,   on the edge of a honeyed field
with a golden grass-stalk by her loins,   a silver grass-stalk on her belt.
It wet its wing in the honey,   its plumage in the liquid honey
on the bright-colored tip of a grass-stalk,   at the top of a lovely bloom.
It carried it to the young girl's hand,   to the lovely virgin's fingertips.
The Osmo descendant stuck it into her beer,   the young girl into her table
   beer.
Then the young beer began to ferment,   then the young drink rose up
in the new wooden cask,   in the birchwood keg.
It foamed up to the top of the kegs,   it bubbled up to the brims,
it sought to run to the ground,   to go down to the floor.

"It was only a little while,   a short time passed quickly.
Men came to drink,   especially Lemminkäinen.
Ahti got drunk, the man with a far-roving mind got drunk, the ruddy-cheeked
   rascal got drunk
on the beer of the Osmo descendant,   on the table beer of the Kaleva descendant.
The Osmo descendant, brewer of beer,   the maiden, maker of table beers,
uttered these words: 'Woe my day, poor wretch,
when I brewed a bad beer,   made a peculiar table beer;
it rose up out of the keg,   billowed out onto the floor.'
A bullfinch sang in a tree,   a thrush on the edge of the eaves:
'It is not a bad sort of beer,   the drink is a good sort of beer,
to be emptied into barrels,   kept available in cellars
in oak barrels,   inside copper hoops.' "

That was the origin of beer,   the beginning of the table beer of the people
   of the Kaleva District;

thus it got its good name,   thus its high repute
since it was a good sort of beer,   a drink good for the righteous.
It set women to laughing,   put men in a good humor,
the righteous to making merry,   fools to joking.

Then the mistress of North Farm,   when she heard about the origin of beer,
got a big tub of water,   a new wooden tub half full,
with barley enough in it   and a lot of hop pods.
She began to boil the beer,   to prepare the strong liquor
in the new wooden cask,   in the birchwood keg.
For months rocks were heated,   for summers water was boiled,
wildernesses of trees were burned,   wells of water were carried.
Now the wildernesses were thinned of trees,   the water of the springs grew less
as she brewed batches of beer,   as she made batches of table beer
for the big feast at North Farm,   for the drinking party of the fine crowd.
Smoke is billowing up on the island,   fire at the tip of the headland.
Dense smoke was indeed rising up,   a haze going up in the air
from the fiercely burning hearths,   from the many fires;
it filled half the North Farm area,   it darkened all Karelia.
All the people take a look,   take a look, ask suddenly:
"Where indeed is the smoke coming from,   the haze rising into the sky?
Isn't it small for the smoke of war,   big for a herdsman's fire?"
Lemminkäinen's mother   very early in the morning
went to get water from a spring,   sees the dense smoke
in the north.   She uttered a word, spoke thus:
"That is surely smoke signals of war,   indeed war fires."
Island-Ahti,   that handsome man with a far-roving mind,
looks about, turns about,   ponders, reflects:
"Suppose I trudge off to look,   to investigate from nearby
where that smoke is coming from,   whence the haze is filling the air,
whether it is smoke signals of war   or war fires."

The man with a far-roving mind trudged off to look   at where the smoke
    was coming from.
They were not signal fires of war   nor war fires;
they were beer fires,   fires where table beer was boiling
at the entrance to the bay of Sedgy Farm,   in a bend in the narrow headland.
Then the man with a far-roving mind keeps looking;   one eye in the head
    of the man with a far-roving mind is squinting,
one eye squinting, the other with a cast,   his mouth slightly askew.
At last while he is looking he speaks,   says from across the sound:
"O my dear mother-in-law-to-be,   sweet mistress of North Farm!
Make first-rate batches of beer,   boil good batches of table beer
for the big crowd to drink,   especially for Lemminkäinen
at that very wedding of his   with your young daughter."

The beer was got ready,   the elixir of man ready to drink.
The red beer was brewed,   the fine table beer made ready
to lay away underground   in a stone cellar,
in oak barrels   behind a copper bung.
Then the mistress of North Farm   had stews cooked,
made kettles bubble,   skillets sizzle.
Then she baked big loaves,   shaped big barley loaves
for the good country people,   to feed the big crowd
at the big feast at North Farm,   at the drinking party at Sedgy Farm.
The bread was baked,   the barley loaves shaped.
A short time passed,   a little while passed quickly.
The beer worked in the barrels,   the table beer made a noise in the cellar.

"If now my drinkers would come,   my guzzlers get ready,
my competent warbler,   my skilled singer!"
They sought a singer,   a skilled singer,
a capable warbler,   a splendid magician in a trance.
A salmon was brought as a singer,   a pike as a warbler of competence;
the salmon was no singer,   the pike no magician in a trance;
the salmon's jaws were crooked,   the pike's teeth sparse.
They sought a singer,   a skilled singer,
a competent warbler,   a splendid magician in a trance.
A baby was brought as a singer,   a boy as a singer of competence;
the child was no singer,   the slobbering child no warbler;
the baby's tongue got stiff,   the root of its tongue rigid.
The red beer grew threatening,   the young drink began practicing magic
in an oak keg   behind a copper bung:
"If you do not produce a singer,   a skilled singer,
a competent warbler,   a splendid magician in a trance,
I will kick off my hoops,   force out the bottom of my barrel."

Then the mistress of North Farm   got the invitations going,
messengers going about.   She utters these words:
"O little maid,   my perpetual slave,
call the country people together,   a crowd of men to the drinking party.
Invite the miserable, invite the poor,   the blind, too, the wretched, too,
also cripples, also the lame who must go by sleigh.   Row the blind in boats,
drive the cripples on horseback,   bring the lame on sleds.
Invite all the people of North Farm   and all the Kaleva people;
invite old Väinämöinen   to be the official singer.
Do not invite the man with a far-roving mind,   that Island-Ahti!"
The little maid   uttered a word, spoke thus:
"Why do I not invite the man with a far-roving mind,   only not Island-
   Ahti?"

That mistress of North Farm   says a word in reply:
"You are not inviting the man with a far-roving mind,   that reckless Lemminkäinen,
because he is always quarrelsome,   a very skillful fighter;
he has done shameful things at weddings,   wrought great havoc at feasts,
violated pure maidens   in their festival clothes!"
The little maid   uttered a word, spoke thus:
"How will I recognize the man with a far-roving mind   so as to leave him
   uninvited?
I do not know Ahti's home,   the farmstead of the man with a far-roving
   mind."
The mistress of North Farm spoke,   uttered a word and said:
"You will easily recognize the man with a far-roving mind,   that Island-
   Ahti.
Ahti lives on an island,   the rascal lives by the water,
by a very extensive bay,   in a cove on Faraway Headland."

The little maid,   the paid drudge,
carried the invitations in six directions,   the bids in eight.
She invited all the people of North Farm   and all the Kaleva people,
also those skinny dependent landless people,   hired hands in close-fitting
   kaftans.
Only and solely the lad Ahti,   him she left uninvited.

POEM 21

The bridegroom and his retinue are received at North Farm (1–226).
The guests are fed and given drink in profusion (227–252).
Väinämöinen sings and praises the people of the farm (253–438).

That mistress of North Farm,   the old woman of Sedgy Farm,
was outdoors,   was about her household duties.
From the fen she heard the crack of a whip,   from the shore the rattling of
   a sled.
She cast her eyes to the northwest,   she turned her head south,
she ponders, reflects:

THE LAY OF THE COMING OF A BRIDEGROOM, LINES 10–252
               "Why are these people spying
on the shores of wretched me?   Is it a big armed force?"
She trudged off to look at that,   to examine it from near at hand.
It was not an armed force,   it was the big bridegroom's retinue,
the son-in-law in the midst of his train,   amid good country people.

The mistress of North Farm,   the old woman of Sedgy Farm,
when she recognized that the bridegroom was coming,   uttered a word, spoke
   thus:
"I thought the wind was blowing,   a pile of stacked wood toppling over,
the shore of the sea resounding,   gravel rippling down.
I trudged off to look at that,   to examine it from near at hand;
the wind was not blowing,   no pile of stacked wood toppling over,
the shore of the sea not resounding,   gravel not rippling down.
My son-in-law's people are coming,   winding along with two hundred men.
How will I recognize my son-in-law,   my son-in-law among the people?
My son-in-law will be recognized among the people   as a chokecherry is
   recognized among other trees,
an oak among slender shoots,   the moon among the stars of heaven.
The son-in-law is on a black stallion   as if on a ravenous wolf,
a powerful raven,   a flying griffin;
six golden oriole bells   singing on his shaft-bow,
seven bluish cuckoo bells   calling on the traces."

A rumbling is heard in the lane,   a clatter of shafts on the path to the well;
now the son-in-law reaches the farmyard,   the son-in-law's people the farmstead.
The son-in-law is among the people,   amid good country people;

he was not indeed the foremost   or quite the hindmost.

"Off and away, lads! Outdoors, men!   To the farmyard, you tallest people,
to unbuckle the breast straps,   to pull away the traces,
to let down the shafts,   to bring the son-in-law into the house!"

The son-in-law's stallion is racing along,   the decorated basket sleigh is speed-
    ing on
over the mother-in-law's farmyard.   The mistress of North Farm said:
"O you slave working for hire,   handsome neighborhood laborer,
take the son-in-law's stallion,   take the horse with a blaze
out of the copper-adorned harness,   the tin-adorned breast straps,
the leather traces,   the shaft-bow made of a sapling.
Lead the son-in-law's stallion,   take it properly out of the silken bits,
out of the silver-tipped bridle   to soft places to roll on, to a level field,
to some soft new-fallen snow,   to milk-white ground.
Water my son-in-law's colt   at the nearby spring
which stands unfrozen,   which still open is bubbling
at the foot of the lovely fir,   under the flourishing evergreen.
Feed my son-in-law's colt   from a golden splint basket,
from a copper bushel   with clean barley, with loaves of bolted meal,
boiled summer wheat,   ground summer rye.
Then lead the son-in-law's stallion   to the most suitable manger,
the most superior place,   to the part of the farmyard farthest back.
Tie up the son-in-law's stallion   to a golden hoop
in an iron ring,   to a post of curly-grained wood.
Put in front of the son-in-law's stallion   half a peck of oats,
a second of hay chaff,   a third of fine chaff.
Groom the son-in-law's stallion   with a walrus-bone brush
so that the hair is not broken,   no long hair comes out.
Cover the son-in-law's stallion   with a silver blanket,
with gold material,   with copper cloth.

"Neighborhood boys, dear fellows,   escort the son-in-law into the house
without a hat on his hair,   without mittens on his hands.
Wait till I look at the son-in-law   to see whether the son-in-law fits into the
    house
without taking away the door,   pulling down the doorjamb,
without raising the lintel,   lowering the threshold,
tearing down the wall where the door is,   without changing the beams
    supporting the wall.
The son-in-law will not fit into the house,   the fine gift under the ceiling
without taking away the door,   pulling down the doorjamb,
without raising the lintel,   lowering the threshold,

without tearing down the wall where the door is,   without changing the
     beams supporting the wall.
The son-in-law is a head taller,   an ear higher.
Let the lintels be raised   so as not to knock his cap off;
let the thresholds be lowered   so as not to touch the heel of his shoe;
let the doorjambs be moved out of the way;   let the doors open of them-
     selves
when the son-in-law comes into the house,   when the splendid man steps
     along.

"Gracious God be praised!   The son-in-law is already coming inside.
Wait till I look at the house,   inside the house with my eyes
to see whether the tables here are washed,   the wall benches flushed down
     with water,
the smooth planking cleaned,   the floorboards swept.
I look at this house   —I do not recognize it at all,
not recognize of what kind of wood the cabin is made,   whence the room
     was got here,
with what the walls are built up,   and the floors laid.
The side wall is of hedgehog bones,   the back wall of reindeer bones,
the wall on the side of the door of wolverine bones,   the doorjamb of lamb's
     bones.
The beams are of apple wood,   the post of curly birch,
the food shelf over the stove of water lilies,   the ceilings of bream scales.
The long bench is made of iron,   the wall benches of German split logs,
the table decorated with gold,   the floor covered with silk.
The stove is cast of copper,   the hearth bench of lovely rocks,
the firestones of stones of the sea,   the inglenook of Kaleva trees."

The bridegroom makes his way into the house,   comes in under the roof.
He uttered a word, spoke thus: "Hail, God, to this place,
under the splendid rooftree,   under the lovely roof!"
The mistress of North Farm said: "Hail, hail your arrival
here in the little house,   the humble cottage,
in the evergreen room,   piny nest!
O my slavey,   neighborhood hired girl,
light the tip of a birchbark roll,   strike a light to the tip of a resinous splint
so that I may look at the son-in-law,   see the bridegroom's eyes,
see whether they are blue or red   or white as linen."
The little slavey,   the neighborhood hired girl,
lit the tip of a birchbark roll,   struck a light to the tip of a resinous splint.
"The crackling fire is birchbark,   the black smoke resinous fir;
it would dirty up the son-in-law's eyes,   blacken his fine figure.
Light up with a candle,   with a wax taper."

The little slavey,   the neighborhood hired girl,
lit up with a candle,   with a wax taper.
The bright wax smoke,   the clear taper flame
lighted the son-in-law's eyes,   the son-in-law's face clearly.
"Now I see my son-in-law's eyes;   they are neither blue nor red
nor linen white,   they are white as sea foam,
brown as seaweed,   beautiful as sedge in the water.
Neighborhood boys, dear fellows,   escort this son-in-law
to the biggest seats,   to the highest places
with his back to the blue wall,   facing the red table,
facing the invited guests,   the clamor of the country people."

Then the mistress of North Farm   provided the guests with food, with drink,
fed their mouths with soft butter,   filled their hands with cream cakes,
those invited guests,   above all her son-in-law.
There was indeed salmon on a plate,   pork besides,
bowls brimful,   dishes spilling over
for the invited guests to eat   and above all for the son-in-law.
The mistress of North Farm said: "O you little maid,
bring beer in stoups,   carry it in a two-eared mug
to those invited guests,   above all to my son-in-law."
The little maid,   the hired drudge,
gave satisfaction with the stoups,   let the five-banded mug pass around
     swiftly,
to rinse beards with beer,   to whiten with froth the beards
of those invited guests   and above all the son-in-law's.

What could the beer do now,   what did the five-banded mug say
when its singer was there,   its competent warbler?
It was indeed old Väinämöinen,   eternal prop of song,
able singer,   the best expert.
First he takes some beer,   then he utters these words:
"Beer, fine drink!   Do not give a drink to an idling man.
Make the men sing,   the golden voices ring out.
Masters of households are wondering,   mistresses reflecting
whether the songs have faded away,   the musical tongues dropped off,
or 'did I brew poor beer,   make a bad drink flow'
since our singers are not singing,   our good bards not intoning,
our cherished guests not singing out,   our joyous cuckoos not making joyous
     music.
Who then here will perhaps sing out,   who sing with their tongues
at this feast at North Farm,   at this drinking party at Sedgy Farm?
Here the benches will indeed not sing   if the bench-sitters will not,
the floors not burst into song   if the walkers on the floor will not;

the windows will not utter joyful music   if the window's masters will not
nor will the edges of a table peal out   if those at the table will not
nor will these flues resound   if those under the flue will not."

There was a child on the floor,   a milk-beard on the fire bench.
The child spoke from the floor,   the boy spoke from the stove bench:
"I am not old in years,   sturdy of frame,
but be that as it may,   if other brawny people will not sing,
sturdier men not break into song,   the fuller-blooded not sing songs,
then I, scrawny lad, will sing,   I, lean boy, will pipe away.
I will sing from out of my scrawny body,   out of my lean loins
to make joyous music for this evening of ours,   to honor the great day."

There was an old man up on the stove.   The latter uttered these words:
"There is nothing in children's songs,   in the cooings of the wretches;
children's songs are deceptions,   girls' songs are empty.
Turn the lay over to a sage,   the song to him sitting on the bench."
Then old Väinämöinen   uttered these words:
"Is there among the young people,   in the whole great clan,
anyone who would clasp hands,   one clenched hand in another,
and who might sing along,   give himself up to song
to make the joyous music of the closing day,   as an honor for the great
    evening?"

From on the stove the old man said: "There has not been heard here before,
neither seen nor heard   ever, ever at all
a better singer,   a more accomplished expert
than I when I used to coo,   sing along as a mere child,
sing along by the waters of the bay,   sing resoundingly on heaths,
sing loudly in fir groves,   sing magic in the forest wilds.
My voice was big and graceful,   my melody exceedingly beautiful.
At that time it flowed like a river,   glittered like a stream of water,
ran on like a left ski on the snow,   like a sailboat on the billows.
Now, however, I cannot sing;   I just do not understand at all
what suppressed the great voice,   cut down the precious tone.
Now it does not flow like a river,   ripple along like billows;
it is like a harrow in stubble,   a pine branch grating on crusted snow,
a sled on the sands of the shore,   a boat on dry rocks."
Then old Väinämöinen   utters these words:
"If no one else may be coming   to sing along with me,
I may well start out alone on the poems,   burst into song.
Since I was created a singer,   became a singer of magic songs,
I do not ask the way from a neighbor   or conclude a song with the help of an
    outsider."

Then old Väinämöinen, eternal prop of song,
seated himself for the joyous task threw himself into the task of singing
as he gave voice to joyful lays, the magic charms at his disposal.
Old Väinämöinen sang, both did and could sing.
Words were not lacking to his songs, no lays were shortened while he was
chanting;
rather do crags lack rocks, landlocked ponds pond lilies.
Then Väinämöinen sang, delighted them long through the evening.
The women all wreathed in smiles, the men in good spirits
listened, kept marveling at Väinämöinen's flow of song which was a miracle
to the listener,
a marvel to those present, and no wonder.

Old Väinämöinen spoke, said at the end of his song:
"What indeed am I in the way of a singer, in the way of an expert?
I can do nothing, am capable of nothing at all.
Were the Creator singing, reciting songs with his sweet mouth,
the Creator would be singing a magic song, singing, be practicing his art.
He would sing the seas to honey, the sands of the sea to peas,
the ooze of the sea to malt, the gravel of the sea to salt,
vast groves to grainfields, sides of clearings to wheatfields,
hills to sweet cakes, rocks to hens' eggs.
He would sing, would practice his art, sing magically, sing competently,
would sing into this farm cattlesheds full of heifers,
sheds full of horned cattle, clearings full of givers of milk,
a hundred bearers of horns, a thousand carriers of udders.
He would sing, would practice his art, sing magically, sing competently,
sing up lynx pelts for the masters, long broadcloth coats for the mistresses,
low-heeled slippers for the daughters, red shirts for the sons.

"Grant indeed, God, always, another time, true Creator,
that one may live here thus, another time act the same way
at a feast at North Farm, at a drinking party at Sedgy Farm,
that the beer may run like a river, the mead flow like a stream
in this house at North Farm, in the log house of Sedgy Farm,
so that there may be singing by day, joyous music made evenings
during the lifetime of this master, the life of the mistress.
May God recompense, may the Creator repay
the master at the head of the table, the mistress in her storehouse,
the sons at their seining ground, the daughters at their looms,
so that there may never be regrets, never a cause to complain next year
about this big feast, the drinking party of the big crowd."

POEM 22

The bride is got ready to set out and is reminded
of former days as well as of those to come (1–124).
The bride becomes distressed (125–184). The bride is made to weep (185–382).
The bride weeps (383–448). The bride is comforted (449–522).

When the wedding party had drunk plenty,   when the feast was over,
the wedding in the house at North Farm,   the feast at Gloomy Farm,
the mistress of North Farm said   to Ilmarinen, the son-in-law:

THE LAY OF THE HANDING OVER OF A BRIDE, LINES 7–124

"What are you sitting around for, man of a great clan?   What are you waiting
   for, pride of the countryside?
Are you sitting around on account of the father's favor   or the mother's
   tender affection
or is it on account of brilliance of the cabin   or the elegance of the wedding
   party?
You are not sitting around on account of the father's favor   or the mother's
   tender affection
or the tidiness of the cabin   or the elegance of the wedding party.
You are sitting around for your virgin's favor,   the young girl's love,
for the radiance of the one you longed for,   for the beauty of your girl with
   luxuriant hair.
Bridegroom, my very dear friend,   you waited a long time; wait some more.
The one you longed for is not ready,   your eternal comrade not prepared.
Half her hair is braided,   half unbraided.
Bridegroom, my very dear friend,   you waited a long time; wait some more.
The one you longed for is not ready,   your source of eternal harmony not
   prepared.
One sleeve is sewed on,   the other still to be sewed on.
Bridegroom, my very dear friend,   you waited a long time; wait some more.
The one you longed for is not ready,   your source of eternal harmony not
   prepared.
Only one foot is shod,   the other still to be shod.
Bridegroom, my very dear friend,   you waited a long time; wait some more.
The one you longed for is not ready,   your source of eternal harmony not
   prepared.
One hand has been gloved,   the other still to be gloved.
Bridegroom, my very dear friend,   you waited a long time; you are not
   tired.
Now the one you longed for is ready,   your mallard prepared.

"Go along now, bartered maiden,   go along, chick that has been sold.
Now your departure is near at hand,   your time to go very imminent
since your escort is at your side,   your abductor at the door;
his stallion is champing at the bit,   the sled is waiting for the maiden.
After being eager for money,   quick to give your hand,
eager to get the engagement presents,   for the fitting of your ring,
now be desirous of the sled,   eager for the decorated basket sleigh,
quick to go to a neighboring farm   and swift to set out.

"Not much indeed, young maiden,   have you looked at your two courses,
really understood   whether you were making a regrettable bargain,
something forever to bewail,   for years to bemoan
after you set out from your father's home,   moved away from your birthplace
from your dear mother's,   from the farmstead of the one who bore you.
How fine it was for you to live   on your father's farm!
You grew up as a flower in the lanes,   as a strawberry on clearings.
You got up from bed to eat butter,   from lying down to drink milk,
from stretching out to eat wheaten bread,   from your straw litter to eat fresh
    butter.
When you could not eat butter,   you sliced off some pork.
There was nothing to worry about at all,   never anything to ponder over;
you let the tall evergreens worry,   the fences ponder,
the bog-pine grieve in the fen,   the heath birch on the heath.
You fluttered about like a leaf,   went round and round like a butterfly,
like a berry on your mother's lands,   like a raspberry in the fields.

"Now you are setting out from this farm,   going to another farm,
to another mother's region,   to a strange family.
One way there, another way here,   another way at the other farm.
There the herdsmen's horns sound different,   the doors screech differently,
the gates sound different,   the hinges speak differently.
You cannot go in the door,   enter the gate
like a daughter of the farm;   you do not know how to blow up the fire
nor warm the hearth   according to the ideas of the master of the farm.
Did you really think, young maiden,   really know or think,
did you think that you were setting out for the night,   coming back the next
    day?
You have not set out for the night,   not for one night, not for two;
you have gone for a longer time,   have disappeared for ever and ever,
forever from your father's cottage,   forever from your mother's.
The farmyard will be a step longer,   the threshold a log higher
when next you come,   when you do it again."

The poor girl sighed,   sighed, gasped;
grief bore down on her heart,   tears came to her eyes.

She put that into words: "So indeed I knew, so indeed I thought,
so I always presumed,   said all the time I was growing up:
'You will probably not, maiden, be a maiden   dependent on your own parent,
in the fields of your own father,   in the cottages of your own mother;
you will be a woman   when you are married,
only when one foot is on the threshold,   the other in your bridegroom's sleigh.
You will be a head taller,   more than an ear higher.'
I hoped for that all my life,   looked forward to that all the time I was growing up,
waited for that as for a good crop year,   looked forward to it like the coming
   of summer.
Now my hope has come true,   my departure has got nearer;
one foot is already on the threshold,   the other in the bridegroom's sleigh.
I do not understand   what has changed my state of mind;
I am not setting out with a joyous heart   nor joyfully parting
from this lovely home,   from the dwelling of my youthful years,
from this farmstead where I grew up,   from the dwelling place got by my
   father.
I am setting out, little one, anxiously,   am parting in sorrow
as if into the embrace of an autumn night,   to the glare ice of spring,
without recognizing my track on the ice,   my footprint on the slippery ice.

"What then may be the state of mind of others,   the state of mind of other
   brides?
Others probably do not feel sorrow   do not carry a heavy heart
as I, poor wretch, carry,   carry dark sorrow,
a heart looking like charcoal,   charcoal-black anxiety.
Such is the state of mind of the lucky,   the thought of the fortunate—
like a spring sunrise,   the sun on a spring morning.
What of my state of mind then,   my gloomy disposition?
It is like the flat shore of a pond,   like the dark edge of a cloud,
like a gloomy autumn night,   a dark winter's day;
it is even blacker still,   gloomier than an autumn night."

There was indeed a woman, a housekeeper   always living on the farm;
she uttered these words: "There, there, young girl!
Do you not remember how I used to keep saying,   saying even hundreds of
   times:
'Do not get infatuated with a suitor,   not by the suitor's mouth;
do not trust the expression,   do not look at his fine legs.
He will hold his mouth charmingly,   fix his eyes on you sweetly
though the devil were in his jaw,   death be living in his mouth.'
Thus indeed I always advised the girl,   instructed my young girl:
'When serious suitors come,   serious suitors, wooers from the countryside,

always say in reply   and say for your part,
always say these words,   make this remark:
"It will not be at all right for me,   not right for me, probably not at all fitting
    for me
to be taken away to be a daughter-in-law,   taken to be a slave.
A girl like me   cannot live as a slave,
cannot remember to give way,   not be always under somebody's thumb.
If another person should say one word,   I would answer with two;
if anybody should go for my hair,   make the mistake of grabbing my locks,
I would wrench him from my hair,   snatch him away from my locks." '

"You did not obey that,   did not listen to my words.
You walked defiantly into the fire,   knowingly into a batch of tar;
you hurried into the fox's sled,   set out on the bear's sled runners,
for the fox to pull its sled,   for the bear to take far away
as the master's eternal slave,   as the mother-in-law's lifelong slave.
You set out from home to school,   from your father's farmyard to a torment.
The school will be hard for you to go to,   be a long torment for you to be
    there;
there slaves are bought,   prisoners' irons provided,
not for anyone else,   just for wretched you.
Soon you will get to experience, unhappy girl,   to experience, you of hard lot,
the father-in-law's bony jaw,   the mother-in-law's stony tongue,
the brother-in-law's cold words,   the tosses of the sister-in-law's head.

"Listen, girl, to what I am saying,   what I am saying, what I am speaking.
At home you were like a flower,   a delight in your father's farmyard;
your father called you 'Moonlight,'   your mother 'Sunbeam,'
your brother 'Gleam of Water,'   your sister 'Blue Broadcloth.'
You are going to another farm,   to be under a strange mother,
the strange mother unlike your mother,   the other woman unlike the one
    who bore you.
Seldom did the strange one reprimand nicely,   seldom give instruction prop-
    erly;
the father-in-law will call you 'Fir-sprig Doormat,'   the mother-in-law call you
    'Clumsy Lappish Reindeer Sled,'
the brother-in-law 'Threshold of the Outer Stairs,'   the sister-in-law will call
    you 'Worst of Women.'

"You would only be good,   only be effective,
should you go out of doors like a mist,   get to the farmyard like smoke,
flutter around like a leaf,   speed off like a spark.
You are not a bird to fly,   not a leaf to flutter
or a spark to speed off,   smoke to get out to the farmyard.

"Woe is you, maiden, my sister!   Now you have made an exchange; what an exchange!
You have exchanged your loving father   for a very bad father-in-law;
you have exchanged your sweet mother   for a really strict mother-in-law;
you have exchanged your dear brother   for a wry-necked brother-in-law;
you have exchanged your patient sister   for a popeyed sister-in-law.
You have exchanged your bed with linen sheets   for sooty log fires,
you have exchanged your bright waters   for dirty mud,
you have exchanged your sandy beach   for black oozy bottoms,
you have exchanged your beloved clearings   for heather-grown heaths,
you have exchanged your berry-grown hills   for the hard stumps of burned-over land.

"Did you think this way, young girl,   this way, chick, while growing up?
Did you think that cares were over, work easing up   by this evening's sitting around,
that you would be led there to lie down,   be taken to sleep?
You will by no means be led to lie down,   be taken to sleep.
Then one must stay awake,   then they will cause you trouble,
give you cause for thought,   produce an unhappy state of mind.
As long as you flitted about unkerchiefed,   just that long you went about free from care;
as long as you went about without a linen coif,   you went about without excessive sorrow.
Now your kerchief will bring trouble,   your linen coif an unhappy state of mind,
your linen coif excessive sorrows,   your flaxen one endless ones.

"How is it in a girl's home?   'A girl in her father's home
is like a king in his castle,   lacking only a sword.'
Differently a poor wretch of a daughter-in-law!   'A daughter-in-law in her husband's home
is like a prisoner in Russia,   lacking only a guard.'
She worked in working hours,   she toiled with might and main,
her body sweating,   forehead glistening with foamy sweat.
When another time comes,   then she will be committed to fiery toil,
toil as hot as a forge,   be delivered into the hands of the Evil One.
She should have,   have, poor girl,
the mind of a salmon, the tongue of a ruffed grouse,   the understanding of a perch in a pond,
the mouth of a dace, the belly of a bleak,   have the knowledge of a scoter duck.
Not one person knows,   not even nine
daughters born of a mother,   cherished by their parent, understand

where a devourer may be born,   a gnawer grow up,
an eater of flesh, a biter of bone,   a scatterer of hair to the winds,
a disperser of locks,   one to abandon her to the cold spring wind.

"Weep, weep, young girl!   When you weep, weep hard indeed;
weep your tears by the handful,   your bitter water by the double handful,
teardrops on your father's farmyard,   ponds on your father's floor.
Weep a flood in the house,   billows on the floorboards.
If you do not weep when weeping is in order,   you will weep when next you
    come,
when you come to your father's home,   when you find your old father
in a smoked-up sauna   with a dry bath whisk under his arm.

"Weep, weep, young girl!   When you weep, weep hard.
If you do not weep when weeping is in order,   you will weep when next you
    come,
when you come to your mother's home,   when you find your old mother
in the cattle barn suffocated [by the smudge],   dead with a big bundle of
    straw in her arms.

"Weep, weep, young girl!   When you weep, weep hard.
If you do not weep when weeping is in order,   you will weep when next you
    come,
when you come into this home,   when you find your ruddy-cheeked brother
collapsed in the cattle shed,   fallen down in the farmstead.

"Weep, weep, young girl!   When you weep, weep hard.
If you do not weep when weeping is in order,   you will weep when next you
    come,
when you come to this farm,   when you find your lovely sister
sunk down on the path to the laundry   with an old battling paddle under her
    arm."

The poor girl sighed,   sighed, gasped;
she began to weep,   began to shed tears.
She wept tears by the handful,   bitter water by the double handful,
teardrops on her father's clean yard,   ponds on her father's floor.
Then she uttered these words,   remarked and said:
"O sisters, my finches,   former lifelong companions,
all the comrades I grew up with!   Listen to what I am saying.
I do not understand   what may have caused me
this dreariness,   occasioned this anxiety,
what may have brought this distress,   have brought along grief.
I knew otherwise, I thought otherwise,   always promised otherwise.

I vowed to go about like a cuckoo,   to call out on knolls
once I reached this day,   once arrived at this goal.
Now I will probably not go about like a cuckoo,   not call out on knolls;
I am like an old squaw on the surge of the sea,   a teal on a broad bay
swimming in chill water,   moving about on the icy water.

"Woe is my father, woe my mother,   woe my esteemed parents!
Where indeed did you cast me?   Where indeed did you take the wretched
  one
to weep these tears,   to sustain these griefs,
to bemoan these anxieties   and to lament sorrows?
You might rather, poor mother,   might rather, fair one who bore me,
my beloved giver of milk,   my lovely wet nurse,
have swaddled tree stumps,   washed little pebbles
than to have washed this daughter,   swaddled your beauty
to end up in these great sorrows,   grievous states of mind.
Many say otherwise,   many reflect:
'The silly fool has no anxiety,   never a worrisome thought.'
Do not, good people,   do not say that!
I have more anxiety   than there are stones in a rapid,
willows on bad ground,   heather on a heath.
A horse would not go on pulling,   an iron-shod one not haul
these anxieties of mine, of slight me,   my dark griefs
without the shaft-bow quivering,   the shaft-bow shivering."

A CHEERING-UP LAY, LINES 451-522

A child was singing on the floor,   a growing child near the inglenook:
"What a weeping of girls,   what a great grieving!
Let a horse worry,   a black gelding grieve;
let a horse with a bit have sorrows,   a horse with a big head lament!
A horse has a better head,   a better head, a sturdier frame,
a better arch to its neck,   the whole body ampler.
There is nothing to weep about,   greatly to grieve about.
You are not being led to a fen,   taken to the edge of a ditch.
They are leading you from a tussock of grain,   leading you to a place with
  even more grain;
they are taking you from a house where beer is drunk,   taking you to a house
  where more beer is drunk.
If you look to your flank,   to your right side,
there is the bridegroom in your house,   the ruddy-cheeked man at your side.
Good the husband, good the horse,   good the whole character of his farm;
the ruffed grouse are preening their feathers,   singing on the shaft-bow;
the thrushes rejoicing,   giving voice on the traces,
six golden cuckoo bells   are hopping about on the hames,

seven bluish bird bells   are calling at the front of the sled.
Do not be upset at that,   child born of your mother, at that at all.
You will not be put in a worsening situation,   you will be put in a situation
    that is getting better
at the side of your plowman husband,   under the guardian's mantle,
by the breadwinner's jaw,   in the crook of the fisherman's arm,
in the sweat of a man who has been skiing after elk,   in the bear-catcher's
    sauna.

"You got the finest husband,   the most daring of men;
his bows will probably not be idle,   the quivers probably not lie unused on
    the pegs,
the dogs not lie stretched out at home,   the puppies not lie resting on their
    litter.
Three times this spring   very early in the morning
he got up from his campfire,   awakened from a bed of pine needles;
three times this spring   dew has dropped on his eyes,
pine needles brushed his head,   saplings stroked his body.

"The husband is the breeder of a herd,   the man a cattle raiser.
This bridegroom of ours indeed   has creatures roving the backwoods on foot,
running over the ridges on their legs,   seeking out swales.
There are a hundred horned cattle,   a thousand with udders.
There are windrows on every clearing,   grain sheds by every brook,
grain fields instead of alder groves,   barley fields instead of ditch sides,
oat fields instead of riverbanks,   wheat fields beside watered lands,
coins instead of stone piles,   silver coins instead of little stones."

POEM 23

A bride is instructed and counseled
as to how she will live in her husband's home (1–478).
An old gossip tells of the events of her life as a girl
in a husband's home and of her parting from the husband's home (479–850).

Now a girl must be counseled,   a bride instructed.
Who indeed is there to counsel the girl,   to instruct the virgin?
Why, an Osmo descendant, flourishing woman,   a Kaleva descendant,
beautiful virgin,   she is the one to counsel the girl, to instruct the young
  woman
how to be sensible,   how to live above reproach,
sensible in her husband's home,   above reproach in her mother-in-law's home.

INSTRUCTION LAY [HOUSEHOLD DUTIES], LINES 15–478

She spoke these words,   made these remarks:
"Bride, my sister,   dear heart, my loved one!
Listen to what I am saying,   what I am stating in varied form.
You are setting out now, flower, to go away,   strawberry, to creep along,
nap of broadcloth, to proceed forward,   piece of velvet, to wander away
from this fine home,   from the beautiful farmstead.
You are coming to a different farm,   to a strange family.
It will be different at the other farm,   otherwise among other strangers.
One must step thoughtfully,   act with reflection;
it is not as in your father's meadow,   not as on your mother's land
with singing in the valleys,   cuckooing in the lanes.
When you set out from this farm,   remember to take all of your other goods,
these three things leave at home: sleeping late in the morning,
a mother's loving words,   butter fresh from the churn.
Remember all your movables;   forget your store of sleep,
left to the daughters of the house,   by the side of the family stove.
Throw the songs on top of the bench,   joyful lays to the windows,
girlish ways to the grip of the bath whisk,   youthful spirits to burlap selvage,
your bad habits to the hearth,   your lazy ways to the floor.
Or else hand them to the maid of honor,   thrust them under the maid of
  honor's arm,
for the maid of honor to convey to a grove,   to carry to a heath.

"A new course must be adopted,   the former forgotten.
A father's love must be left behind,   a father-in-law's accepted;
one must bow lower,   vouchsafe pleasant speech.

A new course must be adopted,   the former forgotten.
A mother's love must be left behind,   a mother-in-law's accepted;
one must bow lower,   vouchsafe pleasant speech.
A new course must be adopted,   the former forgotten.
A brother's love must be left behind,   a brother-in-law's accepted;
one must bow lower,   vouchsafe pleasant speech.
A new course must be adopted,   the former forgotten.
A sister's love must be left behind,   a sister-in-law's accepted;
one must bow lower,   vouchsafe pleasant speech.

"Do not ever at all,   not while the moon shines gold-bright,
enter a household with bad manners,   a husband's house if you are
    incompetent.
A house calls for manners,   even a good house, for manners;
a husband will test your intelligence,   even the very best husband your in-
    telligence.
Straight off one needs to be heedful   if a household is unstable
and one must be steadygoing   if the husband is incompetent.

"If the old father-in-law is a wolf in the corner,   the old mother-in-law a
    bear by the hearth,
the brother-in-law like snakes on the threshold,   the sister-in-law like nails in
    the farmyard,
the same respect must be paid,   the bowing lower
than formerly at your mother's,   than in your father's house,
than the bowing to your father,   the respect paid your mother.

"You must keep   your head clear, your temper even,
your thinking always vigorous,   understanding consistent,
in the evening your eyes alert   to tend the torch,
in the morning your ears sharp   to hear the cock's crow.
When the cock has crowed once,   yet not called twice,
then it is time for the young to get up,   for the old to rest.
If the cock does not crow,   the master's bird not give voice,
keep the moon as your cock,   the Great Bear as your guide.
Go outdoors often,   go looking at the moon,
learning from the Great Bear,   scanning the stars.
When the Great Bear is in the right position   with horns toward the south,
tail toward the north,   then is the time for you
to rise from beside the young bridegroom,   to leave the side of the ruddy-
    cheeked man,
to get a light from the ashes,   flame from a tinder box,
to blow fire into the kindling,   not scatter the embers carelessly.
If there is no fire in the ashes,   flame in the tinder box,
caress your dear one,   pet your handsome man:

'Give us a light, my dear,   a flame, my berry.'
You will get a small flint,   a very little piece of tinder;
hurry and strike fire,   light a splint of wood in a holder.

"Set out to clean the cattle shed,   to feed the cattle.
Your mother-in-law's cow is lowing,   your father-in-law's horse is neighing,
your brother-in-law's cow is shaking its chain,   your sister-in-law's calf is
    wailing
for someone to throw it soft hay,   to hand it clover.
Go to the cattle shed with your body bent,   to the cattle shed with your back
    stooped;
feed the cows gently,   the sheep quietly.
Hand straw to the cows,   water to the wretched people's calves,
choice straw to the colts,   soft hay to the lambs.
Do not speak harshly to the pigs,   do not kick the young pigs;
bring a trough to the pigs,   their troughs to the young pigs.

"Do not linger in the cattle shed,   lounge in the sheepfold.
When you have cleaned the cattle shed,   looked to all the cattle,
then go back from there,   come into the house like a whirlwind.
A baby will be crying there,   a little one under the covers.
The poor child cannot talk,   being speechless cannot say
whether it is cold or hungry   or whether something else has happened
until a familiar person comes,   until it hears its mother's voice.

"But as you come into the house,   come into the house as one of four things:
a water scoop in the hand   a birch twig broom under the arm,
a burning splint between the teeth;   your yourself will be the fourth thing.
Begin to clean the floors,   sweep the floor boards;
throw water on the floor,   do not throw it on the baby!
You may see a baby on the floor,   even your sister-in-law's baby;
lift the baby onto a wall bench,   wash its face, smooth its head,
give it a piece of bread in its hand,   spread butter on the bread.
If there is no bread in the house,   put a chip of wood in its hand.
When you get to washing the tables   at the end of the week at the latest,
wash the tables, remember the edges,   do not forget the legs.
Wash the wall benches with water,   clean the walls with birds' wings,
all the wall benches and their sides,   the walls and their chinks.
Where dust is on the table,   dust on the window hatches,
brush them, too, with a wing,   pass a wet rag over them
so that dust will not fly about at all,   dust not swirl up to the ceiling.
Scrape the bits of caked soot from the ceiling,   wipe the soot off the stove
    stones,
keep in mind the stove post,   do not forget the lintels
so that it should seem like a house,   be reckoned as a dwelling place.

"Listen, girl, to what I am saying,   to what I am saying, how I am talking.
Do not flutter about without a dress   or lounge about without a smock,
do not move about without a kerchief   or saunter about without shoes.
The bridegroom might get angry at that,   the young man be displeased.

"Be very careful about   those rowans in the yard.
The rowans in the yard are sacred,   sacred the branches on the rowans,
sacred the leaves on the branches,   more sacred still their berries
by which a girl is counseled,   a young woman taught
the way to a young man's preferences,   to a bridegroom's heart.

"Have the sharp ears of a mouse,   the swift legs of a hare.
Bow your young nape,   bend your beautiful neck
like a growing juniper   or the fresh crown of a chokecherry.
You must be wide-awake,   always wide-awake, on the lookout
not to sit on your seat,   nor lie stretched out on the stove bench
nor sink down on your bedding,   drag yourself off to bed.
Your brother-in-law will be coming in from plowing,   your father-in-law from
    setting fence posts,
your man from outdoor work,   your handsome fellow from cutting down a
    clearing.
A birchbark water measure must be brought,   a hand towel fetched;
there must be low bowing,   friendly words spoken.
The mother-in-law will be coming from the storehouse   with a grain basket
    under her arm;
run to the yard to meet her,   bow low,
ask to take the basket from her arm   to bring it into the house.

"If you cannot determine,   yourself not understand
what task must be pressed forward,   what must be begun,
then find out from the mistress: 'O my dear mother-in-law,
how are the tasks done here,   the household duties determined?'
The woman will indeed answer,   the mother-in-law say:
'This is how the tasks are done here,   the household duties determined:
grain is pounded up, ground;   one rocks to and fro on the quern staff;
further, water is carried,   dough kneaded,
sticks of firewood brought into the house   for heating the stove.
Then one bakes the loaves,   bakes thick loaves;
the dishes are washed,   the firkins rinsed out.'

"When you have heard about your work from the mistress,   the household
    duties from the mother-in-law,
take grain being dried on the hearthstone,   hurry to the quern shed.
Then after you have got there,   reached the quern shed,
do not sing as you go,   not shout with your throat.

Sing out by the noise of the quern stone,   by the singing of the quern staff.
Do not puff loudly,   do not pant on the quern staff
lest your mother-in-law think,   your father-in-law suppose
you were puffing in anger,   pushing in rage.
Sift the flour briskly,   bring it into the house in a birchbark measure.
Knead the loaves thoroughly,   blend the dough very skillfully
so that no flour is left here and there,   but even mixtures, on the contrary.

"You see a bucket tilted over;   take the bucket on your shoulder,
the water cowl under your arm;   start to go for the water,
carry the cowl nicely,   carry it on the end of a cowl staff.
Come back like the wind,   walk on the crest of the cold spring wind
without delaying long by the water,   without lingering by the well
lest your father-in-law think,   your mother-in-law suppose
you are looking at your image,   admiring yourself,
your rosy complexion in the water,   your beauty in the well.

"You go to the big woodpile   to fetch firewood:
do not scorn any wood;   even take poplar for firewood.
Toss the wood quietly   without banging it hard
or your father-in-law will think,   your mother-in-law suppose
you are throwing it in anger,   making a noise in rage.

"When you step out to the storehouse,   set out to fetch meal,
do not settle down in the storehouse   or delay long on the way to the
    storehouse
or your father-in-law will think,   your mother-in-law suppose
you are handing out meal,   giving it to neighborhood women.

"You set out to wash a receptacle,   to rinse out firkins:
wash the pots and their handles,   the stoups and their grooves;
rinse out the bowls,   remember their lips,
the spoons, remember the handles.   Keep count of the spoons, keep track
    of your receptacles
so that the dogs do not trot off with them,   the cats not keep them,
the birds not move them either,   children not leave them scattered about.
There are plenty of children in the community,   lots of little heads
who would carry off the pots,   scatter the spoons about.

"When preparing the evening sauna,   fetch the water, bring the whisks,
have the whisks warm and ready   in a smoke-free sauna
without delaying long,   without lingering in the sauna
or your father-in-law will think,   your mother-in-law suppose
that you are lounging on the sauna platforms,   lolling about on a bench.
When you come back into the house,   invite your father-in-law to bathe:

'O my dear father-in-law,   the sauna is now ready,
the water fetched, the whisks got,   all the platforms swept;
go bathe to your heart's content,   douse the water as you please.
I will be the one to produce dry steam,   will take my place under the
   platforms.'

"When the time comes to spin,   the time to weave cloth,
do not go to get the art from neighbors   or information from beyond your
   own ditch,
skill from another house,   a weaver's reed from an outsider.
You yourself spin the woolen warp thread,   the weft threads with your own
   fingers;
make the weft threads rather loose,   the warp threads always rather tight.
Wind the ball of yarn firm,   reel it up on the mill,
arrange it for the warp beam,   dress it then for the loom.
Strike the batten firmly,   raise the heddles briskly,
weave homespun jackets,   get woolen skirts
out of one unbroken fleece,   from the shaggy coats of winter sheep,
from the fleeces of a spring lamb,   from the down of a summer ewe.

"Listen now to what I am saying,   once more to what I am reporting.
Brew batches of barley beer,   delicious malt drinks
from one barleycorn,   by burning half a tree.
When you make barleycorn sprout,   flavor up the malted grains,
do not lift them with a hook   or turn them with a forked stick;
always arrange them with your hands,   turn them with your palms.
Go into the sauna often,   do not let a sprout get damaged,
do not let the cat sit on the sprouts,   kitty lie on the malted grains.
Do not worry about wolves,   be afraid of forest animals
when strolling to the sauna,   when going there in the middle of the night.

"If ever a stranger comes,   do not be cross at the stranger.
A good house always   keeps reserves for a stranger,
lots of broken meats,   nice buns.
Bid the stranger sit down,   speak politely,
feed the stranger with words   until the stew is done.
Again when he sets out from the house,   makes his farewells,
do not escort your guest   outside the door;
the bridegroom would get angry at that,   your handsome man frown on it.

"If sometime the desire comes to you   to visit a neighboring farm,
visit the neighboring farm after asking leave,   after requesting to visit the
   neighbors.
Then while you are there,   carry on sensible talk;
do not disparage your home,   run down your mother-in-law.

The neighborhood brides will ask   or the other neighborhood women:
'Did your mother-in-law give you butter   as your mother formerly did at home?'
Do not ever say: 'Mother-in-law does not give me butter';
always say that she does give it,   serves it with a ladle,
even though you happen to get it once a summer,   that, too, winter-before-last's!

"Listen further to what I am saying,   a second time to what I am reporting.
When you go out of this house away from here,   come into the other house,
do no forget your mother,   do not disparage your mother.
Your mother indeed brought you up,   her lovely breasts nursed you
from her own lovely self,   from her white body.
Many nights she spent without sleep,   many meals she forgot
while rocking you,   looking after her little one.
Whoever forgets her mother,   disparages her mother,
may she not go to the Abode of the Dead,   to Death's Domain with a good conscience.
In the Abode of the Dead the fine is heavy,   in Death's Domain the penalty severe
for one who forgets her mother,   who disparages her mother.
Death's daughters will scold,   the maidens of the Abode of the Dead will shrill:
'How did you forget your mother,   disparage your own mother?
Your mother experienced great pain,   she who bore you suffered, suffered severely
while lying on the sauna floor,   while on the straw,
while giving birth to you,   bearing the wretched one.' "

A woman was on the floor,   an old woman with a cloak on,
a haunter of neighborhood thresholds,   a reconnoiterer of the roads of the district.
She uttered these words,   remarked and said:

A DAUGHTER-IN-LAW'S LAY, LINES 485-850

"A cock crowed to his dear one,   a chicken to his beauty;
a crow cawed in the late winter,   sang rocking to and fro in the early spring.
I ought to sing,   they ought not to sing;
they have their loved ones at home,   their dear ones always there;
I have no dear one, no home,   I am ever without loving tenderness.

"Listen, sister, to what I am saying.   When you go to a husband's home,
do not heed the husband's whim,   as I, poor wretch, heeded
the man's desire, obeyed the lark's gabble,   the heart's desire of my great bridegroom!

In my time I was a flower,   a sprig of heather when growing up,
a sapling when shooting up,   a little bud when getting taller,
when I was called 'Arctic Bramble,'   called in a whisper 'Precious Thing,'
in my father's farmyard 'Teal,'   on my mother's floor 'Wild Goose,'
'Waterfowl' at my brother's,   'Bunting' at my sister's.
I walked like a flower in the lanes,   like a raspberry on the meadow;
I used to flutter along the sandy beaches,   swing along on the flowery knolls;
I sang in every valley,   caroled on every rise,
sported in copses,   ever rejoiced in clearings.

" 'A fox's appetite lures it into a snare,   a weasel's tongue into a trap,
a girl's inclination to a husband's home,   her disposition to another house.'
Indeed a girl is really created,   a daughter really rocked
to be a daughter-in-law in a husband's home,   a slave in her mother-in-law's.
I, berry, got to other lands,   I, chokecherry, to other waters;
I, whortleberry, got to be snapped at,   I, strawberry, to be execrated.
Every tree bit me,   every alder kept cutting me,
every birch scolding me,   every aspen barking at me.
I was married off to a husband's home,   was escorted to a mother-in-law's.
They said, when marrying the girl off,   that there were there
six fir-log houses,   twice as many rooms,
that the sides of the clearings were the sites of storehouses,   the sides of the
    lanes the sites of flower beds,
the sides of the ditches barley fields,   the sides of the heaths oat fields,
bins of threshed grain,   other bins of grain to be threshed,
a hundred coins acquired,   another hundred to be acquired.
I, fool, managed to get there,   I, foolish creature, managed to shake hands.
The house was on six studs,   seven posts,
the clearings were full of mercilessness,   the copses full of lack of affection,
the lanes of poor me's cares,   the woods of evil thoughts,
bins of threshed hostility,   other bins of unthreshed hostility,
a hundred reproaches acquired,   another hundred to be acquired.

"I paid no attention at all to that,   I tried to live above reproach.
There I hoped for respect,   hoped for affection there
by bringing fire into the house,   by snuffing the charred end of the torch
    splints.
I bumped my forehead on the door,   my head on the doorjamb.
In the doorway are strange eyes,   grim-looking eyes in the inglenook,
squinting eyes in the middle of the floor,   at the back very hostile ones.
Fire sparkles from the mouth,   firebrands from under the tongue,
from the mouth of the disagreeable master,   from under an unloving tongue.

"I paid no attention at all to that,   I tried to live on somehow,
always to be in favor   and be meek under instruction.

I skipped about with the legs of a hare, went about with the paws of a
  weasel,
went to lie down terribly late, got up extremely early.
I did not, poor wretch, gain respect, did not, sorry me, encounter love
though I might move mountains, split crags in two.
In vain I pounded coarse meal, to no purpose sifted out the grits
for my strict mother-in-law to eat, for the old witch to guzzle
from golden bowls at the long deal table.
As for myself I, wretched daughter-in-law, ate, greedily devoured meal from
  the quern stone,
the stove bench my table, a wooden ladle my spoon.
Often I, sad of heart, as a daughter-in-law in my husband's home,
brought mosses from the fen; those I baked as my bread;
I brought water from the well with a stoup, that I sipped as my drink.
I, a girl of hard lot, ate fish, I, wretched one, ate smelts,
as long as I rocked on the seine-poles, swung in the middle of the boat.
I never got such a fish as a gift from my mother-in-law,
as would suffice for a day, do for a moment.

"Summers I gathered cattle fodder, winters I plied the handle of a dung fork
like a hired hand of yore or a slave, a paid laborer.
At my mother-in-law's the biggest flail in the threshing barn
was always thrust upon me, the heaviest flax brake in the sauna,
the heaviest battling paddle on the shore, the biggest dung fork in the
  barnyard.
No one believed I got tired nor worried about my collapsing
even though the men grew tired, the horses collapsed.

"Thus I, wretched maiden, worked in working hours,
toiled with might and main. Let another time come.
Now I was committed to fiery toil, delivered into the hands of the Evil One.
Without cause disparaging talk was raised, without reason tongues gossiped
about my good habits, my well-known honor;
words rained down upon me, words kept dropping
like fiery sparks or iron hailstones.

"I did not doubt but that I would have lived on
as a help to the strict mistress, as a companion to the firebrand,
but that evil came, that grief of mine increased
when my bridegroom turned into a wolf, when the handsome fellow became
  a bear,
ate sideways to me, slept back to me, did his work back to me.
I wept over this to myself, thought about it in my storehouse.
I remembered my other days, my former way of life
in my father's big farmyard, in my lovely mother's homestead.

I began to speak of that, spoke, talked away to myself:
'My mother knew how, knew how to get her apple,
knew how to grow the young plant; she did not know how to set it out.
She set the lovely plant in a bad spot,
put it in bad places, in the hard roots of a birch
to weep all its life, to lament its life long.

" 'I had it in me for better places,
bigger farmyards, more spacious floors,
for something like a better body, something like a ruddier-cheeked husband.
I was saddled with that lout, stuck with that hulking fellow;
he got his trunk from a crow, grabbed his nose from a raven,
his mouth from a ravening wolf, his total form from a bear.
I would indeed have got such a one if I had just gone outdoors,
got a resinous pine stump by the wayside, a rotten alder log from a copse,
had made his snout from a piece of turf, his beard from bad lichens,
his mouth from a stone, his head from clay, his eyes from hot coals,
gnarls of birch as his ears, the fork of a willow as legs.'

"I was singing this in my grief, sighing over it in my anxiety.
The oh so handsome fellow happened to hear it, happened to be standing by
   the wall.
So when that fellow comes from there, stepped on the storehouse stairs,
I was already aware of his coming, guessed from his step.
His hair was flying though there was no wind at all, his locks were tossing
   about though there was not even a draught.
His gums were bared, his eyes popping out,
with a gnarled piece of rowan in his grip, a gnarled billet under his arm
with which he comes forward to strike, clubs me on the head.
Then let evening come! When he went to go to bed
he put a whip by his side, took a leather whip from its peg,
not for anyone else, just for anguished me.
I myself went to go to bed in the evening,
stretched out quickly beside my bridegroom. The bridegroom lay on his
   side;
he struck plenty with his elbow, with his angry hand,
with a lot of thick willow branches, a walrus-bone whipstock.
I got up from the cold flank, from the chill bed.
The bridegroom set out after me, drove me out the door with threats.
His hand goes into my hair, fumbles around in my hair,
scatters my hair to the winds, gives it to the cold spring wind.

"What was there for me to do, what counsel to adopt?
I had shoes made of steel, had copper laces put in them
in which I stood outside the wall, listened at the end of the lane

until the enemy might quiet down, the violent man settle down.
He does not finally quiet down, never settles down.
At last it gets cold as I, hated one, was going away,
was standing by the wall, was behind the door.
I pondered, I reflected: 'I cannot stand the long-lasting hatred,
the aloof disdain in this hellish crew, in these devils' nest.'
I left the charming house, my lovely dwelling place.
I, gentle girl, set out to wander; I walked the fens, walked the countryside,
I journeyed over deep waters, walked to the head of my brother's field.
Then the dry firs shouted, the bushy-crowned pines sang out,
all the crows cawed, the magpies chattered:
'Your home is not here nor the place of your birth!'
I paid no attention at all to that, I walked into my brother's farmyard.
Now the gates spoke to me, all the fields complained:
'Why are you coming home, what are you coming home, poor wretch, to
   hear?
Your father died long since, the fair one who bore you departed,
your brother is a total stranger to you, your brother's wife is like a Russian
   woman.'

"I paid no attention at all to that. I went into the house just the same.
I put my hand on the door handle, the handle was cold to my hand.
When I came into the house from outside, I stood in the doorway.
The lady of the house is haughty, does not come to embrace me,
does not give her hand. I am haughty myself;
I do not embrace her, do not give her my hand.
I pressed my hand on the stone stove, the stones of the stove were cold;
I moved my hands to the ashes, the coals in the ashes were cold.
My brother is lounging on the bench, sitting gaping on the wall bench
with a fathom of soot on his shoulders, a foot on the rest of his body,
an ell of fluffy ash on his head, half a foot of caked soot.
The brother questioned the stranger, inquired of the newcomer:
'Whence comes the stranger from beyond the water?' I just answered:
'Do you not recognize your sister, child of your late mother?
We are the children of one mother, were rocked by one bird,
warmed by one goose, got from the nest of one ruffed grouse.'
At that my brother began to weep, his eyes began to shed tears.

"My brother said to his wife, whispered to his dear one:
'Fetch something to eat for my sister.' My brother's popeyed wife
brought from the cookhouse cabbage stew from which the cur had eaten the
   fat,
the dog tasted the salt, from which Blackie had had his midmorning meal.
My brother said to his wife, whispered to his dear one:

'Bring the guest some beer.'   My brother's popeyed wife
brought the guest water,   it was not decent water,
it was water her sisters had washed their faces in,   my sisters-in-law their
   hands in.

"I wandered again from my brother's house,   went away from the place of
   my birth;
I, poor wretch, began to walk,   I, poor wretch, got wandering on,
I, miserable one, to rove the shores,   I, anguished one, to wander
ever to strange doors,   to strangers' gates,
'as a poor wretch's children to desolate shores,   miserable people to be community charges.'

"There is now many a one,   is many a one
who utters hostile words to me,   many a speaker with a harsh voice;
there are not many   who bestow a word of affection on me,
who speak in kindly fashion,   invite me to the stove
when I have come in out of the rain,   when with difficulty I get in out of
   the cold
with the hem of my dress covered with rime,   the hem of my fur coat covered
   with swirling snow.
Not indeed when younger   would I have believed,
had a hundred tongues said,   a thousand repeated,
that I would get into these difficulties,   fall upon such days
as the days that have befallen me,   the difficulties that have come to hand."

POEM 24

A bridegroom is counseled how he must treat a bride,
and is enjoined not to treat her badly (1–264). An old man of the neighborhood
tells how in days gone by he was able to make his wife like him (265–296).
With tears in her eyes the bride remembers that she must now leave forever
the beloved home of her birth and takes leave of all (297–462).
Ilmarinen snatches the bride into his sled, sets out on the journey,
and gets to his home on the evening of the third day (463–528).

Now the maiden has been counseled,   the bride instructed.
I will speak further to my dear friend,   speak to the bridegroom with my mouth:
"Bridegroom, my boon companion,   even better than a brother,
more affectionate than a mother's child,   gentler than a father's child!
Listen to what I am saying,   to what I am saying, to what I shall utter
about this linnet of yours,   the chick which you have acquired.
Bridegroom, thank your good luck   for having made a good acquisition!
When you express your thanks, express it well indeed.   You got a good
    thing, came upon a good thing,
your Creator granted you a good thing,   the Gracious One gave you a good
    thing.
Express your thanks to the father,   still more to the mother
who rocked such a child,   just such a bride.
Pure is the maid at your side,   the girl resplendent in your betrothal gifts,
radiant under your sovereignty,   graceful in your keeping,
sprightly daughter, thresher of grain,   fair pitcher of hay,
fine-looking washer of laundry,   sturdy bleacher of linen,
strong spinner of thread,   quick weaver of cloth.

"The sound of her batten creaked   like a cuckoo calling on the hill,
her shuttle rustled   like a weasel in a woodpile,
her bobbin turned   like a pine cone in a squirrel's mouth.
The community has not slept soundly,   the people of the great house not
    slumbered
because of the creaking of the maiden's batten,   the rustle of the shuttle.

"Bridegroom, young man,   fine figure of a man,
forge a steel scythe,   make a good handle, too
whittle it by the gateway,   shape it sitting on a stump.
When sunshine comes,   take the girl to a meadow:
you will see how the hay crackles,   the coarse hay rattles,

the sedge whistles, the sorrel swishes,
tussocks are leveled off, suckers snapped off.

"When another day comes, get her a proper shuttle,
a sturdy batten, a proper warp beam;
carve nice treadles, equip a complete loom.
Establish the girl at the loom with batten in hand;
then and there the batten will creak, the loom groan;
it will be heard to the next farm, the rustling of the batten farther still.
The women will wonder at that, the neighborhood women will ask:
'Who is weaving cloth?' It will befit you to answer:
'My own darling is weaving, my sweetheart is clattering along.'
'Did the cloth show any flaws, the reed break any warp threads?'
'The cloth did not show any flaws, the reed not break any warp threads;
it is like the weaving of Moon Spirit, the spinning of Sun Spirit,
the skill of the Spirit of the Great Bear, the finished work of Star Spirit.'

"Bridegroom, young man, fine figure of a man,
when now you start to go, get driving from here
with your young maiden, with your beautiful chick,
just do not drive your sparrow, this little linnet of yours,
up on embankments, not drive into wattled fence corners,
not throw her out on a stump, not stretch out in the stones.
Not previously in her father's home, in her lovely mother's homestead,
was the girl driven up on embankments, driven into wattled fence corners,
thrown out on a stump, stretched out on stones.

"Bridegroom, young man, fine figure of a man,
do not transport your maiden, drag your dear one
to slink off into nooks, to be idle in corners.
In her father's home, in the house of her mother of yore,
the girl did not slink off into nooks, not be idle in corners;
she used always to sit by the windows, to rock in the middle of the floor,
evenings as her father's joy, mornings as her mother's darling.

"Just do not, wretched bridegroom, do not take this chick
to an arum mortar, not set her to pounding up bark,
to baking straw bread, to pounding up pine bark.
In her father's home, in her lovely mother's farmstead
the girl was not taken to an arum mortar, not set to pounding up bark,
to baking straw bread, to pounding up pine bark.
Take this chick, take her to a mound of grain,
to empty the rye bin, to take oats from a bin,

to bake a thick loaf,   to brew beer,
to bake wheaten bread,   to knead dough.

"Bridegroom, my boon companion,   do not make this chick,
do not make our gosling   weep from loneliness.
If the oppressive feeling should come,   loneliness seize hold of the girl,
put the dark brown horse in the shafts   or the white horse in the harness;
bring the girl to her father's home,   to her dear mother's house.
Do not treat this chick,   our little linnet,
as your slave,   do not regard her as a hired girl;
do not forbid her the cellar   nor keep her out of the storehouse.
In her father's home,   in her lovely mother's farmstead
she was not treated with the esteem of a slave,   not regarded as a hired girl,
not forbidden the cellar,   not kept out of the storehouse.
She used always to slice wheaten loaves,   to look for hen's eggs
around the milk tubs,   inside beer measures,
mornings opening the storehouse,   evenings shutting up the storehouse lofts.

"Bridegroom, young man,   fine figure of a man,
if you treat the girl well   it will be looked upon favorably;
when you come to your father-in-law's house,   to the home of your dear
    mother-in-law,
you will be fed,   fed, given drink;
your horse will be unharnessed,   led to the stable,
fed, watered,   the oat bushel fetched.

"Just do not say of our girl,   this of our linnet,
that she has no clan,   has no relatives.
This girl of ours has   a big clan, many relatives.
Should one sow a peck of peas,   a pea would get to each person;
should one plant a peck of flaxseed,   a thread would get to each.
Just do not, wretched bridegroom,   treat the girl badly,
instruct her with slave whips,   flog her with whip thongs,
make her whimper with five whips,   make her cry out at the head of the outer
    stairs.
Formerly the girl was not,   formerly in her father's house was by no means
instructed by slave whips,   flogged with whip thongs,
made to whimper with five whips,   made to cry out at the head of the outer
    stairs.
Stand before her like a wall,   stay there like a doorpost.
Do not let the mother-in-law strike   or the father-in-law scold
or an outsider be hateful to her   or another farm slander her.
The family bade you whip her,   other people bade you beat her;
you just do not have the heart to whip your poor girl   nor can you bear to
    beat your darling

after seeking her for three years,   continuously suing for her.

"Bridegroom, counsel your girl,   instruct your apple,
counsel the girl in a bed,   instruct her behind a door,
a year in each place,   one year by word of mouth,
the second by a glance of the eye,   a third year by a stamp of the foot.
If then she does not heed this   nor obeys that at all,
take a reed from a reedbed,   a stalk of horsetail from the heath.
Counsel your girl with that,   counsel the girl during the fourth year,
touch her lightly with the horsetail,   poke her with the side of a piece of
    sedge;
do not yet strike her with a lash,   not hit the girl with a switch.
If, however, she then does not heed this,   still does not obey that at all,
fetch a switch from a thicket,   a birch switch from a backwoods dell—
be sure to carry it under your fur coat   so that no other farm will know.
Show it to your girl,   shake it; do not strike her.
If she still does not heed this,   does not obey that at all,
counsel your girl with a switch,   instruct her with a birch branch.
Counsel her in a four-cornered room,   speak to her in a moss-caulked
    house;
do not strike her on a meadow,   not lash her on the edge of a field:
one would hear the noise at a neighboring farm,   the din at the next farm,
the woman's weeping as far as the neighbors',   the great uproar as far as the
    forest.
Keep warming up her shoulders,   softening up her back muscles;
do not graze her eyes   or touch her ears;
a lump would come on her eyebrow,   a black and blue spot on her eye.
The brother-in-law would indeed ask about that,   the father-in-law would
    ponder it,
the plowmen of the next farm would see,   the neighborhood women would
    laugh:
'Has that woman been to the wars,   gone to battle
or was she scratched by a wolf,   clawed by a forest bear?
Or was a wolf her bridegroom,   a bear her boon companion?' "

There was an old man on the stove,   a beggar by the stove stones.
The old man spoke from the stove,   the beggar from the stones:
"Just do not, unhappy bridegroom,   pay attention to a woman's desire,
to a woman's desire, to a lark's gabble   as I, poor lad.
I bought meat, I bought loaves,   bought butter, bought beer,
bought all kinds of fish,   many kinds of soft delicacies,
domestic beers,   wheat from foreign lands.
By that I got nothing good   nor did I encounter anything decent.
When the woman came into the house,   she came as if to tear my hair,
making faces,   rolling her eyes;

in her bad temper she always spoke angrily,   spoke in a hostile way,
called me a clumsy lout,   barked out I was a blockhead.
Now I remembered a new trick,   now I knew another way:
when I peeled a birch branch,   then she embraced me as her little bird;
when I lopped off the top of a juniper bush,   then she bowed as my darling;
when further I struck her with willow switches,   then she flung herself on my
   neck."

A LAY OF A BRIDE'S GOING AWAY, LINES 297–462

The poor girl sighs deeply,   sighs deeply, gasps;
she burst out crying.   She uttered a word, spoke thus:
"Now the departure of the others is at hand,   the time of departure of the
   others has got near,
my departure nearer,   my time of leaving nearer
though it is hard to set out, too,   difficult the hour of parting
from this splendid community,   from the beautiful farmstead
where I grew up happily,   grew up very finely
during my whole growing-up period,   the time of my childhood.
I never thought so before   nor ever believed it,
I did not think that I would part,   believe I would go away
from the vicinity of this fine house,   from the shoulder of this ridge.
Now I am already thinking that I am departing,   indeed believe it and am
   departing.
The parting stoups have been emptied,   the parting beers drunk;
soon the sleighs will be turned around,   front end outward, rear end toward
   the house,
sideways to my father's barn,   aslant toward the cattle shed.

"With what, now that I am departing,   setting out, poor girl,
with what shall I repay my mother's milk   and my father's kindness,
with what my brother's affection,   my sister's tenderness?
I thank you, father,   for my former way of life,
for the lunches of days gone by,   for the best snacks.
I thank you, mother,   for rocking me when young,
for tending me when tiny,   for feeding me at your breasts.
I further thank my brother,   my brother, my sister,
repay the whole family,   all the companions I grew up with,
in whose company I lived,   grew up with at my growing-up time.
Do not now, my dear father,   do not, my beloved mother
or the rest of my big clan,   my fine kindred,
get distressed at this,   become sorrowful
because I am going to other parts,   taking my way somewhere.
The Creator's sun will probably shine,   the Creator's moon gleam palely,
the stars in heaven twinkle,   the Big and the Little Bear be spread out

in the sky farther away,   elsewhere in the world, too,
not alone in my father's farmyard,   in this farmstead I grew up in.

"Now I am setting out from here, leaving, so to speak,   this lovely home,
from the house acquired by my father,   from my mother's well-stocked cellar.
I am leaving my fen, leaving my farm,   leaving my grass-grown farmyard,
leaving my sparkling waters,   leaving my sandy beach
for the neighborhood women to bathe on,   for herdsmen to splash about on.
I am leaving the fens for people to tramp over,   leaving the fields for people
   to loiter on,
the clumps of alder for people to rest in,   the heaths for people to walk over,
fence sides for people to step along,   the sides of lanes for wanderers,
farmyards for people to run across,   sides of walls for the people who stand
   there,
floorboards for the people who clean them,   floors for the people who sweep
   them.
I am leaving the fields for a wild reindeer to run over,   wildernesses for a lynx
   to roam in,
clearings for wild geese to live on,   groves for birds to rest in.
I am setting out from here, leaving, so to speak,   with another person who is
   setting out
into the embrace of the autumn night,   on the glare ice of spring,
so that my track will not be recognized on the ice   nor my footprint on the
   slippery ice
nor the warp of my skirt on the crusty snow,   the contact of my hem on the
   snow.

"Then the next time I come,   visit my home,
my mother will probably not hear my voice,   my father not be aware of
   weeping
when I sing plaintively on his brow,   sing on the crown of his head.
Young grass will already have come up,   a juniper bush grown
on the skin of the one who nursed me,   on the cheeks of the one who bore
   me.

"The next time I come   to this big farmyard,
the others will probably not recognize me   except those two things:
the lowest withe of the wattled fence,   the post farthest back in the field,
the ones stuck in by me when little,   wattled by me as a girl.
My mother's farrow cow,   watered by me when young,
tended by me when a calf,   will start to bellow
on the rubbish pile in the farmyard,   on the winter feeding grounds;
that one will probably recognize me   as a daughter of the house.
My father's very old stallion,   fed by me when little,

given fodder by me as a girl,   will start to neigh
on the big rubbish pile in the farmyard,   on the winter feeding grounds;
he will recognize me   as a daughter of the house.
My brother's old dog,   fed by me as a child,
trained by me when a girl,   will start to bark
on the big rubbish pile in the farmyard,   on the winter feeding grounds;
he will recognize me   as a daughter of the house.
Other things will not recognize me   when I come home,
not even my old landing sites,   my dwelling places of yore,
the whitefish sounds in their places,   the seining sites where they were.

"Farewell now, cabin,   cabin with your planked roof!
It will be fine for me to come next time,   lovely for me to come tripping
    along.
Farewell now, entryway,   entryway with your planked floor!
It will be fine for me to come next time,   lovely for me to come tripping
    along.
Farewell indeed, farmyard,   farmyard with your rowans!
It will be fine for me to come next time,   lovely for me to come tripping
    along.
I bid farewell to all: the fields and the forests with their berries,
the sides of lanes with their flowers,   the heaths with their heather,
the lakes with their hundred islands,   the deep sounds with their whitefish,
the fair knolls with their firs,   the wilderness swales with their birches."

Then craftsman Ilmarinen   snatched the girl into his sleigh,
struck the spirited steed with the whip,   uttered a word, spoke thus:
"Farewell, lake shores,   lake shores, edges of fields,
all the pines on the hill,   tall trees in the pine groves,
the stand of chokecherries back of the house,   the juniper bushes on the way
    to the well,
all the berrystalks on the ground,   berrystalks, straws of hay,
willow bushes, roots of the fir,   leafy alder twigs, bark of the birch."

Then craftsman Ilmarinen   set out from the yard of North Farm.
The children stayed on to sing,   the children sang and said:
"A blackbird flew here,   winged its way through the backwoods,
enticed the mallard from us,   lured the berry away from us,
it took the apple from us,   took away our little fish of the water,
tricked her away with a little money,   enticed her with silver pieces.
Who will now take us to the water?   Who will lead us to the river?
The cowls will get to standing still,   the cowlstaffs to rattling idly,
the flooring not be cleaned,   the floors not swept,
the sides of the mug will get streaked with dirt,   the stoup handles get dark."

Craftsman Ilmarinen   with his young bride
speeds along   those shores of North Farm,
along the sides of lovely sounds,   along the shoulders of sandy ridges.
The shingle rang out, the sand sang,   the sled went on, the road flashed by,
iron trace hooks creaked,   the birchwood runner clattered,
the curly-grained shackles squeaked,   the chokecherry shaft-bow quivered,
the withe-fastening creaked,   the copper fitting shook
as the good horse raced on,   as the good horse with a blaze galloped.
He drove one day, then a second,   soon drove a third, too,
one hand guiding the stallion,   the other holding the girl in his arm,
one foot on the side of the sled,   the other under the woolen rug.
The spirited steed races, the journey sped on,   the day went forward, the
   distance shortened.
On the third day   as the sun was going down,
the craftsman's home appears,   the dwellings at Ilma Farm loom up.
Soot was going up straight as a string,   dense smoke was escaping,
smoke was belching forth from the house,   rising up to the clouds.

POEM 25

The bridegroom, the bride, and the escorts are received
in Ilmarinen's home (1–382). The crowd is fed and give drink in profusion;
Väinämöinen sings and praises the master, the mistress, the master of ceremonies,
the maid of honor, and the rest of the wedding party (383–672).
On the way home from the wedding Väinämöinen's sled is broken;
he repairs it and drives home (673–728).

Now they had been waiting a long time,   waiting, looking
to see if the girl's retinue was coming   to craftsman Ilmarinen's home.
The old people's eyes are running   as they sit by the windows,
the young people's knees are shaking   as they wait at the gates,
the children's feet were getting cold   as they stood by the walls,
the middle-aged people's shoes were wearing out   as they walked on the pier.
So on a certain morning,   on a certain day
a rumbling is heard in the wilderness,   the clatter of a sled on the heath.

Lokka, gracious mistress,   a Kaleva descendant, beautiful wife,
uttered a word, spoke thus: "That is my boy's sled;
now he is coming from North Farm   with his young maiden!
Now he is near these parts,   near this farmstead,
the house provided by his father,   fixed up by his parent."
Craftsman Ilmarinen   is coming home right now
to the farmyard provided by his father,   fixed up by his parent.
Hazelgrouse bells are whistling   on the sapling shaft-bows,
cuckoo bells are calling   on the prow of the decorated basket sleigh,
carved squirrels lie stretched out   on the maplewood shafts.

LAYS OF THE RECEPTION OF A BRIDE AND THE RETURN
OF A BRIDEGROOM, LINES 37–382

Lokka, gracious mistress,   a Kaleva descendant, beautiful wife,
then uttered these words,   said, spoke thus:
"The community has been waiting for a new moon,   the young people
    waiting for a sunrise,
the children for land grown with berries,   the water waiting for a tarred boat.
I have not been waiting for even half a moon,   for the sun at all;
I have been waiting for my dear son,   my dear son, my daughter-in-law.
I looked mornings, looked evenings,   I did not know where he had vanished
    to,
whether he was letting a little bride grow up   or fattening up a lean one

when he did not come at all   though he had indeed sworn
to come while the trail was recognizable,   come before the trail had got cold.
Mornings I was always looking,   in the daytime I had my mind
on whether my dear son's sleigh would not come,   my dear son's sled not
   rattle along
to this little farmyard,   to the small homestead.
Whether the stallion was of straw   or the sled had only two shackles,
I would call it a sleigh just the same,   would exalt it into being a basket
   sleigh
if only it might transport my dear son,   bring my handsome fellow home.
So indeed I always hoped,   looked for every day;
I have looked with my head bowed,   my rolled up braids askew,
my straight-set eyes squinting.   I hoped my dear son was coming
to this little farmyard,   to the small homestead.
Now he is finally coming,   at long last arriving,
a pink-cheeked form at his side,   a rosy-cheeked girl beside him.

"Bridegroom, my dear boon companion,   unharness the horse with a blaze,
lead the good horse   to the hay it is used to,
to its accustomed oats.   Greet us,
greet us, greet the others,   greet the whole community.
After you have conveyed your greetings,   tell your tales.
Did you journey uneventfully,   make your trip safe and sound
when you set out for your bride's mother-in-law's,   to the home of her dear
   father-in-law?
Did you get the girl, win sovereignty,   overthrow the barricade,
break down the girl's fortress,   demolish the upright wall,
step on your mother-in-law's floor,   sit on the master's wall bench?
I see this already without asking,   understand without inquiring:
he made the journey safe and sound,   the trip comfortably;
he got the gosling, won sovereignty,   overthrew the barricade,
broke down the wooden fortress,   tore down the lindenwood wall
when he visited his mother-in-law,   in the home of his dear father-in-law.
The goldeneye is in his keeping   the chick by his side,
the pure maiden at his side,   the radiant girl in his sovereignty.
Who brought this lie,   who told the bad news
that the bridegroom had come empty-handed,   the stallion run in vain?
The bridegroom has not come empty-handed,   the stallion not run in vain.
There is something for the stallion to pull,   for the flaxen-maned horse to
   move.
The good horse was in a sweat,   the excellent colt in a lather
when it brought the chick here,   conveyed the pink-cheeked girl.
Get up now from the sleigh, lovely one,   fair gift from the long sleigh.
Get up without being lifted,   rise without being raised

even if your young man would lift you,   your proud escort raise you.
After you have got up out of the sleigh,   got from the back of the sled,
step on the brownish path,   on the liver-colored soil
worn smooth by swine,   trampled down by pigs,
trod hard and smooth by a sheep,   brushed by a horse's mane.
Step with the step of a goose,   tap along with the gait of a teal
on this clean farmyard,   on the level ground,
on the farmyard provided by your father-in-law,   established by your mother-in-law,
where the brother whittles,   on the sister's woad-grown meadows.
Press your foot lightly on the outer stair,   go to the floor of the entry,
step into the lovely entryway;   then betake yourself inside,
under the fine ridgepole,   under the lovely roof.

"Already here this winter indeed,   even last summer,
the fishbone floor was singing   waiting for her who was to stand on the floor;
the lovely roof was resounding   waiting for her who was to walk under the roof;
the windows were rejoicing   waiting for her who was to sit by the windows.
Already here this winter indeed,   even last summer,
the door handles were creaking   waiting for her with a ring-adorned hand who was to close them;
the thresholds were making a noise   waiting for the elegant one in a fine kirtle;
the doors kept opening   waiting for her who is to open the doors.
Already here this winter indeed,   even last summer,
the cabin spun right around   waiting for her who was to wipe up the cabin;
the entry took up its position   waiting for her who was to clean the entry;
the sheds were making a noise   waiting for her who was to sweep the sheds.
Already here this winter indeed,   even last summer
the farmyard was turning around furtively   waiting for her who was to trim the burned end of the long torch splint;
the storehouses bowed down   waiting for her who was to step into the storehouses;
the lintels swayed, the rafters bent   waiting for the young wife's clothing.
Already here this winter indeed,   even last summer
the cattle sheds were cooing   waiting for her who is to go about in the cattle sheds;
the cow barns were drawing nearer   waiting for her who is to clean out the cow barns;
the cattle pens moved straight back   waiting for the teal who is to be in charge of the cattle pens.
Already here today indeed,   even yesterday, too,
the full-grown cow lowed early   waiting for her who is to give the morning snack of hay;

the colt whinnied   waiting for her who is to throw it its snack of hay;
the spring lamb bleated   waiting for her who is to prepare its morsel.
Already here today indeed,   even yesterday, too,
the old people were sitting by the windows,   the children were moving about
    on the shores,
the women were standing by the walls,   the boys at the doors of the entry
awaiting the young wife,   waiting for the bride.

"Hail now farmyard with your crowd,   outer yard with your men!
Hail roofed stairs with your crowd,   top landing of the roofed stairs with your
    guests!
Hail entry with your crowd,   birchbark roof with your people!
Hail cabin with your crowd,   hundred-planked cabin with your children!
Hail moon, hail king,   hail their young escorts!
There was not here before,   not before, not yesterday
the splendor of this crowd,   the handsomeness of this company.
Bridegroom, my dear boon companion,   take off her red kerchiefs,
seize hold of her silken veils.   Display that marten of yours
after admiring her for five years,   eyeing her for eight.
Did you really bring the one you tried to?   You were trying to bring a cuckoo,
to choose a white one from the land,   to get a pink-cheeked one from the
    waters.
That I already see without asking,   understand without inquiring.
You brought the cuckoo when you came,   a blue goldeneye in your keeping,
the greenest twig of a treetop   from a green copse,
the leafiest chokecherry twig   from a leafy chokecherry grove."

There was indeed a baby on the floor;   the baby spoke from the floor:
"Alas, brother, what are you fetching?   The beauty of a pitchy pine stump,
the length of a keg of pitch,   the height of a windle reel!
There, there, poor bridegroom!   You ever hoped for that,
said you were getting a maiden   worth hundreds, were bringing one worth
    a thousand.
Now you have got a good one worth hundreds,   that wretched girl worth a
    thousand!
You got a curlew from a fen,   a terror to magpies from a fence,
a scarecrow from a field,   a blackbird from a new-plowed field.
What may she always have been doing,   what last summer,
if she did not weave a mitten,   if not at least start on a sock?
She came empty-handed ino the house,   without a trousseau to her father-in-
    law's;
mice were rustling in the splint basket,   prick-ears in the little box."

Lokka, gracious mistress,   a Kaleva descendant, beautiful wife,
heard the strange tale;   she uttered a word, spoke thus:

"What were you saying, wretched baby?   What did you utter, worthless
  creature?
Let us hear strange things about other people,   let scandalous words hover
  about
but not about this girl,   not about the people of this farm.
Now you said a bad word,   uttered an evil word
from the mouth of a night-old calf,   from head of a day-old puppy.
The bridegroom has got a good girl,   brought the region's best from there;
she is like a half-ripe whortleberry,   like a strawberry on a hill
or a cuckoo on a tree,   a little bird in a rowan,
a fine-feathered bird in a birch,   a light-breasted bird in a maple.
One could not possibly have got from Germany,   not met beyond Estonia
the elegance of this girl,   the loveliness of this old squaw,
the beauty of this plant,   the stateliness of this figure,
the whiteness of arm,   the arch of the slender neck.
The girl did not come empty-handed: furs had to be brought,
capes especially fetched,   fine clothes brought.
This girl has a lot of things,   the product of her own distaff,
spun with her own spindle,   finery prepared by her own hands,
white garments   got ready on the winter washday,
bleached on a spring day,   dried in the summer months:
good fluttering sheets,   soft puffy pillows,
rustling silk kerchiefs,   swishing woolen capes.

"Dear young woman, beautiful young woman,   brilliantly pink-cheeked
  young woman!
You were very illustrious at home   as a daughter in your father's home;
you will be illustrious forever   as a daughter-in-law in your husband's home.
Do not start to worry,   do not concern yourself with anxieties.
You have not been brought to a fen,   not taken to the edge of a ditch;
you were fetched from a heap of grain,   fetched to a place still richer in
  grain,
taken from a house with much beer,   taken to one with more beer.
Dear girl, fair young woman!   That indeed I ask you:
As you were coming here   did you see the rounded ricks of grain,
the high-topped hurdles?   They all belong to this farm,
things plowed by this bridegroom,   things plowed, sown.
Maiden, young woman!   That I now say to you:
Since you knew enough to come to this farm,   then know how to get along
  on this farm.
It is good for a young mistress to be here,   fine for a daughter-in-law to grow
  up here,
with a wooden mug of clotted cream in your hand,   a dish of butter in your
  possession.

It is good for a girl to be here,   fine for a chick to grow up here.
Here the sauna platforms are broad   and the wall benches of the cabin wide;
the masters are like your father,   the mistresses like your mother,
the sons are like a brother,   the daughters like a sister.

"If it is your wish,   if it is your desire to have
the kind of fish your father caught,   the kind of ruffed grouse your brother
    snared,
then do not ask your brother-in-law,   do not request your father-in-law;
ask your bridegroom straight out,   find out from the man who brought you
    here.
In the forest there is not that thing   running on four feet
nor birds of the air   whizzing along on two wings
nor yet in the water indeed   the best school of fish
which the man who got you will not snare,   the snarer not snare, the fetcher
    not fetch.
It is good for a young woman to be here,   fine for a chick to grow up here.
There is no hurry to get to the quern stone   nor is there worry about getting
    to the mortar;
here water ground the wheat,   the rapids milled the rye;
a wave washes the wooden dishes,   the sea foam bleaches them.
O lovely community,   my favorite place in the land!
Meadows down there, fields up there,   the settlement in between.
There is a lovely shore below the settlement,   lovely water on the shore;
it is fit for a mallard to swim in,   for a waterfowl to move about in."

Then the crowd was given drink,   given drink, fed,
with plenty of pieces of meat,   fine cakes with pudding filling,
barley beer,   wheat wort.
There was indeed plenty of roasted meat to eat,   plenty to eat, plenty to
    drink
in the red trenchers,   in the fine troughs,
pasties to break up,   buttered bread to slice,
whitefish to cut up,   salmon to slice up
with a silver knife,   with a gold sheath knife.
The beer flowed for nothing,   mead not paid for in marks,
beer from the end of the lintel,   mead from inside wooden kegs,
beer as a rinse for lips,   mead as a diversion for minds.

Who there indeed will become a cuckoo,   a proper singer?
Steadfast old Väinämöinen,   eternal singer,
started out to sing,   set upon the task of versemaking.
He speaks these words,   gave utterance to this:
"Beloved brothers, my friends,   my companions in fluent speech,

my comrades in discourse! Listen to what I say.
Rarely are geese mouth to mouth, sisters eye to eye,
rarely brothers side by side, a mother's children shoulder to shoulder
on these wretched marches, in the miserable northern parts.
Shall we now set out on a song, apply ourselves to versemaking?
The singing of songs is the work of singers, cuckooing the work of spring
  cuckoos,
dyeing the work of Woad Spirits, weaving the work of Fabric Spirits.
The children of Lapland sing, the people in hay-stuffed shoes sing resoundingly
of tough elk meat, of the flanks of a small wild reindeer,
so why do not I, too, sing, why do our children not sing
of rye bread, of a mouth well filled with bread?
The children of Lapland sing, the people in hay-stuffed shoes sing resoundingly
after they have drunk a bowl of water, have bitten off a piece of pine-bark
  bread;
so why do not I, too, sing, why do our children not sing
of their drink made from grain, of their barley beer?
The children of Lapland sing, the people in hay-stuffed shoes sing resoundingly
of their sooty campfires, soot-covered sleeping places;
so why do not I, too, sing, why do our children not sing
under a fine ridgepole, under a lovely roof?

A LAY OF PRAISE [FOR THE PRINCIPALS], LINES 453-672

"It is good indeed for men to be here, lovely for women, too, to live
near the beer tun, near the mead tub,
at our side sounds with whitefish, by us salmon-seining places,
where, when eating, food is not lacking, when drinking, drinks do not run
  short.
It is good indeed for men to be here, lovely for women, too, to be alive here.
Here one does not eat in sorrow, not live in the company of care;
here one eats without sorrow, one lives carefree
during the life of this host, the lifetime of the hostess.

"Which of the two here shall I praise first, the master or the mistress?
Men of yore always first praised the master
who created a dwelling in the fen, raised up a home in the wilderness,
brought sturdy pine trees with their butts, lopped pines with their crowns,
put them in a good spot, set them firmly
to be a big house for the clan, a beautiful farmstead;
he shaped the walls in the wilderness, the beams on a terrible hill,
the roofpoles on stony ground, the poles to top off the roof on a berry-grown
  heath,

pieces of birchbark from Chokecherry Hill,   mosses from lovely fens.
The house is built just right,   the roofed building put in its proper place.
A hundred men were engaged in raising it,   a thousand busy on the roof of
    the house
while building the house,   laying the floor.
Already, however, while the host   was making this house,
his shock of hair experienced many a gale,   his hair terrible weather.
Often the good master's mitten   was left on a stone,
his hat on an evergreen spray,   a stocking sunk in the fen.
Often the good master   very early in the morning
before others got up,   before a neighborhood cock was heard,
got up from his campfire,   waked up in his hut of evergreen sprays;
an evergreen spray brushed his head,   dew washed his keen eyes.

"Then indeed the good master   receives his dear one in the house
with the benches full of singers,   the windows full of rejoicing people,
the floorboards loaded with magicians,   inglenooks full of sorcerers,
people standing outside by the wall of the house,   people walking along the
    side of the field,
people walking along the farmyard,   people milling about on the place.

"First I praised the master;   now I will praise the gracious mistress
for preparing the food,   for loading the long table.
She indeed baked the thick loaves,   patted into shape the big cakes of barley
    mush
with her deft hands,   with her ten curved fingers.
She brought the loaves in kindly fashion,   quickly fed the guests
with abundant pork,   with fish pasties.
The blades worked loose from our knives,   the points dropped from our
    sheath knives
while severing the salmon heads,   cleaving the pike heads.
Often the good mistress,   that meticulous housewife
sensed the time to get up without a cock,   to hurry without a chicken,
while she was getting ready for that wedding,   was busy at work
making drinks with hops,   brewing batches of beer.
The good mistress,   that meticulous housewife
knew well how to brew beer,   to make the tasty drink flow
from the sweetened malt sprouts,   from sweet malt
which she did not stir with a stick,   not turn over with a cowlstaff,
on the contrary only stirred with her hands,   turned with her arms
in a smoke-free sauna,   on the clean-swept platforms.
Nor did that good mistress,   that meticulous housewife
let the sprouts cake together,   drop the malted grains on the ground;
she often goes to the sauna   alone in the dead of night,
does not bother to worry about wolves,   to fear the beasts of the forest.

"Now I have praised the mistress; let me praise my master of ceremonies.
Who was chosen master of ceremonies, who elected leader?
The best one in the community was chosen master of ceremonies, the
  community's Good Luck engaged as the leader.
Our master of ceremonies has on a coat of imported broadcloth;
it is close fitting under the arms, trim in the waist.
Our master of ceremonies has indeed a snug-fitting kaftan;
with hems brushing the sand, the back the ground.
A little of his shirt shows, a little sticks out;
it is as if woven by Moon Spirit, thumped out on a loom by a maid with a
  tin brooch on her breast.
Our master of ceremonies has a soft woolen belt around his waist
woven by Sun Spirit, embroidered by a girl with beautiful fingernails
at a time before there was fire, before fire was known.
Our master of ceremonies has silk stockings on his legs,
silk garters for his stockings, satin ribbons on his legs
which are woven of gold, elaborately worked of silver.
Our master of ceremonies has serviceable German shoes
like swans on a river, like pigeons on the banks
or geese on an evergreen spray, birds of passage in a windfall.
Our master of ceremonies has golden curls,
his beard in golden braids, with a high-peaked hat on his head,
towering through the clouds, gleaming through the forest,
a hat which may not be acquired for hundreds, got for thousands of marks.

"I have now already praised my master of ceremonies; let me praise the
  maid of honor.
Whence was got the maid of honor, whence fetched that happy choice?
From yonder was got the maid of honor, from yonder fetched the happy
  choice,
from beyond Tallinn, from around Novgorod.
She was not got from there at all, not by any means!
The maid of honor was got, the happy choice fetched
from the headwaters of the Dvina, from the open waters of the White Sea.
She was not got from there at all, not by any means.
She grew up as a strawberry on the ground, as a red whortleberry on a heath,
as bright grass in a field, as a golden cuckoo in a clearing.
Thence the maid of honor was got, thence the happy choice was fetched.
The maid of honor's pretty mouth is like a Finnish shuttle,
the maid of honor's keen eyes like the stars in heaven,
the maid of honor's splendid brows like the moon when over the sea.
On our maid of honor's throat are gold necklaces,
on her head golden spangles, gold bracelets are on her arms,
gold rings on her fingers, gold beads in her ears,

knotted gold threads on her brows,   beads on her eyebrows.
I thought the moon was gleaming palely   when her gold brooch gleamed
palely,
I thought the sun was shining   when the collar of her blouse shone,
I thought a ship was glistening   when her cap glistened on her head.

"Now I have praised the maid of honor;   let me take a look at the whole
company
to see whether the people are handsome,   the old people splendid
and the young people comely,   the whole crowd lively.
Now I have looked at the whole company;   perhaps I knew it beforehand:
there has not been here before   nor will there probably be indeed in the
future
the liveliness of this crowd,   the fine appearance of this company,
the splendidness of the old people,   the comeliness of the young people.
The whole company in light grey garb   is like a forest white with rime;
at the bottom it is like the light of dawn,   at the top like the break of day."

Silver pieces were cheap;   gold pieces were given freely by the invited guests,
purses lay on the ground,   moneybags were left in the lanes
by these invited guests   as an honor to the party.

Steadfast old Väinämöinen,   eternal prop of song,
then got into his sled,   sets out toward home;
he sings his lays,   sings, performs skillfully.
He sang one lay,   sang a second
but by the third lay   his sled runner rang out on a rock,
a shackle caught   on the top of a stump.
The singer's sled was broken,   the singer's runner caught;
a shackle cracked off,   the sides cracked loose.
Old Väinämöinen said,   uttered a word, spoke thus:
"Is there in this young group here,   among the rising generation
or in this assembly place of old people,   a folk which is getting fewer,
anyone who would pay a visit to Death,   set out for the dwellings of the
Abode of the Dead,
bring a gimlet from Death,   an auger from the people of the Abode of the
Dead,
for me to make a new sled,   for me to repair the sleigh?"
Both the younger people say   and the elderly reply:
"There is not in this young group   nor indeed among the elderly
in the whole big clan   so brave a man
as would go to Death,   set out for the dwellings of the Abode of the Dead,
to bring a gimlet from Death,   an auger from the Abode of the Dead
for you to make a new sled,   for you to repair the sleigh."

Then old Väinämöinen,   eternal singer,
set out a second time for Death's Domain,   journeyed to the dwellings of the
    Abode of the Dead.
He brought a gimlet from Death's Domain,   an auger from the dwellings of
    the Abode of the Dead.
Then old Väinämöinen   sings up a hazy blue wilderness,
into the wilderness he sings a sturdy oak   and a strong rowan.
These he made into his sleigh,   bent into his runners;
from these he selected his shackle-stakes   and bent his shaft-bows;
he managed to repair the body,   to make a new sled.
He put the colt into harness,   the brown horse in front of the sled;
he sat down in the sled,   got down into his basket sleigh.
Without a whip the spirited steed ran,   the horse ran to its familiar grits
without being struck with a knotted whip,   ran to its accustomed mash.
It brought old Väinämöinen,   eternal singer,
to the opening of his own door,   to in front of his own threshold.

POEM 26

Lemminkäinen, in bad humor at being left uninvited to the wedding,
decides, however, to set out for North Farm
regardless of his mother's forbidding him and of those many deaths
which his mother said would overtake him on the way (1–382).
He sets out on his journey and, by virtue of his knowledge,
luckily gets through all the mortally dangerous places (383–776).

Ahti is living on an island,   in a cove in Faraway Headland.
He was plowing a field,   furrowing a field.
He was very keen of ear,   very sharp of hearing.
He hears a roar from the settlement,   a din beyond the lakes,
the beat of hoofs on the slippery ice,   the clatter of a sled on the heath.
The idea entered his mind,   the thought struck him:
North Farm is having a wedding,   a drinking party of a crowd meeting in
   secret.
He screwed up his mouth, twisted his head around,   clawed at his black
   beard;
the blood rushed in ugly fashion   from the wretched man's cheeks.
He at once left off his plowing,   left the furrow unfinished in mid-field;
from the ground he mounted the horse's back,   set out straight from home
to his dear mother's,   to his esteemed parent's.

When he got there he said,   when he arrived he announced:
"O mother mine, aged woman,   put out some food quickly
for a hungry person to eat,   for a ravenous man to take a bite of.
Heat up the sauna at once,   warm up the cabin quickly
where a man is to clean himself,   the best of persons fix himself up."
Lemminkäinen's mother   quickly put out food
for the hungry person to eat,   for the ravenous man to take a bite of
while she was hurrying to prepare a bath,   to get a sauna ready.
Then reckless Lemminkäinen   ate the food quickly,
went at once into the sauna,   went to the bath cabin.
There the chaffinch washes himself,   the snow bunting cleans himself,
cleans his head till it is like a bunch of flax,   cleans his neck white.

He came from the sauna into the house,   uttered a word, spoke thus:
"O mother mine, aged woman,   step outside to the storehouse,
bring from there my fine clothing,   carry the faultless garments

in which I might dress myself,   might put on my body."
His mother managed to ask,   the aged woman to inquire:
"Where are you setting out for, my son?   Are you setting out to hunt a lynx
or to ski after an elk   or to shoot a squirrel?"
Reckless Lemminkäinen spoke,   the handsome man with a far-roving mind
  said:
"O mother mine who bore me,   I am not setting out to hunt a lynx
or to ski after an elk   or to shoot a squirrel;
I am setting out to the feast at North Farm,   to the drinking party of a crowd
  meeting in secret.
Bring me my fine clothing,   my faultless garments
for me to parade in at the wedding,   to wear at the feast."

The mother forbade her son,   the wife tried to stop her husband;
the two women tried to stop him;   three Nature Spirits forbade
Lemminkäinen to set out   to the feast at lovely North Farm.
The mother spoke thus to her son,   the very old woman said to her child:
"Do not go, my son,   my son, my boy with a far-roving mind,
to that feast at North Farm,   to the drinking party of the big crowd.
You were not invited there,   you are really not wanted at all."
Reckless Lemminkäinen   uttered a word, spoke thus:
"Wretched people go by invitation,   a good man skips along without one.
In that are invitations as old as the moon,   perpetual messengers:
in a sharp sword,   in a flashing blade."

Lemminkäinen's mother   kept trying to stop him:
"Just do not, my son,   go to the feast at North Farm.
There will be many terrible things on your journey,   great prodigies on your
  route,
three most terrible deaths,   three things to kill a man."
Reckless Lemminkäinen spoke,   the handsome man with a far-roving mind
  said:
"There are always deaths for women,   deaths everywhere;
a man does not worry about those,   is not indeed likely to hold back.
But be this as it may,   say for me to hear with my ears
what the first death is,   the first, the last, too."

Lemminkäinen's mother spoke,   the aged woman answered:
"I will tell you the deaths according to the cause,   not according to a man's
  desire.
I will tell you the first death.   That death is the first death:
you will go a short distance,   get a day's journey on your way;
a fiery river   will come athwart you,
in the river a fiery rapids,   in the rapids a fiery islet,
on the islet a fiery knoll,   on the knoll a fiery eagle.

By night it hones its beak,   by day gently whets its talons
for the stranger who will come,   for one who intends to come."
Reckless Lemminkäinen spoke,   the handsome man with a far-roving mind
    said:
"That death is a woman's death;   it is not death to a man.
Indeed I will devise something for that,   I know something good:
I will sing up an alderwood horse,   sing up an alderwood man
to go along beside me,   to walk in front of me.
I will dive in the form of a mallard,   go down in the form of an old squaw
along under the eagle's clenched talons,   along under the toes of the griffin.
O mother mine who bore me,   tell the middle death."

Lemminkäinen's mother said: "That death will be the second death:
You will go a short distance,   just a second day's journey.
A fiery pit will appear,   it will be across your way,
ever far to the east,   without end to the northwest,
full of hot stones,   burning boulders.
Hundreds have got into it,   thousands been crammed into it,
a hundred sword-girt men,   a thousand iron stallions."
Reckless Lemminkäinen spoke,   the handsome man with a far-roving mind
    said:
"There is no man's death in that   nor a fellow's death.
Indeed I remember a trick for that,   remember a trick, will devise a means:
I will sing up a man of snow,   quickly construct a person out of crusted snow,
push it into the power of the fire,   thrusting it into the blaze
to bathe in the hot sauna   with a copper bath whisk.
I will go along beside it,   will push myself through the fire
so that my beard will likely not burn,   the locks of my hair not be singed.
O mother mine who bore me,   tell the last death."

Lemminkäinen's mother said: "That death is the third death:
you will go still a bit farther,   you will get a day's journey from there
to the gateway of North Farm,   at the really narrowest point.
A wolf will make a sudden attack,   a bear as a second will join in the attack
at the gateway of North Farm,   in the narrowest lane.
It has indeed eaten a hundred men,   destroyed a thousand people,
so why should it not eat you,   not destroy a defenseless man?"
Reckless Lemminkäinen spoke,   the handsome man with a far-roving mind
    said:
"Let a ewe be eaten uncooked,   be torn to pieces raw,
however not even a really rather inferior man,   a really less enterprising
    person!
I have girded myself with a man's belt,   equipped myself with a man's
    buckle tongue,

fastened myself with a man's buckle   so that I will by no means yet get
into the mouth of Untamo's wolves,   into the cursed creatures' maws.
I remember a trick for a wolf,   will devise something for a bear, too.
I will sing muzzles onto the wolves,   fetters onto the bears
or grind them to chaff,   sift them fine through a sieve.
Thus I will rid myself of them,   get to my destination."

Lemminkäinen's mother said: "You have not yet reached your destination.
As you are going there,   on your journey there will have been great marvels,
three terrible irresistible things,   three deaths for a man.
The worst horrors will be   after you have got right into the place.
You will go a little way,   will come into the yard at North Farm;
the fence is made of iron,   a simulated steel enclosure
reaching from earth to heaven,   from heaven to earth,
staked about with spears,   wattled with reptiles of the earth,
interlaced with snakes,   bound together with lizards,
the tails free to lash,   the clublike heads to writhe,
the pates to hiss,   heads outward, tails inward.
In the ground are other reptiles,   a long line of adders, snakes
hissing at the top with their tongues,   at the bottom lashing with their tails.
In front across the gateway is   one more frightful than the others,
longer than a rooftree of a log cabin,   thicker than the uprights of the cattle
   shed,
hissing at the top with its tongue,   whistling at the top with its mouth,
not for anyone else,   just for poor you."

Reckless Lemminkäinen spoke,   the handsome man with a far-roving mind
   said:
"That death, too, is a child's death,   it is not death for a man.
I know how to enchant fire,   to quench a blaze,
and I know how to exorcise reptiles,   to transform snakes.
Only yesterday   I was plowing adder-ridden land,
was turning over snake-infested ground   with absolutely bare hands.
I held the adders in my fingernails,   the snakes in my hands;
I killed a good ten adders,   a hundred black reptiles.
There is still adder blood under my nails,   snake fat on my hands.
Therefore I am not at all likely to become,   not likely indeed to end up
as a snack for a big reptile,   as a snake's prey.
I will wring the loathsome creatures,   forever squeeze the nasty things;
I will sing the adders farther to the side,   remove the reptiles to the wayside.
I will step from the yard of North Farm,   force my way inside the house."

Lemminkäinen's mother said: "Just do not, my son,
go into the house at North Farm,   into the log buildings of Sedgy Farm.

There are men there with sword in belt,   people with weapons of war,
men crazy drunk,   bad after they have drunk a lot.
They will sing you, poor wretch,   onto a very sharp sword;
already better men have been enchanted,   mightier, too, been vanquished."
Reckless Lemminkäinen spoke: the handsome man with a far-roving mind
   said:
"I have spent time before   in those buildings at North Farm.
No Lapp will enchant me   no Finnmark Lapp put me under compulsion.
I myself will enchant the Lapp   and put the Finnmark Lapp under com-
   pulsion;
I will sing his shoulders apart,   will talk his chin apart,
his shirt collar in two,   his breastbone to pieces."

Lemminkäinen's mother said: "O my poor boy!
You still remember your past,   still boast of your former visit!
Indeed you have spent time before   in those buildings at North Farm;
you swam in all the landlocked ponds,   you made trial of ponds grown with
   dog's tongue.
Banging along you went down the rapids,   rushing along you went with the
   current,
made the acquaintance of Death's rapids,   sounded the currents of the
   Abode of the Dead.
You would be there this very day   but for your poor mother.
Remember what I am saying.   You will come to the buildings of North
   Farm;
there will be a rise studded with stakes,   the farmyard full of posts;
these are full of human heads.   One stake is a stake without a head;
for the end of that stake   they will cut off your head."
Reckless Lemminkäinen spoke,   the handsome man with a far-roving mind
   said:
"A crazy person will perhaps worry about those things,   a good-for-nothing
   take notice
of five, six years of conflict,   of seven summers of warfare.
A man is not likely to pay attention to them,   to turn aside from them in the
   least.
Bring me my war harness,   my tried and true battle dress.
I will go fetch my father's sword,   will select my father's blade.
It has been in the cold a long time,   long in a dark place;
it has been weeping there a long time,   longing for someone to carry it."

Then he got his war harness,   his tried and true battle dress,
his father's ancient sword,   that battle comrade of his father.
He jabbed it into the floor,   pushed the point into the floor;
the sword gave in his hand   like the fresh top of a chokecherry

or a growing juniper.   Reckless Lemminkäinen said:
"In the buildings at North Farm,   in the log buildings at Sedgy Farm
there is scarcely anyone to measure this sword,   to appraise this blade."
He snatched his crossbow from the wall,   his strong bow from a peg.
He speaks these words,   made this remark:
"Him I would call a man,   him esteem as a person
who might draw my crossbow,   bend my springy bow
in those buildings at North Farm,   in the log buildings at Sedgy Farm."

Then reckless Lemminkäinen,   that handsome man with a far-roving mind,
adjusted his war harness,   put on his battle dress.
He spoke to his slave,   uttered a word, spoke thus:
"O my boughten slave,   my drudge got with money,
get my war horse,   harness the steed of battle
so that I may set out to the feast,   to the drinking party of the devil's crew."
Humble, obedient, the slave   quickly betook himself to the farmyard,
put the colt into the harness,   the fiery-red animal into the shafts.
When he returned from there he said: "I have done my job,
have fixed up that stallion of yours,   harnessed the splendid colt."

Then it was up to reckless Lemminkäinen   to set out.
One hand said yes, the other said no;   his sinewy fingers insisted.
Now he set out as he had vowed,   set right out, suffered no anxiety.
The mother counseled her son,   the very aged woman cautioned her child
in the doorway, under the lintel,   where the kettle is kept covered:
"My son, my one and only,   my child, my baby!
If you get to the drinking party,   get anywhere at all,
drink half your stoup,   your bowl to the middle;
give the other half to another,   the worse half to a worse man.
A reptile will be stretched out in the bowl,   a maggot on the bottom of the
    stoup."
She counseled her son further,   admonished her child emphatically
from the farthest field,   from the last gate:
"If you get to the drinking party,   get anywhere at all,
sit on half a seat,   step with a half-length step;
give the other half to another,   the worse half to a worse man.
Thus you will emerge as a man,   become so obviously a distinguished person
that you can wander through folk assemblies,   carry forward lawsuits
in a crowd of people,   a group of men."

Then Lemminkäinen set out,   sitting in the stallion's sled;
he hit the spirited steed with a whip,   struck it with a whip with a bead-
    adorned handle.
The spirited steed started to go,   the horse to trot along.

He drove for a little time,   jogged along for a good while.
On the road he saw a covey of black grouse;   the grouse took off in flight,
the flock of birds fluttered   in front of the trotting horse.
A few feathers were left,   grouse-feathers on the road.
Lemminkäinen gathered them up,   groped in his wallet;
he does not know what might turn up,   what might happen on the way;
on a farm everything may be necessary,   be of use as a makeshift.

He drove ahead a little,   proceeded a short way;
now the horse pricks up its ears,   lop-ears moves uneasily.
Reckless Lemminkäinen,   that handsome man with a far-roving mind
rose up out of his basket sleigh;   he leaned over to look.
Yes indeed, just as his mother said,   as his own parent assured him.
There really is a fiery river   right in front of and athwart the horse.
In the river is a fiery rapids,   in the rapids a fiery islet,
on the islet a fiery knoll,   on the knoll a fiery eagle;
its throat foamed fire,   its mouth gushed flame,
its feathers flashed like fire,   sparkled like sparks.
From afar it sees the man with a far-roving mind,   Lemminkäinen from quite
    far off:
"Where indeed is the man with a far-roving mind going?   Where are you
    setting out for, son of Lempi?"
Reckless Lemminkäinen spoke,   the handsome man with a far-roving mind
    said:
"I was setting out for the feast at North Farm,   to the drinking party of the
    company meeting in secret.
Move over a little to the side,   turn off the road,
let a traveler go on,   especially Lemminkäinen,
so as to get past you,   to walk by."
The eagle knew how to speak,   fiery-throat knew how to hiss:
"I will let a traveler go ahead,   especially Lemminkäinen,
to go through my mouth,   to proceed through my throat.
Thence goes your way of no return to that long-lasting feast,   to those dwel-
    lings forever."
What did Lemminkäinen care!   He did not worry much about it.
He groped in his wallet,   felt in his pouch,
took some black grouse feathers,   gently rubs them
between his two palms,   between his ten fingers.
Thence a covey of black grouse was created,   a whole covey of capercailie
    hens.
He plunged them into the eagle's mouth,   put them into the ravenous bird's
    maw,
into the throat of the fiery eagle,   into the gums of the bird of prey.
Thus he got clear from there,   escaped the first day.

He hit the spirited steed with the whip,   made a ringing sound with the bead-
  adorned handle.
The stallion set out at a canter,   the horse to trot along.
He drove along a little way,   sped on a little distance.
Now the stallion acts strangely,   the horse snorts.
He lifts himself up from his sleigh,   cranes his neck to look.
It is just as his mother said,   as his own parent assured him.
In front is a fiery pit,   it is right across the road,
extending ever far to the east,   endlessly to the northwest,
full of hot stones,   burning boulders.
What did Lemminkäinen care!   He prays to Ukko:
"O Ukko, god on high   or heavenly father,
raise a cloud bank in the northwest,   send another in the west,
build up a third in the east,   raise it in the northeast.
Push them right together,   bang them together side by side.
Let a ski pole's depth of snow fall,   build up a spear's depth
on those hot stones,   burning boulders."
That Ukko, god on high,   old heavenly father,
raised a cloud bank in the northwest,   sent a second in the west,
produced a cloud in the east,   raised a wind in the northeast,
joined them together,   banged them together side by side.
He let fall a ski pole's depth of snow,   built up a spear's depth
on those hot stones,   burning boulders.
There came indeed a pond of snow,   a slushy lake is formed.
Then reckless Lemminkäinen   sang a bridge of ice there
across the pond of snow   from side to side.
Thus he got over that obstacle,   got clear of the second day's journey.

He struck his spirited steed with the whip,   made a ringing sound with the
  beaded lash.
The spirited steed started to run fast,   the horse to trot along.
The horse ran one verst, a second;   the best of horses in the land flew along a
  bit;
then it came to a sudden stop,   does not stir from the spot.
Reckless Lemminkäinen   jumped up to look:
a wolf is in the gateway,   a bear opposite in the lane,
in the gateway of North Farm,   at the end of the long lanes.
Then reckless Lemminkäinen,   the handsome man with a far-roving mind,
groped in his wallet,   felt in his pouch;
he took some ewe's wool,   rubbed it gently
between his two palms,   between his ten fingers.
He blew once on his palm: the ewes suddenly rushed off,
a whole drove of sheep,   a big flock of lambs.
The wolves made a rush there,   the bears attacked along with them.
Reckless Lemminkäinen   drove ahead on his journey.

He proceeded a bit of a way,   came to the yard of North Farm.
An iron fence had been built,   a steel enclosure made,
a hundred fathoms into solid ground,   a thousand fathoms up to the heavens,
staked about with spears,   wattled with reptiles of the earth,
interlaced with snakes,   bound together with lizards.
Their tails were free to lash,   their clublike heads to writhe,
their big heads to sway back and forth,   heads outward, tails inward.
Reckless Lemminkäinen   now reflects on that:
"It is just as my mother said,   as she who bore me complained:
there is such a fence there   set up from the earth to the heavens.
Deep down an adder is crawling about,   but the fence is set deeper.
High aloft a bird is flying about,   but the fence is erected higher."
Lemminkäinen did not, however,   bother to worry much about that;
he drew his knife from its sheath,   the sharp blade from its sheath;
with it he slashed the fence,   broke the posts in two,
opened up the iron fence,   thrust aside the snake-ridden enclosure
for a space of five posts,   of seven poles.

He drives ahead   to in front of the main entrance of North Farm.
A snake is writhing on the road   athwart the entrance,
longer than the upright of the cabin,   thicker than the doorjamb.
The reptile has a hundred eyes,   the snake a thousand tongues,
eyes the size of a flour sieve,   tongues as long as a spear shaft,
teeth like the handle of a hayrake,   its back seven boatlengths long.
Then reckless Lemminkäinen   does not dare to lay hold
of the hundred-eyed reptile,   the thousand-tongued snake.
Reckless Lemminkäinen spoke,   the handsome man with a far-roving mind
    said:

A CHARM TO CALM DOWN SNAKES, LINES 633–670

"Black reptile, underground creature,   maggot the color of Death,
rover about in dead grass,   wanderer among the roots of bracken,
passer through a tussock,   slinker in a tree root!
Who raised you up from the withered grass,   roused you up from the grass
    roots
to crawl about on the ground,   to wriggle about on the road?
Who raised your head,   who ordered you, who encouraged you
to hold your head erect,   your neck stiff?
Your father or your mother   or your eldest brother
or youngest sister   or someone else of your great clan?
Now close your mouth, cover your head,   hide your quick-moving tongue,
roll yourself up into a bundle,   curl yourself up into a coil,
yield the road, half the road,   the roadside for the traveler to pass by.
Or move away from the road,   go, wretch, into the underbrush,
lumber off onto a heath,   hide yourself in the moss,

take yourself off like a tuft of wool, turn into a faggot of aspen,
stick your head into the turf, stuff it inside a tussock—
your house is in the turf, your hut under a tussock.
If you raise your head from there, Ukko will likely crush your head
with steel-tipped nails, with iron hailstones."

That is what Lemminkäinen said. The reptile did not obey that;
it keeps on hissing, whistles with its tongues up,
hisses with mouths raised, ready for Lemminkäinen's head.
Then reckless Lemminkäinen remembered some old charms
recommended formerly by an old woman, taught by his mother.
Reckless Lemminkäinen spoke, the handsome man with a far-roving mind
    said:
"If you do not obey that nor yield a little,
you will indeed swell up in agony, puff up in anguish;
you will split, evil one, in two, into three pieces, loathsome one,
if I seek out your mother of former days, fetch your esteemed parent.
I know, coiled creature, your origin, your growing up, horrible creature of
    the earth.

THE ORIGIN OF SNAKES, LINES 693–758

"An ogress was your mother, your parent a water witch.
The ogress spat in the waters, let her slaver fall onto the billows.
That the wind rocked, the spirit of the water swayed,
rocked it for six years, rocked it indeed seven summers
on the clear expanse of the sea, on the arching billows.
The water stretched it way out, the sun warmed it soft,
the lapping water forced it to land, a wave drove it ashore.
Three Nature Spirits were walking on the shore of the surging sea,
on the edge of the thundering sea. They saw that on the shore,
spoke these words: 'What would come of that
if the Creator should create life in it, bless it with eyes?'
The Creator happened to hear this; he uttered a word, spoke thus:
'Evil would come of evil, a loathsome creature from the vomit of a loath-
    some creature
if I were to put the breath of life in that, bless the head with eyes.'
The Demon got to hear of it, the wicked man to examine it.
He began to create; the Demon gave the breath of life
to the slaver of the foul loathsome creature, to what was spewed out by the
    ogress.
Thus it was turned into a snake, was changed into a black reptile.
Whence did the breath of life get into it? The breath of life came from the
    Demon's ember.
Whence was its heart spewed out? The heart was spewed out by the ogress.

Whence comes the brain of the evil thing?   From the foam of a mighty current.
Whence does the rascal get its disposition?   From the foam of a fiery rapids.
Whence was the head put on the bad thing?   The head is from the seed of a bad pea.
Whence were its eyes created?   From the Devil's flaxseed.
Whence are the ears of the loathsome creature?   From the leaves of the Devil's birch tree.
Whence was the mouth formed?   The mouth is from ogress' belt buckle.
Whence is the tongue in the wretch's mouth?   From the evil elf's spear.
Whence does the evil creature get its teeth?   From an awn of Death's barley.
Whence are the wretch's gums?   From the gums of the Grave Spirit's virgin.
What is the back supported by?   By the Demon's charcoal fork.
What is the tail put together from?   From the braided hair of the Evil One.
From what were the intestines made?   The intestines were from Death's belt.
There was your clan,   there your fine reputation!

"Black reptile from under the earth,   grub the color of Death,
dirt-colored, heather-colored thing,   color of the whole rainbow!
Now get out of the traveler's way,   from in front of the man who is
    proceeding.
Let the journeyer go,   let Lemminkäinen step lightly along
to that feast at North Farm,   to the banquet of the good clan!"

Now the snake moved off eerily,   hundred-eyes moved,
the fat snake turned,   shifted into a bend in the road;
it let the traveler go,   let Lemminkäinen step along lightly
to the feast at North Farm,   to the drinking party of the crowd meeting in
    secret.

POEM 27

Lemminkäinen gets to North Farm
and in many ways behaves arrogantly (1–204).
The master of North Farm gets angry and,
when he does not overcome Lemminkäinen by magic arts,
challenges him to swordplay (205–282).
While they are fencing, Lemminkäinen
strikes off the head of the master of North Farm; to avenge this
the mistress of North Farm assembles an
armed force to proceed against him (283–420).

Now indeed I have guided my man with a far-roving mind,   have escorted
   Island-Ahti
past the mouth of many deaths,   beyond the reach of the Grave Spirit's
   tongue
to that feast at North Farm,   to the farmstead of that crowd meeting in
   secret.
Now must be told,   reported by tongue,
how reckless Lemminkäinen,   that handsome man with a far-roving mind,
came into the dwellings at North Farm,   into the log cabins at Sedgy Farm,
uninvited to the feast,   without escorts to the drinking party.

As soon as reckless Lemminkäinen,   the lad, ruddy-cheeked rascal,
came into the house,   he stepped onto the middle of the floor;
the lindenwood floor shook,   the firwood house resounded.
Reckless Lemminkäinen said,   uttered a word, spoke thus:
"Hail my arrival here,   hail the hailer!
Listen, master of North Farm!   Would there be on this farm
some barleycorns for a stallion to nibble,   beer for man to drink?"
The master of North Farm   was sitting at the head of a long table;
from there he answers,   uttered a word, spoke thus:
"There may be on this farm   a place for your horse to stay
nor are you forbidden,   while you are in the peaceful house,
to stand in the doorway,   in the doorway, under the lintel,
between the two kettles,   close by the three pothooks."
Then reckless Lemminkäinen   clawed at his black beard
the color of a kettle.   He uttered a word, spoke thus:
"May the devil come here   to stand in the doorway,
to clear out your soot,   to scrape off bits of caked soot!
Formerly my father did not, indeed,   not my esteemed parent,
stand in that place,   in the doorway, under the lintel.

In those days there was indeed room,   a shed for a horse to be in,
a house washed clean for men to come into,   nooks to toss their gloves into,
pegs for men's mittens,   walls to stack swords against.
Why, indeed, is it not for me   as formerly for my father?"
Then he moved farther up the room,   swung around to the head of the table,
sat down at the end of the seat,   at the end of the deal bench;
the bench rattled,   the deal bench shook.
Reckless Lemminkäinen said: "I am probably no favorite guest
since probably no beer will be brought   to the newly arrived visitor."

Ilpo's daughter [Louhi], good mistress,   uttered a word, spoke thus:
"O my lad Lemminkäinen,   what a guest you are!
You came to trample on my head,   to bash my brains in!
We have beer in the form of barleycorns,   a tasty drink in the form of malt
   sprouts;
the wheaten bread is not baked,   the beef stew not cooked.
You might rather have come last night   or a day later."

Then reckless Lemminkäinen   screwed up his mouth, twisted his head
   around,
clawed at his black beard.   He uttered these words:
"Here the food has already been eaten,   the wedding drunk out, the feast
   over,
the beer portioned out,   the mead measured out to the men,
the mugs all collected,   the stoups piled up in stacks!
O you mistress of North Farm,   long-fanged woman of Gloomy Farm,
you celebrated the wedding like a wicked woman,   the feast in a way to honor
   a dog.
You baked big loaves,   you brewed barley beer,
you sent out invitations in six directions,   bearers of invitations in nine
   directions.
You invited wretches, you invited the poor,   invited outcasts, invited scoundrels,
all the skinny tenants,   workmen with snug-fitting coats.
You invited a whole crowd of other people,   you left me uninvited.
Why this refusal to me   of my own barleycorns?
Some brought them by the spoonful,   others dribbled them by the cupful;
I dumped them out by the bushel,   poured them out by the half-kegful,
my own barleycorns,   grains I had sown.
Maybe I am not Lemminkäinen,   not a guest of good repute
since no beer is likely to be brought,   no pot put on the fire,
no stew in the pot,   no twenty-pound weight of pork
for me to eat, nothing for me to drink   after I reached the end of my
   journey."

Ilpo's daughter, good mistress,   uttered these words:
"O little maidservant,   my perpetual slave,
put stew in the pot,   bring beer to the guest."
The little maid, desolate child,   washed a dish badly,
cleaned the spoons badly,   scraped off the wooden ladles badly.
She put stew in the pot: meat bones, fishheads,
old turnip stalks,   crusts of hard bread.
Then she brought a stoup of beer,   a jug of the worst brew
for reckless Lemminkäinen to drink,   for the ravenous man to drain.
She uttered these words: "I wonder if there is anything of a man in you,
drinker of this beer,   drainer of this jug?"

Lemminkäinen, reckless lad,   then looked into his stoup;
a grub was at the bottom of the mug,   snakes in the middle,
on the edges reptiles were creeping,   lizards slithering about.
Reckless Lemminkäinen spoke,   the man with a far-roving mind said suddenly:
"Bearers of the stoup, to Death's Domain with you,   carriers of the mug, to the Abode of the Dead with you,
before the moon comes up,   before the end of this day!"
Then he uttered these words: "O you miserable beer,
now you have already become pointless,   become useless.
Perhaps one may take the beer into one's mouth,   throw the refuse onto the ground
with the third finger,   with the left thumb."
He groped in his wallet,   felt in his pouch;
he took a fishhook from his wallet,   a barb from his pouch.
That indeed he thrust into his stoup,   began to angle in the beer;
reptiles caught fast on his hook,   angry adders on his barb.
He brought up a hundred frogs,   a thousand black reptiles;
those he cast onto the ground for the ground,   threw them all onto the floor.
He pulled out his sharp knife,   that keen sheath knife;
with it he cut of the reptiles' heads,   broke off the snakes' necks.
He drank the beer to his own good health,   the dark mead to his own good luck.
He uttered a word, spoke thus: "I am probably no favorite guest
since no beer is likely to be brought me,   nothing better to drink,
by a more liberal hand,   in a bigger vessel,
nor is a ram slaughtered   or a big bull killed
or a steer brought into the dwelling,   no cloven-hoofed animal into the house."

The master of North Farm   uttered a word, spoke thus:
"Why did you come here?   Who invited you to the gathering?"

Reckless Lemminkäinen spoke,   the handsome man with a far-roving mind
    said:
" 'An invited guest is splendid   more splendid is an uninvited stranger.'
Listen, chap of North Farm,   you master of North Farm!
Let me buy some beer,   a drink had for money."

The master of North Farm   got angry at that and lost his temper,
got very angry and mad.   He sang up a pond onto the floor
in front of Lemminkäinen.   He uttered a word, spoke thus:
"There is a river there for you to drink,   a pond for you to splash about in."
What did Lemminkäinen care!   He uttered a word, spoke thus:
"I am no women's calf   nor a steer with a tail
to drink river water,   to splash about in pond water."
He began to practice magic,   suddenly started to sing.
He sang up a bull onto the floor,   a big steer with golden horns;
that was the one that splashed about in the pond,   drank up the river to its
    own good luck.
The man of North Farm, tall fellow,   by his words created a wolf,
that he sang onto the floor   as a death to the fat bull.
Lemminkäinen, reckless lad,   sang up a white hare
onto the floor to hop about   in front of the wolf's mouth.
The man of North Farm, tall fellow,   sang up a dog with an undershot jaw
to kill that hare,   to tear up slant-eyes.
Lemminkäinen, reckless lad,   sang up a squirrel onto the lintel
to climb about on the lintels,   for the dog to bark at.
The man of North Farm, tall fellow,   sang up a golden-breasted marten;
the marten snatched the squirrel   from where it was sitting on the lintel.
Lemminkäinen, reckless lad,   sang up a russet fox;
it ate the golden-breasted marten,   destroyed the one with a handsome coat.
The man of North Farm, tall fellow,   by his words created a chicken
to patter about on the floor   in front of the fox's mouth.
Lemminkäinen, reckless lad,   by his words created a hawk,
by his utterance created one with fast-working claws;   it tore the chicken to
    pieces.

The master of North Farm said,   uttered a word, spoke thus:
"The feast here is not likely to get better   unless the guests get fewer.
The house to work! The guest away,   even from a good drinking party!
Get out of here, demon's rascal,   away from all human kind!
Make for your home, rogue,   flee to your land, evil one!"
Reckless Lemminkäinen spoke,   the handsome man with a far-roving mind
    said:
"By exorcism one does not get a man,   not even an inferior man,
to move from his position,   to flee from where he is."

Then the master of North Farm   seized his sword from the wall,
snatched up his keen blade.   He uttered a word, spoke thus:
"O you Island-Ahti   or handsome man with a far-roving mind,
let us measure our swords,   appraise our blades
to see whether mine is the better sword   or just Island-Ahti's."
Reckless Lemminkäinen said: "What is left of my sword
now that it has splintered on bones,   smashed to bits on skulls!
But be that as it may,   if that feast is not likely to get better,
let us measure them, appraise them   to see which of our swords is the more
    eager.
Formerly my father   did not hold back in the measuring off of swords;
has his son's generation changed,   his child's clan degenerated?"
He took the sword, bared the blade,   snatched the sharp steel
from its leather sheath,   from the bast-lined belt.
They measured, appraised   the length of those swords;
the sword of the master of North Farm   was a little longer,
longer by the edge of one fingernail,   by the joint of half a finger.

Island-Ahti said,   the handsome man with a far-roving mind spoke:
"Your sword is indeed longer;   yours must be the first to strike."
Then the master of North Farm   struck out, made a pass,
made a try, did not hit   the crown of Lemminkäinen's head.
Once he hit a beam,   knocked against a lintel;
the beam cracked,   the lintel flew apart.
Island-Ahti said,   the handsome man with a far-roving mind spoke:
"What harm did the beams do,   what evil deed the lintel,
that you are aiming at the beam,   knocking down the lintel?
Listen, chap of North Farm,   you master of North Farm!
A fight in a house is grievous,   adventures among women grievous;
we will damage the new house,   get blood on the floors.
Let us go out to the farmyard,   outside to a field for the fight,
to the meadow for the fray.   Blood is better in a farmyard,
more beautiful out in a yard,   more fitting on snow!"
They went out to the farmyard,   they come upon a cowhide;
they spread it out on the yard   so as to stand on it.
Island-Ahti said: "Listen you fellow of North Farm!
Your sword is indeed longer,   your blade more terrible;
perhaps you will need it   before we part
or a neck is broken.   Strike first, fellow of North Farm!"
The fellow of North Farm struck offhandedly;   he struck once, struck twice,
he soon lay on a third time.   He did not aim right,
he just grazed some flesh,   does not even scratch the skin.
Island-Ahti said,   the handsome man with a far-roving mind spoke:
"Please let me try, too;   it is my turn now."

The master of North Farm   paid no heed to that:
he struck again, did not hesitate,   took aim, did not hit.
The sharp blade flashed fire,   the steel blade really flamed
in reckless Lemminkäinen's hand;   its gleam extended farther,
slipped against the neck   of that fellow of North Farm.
The handsome man with a far-roving mind said: "O master of North Farm!
Indeed, your neck, wretch,   is ruddy like the dawn."
The lad of North Farm,   the master of North Farm himself,
shifted his gaze there   toward his own neck.
Reckless Lemminkäinen   then lashed out with a blow,
struck the man with his sword,   gave a quick cut with his blade.
He gave one lashing blow: he struck the head from the shoulders,
whipped the pate from the neck;   he took it like a turnip from its stalk
or an ear of grain from a straw,   a fin from a whole fish.
The head rolled onto the courtyard,   the man's pate onto the yard
as, when hit by an arrow,   a capercaillie hen falls from a tree.
Outside there were a hundred stakes,   a thousand upright in the farmyard,
heads by the hundred on the stakes;   there was one stake without a head.
Reckless Lemminkäinen   took the capable fellow's head,
carried the skull from the yard   to the tip of that very stake.

Then after Island-Ahti,   that handsome man with a far-roving mind,
had returned to the house,   he uttered a word, spoke thus:
"Bring some water, hateful maid,   for me to wash my hands
clean of the blood of the bad master,   of the gore of the wretched man."
The dame of North Farm began to get angry,   to get angry, to get furious.
She sang up a man with a sword,   an armed man,
a hundred men with swords,   a thousand bearers of swords
to go for Lemminkäinen's head,   to get the neck of the man with a far-roving
    mind.
Now the time is really coming to set out,   the day advancing to the time of
    departure;
truly it is getting more unpleasant,   becoming harder
for the lad Ahti to stay on,   for Lemminkäinen to remain comfortable
at that feast at North Farm,   at the drinking party of the crowd meeting in
    secret.

POEM 28

Lemminkäinen flees in haste from North Farm,
comes home, and inquires of his mother where he should set out for
in order to hide from the people of North Farm, of whom,
he says, a lot will soon be coming with a whole troop to wage war on him,
against the solitary man (1–164).
His mother reproaches him for having gone to North Farm,
first suggests one or two dangerous places, and finally advises him
to set out for an island beyond several seas where his father
likewise earlier lived in peace during the great war years (165–294).

Now Island-Ahti,   that reckless Lemminkäinen,
betakes himself into hiding,   hastens to flee from gloomy North Farm,
from great Sedgy Farm.   He set out from the house like a blizzard,
gets to the farmyard like smoke   to flee bad acts, to hide his evil deeds.
Then after he had got out into the yard,   he looks around, turns around,
looks for the stallion he used to have.   He does not see the stallion he used
   to have;
he saw a boulder at the end of the field,   a willow bush on the side.
Who will come to advise him,   who to give advice
so that his head may not come to grief,   his shock of hair not get ruined,
not a single fine hair be lost   in this yard at North Farm?
Already a din was heard in the neighborhood,   an uproar on other farms,
the twinkling of lights about in the vicinity,   the glance of eyes from windows.

Then reckless Lemminkäinen,   that Island-Ahti,
had to become something different,   had to change himself into other things.
He rose up in the form of an eagle,   he wanted to rise to the heavens.
The sun burned his cheeks,   the moon lighted his brows.
Then reckless Lemminkäinen   prays to Ukko:
"O Ukko, gracious god,   sharp-witted man of the heavens,
keeper of thunder clouds,   ruler of cloud patches!
Do make the air hazy,   create a little cloud
in the lee of which I might go,   might try to get home
to my beloved mother,   to my esteemed parent."

He flaps along.   Once he looked behind him,
spied a gray hawk   —its eyes burned like fire,
like the fellow of North Farm,   the former master of North Farm.

The gray hawk said: "O my good friend Ahti,
do you remember the combat of old, the equally matched fight?"
Island-Ahti spoke, the handsome man with a far-roving mind said:
"My hawk, my bird! Turn back toward home.
After you get there say to gloomy North Farm:
"It is hard to catch an eagle with one's claws, to eat with one's talons a
    bird with strong wing feathers."

Now he got straight home to his beloved mother
with mouth sad-looking, with heart gloomy.
His mother comes to meet him as he is walking along the lane,
stepping along the side of the fence. His mother hastened to inquire:
"My son, my young boy, my child, my steadygoing lad!
Why are you low in mind as you come from North Farm?
Did they treat you unfairly with flagons at the feast at North Farm?
If they treated you unfairly with the flagons, you will get a better flagon
    here,
got by your father in combat, acquired in battle."
Reckless Lemminkäinen said: "O mother mine who bore me,
who would hurt me with flagons? I myself would hurt the masters,
would hurt a hundred people, would put a thousand men to the test."
Lemminkäinen's mother said: "Why are you low in mind?
Were you defeated by stallions, put to shame by colts?
If you were defeated by stallions, buy a better stallion
with riches got by your father, provided by your parent."
Reckless Lemminkäinen said: "O mother mine who bore me,
who would shame me in with horses or defeat me with colts?
I would shame the masters, defeat the stallion-drivers,
strong men with their colts, men with their stallions."
Lemminkäinen's mother said: "Why are you low in mind,
why gloomy of heart after coming from North Farm?
Were you laughed at by the women or mocked by the girls?
If you were laughed at by the women or mocked by the girls,
there are others to be mocked next time, women to be laughed at in the
    future."
Reckless Lemminkäinen said: "O mother mine who bore me,
who would make me laughed at by women or mocked by girls?
I would laugh at the masters, mock all the girls,
would bring shame to a hundred women, to a thousand other brides."

Lemminkäinen's mother said: "What is the matter with you, my son?
Did some strange thing happen to you while you were visiting North Farm
or, after you had eaten too much, eaten too much, drunk too much,
did you dream strange dreams in your night's resting place?"

Then reckless Lemminkäinen managed to say:
"Let women brood over those dreams in the night!
I remember my dreams at night, better still those by day!
O mother, aged woman, prepare provisions for my rucksack,
put flour in my linen bag, fit lumps of salt into my cloth bag.
The hour of departure has come for your son; he must journey out of the
    country,
away from this lovely home, this beautiful farmstead.
Men are whetting their swords, sharpening their spears."
The mother managed to ask, seeing his distress inquired:
"Why are they whetting their swords, sharpening their spears?"
Reckless Lemminkäinen spoke, the handsome man with a far-roving mind
    said:
"This is why they are whetting their swords, sharpening their spears:
for the head of wretched me, for the miserable man's neck.
Trouble came, an adventure happened in that yard at North Farm;
I killed the fellow of North Farm, the master of North Farm himself.
North Farm rose up for war, that source of danger up north for battle
against miserable me, around solitary me."

His mother uttered these words, the very old woman said to her child:
"I already told you, in fact warned you,
further tried to forbid you to set out for North Farm.
If you had done as you should, lived on in your mother's house,
in the protection of your own parent, on the farmstead of her who bore you,
no war would have come about, no fighting occurred.
Where now, my poor son, where, unfortunate offspring,
will you set out for, to conceal your evil deed, flee the bad act,
that your head may not come to grief, your handsome neck not be cut off,
your shock of hair not get ruined, not a single fine hair be lost?"

Reckless Lemminkäinen said: "I do not know a place
where I might flee to hide my evil deeds.
O mother mine who bore me, where do you advise me to hide?"
Lemminkäinen's mother said, gave utterance, spoke thus:
"I do not know where to suggest, where to suggest and urge you to go to.
If you go to a hill as a pine, to a heath as a juniper,
disaster will come there, hard luck will occur.
Often a pine on a hill is cut down for kindling,
often a heath juniper cropped off for poles.
If you rise up as a birch in a swale or as an alder in a grove,
disaster would come there, too, hard luck occur right there.
Often a birch in a swale is split into firewood,

often a clump of alders   cut down to make a clearing.
If you go to a hill as a berry,   to a heath as a whortleberry,
to these places as strawberries,   to other places as bilberries,
disaster would come there, too,   hard luck would occur.
Young girls would pick them,   girls with tin ornaments on their breasts
   would strip them all.
If you go to the sea as a pike,   as a whitefish to the open sea,
disaster would come there, too,   a hard end would come about suddenly.
A young man, a fisherman from by his campfire,   would put his seine in
   the water,
young men would haul you in with a net,   old men would get you with
   their seines.
If you go to the forest as a wolf,   to the deep forest as a bear,
disaster would come there, too,   hard luck occur.
A young man, sooty-looking from his fire,   would sharpen his spear
in order to kill the wolves,   to lay low the forest bears."

Then reckless Lemminkäinen   uttered a word, spoke thus:
"I myself know the most dreadful spots,   am aware of the worst places
where Death might hold me with his mouth,   where a hard end might
   come about suddenly.
O mother mine who brought me up,   mother who gave me milk,
where do you advise me to hide,   where do you advise and urge?
Death is right in front of my mouth,   an evil day by my beard;
this man will keep his head for one day,   keep it indeed for hardly a
   full day."
Then Lemminkäinen's mother   uttered a word, spoke thus:
"I will mention a really good place,   will name a very lovely one
for the wrongdoer to escape to,   for a wretch to flee to.
I recall a little bit of land,   I know a bit of space,
unplundered, unconquered,   unvisited by the sword of man.
Swear eternal oaths,   unequivocal ones,
firm ones, that for six, ten summers   you will not go to war
from a desire for silver   or a craving for gold, either."
Reckless Lemminkäinen said: "I swear firm oaths
that not during the first summer   or even during the second
will I set out to big wars,   to those clashes of swords.
There are still wounds in my shoulders,   deep holes in my chest
from former delights,   from bygone tumults
on fought-over hills,   on the battlefields of men."

Then Lemminkäinen's mother   uttered a word, spoke thus:
"Take your father's vessel,   set out to hide there
across nine seas,   halfway across a tenth sea,

to an island out in the open water,   to a little island in the sea.
Your father formerly hid there,   both hid and kept himself
during the summers of severe fighting,   during years of hard warfare.
It was good for him to be there,   pleasant for him to spend time there.
Hide there one year, hide a second,   come home the third year
to your father's familiar dwellings,   to your parent's landing places."

POEM 29

Lemminkäinen sets out to sail across the sea and luckily comes to the island (1–78).
On the island he lives too recklessly with the daughters and other womenfolk,
for which reason the men in their rage decide to kill him (79–290).
Lemminkäinen sets out to take flight while there is time and leaves
the island to the great sorrow of both the virgins and himself (291–402).
At sea a big storm wrecks Lemminkäinen's ship,
he himself reaches land by swimming, gets a new boat and, with it,
arrives at his home shores (403–452).
He sees that his former house has burned down and the whole place is
laid waste; because of this he begins to weep and lament,
especially since he fears that his mother, too, is now dead (453–514).
His mother, however, is alive and is living in a new place in the backwoods,
where to his great joy Lemminkäinen finds her (515–546).
His mother relates how the people of North Farm came
and burned the buildings to ashes;
Lemminkäinen vows to make new, even better buildings, just as he will
also take revenge on North Farm for her sufferings, and tells his mother
of his jolly life during the time of hiding on the island (547–602).

Lemminkäinen, reckless lad,   that handsome man with a far-roving mind,
got provisions in his rucksack,   summer butter in his box,
butter for him to eat for one year,   pork for a second.
Then he set out to go into hiding,   both set out and made haste.
He uttered a word, spoke thus: "Now I am setting out, now taking flight
for three whole summers,   for five years.
I am leaving the land for reptiles to consume,   the groves for lynxes to
   rest in,
fields for wild reindeer to roll about in,   clearings for geese to live in.
Farewell, my good mother!   When North Farm's people come,
the big troop from Gloomy Farm   to ask for my head,
say I have wandered off,   gone away from here
after felling for burning the same clearing   which has already been cut
   down."

He hauled his boat to the water,   brought the ship down to the billows
from the steel rollers,   from the copper rollers.
He hoisted the sails on the mast,   the canvas on the main spar;
he sat down in the stern,   got ready to get going,
depending on the birchwood prow,   relying on the sturdy steering oar.

He uttered a word, spoke thus,   spoke and said:
"Blow, wind, into the sail,   cold spring wind, drive the craft on.
Let the wooden vessel run along,   the pinewood boat go
to the uninhabited island,   to the unknown headland."
The wind rocked the boat,   the lapping of the sea drove it along
on the surface of the clear waters,   on the open expanses of the sea;
it kept rocking for two months,   soon a third month too.

There the maidens of the headland were sitting   on the shore of the blue sea;
they are looking about, turning about   with their eyes toward the blue sea.
One was waiting for her brother,   was hoping to see her father come;
she indeed was waiting eagerly,   who was waiting for her suitor.
The man with a far-roving mind is seen from afar,   the ship of the man
    with a far-roving mind from farther still;
it is like a little cloud patch   between the water and the sky.
The girls of the headland reflect,   the virgins of the island say:
"What is that odd thing on the sea,   what the remarkable object on the
    billows?
If you happen to be a ship of our kin,   a sailing vessel of the island,
then turn toward home,   toward the landing places of the island.
We may get to hear news,   reports from distant parts,
whether the coastal peoples are at peace   or in a state of hostility."
The wind makes the sail jibe,   a wave drove the craft on.
Quickly reckless Lemminkäinen   steered the vessel toward the little island,
brought the ship to the end of the island,   to the tip of the headland of
    the island.

After he got there he said,   after he arrived he inquired:
"Is there room on the island,   space on the main part of the island,
for me to haul the boat ashore,   to turn the vessel over on dry ground?"
The virgins of the island speak,   the girls of the headland reply:
"There is room on the island,   space on the main part of the island,
for you to haul the boat ashore,   to turn the vessel over on dry ground.
There are spacious landing places here,   shores full of rollers
should you arrive with a hundred ships,   come with a thousand vessels."
Then reckless Lemminkäinen   hauled the boat ashore,
the vessel onto the wooden rollers.   He uttered these words:
"Is there room on the island,   space on the main part of the island
for a smallish man to hide in,   for a feeble one to flee to
from the great din of battle,   from the clashes of sharp swords?"
The virgins of the island speak,   the girls of the headland reply:
"There is room on the island,   space on the main part of the island
for a smallish man to hide in,   for a feeble one to flee to.
We have an excess of fine houses here,   fine farmsteads to live in

if a hundred people arrive,   a thousand men come."
Then reckless Lemminkäinen   uttered a word, spoke thus:
"Is there room on the island,   space on the main part of the island,
a little corner of a birch grove   and a bit of other ground
for me to fell a clearing,   for me to clear a nice piny tract?"
The virgins of the island speak,   the girls of the headland reply:
"There is no room on the island,   no space on the main part of the island
as large as your back,   a piece of land as large as a five-peck measure,
not enough for you to fell a clearing,   to clear a nice piny tract.
The lands of the island have been divided into strips,   the field strips
      measured off into parcels;
lots are drawn for clearings,   one goes to folk assemblies for grasslands."
Reckless Lemminkäinen spoke,   the handsome man with a far-roving mind
      asked:
"Is there room on the island,   land on the main part of the island
for me to sing my songs,   intone my long lays?
Words melt in my mouth,   sprout on my gums."
The virgins of the island speak,   the girls of the headland reply:
"There is room on the island,   land on the main part of the island
for you to sing your songs,   intone your good lays;
there are groves for you to have fun in,   a meadow for you to dance on."

Then reckless Lemminkäinen   now began to sing.
He sang up rowans in farmyards,   oaks in the middle of farmyards,
sturdy boughs on the oaks,   an acorn on a branch,
on the acorn a golden ball,   on the golden ball a cuckoo.
When the cuckoo calls,   gold foams from its mouth,
copper streams from its jaws,   silver gleams
on the golden knoll,   on the silver hill.
Lemminkäinen kept on singing,   kept on singing and speaking magically,
sang the sands into fresh-water pearls,   all the rocks till they were glistening,
all the trees till they were reddish,   the flowers the color of gold.
Then Lemminkäinen sang,   sang up a well on the farmstead,
a golden cover on the well,   a golden scoop on the cover
from which brothers drink water,   sisters wash their faces.
He sang up a pond onto the meadow,   onto the pond green mallards
with brows of gold, heads of silver,   all their toes of copper.
The virgins of the island marveled,   the maidens of the headland were
      astonished
at Lemminkäinen's singing,   at the man's skill.
Reckless Lemminkäinen spoke,   the handsome man with a far-roving mind
      said:
"I would sing a fine song, too,   resoundingly sing a beautiful one, too,
if I might be under a roof   at the end of a long deal table.

If no house is relinquished,   no floor lent out,
then I will recite my words to the backwoods,   drop my songs into a
   thicket."

The virgins of the island speak,   the maidens of the headland ponder:
"We have houses to come to,   spacious farmsteads to live in,
to take your songs to from out of the cold,   to bring your words in from
   outdoors."
Then as soon as reckless Lemminkäinen   came into the house
he sang the stoups from farther off   toward his end of the long deal table,
stoups full of beer,   beautiful pots of mead,
dishes spilling over,   bowls brimful.
Stoups of beer,   pots of mead
were indeed brought,   butter was put in readiness and pork put there
for reckless Lemminkäinen to eat,   for the man with a far-roving mind to
   enjoy.
The man with a far-roving mind is very grand,   nor does he start to eat
without a silver-hilted knife,   a gold sheath knife.
He got a silver knife,   sang up a gold sheath knife;
then he eats his fill,   drank beer to his contentment.

Then reckless Lemminkäinen   strolled about the communities
enjoying the virgins of the island,   in the lovely bevy of those with luxuriant
   hair.
Wherever he turned his head   then his mouth was quickly kissed,
wherever he reached out his hand   then his hand was gently pressed.
Evenings he went out for some fun   in the pitch dark.
There was not a community   in which there were not ten farms
nor was there a farm   in which there were not ten daughters,
not that daughter,   not that mother's child
by whose side he did not stretch out,   press down the arm.
He knew a thousand brides,   lay with a hundred widows.
There were not two in ten,   three in a whole hundred maids
who were not had,   widows not lain with.

Thus indeed reckless Lemminkäinen   lives in an easygoing way
all of some three summers   in the big communities of the island.
He delighted the virgins of the island,   satisfied all the widows, too.
One was left unsatisfied,   one wretched old virgin;
she is at the end of the long headland   in the tenth settlement.
Now his mind was on a journey   to set out for his own land.
The wretched old virgin came,   she spoke these words:
"Wretched man with a far-roving mind, handsome man!   If you will not
   notice me,

I will, when you go from here,   let your ship run onto a rock."
Without a cock he did not sense the time to get up,   without a chicken
   he did not hurry,
to the delight of that virgin, too,   to the laughter of the wretched woman.
So on a certain day,   on a certain evening
he resolved to get up   before the moon set, before the cock crew, too.
He got up before the time decided,   before the time agreed on.
He set out at once to walk,   to stroll about the communities
to the joy of that virgin, too,   to the laughter of the wretched woman.
That night as he was walking alone,   was going about the communities
over there at the end of the long headland,   to the tenth community,
he did not see a farm   on which there were not three cabins,
not see a cabin   in which there were not three men,
not see a man   who was not whetting his sword
not sharpening his battle ax   for Lemminkäinen's head.
Then reckless Lemminkäinen   uttered a word, spoke thus:
"Alas, a fine day has dawned,   a lovely sun has risen
on me, poor lad,   on my wretched neck!
May the Devil shelter a single man   in his cloak,
protect him in his tunic,   guard him in his mantle
when hundreds assail him,   thousands press upon him!"

He left the girls unembraced,   those he had embraced he left unhugged.
Now he walked to the rollers,   the poor fellow to his vessel.
The vessel was burned to ashes,   reduced to fluffy ashes.
Now he recognized that disaster was coming,   a day of trouble coming on.
He began to fashion a boat,   to busy himself with a new vessel.
The craftsman lacked wood for the vessel,   the wright lacked planks for
   the boat.
He gets a tiny bit of wood,   a very tiny plank,
five little bits of a distaff,   six small fragments of a spindle.
Then he fashions a boat,   busies himself with a new vessel.
He made a boat artfully,   with magic words.
He struck one blow: one side was formed;   he struck a second time: the
   other side was formed;
he struck a third time: then the whole boat was produced.

Now he shoved the boat into the water,   put the ship down on the billows.
He uttered a word, spoke thus,   spoke and said:
"Go, boat, like bubbles onto the water,   like water lilies onto the billows.
Eagle, three of your feathers!   Eagle three, raven two,
as a protection for the little boat,   as a gunwale for the poor vessel."
He steps into his craft,   turned to the stern of the boat
downcast, low in mind,   high-peaked hat all askew,

since he could not stay nights   nor live his days
to delight the maidens of the island,   to dance with the girls with luxuriant
  hair.

Reckless Lemminkäinen spoke,   the handsome man with a far-roving mind
  said:
"The time of departure has come for the lad,   his trip from these dwellings,
from the delights of the virgins,   from the dances with the beauties.
However, after I have indeed set out,   have gone from here
the virgins will not be joyous,   the girls with luxuriant hair will not chat
  gaily
in these wretched houses,   on the mean farmsteads."
Now the virgins of the island wept,   the girls of the headland moaned:
"Why did you set out, Lemminkäinen?   Why depart, best of men?
Did you set out because of the girls' prudery   or just for lack of women?"
Reckless Lemminkäinen spoke,   the handsome man with a far-roving mind
  said:
"I am not setting out because of the girls' prudery   nor for lack of women;
I could even get a hundred women,   a thousand maidens to fondle.
For this reason I, Lemminkäinen, am setting out,   best of men departing,
because a strong longing came,   a longing for my own lands,
for the strawberries of my own country,   for the raspberries of my own hill,
the maidens of my own headland,   the chicks of my own farmstead."
Then reckless Lemminkäinen   put his ship farther out.
The wind came, it blew it along;   a wave came, it drove it along
to the surface of the blue sea,   to the open expanse of the deep.
The wretched girls remained on the shore,   the tender-hearted ones on a
  rock in the water,
the virgins of the island remained to weep,   the lovely ones to lament.
The virgins of the island wept,   the girls of the headland lamented
as long as the sailing vessel was visible,   the ship with iron tholepins dimly
  to be seen.
They are not weeping for the sailing vessel,   not longing for the ship with
  iron tholepins;
they are weeping for the helmsman of the sailing ship,   the master of the
  main sheet.
Lemminkäinen himself wept,   wept and sorrowed
as long as the shores of the island were visible,   the ridges of the island
  dimly to be seen.
He did not weep for the shores of the island,   not long for the ridges of
  the island;
he was weeping for the virgins of the island,   for those wild geese of the
  ridge.

Then reckless Lemminkäinen   proceeds on the blue sea.
He proceeded one day, proceeded a second.   On the third day indeed
a wind got to blowing,   the horizon to rumbling,
a great northwest wind,   a strong northeast wind blew.
It caught one plank, caught a second,   it capsized the whole boat.
Then reckless Lemminkäinen   fell straight into the water,
began to row with his fingers,   to paddle with his feet.
After he had swum a night and a day,   after he had paddled along quite a
    distance.
he saw a little cloud,   a cloud patch in the northwest.
That indeed changed into land,   became a headland.
He went onto the headland into a house,   found the mistress baking,
the daughters shaping loaves: "O gracious mistress,
if you only understood my hunger,   appreciated my condition,
you would go running to the storehouse,   to the beer house like a blizzard;
you would bring a stoup of beer,   a sliver of pork;
you would put it to roast,   would slice some butter on it
for an exhausted man to eat,   for one has been swimming to drink.
I have been swimming now nights and days   on the waves of the open sea,
every gale my refuge,   the waves of the sea my source of mercy."
The gracious mistress   went out to the storehouse,
sliced some butter in the storehouse,   a sliver of pork;
she puts it to roast   for the hungry man to eat,
brings beer in a stoup   for the man who has been swimming to drink.
Then she gave him a new vessel,   a really well-equipped boat,
for the man to go to other lands,   to proceed home.

Then after reckless Lemminkäinen   had got home,
he recognized the countryside,   recognized the shores,
both the islands and the sounds,   recognized his old landing places,
his former dwelling sites;   he recognized the hills with their pines, all the
    knolls with their firs;
he does not recognize the site of the house,   the wall of the dwelling place.
There now on the site of the house   a young chokecherry was murmuring,
a stand of pines out by the house,   a stand of juniper on the path to the
    spring.
Reckless Lemminkäinen spoke,   the handsome man with a far-roving mind
    said:
"There is the grove in which I used to go about,   there the rocks on which
    I moved about,
there the meadows I tumbled about on,   the sides of fields I rolled about on.
What took away my beloved dwelling,   who removed the lovely sheds?
The house has been burned to ashes,   the wind has cleared the ashes away."

Then he began to weep;   he wept one day, wept a second.
He did not bewail the house   nor long for the storehouse;
he bewailed the loved one in the house,   his dear mother in the storehouse.

He sees a bird flying,   an eagle moving about.
From where he was he began to ask: "O you eagle, my bird,
would you not have word   as to where my old mother is,
where the fair one who bore me is,   the lovely one who suckled me?"
The eagle recalls nothing at all   nor does the stupid bird know.
The eagle knew she was dead   and the raven knew she had vanished,
been killed by a sword,   struck by a battle ax.
Reckless Lemminkäinen spoke,   the handsome man with a far-roving mind
   said:
"O fair one who bore me,   lovely one who suckled me!
Now you have died, you who bore me,   you, my gracious mother, have
   departed,
your flesh has decayed to dust   with firs grown at your head,
junipers at your heels,   willows at your finger tips.
For revenge, poor wretch,   for revenge I, luckless man,
measured my sword,   carried a fine weapon
to the yard at North Farm,   on the side of the field at Gloomy Farm—
resulting in the death of my own clan,   in the loss of her who bore me."

He looks about, he turns about;   he faintly saw the trace of a footprint
crushed in the grass,   broken off in the heather.
He set out to discover the trail,   to learn the right course.
The way leads into the forest;   he picks up the trail.
Then he went one verst, went a second,   hurries over a bit of country
into a most gloomy wilderness,   into a bend in a corner of the backwoods.
He sees a secret sauna hut,   a little hidden hut
between two crags   at the foot of three firs growing close together;
there sees his gracious mother,   that esteemed parent of his.
Then reckless Lemminkäinen   rejoiced greatly,
speaks these words,   made this remark:
"O my dear mother,   O mother who reared me!
You are still alive, mother,   still awake, my parent,
when I was already thinking you were dead,   that you had probably vanished,
killed by a sword,   struck by a spear.
I wept away my lovely eyes,   ruined my handsome face."

Lemminkäinen's mother said: "I am indeed still alive
though I had to flee,   betake myself into hiding
here in the gloomy wilderness,   in the bend in a corner of the backwoods.
North Farm waged war,   the backwoods crowd battled

against wretched you,   against you, luckless fellow.
They burned the buildings to ashes,   destroyed our whole farmstead."
Reckless Lemminkäinen said: "O mother mine who bore me,
do not be upset by this,   not upset by this, not by that.
New buildings will be built,   better ones constructed;
North Farm will be warred on,   the Devil's crew destroyed."

Then Lemminkäinen's mother   uttered these words:
"You stayed a long time, my son,   long, my man with a far-roving mind,
     you dwelt,
in those alien lands,   always in strange doorways,
on a unknown headland,   on an uninhabited island."
Reckless Lemminkäinen spoke,   the handsome man with a far-roving mind
     said:
"It was fine for me to be there,   lovely for me to amble about.
There the trees shone red,   the trees red, the ground green,
the tall evergreen branches silvery,   the heather-blooms gold.
There the hills were of mead,   the crags of hens' eggs;
withered firs flowed with honey,   rotten pines with milk;
fence corners yielded butter,   the fence posts poured forth beer.
It was fine for me to be there,   lovely to spend my time there.
Then life was bad,   then it was strange for me to be there;
they feared for their maidens,   thought I was treating their loose women
     badly,
those potbellied fellows of the Evil One,   those pudgy waddling fellows
     of the devil
took it amiss   that I was courting them overly at night.
I hid from the maidens,   I was scared of the mother's daughters—
just about as a wolf hides from pigs,   hawks from community hens!"

POEM 30

Lemminkäinen with his former comrade-in-arms Snowfoot
sets out to wage war against North Farm (1–122).
To oppose him the mistress of North Farm produces a severe cold spell
which freezes their ships into the sea
and would have come within an ace of freezing the crewmen themselves
had not Lemminkäinen by means of effective charms and exorcisms
got Jack Frost to desist (123–316).
With his companion Lemminkäinen walks ashore on the ice,
in a woeful condition wanders a long way through the backwoods
until he finally gets to his home farm (317–500).

The lad Ahti, fine lad,   the reckless lad Lemminkäinen,
very early one morning,   very early in the morning,
was walking along to the boat sheds,   setting out toward the ships' landing
    places.
There a wooden vessel was weeping,   a boat with iron tholepins grieving:
"What about me who has been built,   me, poor wretch, who has been
    fashioned?
Ahti has not rowed to war   for six, ten summers
out of a desire for silver,   a craving for gold, either."
Reckless Lemminkäinen   struck the vessel with his mitt,
his mitten with an embroidered wristband.   He uttered these words:
"Do not worry, deck of evergreen,   do not complain, ship with extra free-
    board.
You will yet wage war,   go to battle;
you will be full of rowers   from tomorrow morning on."

He walks to his mother's,   uttered these words:
"Do not weep now, mother mine,   do not complain, my parent,
if I go somewhere or other,   set out to scenes of war.
A scheme has come to my mind,   a plan has entered my brain
to destroy the people of North Farm,   to avenge myself on the wretches."
His mother tried to stop him,   the aged woman warned him:
"Do not go, my son,   to those battles at North Farm.
There your death will come about,   your death occur."

What did Lemminkäinen care!   He just considered going,
vowed to set out.   He uttered a word, spoke thus:
"Where will I get a second man,   both a man and a sword

to help Ahti in battle,   as a reinforcement for the very mighty man?
I know Snowfoot,   Hoarfrosty who is within earshot of me.
From him I will probably get a second man,   both a man and a sword
to help Ahti in battle,   as a reinforcement for the very mighty man.
He walks over there about the community,   along the path to Snowfoot's
   farmstead.
When he got there he said,   when he arrived announced:
"My Snowfoot, my trusty fellow,   my dearest friend, my dear friend!
I wonder if you remember our days of yore,   our former life
when in the past we used to go together   to great scenes of battle?
There was not a community   in which there were not ten farms,
not a farm   on which there were not ten men,
not that man   or a person of consequence
whom we did not destroy   and between us overthrow."

The father happened to be at the window   shaping a spear shaft,
the mother on the threshold of the storehouse   banging the churn,
the brothers by the gateway   fashioning sleighs with long sides,
the sisters on the floor   fulling homespun.
The father spoke from the window,   the mother from the threshold of the
   storehouse,
the brothers from the gateway,   the sisters from the floor:
"Snowfoot has no time for warfare,   Snowfoot's icepick no time for battle;
Snowfoot has made a fine bargain,   struck an everlasting compact:
he has just married a young woman,   taken a mistress for himself;
her nipples are yet unplayed with,   her breasts unwearied."
Snowfoot happened to be by the hearth,   Hoarfrosty by the stove.
He put on one shoe on the hearth,   the other on the side of the stove bench,
at the gate he put on his belt,   outside he anointed himself with snake
   poison.
Snowfoot grabbed his spear;   it was not a very big spear
nor a very small spear,   it was a medium-sized spear.
A horse stood etched on the head,   a colt was swaying on the side of the
   head,
a wolf was howling on the ferrule,   a bear was growling on the stud.
He brandished his spear,   brandished it, shook it;
he hurled the spear shaft a fathom deep   into a clayey field,
into a hard grassless tract,   into a field free of tussocks.
Snowfoot thrust his spear   in with Ahti's spears,
set forth and hastened   to help Ahti in battle.
Then Island-Ahti   launched his boat onto the water
like a snake that lives in withered grass   or a living serpent.
He set out bearing to the northwest   to that sea by North Farm.

217

Then the mistress of North Farm   sent bad Jack Frost
to that sea by North Farm,   to the wide open sea.
She uttered these words,   both commanded and said:
"Little boy Jack Frost,   my own lovely foster child!
Set out yonder to where I order,   to where I order and urge you.
Freeze the rascal's boat,   reckless Lemminkäinen's vessel
on the broad expanse of the sea,   on the wide open sea.
Freeze the master himself, too,   freeze the rascal in the water
so that he will never escape,   never get clear
unless I get to freeing him,   get ready to release him."

A CHARM AGAINST JACK FROST, LINES 143–316

Jack Frost of bad lineage   and an ill-mannered boy
set out to freeze the sea,   to tame the waves.
Now while he was going there,   while traveling over the land,
he bit the trees leafless,   the grass sheathless.
Then after he got there   beside the sea of North Farm,
to the boundless shore,   straight off the first night
he froze the coves, froze the ponds.   He iced up the shores of the sea,
he did not yet freeze the sea over,   not tame the waves.
There is a little chaffinch on the surface of the water,   a wagtail on the
    billows;
its claws are not frozen,   its little head not freezing cold.
Not until the next night after that   did he get violent,
fling himself about shamelessly,   grow very dreadful.
Then he froze in full measure;   Jack Frost's power froze hard.
It froze ice a forearm thick,   it dropped snow a ski pole deep,
it froze the rascal's boat,   Ahti's ship to the billows.
He meant to freeze Ahti, too,   to turn the fine man to ice.
Already he was asking for his fingernails,   from down there requesting his
    toes.

Then Lemminkäinen got angry,   then got angry and took offence;
he pushed Jack Frost into a fire,   shoved him into a bog-iron furnace.
He held Jack Frost with his hands,   squeezed Sharp Air.
He speaks these words,   made this remark:
"Jack Frost, Windblast's son,   icy son of Winter,
do not freeze my fingernails,   do not demand my toes,
do not touch my ears,   do not freeze my head.
You have plenty to freeze   and much indeed to make freezing cold
apart from human skin,   apart from the body of a mother's offspring.
Freeze fens, freeze the countryside,   freeze the stones cold,
make water willows cold,   strike the galls off aspens,
strip bark off birches,   nibble young firs,

not human skin,   not the locks of a maiden's offspring.
If perhaps you do not get enough from that,   freeze other more extraordinary
     things:
freeze hot stones,   burning boulders,
iron crags,   steel mountains;
freeze the fierce rapids of the Vuoksi,   of terrible Imatra,
the mouth of the maelstrom,   the terrible whirling eddy.

"Shall I now recite your lineage,   proclaim your repute?
Indeed I know your lineage,   know all about your growing up.
Jack Frost was born in the willows,   Sharp Air in a birch grove
at the back of a Lappish tent at North Farm,   in a cabin at Gloomy Farm,
of a pernicious father,   a worthless mother.
Who suckled Jack Frost,   nursed Sharp Air,
since the mother was without milk,   the mother without breasts?
A serpent suckled Jack Frost,   a serpent suckled, a snake fed him
with its tipless teats,   with its milkless udder.
The north wind swayed him,   the chill air rocked him
by bad willow-lined streams,   by heaving quagmires.

"The boy got bad-mannered,   became destructive.
The worthless boy   did not yet have a name.
They bestowed a name on the bad fellow,   bestowed the name Jack Frost.
Then he rode the hedges,   rustled in the underbrush.
Summers he moved about on the quagmires,   on the very vast surfaces of
     the fen;
winters he romped in the pine groves,   roared in the pines,
frisked about in the birch groves,   fluttered about in the alder groves.
He froze trees and withered grass,   flattened out fields,
bit the trees leafless,   the heather of its blooms,
scattered scales of bark from tall evergreens,   caused chips to drop off
     the pines.

"Now that you have got big,   grown up to be very handsome,
you thought you would freeze me,   puff my ears up,
beg for my feet from down there,   ask for my fingernails up there.
You are not likely to freeze me,   to chill me badly.
I will thrust fire into my stockings,   embers into my shoes,
fine charcoal into my hems,   fire under my bootlaces,
so that Jack Frost will not freeze me,   Sharp Air not touch me.
I will exorcise you to over yonder,   to the far backwoods of North Farm.
Then after you have come there,   have got to your home,
freeze the kettles to the fire,   the coals to the stove hearth,
a woman's hands in the dough,   a child in a maiden's womb,

milk in ewe's udders, a foal in a horse's belly.
If you will not obey this, then I will exorcise you to over yonder
among the Demon's coals, to the hearthstones of the Demon's fireplace.
There thrust yourself into the fire, put yourself on an anvil
for a smith to smite with his sledge, to pound with his hammer,
strike firmly with his sledge, hard with his hammer.
If you will not obey that, not pay even a little heed,
I will recall still another place, will think of a certain region.
I will conduct your mouth to Summer's place, your tongue to Summer's
    home
whence you will never get away, never at all escape
if I do not come to free you and go to release you."
Jack Frost, Windblast's son, now recognized that disaster was coming;
he began to beg for mercy. He uttered a word, spoke thus:
"Let us make a nice agreement never to harm one another,
never, never at all, not while the moon shines gold-bright.
If you hear that I am going to freeze you, behave foolishly a second time,
then thrust me into a fireplace, sink me into a fire
among a smith's coals, into the bottom of Ilmarinen's forge.
Or bring my mouth to Summer's, my tongue to Summer's home
so that I will never get free, never at all escape."

Then reckless Lemminkäinen left his ship in the glare ice,
the warship stuck fast; he himself goes on ahead.
Snowfoot, there as the second man, turned after the scamp.
He stepped along on the level ice, walked over the smooth ice.
He walked one day, then a second, on the third day, indeed,
Starvation Headland comes into view, the miserable settlement looms up.
He walked along beneath a great house on the headland, uttered a word,
    spoke thus:
"Is there any meat in the house and fish in the farmstead
for weary people, for tired men?"
There was no meat in the house, no fish in the farmstead.
Reckless Lemminkäinen spoke, the handsome man with a far-roving mind
    said:
"Fire, burn the stupid house, let water take such a thing away."
He proceeds farther on, went up into the wilderness
on routes with no cottages, on unfamiliar trails.
Then reckless Lemminkäinen, that handsome man with a far-roving mind,
clipped wool from a rock, pulled hair off crags,
made it into stockings, hurriedly made it into mittens
in Cold's very great domains, in places frozen by Jack Frost.
He set out to inquire about the trail, to learn the course;
the way leads into a forest, the trail leads on.

Reckless Lemminkäinen spoke,   the handsome man with a far-roving mind
   said:
"O my dear friend Snowfoot,   now we have got into something,
we are forever on the move,   ever going toward the horizon."

Snowfoot said these words,   gave utterance, spoke thus:
"To take our revenge, we miserable wretches,   to take our revenge luckless
   ones
we got into a great fight   at gloomy North Farm,
at the risk of our own lives,   of our own ruin
in these evil parts,   on unfamiliar trails!
We do not recognize that,   we neither recognize nor know
what track is leading us on,   what course leads
to the backwoods to death,   to the heath to our fall,
to the dwelling places of ravens,   to the fields of crows.
There the ravens are hovering,   the bad birds soaring;
the birds are getting flesh,   the crows supplies of blood,
the ravens moisture for their beaks   from the bodies of us, poor wretches;
they will throw our bones on stone piles,   will carry them to rocky reefs.
My hapless mother does not know,   not the wretched one who bore me,
where her flesh is going,   her own blood going to,
whether he is in a great war,   in an evenly matched struggle
or on the great open sea,   on the boundless billows
or is staying on a pine-grown hill,   wandering in a wild scrub growth.
My mother knows nothing   of her miserable son.
The mother just knew he had died,   the one who bore him knew he had
   vanished.
Thus indeed will my mother bewail,   my parent lament:
'Yonder is my son, poor wretch,   yonder the miserable one, my prop,
sowing Death's crops,   harrowing the lands of the Guardian of the Grave.
Now my son is letting,   child of hapless me
is letting his crossbows be idle,   the splendid bows dry out,
the birds get very plump,   the hazel grouse preen themselves in the grove,
the bears to live unrestrained,   the wild reindeer to roll about on the field.' "

Reckless Lemminkäinen spoke,   the handsome man with a far-roving mind
   said:
"So it is, so, unhappy mother,   so indeed, poor mother who bore me!
You reared a brood of chicks,   a whole brood of swans.
The wind came and scattered them,   the devil came and dispersed them,
some here, others there,   the third lot anywhere at all.
I will remember my days of old, too   —I esteem them the better time—
when we used to walk about like so many flowers,   like berries on our
   own land.

Many looked at our figures,   gazed at our forms.
It is not like this nowadays,   in this vile time.
Now our one acquaintance is the wind,   the sun the only thing seen before;
even that the clouds cover,   the rains veil.
However, I do not get to worrying,   to grieving greatly,
provided the virgins live happily,   the ones with luxuriant hair chat gaily,
all the women wreathed in smiles,   the brides in a happy state of mind,
not weeping in distress,   not falling into a state of anxiety."

A PROTECTIVE CHARM [AGAINST WIZARDS], LINES 447–480

"The wizards will not yet bewitch us,   wizards not bewitch, seers not
  prophesy
my dying on these tracks,   my succumbing on this journey,
passing on while young,   falling dead while ruddy-cheeked.
Whomever the wizards may bewitch,   whose future soever the seers may see,
may that person reach his home,   get to his cottage.
Let them bewitch themselves,   enchant their children,
slay their clan,   defame their tribe.
Formerly my father did not,   my esteemed parent not
take notice of a wizard's desire   nor did he reward a Lapp.
Thus my father said,   thus I myself say:
'Protect me, steadfast Creator,   guard me, gracious God,
help me with your loving hand,   with your mighty power
against the designs of men,   the schemes of women,
the words of the bearded,   the words of the beardless.
Be a constant aid,   a steadfast watchman
so that no child may depart,   no mother's offspring stray,
from the track created by the Creator,   made by God.'"

Then reckless Lemminkäinen,   that handsome man with a far-roving mind,
from out of his anxieties fashioned horses,   from his sorrows black geldings,
from evil days bridles,   from acts of treachery saddles.
He leaped on the back of the good horse,   on the haunches of the good
  horse with a blaze;
he rumbled along with his companion Snowfoot.   He rattled along the
  shores,
riding easily along the sandy beaches to his dear mother's,   to his esteemed
  parent's.

Then for a long time I will leave   my man with a far-roving mind out of
  my song,
sending Snowfoot on his way   to proceed to his home.
I myself will rattle off my song,   put it on another tack.

POEM 31

Untamo stirs up strife against his brother Kalervo,
slays Kalervo and his troop
so that only one pregnant woman survives out of the whole clan;
he takes the woman with him
and to her is born a son, Kullervo, at Untamo's farm (1–82).
While still in the cradle Kullervo plans vengeance on Untamo
and Untamo tries in many ways to kill him; he does not kill him (83–202).
When he grew bigger Kullervo botches all his work
and in his distress Untamo sells him to Ilmarinen as a slave (203–374).

A mother reared her chicks,   a big brood of swans.
She placed the chicks by a hedge;   she led the cygnets to a river.
An eagle came and picked them up;   a hawk came and scattered them;
a winged bird thus dispersed them: it carried one right to Karelia,
the second it took to Russia,   the third it left at home.
The one it carried to Russia,   from that a merchant grew up;
from the one it carried to Karelia,   from that one Kalervo grew up;
the one it left at home,   that one begot Untamo
to become his father's misfortune,   his mother's distress.

Untamo laid fish traps   in Kalervo's fishing waters;
Kalervo took a look at the traps,   gathered up the fish in his creel.
Untamo, energetic man,   he was the one who got angry and mad.
He waged war merely by gestures with his fingers,   with only his knuckles
    carried on lawsuits,
raised a row over the fish offal,   made an issue over the perch fry.
They quarrel, they fight;   neither defeats the other;
whichever struck the other,   he himself got it back.
Again another time later,   after two, three days,
Kalervo was sowing oats   back of Untamo's house.
A bold ewe from Untamo's farm   ate the oats Kalervo had sown;
Kalervo's fierce dog   ripped up the ewe from Untamo's farm.

Untamo threatens   his brother Kalervo,
threatens to kill Kalervo's clan,   to strike down the grownups, strike down
    the children,
to beat up the whole crowd,   to burn the buildings to ashes.
He got together men with sword in belt,   people with weapon in hand,
little boys with spikes in their belts,   lovely girls with billhooks on their
    shoulders;

he set out for a big fight   against his own brother.
Kalervo's fair daughter-in-law   was sitting by a window.
She looked out of the window,   uttered a word, spoke thus:
"Is that dense smoke   or is it a dark cloud
at the end of those fields,   at the far end of the new cattle shed?"
It was not a misty mist   nor indeed a dense smoke;
these were Untamo's men   getting ready to come to battle.
Untamo's men came on,   men came with sword in belt.
They laid low Kalervo's troop,   killed the great clan,
burned the house to ashes,   leveled it to a trampled-down field.
One virgin of Kalervo survived,   she with a heavy belly.
Her Untamo's men   took home with them
to clean the little cabin,   to sweep the floor.
A short time passed;   a little boy-child was born
to the luckless mother.   What will one name him?
The mother called him Kullervo,   Untamo called him "War-Hero."
They put the little boy,   fixed up the orphan child
in a cradle to rock,   in a swinging cradle to swing.
The child rocked in the swinging cradle,   the child rocked, his hair fluttered.
He rocked one day, rocked a second;   it was already right on the third day
when the boy began to kick;   he kicked, he struggled,
he tore off his swaddling band,   got rid of his covers,
smashed the lindenwood cradle,   tore his whole diaper to ribbons.
It was foretold that he would turn out well,   one foresaw that he would
    be competent.
The people at Untamo's farm expect   him to grow up,
to attain discretion, to become a man,   to get to be right manly,
to get to be worth hundreds of slaves,   to grow to be worth thousands.
He grew for two, three months.   Already in the third month the knee-high
    boy began to reflect:
"If I should get bigger,   become sturdier of body,
I would avenge the blows my father received,   repay my mother's tears."

Untamo came to hear this;   he uttered these words:
"My clan will get its death from him,   a Kalervo will grow up from him."
The men ponder,   all the women reflect,
where one may put the boy,   where bring about his death.
They put him in a keg,   thrust him into a cask;
then they take him to the water,   lower him into the billows.
At the end of two, three nights   they go to see
if he has drowned in the water,   if the boy has died in the keg.
He has not drowned in the water,   the boy not died in the keg.
The boy had got out of the keg.   He was sitting on the surface of the waves
with a copper fishing pole in his hand,   a silken line at the end of it;

he is angling for sea fish, measuring the water of the "sea":
if there is as much as two ladlefuls there is quite a lot of water in the "sea";
should one measure it exactly there would be part of a third ladle!
Untamo reflects: "Where may one put the boy,
where may one destroy him, with what bring about his death?"
He ordered his slave to collect birch trees, hardwood trees,
tall bushy evergreens, reliable resinous trees
to burn the same boy up, to kill Kullervo.
They got together, gathered birches, hardwood trees,
tall bushy evergreens, reliable resinous trees,
a thousand sledloads of birchbark, a hundred cords of rowan.
They set fire to the trees, kindled a blazing pile of wood,
threw the boy into it, in the midst of the burning fire.
It burned one day, then a second, burned even a third day.
They went to take a look: the boy was knee-deep in the ashes,
in fluffy ashes up to his elbow with a charcoal rake in his hand
with which he is stirring the fire, pulling the coals together
without losing a single hair, without ruffling a lock!

Untamo is angry: "Where may one put the boy,
where may one destroy him, bring about his death?"
They hang the boy on a tree, string him up on an oak.
Two, three nights passed, as many days.
Untamo reflects: "It is time to go and see
whether Kullervo perished, whether the boy died on the tree."
He got the slave to look. The slave brought back the word:
"Kullervo has not perished, the boy not died on the tree;
the boy is decorating the tree with a little nail in his hand.
The whole tree is full of pictures, the oak covered with designs:
on it are men, on it swords, on it spears at the side."
What on earth availed Untamo with that wretched boy!
However he arranged for his demise, however he planned his death,
the boy did not land in the jaws of death nor die in any way at all.

One must finally get tired of planning his death,
of bringing up Kullervo, the slave as one's own son.
Untamo says his say, spoke and said thus:
"If you will behave nicely, always act properly,
you can stay on at this farm, perform the tasks of a slave.
The pay will be established afterward, determined according to your work:
a fine belt for your waist or a box on the ear."

When Kullervo had grown taller, had gained a span in stature,
he was put to work, got ready for the job

of looking after a little child, his fingers put to rocking a little one.
"Look after the child nicely, feed the child, eat yourself.
Rinse the diapers in the stream, wash the little clothes."
He looked after the child for one day, for two: he broke off a hand, gouged
  out an eye.
Then right on the third day he killed the child with magic diseases,
threw the diapers for the stream to carry away, burned the swinging cradle
  in the fire.
Untamo reflects: "He is not fit
to look after a little child, his fingers not fit to rock a little one.
I do not know what to apply him to, to what work I should put him.
Shall I set him to felling a clearing?" He set him to felling a clearing.
Kullervo, son of Kalervo, then said these words:
"I will be a man just as soon as I get an ax in my hand,
be much better-looking, nicer than I was before.
I will be a man the equal of five, a fellow the match of six."
He went to the smithy at the smith's place, uttered a word, spoke thus:
"O smith, my dear friend, forge me an ax,
forge an ax suitable for a man, a bit fit for a laborer.
I am setting forth to fell a clearing, to drop a straight slender birch."
The smith forges what is called for, quickly fashions an axhead.
The axhead was suitable for a man, the bit fit for a laborer.

Kullervo, son of Kalervo, then sharpened his ax,
sharpens his ax in the daytime, makes a handle in the evening.
To fell the clearing he set forth to a tall backwoods forest,
to a very fine stand of slender trees, to a dreadful stand of timber pine.
He struck a tree with the ax, broke it off with the even-bladed ax;
good timber trees go with one blow, poor ones with half a blow.
In a rage he felled five trees, eight trees in all.
Then he uttered these words, spoke and said thus:
"Let the Devil do the work, let the Demon fell the big trunks!"
He jumped up on top of a stump, shouted long and loud,
whistled, let out a shrill cry.

[AN ANTIFERTILITY CHARM, LINES 279-294]
He uttered a word, spoke thus:
"May the clearing fall to the ground, the slender birch be broken off
as far as my voice is heard, as my whistle reaches.
Let no shoot spring up, no blade of grass ever rise,
never, never at all while the moon shines gold-bright,
in the clearing of Kalervo's son, in the fine man's new-cleared land.
Should the land start to sprout, a young crop to spring up
and a blade of grain to grow or a stalk to shoot up,
may it form no head, the stalk produce no ear."

Untamo, the bold man,   went to view
the clearing of Kalervo's son,   the place cut by the new slave;
the clearing does not seem like a clearing,   not like a place cut by a young
   man.
Untamo reflects: "He is not fitted for that;
he spoiled a good stand of timber,   felled a good stand of lumber pine. '
I do not know what I should apply him to,   to what work I should put him.
Shall I put him to making a fence?"   He put him to making a fence.
Kullervo, son of Kalervo,   now makes a fence.
He places big pines as palings just as they were,   whole tall firs he sets up
   as posts;
he pulled withes good and hard   from the tallest rowans,
made a fence without an opening,   made it quickly without a gate.
Then he uttered these words,   spoke and said this:
"Whoever does not rise aloft like a bird,   not fly along with two wings,
let him not get over   the fence of Kalervo's son."

Untamo chances   to come to view
that fence of Kalervo's son,   the slash felled by the war slave.
He saw a fence without an opening,   without a chink, without a slit,
a fence which was built up from the ground,   constructed up to the clouds.
He uttered a word, spoke thus: "He is not fitted for this;
he made a fence without an opening,   built it without a gate;
he raised it up to the heavens,   raised it up to the clouds.
I cannot get over it   or inside it through a chink.
I do not know what to apply him to,   to what work I should put him.
Shall I put him to threshing rye?"   He put him to threshing rye.
Kullervo, son of Kalervo,   was now threshing rye.
He threshed the rye to husks,   reduced the straw to chaff.
The master came there,   went himself to look
at the threshing of Kalervo's son,   at Kullervo's flailing.
The rye is like husks,   the straw rustled like chaff.

Untamo grew angry: "There is nothing to be got from this laborer;
to whatever work I put him   he bungles his work stupidly.
Shall I take him to Russia   or sell him to Karelia
to craftsman Ilmarinen,   to pound the craftsman's sledge hammer?"
Then he sold Kalervo's son,   made the sale to Karelia
to craftsman Ilmarinen,   to the skilled smith.
What did the craftsman give for him?   The craftsman gave a lot for him—
two battered old kettles,   three bits of a hook,
five beat-up sickles,   the wrecks of six grub hoes
for the worthless man,   for the good-for-nothing slave.

POEM 32

*Ilmarinen's lady sets Kullervo to herding
and roguishly bakes a stone in his little luncheon loaf (1–32).
The mistress sends the cattle forth to the recitation
of the usual cattle and bear charms (33–548).*

Kullervo, son of Kalervo,   blue-stockinged son of an old man,
with yellow locks, handsome,   with shoes with fine uppers,
as soon as he is in the craftsman's house   that evening asked for work,
asked the master in the evening,   the mistress in the morning:
"Name the jobs here,   give the job a name,
tell me to what work I am to be put,   for what labor I am to prepare
   myself."

Craftsman Ilmarinen's lady   then thinks over
to what work the new slave,   to what labor the hired man can be put.
She made the slave a herdsman,   a tender of big cattle.
That roguish mistress,   the craftsman's wry-faced lady,
baked a loaf for the herdsman,   bakes a fat little loaf,
oaten at the bottom, wheaten at the top;   in the middle she works in a
   stone.
She spread the little loaf with melted butter,   prepared the crust with
   drippings,
gave it to the slave as his share,   to the herdsman as a snack.
She instructed the slave,   uttered a word, spoke thus:
"Do not eat this before   the cattle have gone to the forest."

Then Ilmarinen's lady   dispatched the cattle to pasture.
She utters these words,   recited this charm:

CATTLE CHARMS, LINES 33–314

"I am sending my cows to the grove,   the givers of milk to the clearing,
the longhorns to the aspen grove,   the crumpled horns to the birch grove.
I am driving them out to put on fat,   to acquire suet
in the open clearings,   in the extensive leafy woods,
in the high birch groves,   in the low aspen groves,
in the golden fir groves,   in the silver wildernesses.
Watch over them, gracious God,   guard them, steadfast Creator;
keep them out of harm's way,   protect them from all evils
that they may not get into trouble,   not come to grief.

As you watched them when under a shed,   as you kept them in your
   protection,
so watch them when they have no shed,   take care of them when they are
   without a caretaker,
that the cattle may get fine looking,   the mistress' cattle flourish
according to the idea of a well-disposed person,   not the idea of one
   ill-disposed.

"Should my herdsmen be no good,   the herdswomen, too, bad,
make a willow the herdsman,   an alder the one to watch over the cow,
a rowan the caretaker,   a chokecherry the one to bring them home
without the mistress' searching for them,   without being a worry to other
   people.
If the willow will not tend them,   the rowan not look after them well,
the alder not drive the cattle,   the chokecherry not bring them home,
then send your favorites,   send Nature's daughters
to care for my cattle,   to look after all the cattle.
You have a lot of serving maids,   hundreds who obey your orders,
hundreds living under the heavens,   good Spirits of Nature.

"Summer Spirit, fine woman,   South Wind Spirit, maiden of Nature,
Evergreen Spirit, good mistress,   Juniper Spirit, fair maiden,
Rowan Spirit, little serving maid,   Chokecherry Spirit, Tapio's daughter,
Darling, daughter-in-law of the forest,   Tellervo, Tapio's maid!
May you look after my cattle,   tend my cattle nicely
all summer,   in the growing season
while leaf is fluttering on tree,   grass growing luxuriantly on the earth.
Summer Spirit, fine woman,   Southwind Spirit, maiden of Nature!
Throw down your fine shirts,   spread out your aprons
as a covering for my cattle,   as a cover for my little ones,
and do not let the wind blow hard,   not let it rain hard.

"Guard my cattle from evils,   keep them out of harm's way,
from those quoggy bogs,   from quaking springs,
shaking quagmires,   round pools,
that they may not get into trouble,   not come to grief,
no hoof stumble into a bog,   slip into a quagmire
against God's knowledge,   contrary to His blissful intent.

"Bring a horn from farther off,   from yonder heavenly pole,
a honey-toned horn from the heavens,   sweet-toned horn from mother earth.
Blow into that horn of yours,   boom into your splendid one.
Blow knolls into bloom,   the borders of heaths beautiful,
the borders of clearings lovely,   the borders of groves charming,

the borders of fens into lovely honey,   the borders of springs into wort.
Then feed my cattle,   fodder my cattle,
keep feeding them honeyed food,   keep watering them with honeyed drinks.
Feed them lovely greensward,   fair tassels of grass
from wheyey quagmires,   from plashing springs,
from roaring rapids,   rushing rivers,
from golden knolls,   from silvery clearings."

MILK CHARMS, LINES 141–228

"Make a lovely well   on two sides of the cattle grounds
from which the cattle may drink water,   may drink deep of mead
into the brimful udders,   their aching teats.
The ducts in the teats would get to moving,   rivers of milk to flow,
brooks of milk to discharge,   rapids of milk to foam,
the milk pipes to spout,   the milk tubes to exude,
to give milk every time,   to leak down every time
over a hostile-minded person,   along the fingers of an ill-disposed person
so that he does not take the milk to the devil,   so that the cow's gift does
    not get lost.
There are many of those people, and bad ones,   who take the milk to hell,
make the cow's gift get lost,   take the cow's product elsewhere.
There are a few people, and good ones,   who get their milk from hell,
their buttermilk in spite of neighborhood obstruction,   their fresh milk
    from elsewhere.

"In days gone by my mother   did not seek advice from neighbors,
know-how from another farm;   she got her milk from hell,
her buttermilk in spite of an obstructor,   her fresh milk from somewhere else.
She made it come from over yonder,   made it arrive from farther away,
the milk come from Death's Domain,   from the Abode of the Dead, from
    under the earth,
made it come at night of itself,   secretly in the dark
without a bad person's hearing,   without a malevolent person's finding out,
without an ill-disposed person's spilling it,   without an envious person's
    begrudging it.

"So my mother said,   so I myself say:
'Where did the cow's yield get detained,   where did my milk vanish to?
Was it taken to an outsider,   chained up in neighboring farmyards,
chained to the breasts of community whores,   under the arms of envious
    people?
Or has it got caught in among the trees,   got into trouble in the forests,
spread out about in the leafy woodlands,   vanished into the heaths?
One cannot let milk get to hell,   the cow's yield to an outsider,

to the breasts of community whores,   under the arms of envious people
or get caught in among the trees,   get into trouble in the forests,
spread about in groves,   spilled onto the heath.
The milk is needed at home,   is required all the time;
at home the mistress is waiting   with a juniperwood milk pail in her hand.'

"Summer Spirit, splendid woman,   Southwind Spirit, Nature's daughter,
go now, feed my Eater,   also water my Drinker,
milk Stringy,   increase Freshness' milk,
grant Sweetie milk,   fresh milk to Apple
from the bright tips of grass,   from the lovely dewy herbage,
from the lovely soil,   from the honeyed tussocks,
from honey-yielding grass,   from land with berrystalks,
from the spirits of the heather blooms,   from the spirits of hay chaff,
from the spirits of the clotted cream of the clouds,   from the spirits of the
    heavenly pole,
to provide milk-filled udders,   udders ever full
for a short woman to milk,   for a little maid to press.

"Rise, maiden, from the swale,   in your soft dress from the quagmire,
warm maiden, from the spring,   beautiful one from the ooze!
Take water from the spring   with which you will wet down my cattle
so that he cattle may become lovely-looking,   the mistress' cattle better-
    looking
before the arrival of the mistress,   before the inspection by the herdswoman,
by the incompetent mistress,   the all too timid herdswoman.

"Darling, mistress of the forest,   liberal-handed guardian of cattle,
send the tallest of your maidservants,   the best of your hired girls,
to tend my cattle,   to look out for my cattle
during this lovely summer,   warm summer of the Creator,
vouchsafed by God,   granted by the Gracious One.

"Tellervo, Tapio's maid,   dumpy maid of the forest
in a gauzy shirt, a soft skirt,   with yellow hair, pretty one,
you who are the guardian of cattle,   tender the mistress's livestock
in pleasant Woodland,   among the keen-eyed folk of Tapio's Domain!
Protect the livestock well,   tend the cattle watchfully.
Protect them with your lovely hands,   guide them with your pretty fingers,
curry them sleek as a lynx,   comb them as glossy as fish fins,
like a mermaid's hair,   like the soft fleece of a forest ewe.
When evening comes, when night grows dark,   when the dusk of twilight
    comes,
get the cattle home   to in front of the good mistress

with plashing spring water on their backs,   a pond of milk on their hind-
  quarters."

CHARMS FOR GETTING CATTLE HOME, LINES 273–314

"When the sun is going to its dwelling,   while the bird of the evening is singing,
say to my cattle,   speak to my file of horned cattle:
'Home, crumpled-horns!   Givers of milk of your dwelling!
It is good for you to be home,   pleasant to lie down on the ground;
the backwoods are gloomy for you to walk in,   the shore a bad place for you
  to go bellowing on.
So that you will come home   the women will make a fire
on a honeyed meadow,   on ground covered with berrystalks.'

"Nyyrikki, son of Tapio,   blue-coated boy of the thicket!
Set up tall firs with their butts,   bushy evergreens with their crowns
as a corduroy road over muddy places,   as fill on bad ground,
in watery fens, on wet spots of land,   on quivering pools.
Let crumpled-horn go,   cloven-hoof step along,
get to each smudge fire   unharmed, in good condition
without falling into the fen,   without getting crowded into the muck.

"If the cattle do not heed that,   if they do not walk home at night,
Rowan Spirit, little maid,   Juniper Spirit, fair girl,
cut a birch switch from a grove,   take a twig from a thicket,
fetch a rowan switch,   a juniper cattle whip
from behind Tapio's fine house,   from that side of Chokecherry Hill.
Drive the cattle to the farmstead   at the time of warming up the sauna,
drive the farm animals home,   the forest animals to Woodland."

ADMONITORY CHARMS AGAINST BEARS, LINES 315–542

"Bear, apple of the forest,   honey-paws with arched back,
let us make nice compacts,   let us conclude boundary treaties
forever, for always,   for as long as we live, for all our days,
so that you will not violate a cloven-hoofed shank,   fell a bearer of milk
this whole fine summer,   during the Creator's warm summer.
When you hear the sound of a bell   or the tooting of a horn,
throw yourself down on a tussock,   take a nap on the grass.
Push your ears into the ground,   press your head into a tussock!
Or try to get to the backwoods,   get into your mossy dwelling,
go to other hills,   get back quickly to other knolls,
so that you will not hear the cowbell   or the herdsman's chatter.
My bear, my dear one,   honey-paws, my lovely one!

I do not forbid your wandering about   nor do I deny walking about;
I forbid a tongue to touch,   an ugly mouth to lay hold,
any tearing apart with teeth,   any mauling with paws.
Go skirt the cattle lands,   hurrying by clotted-cream-yielding heaths,
circle the tinkle of bells,   flee a herdsman's voice.

"When the cattle are on the heath,   you tramp off to the fen;
when the cattle are slipping along to the fen,   then you make for the back-
    woods.
When the cattle are walking on a hill,   you walk below the hill;
when the cattle are walking below a hill,   you go along the hill.
When they are walking in a clearing,   you walk in a thicket;
when they are walking in a thicket,   you walk in a clearing.
Walk like a golden cuckoo,   like a silver wood pigeon;
move by like a whitefish,   idle along like a fish of the water;
walk like a tuft of wool,   go like a bunch of flax.

"Sheathe your claws in your fur,   your teeth in your gums
so that the cattle may not be scared,   the small neat not be frightened.
Leave the cattle in peace,   come to terms with the cloven-hoofs;
let the cattle walk about nicely,   step along prettily
across fens, across the countryside,   through backwoods heaths
so that you never touch them at all,   not lay hold of them in the least like a
    glutton.

"Remember your oath of long ago   by that river of Death's Domain,
by the powerful Claw Rapids,   before the Creator's knees.
You were given leave   three times a summer
to go within earshot of a bell,   to districts where little bells tinkle;
you were not, on the contrary, permitted   or given leave
to enter upon evil deeds,   be led into something shameful.
Should a fit of rage come upon you,   your teeth be seized with longing,
throw your rage into a thicket,   your evil desires in among tall evergreen trees.
Hew down a rotten tree,   fell a dry birch,
turn to pine trunks that have rotted in the water,   root up berry tussocks.
When the need for food comes,   when you desire to eat,
eat forest mushrooms,   open up ant hills,
root up red angelica,   woodland's sweet tidbits,
not my fodder grass,   my life-giving hay.
Woodland's honeyed trough   is fermenting at a boil
on a golden knoll,   on a silver rise.
In that is something for a glutton to eat,   for a man craving a drink;
nor in eating will the food run short,   in drinking the drinks grow less.

Thus we make everlasting compacts,   conclude everlasting treaties
to live pleasantly,   nicely all summer;
we have land in common,   separate provisions.

"If, on the contrary, you may want to fight,   to live on a war footing,
let us fight in the wintertime,   have a row when it is snowy.
When summer comes, when the fen thaws,   the pools warm up,
do not come here   within earshot of the golden cattle.
If you come to these parts,   should you get to these backwoods,
here they will always shoot you.   If the bowmen are not at home,
we have competent women,   ever-present housewives
who will spoil your trip,   ruin your journey,
so that you will never touch them at all,   not lay hold of them in the least
   like a glutton
against God's will,   contrary to the Blissful One's intent.
O Ukko, god on high!   If you hear him truly coming,
change my cows into other things,   strike my cattle with a bang,
change my own cattle to stones,   my lovely ones to stumps
while the strange creature is roving the countryside,   the husky fellow roam-
   ing about.

"If I were a bear,   were going about as a honey-paws,
I would never live   where there were women about.
There is land elsewhere,   a corral farther back
for one unoccupied to run about in,   for one unemployed to rush about in,
for the tips of your paws to go through,   your fat calves to go across,
within the hazy-blue wilderness,   in a bend in a lovely backwoods.
There is a piny heath for you to walk on,   sand for you to step lightly on;
a trail has been made for you to walk on,   a lake shore for you to run on
to way back up north,   to the open country of Lapland.
It will be lucky for you to be there,   pleasant to pass your time there,
in summer to walk without shoes,   in the autumn without short socks
on the great big surfaces of a fen,   on broad grassy marshy lands.
If you do not actually go there,   are not rightly able to,
run off on a trip,   step along the path
off there to the wilderness of Death's Domain   or to the Grave Spirit's heath.
There is a fen there to step along,   a heath to walk on;
Brindle is there, Brandle there,   other young bullocks are there
in iron chains,   in ten stanchions.
There the lean ones take on flesh,   even the bones get meaty.

"Be appeased, grove, be favorable, backwoods,   be gentle, hazy-blue wilderness!

Grant peace to the cattle,   amity to the cloven-hoofs
this whole fine summer,   the Lord's hot summer.

"Kuippana, king of the forest,   gray-bearded nimble fellow of the forest!
Call off your dogs,   get rid of your curs!
Stick a mushroom in one nostril,   in the other an apple
so that it will not smell the breath,   sniff the scent of cattle.
Bind its eyes with silk,   wrap its ears with a bandage
so that it will not hear the cattle walking,   not see them moving.
If this may not be enough,   if he is not yet particularly heedful,
order your boy away,   stop your bastard.
Lead him out of these wildernesses,   drive him from these shores,
from confined cattle lands,   from broad meadow-sides.
Hide your dog in a hole,   make your cur fast
in golden chains,   in silver thongs,
so that he may do no damage,   not be misled into something shameful.
If this may not be enough,   if he is not heedful of this,
Ukko, golden king,   silver ruler,
hear my golden words,   my gracious utterance.
Press a rowan muzzle   around the stubby nose;
if the rowan withe does not hold,   then cast one of copper;
if the copper one is not firm,   make an iron muzzle.
If, however, he breaks the iron one,   if he still does wrong,
drive a golden cowlstaff   from jawbone to jawbone,
clinch the ends fast,   fasten them very firmly
so that the bad jaws will not move,   the sparse teeth not part from one an-
    other
unless one rips them open with iron tools,   jerks them apart with steel tools,
gashes with knives,   tears them loose with an ax."

Then Ilmarinen's lady,   the niggardly wife of the craftsman,
sent the cows from the cow house,   sent them off to the cattle pasture,
put the herdsman in the rear,   set the slave to driving the cows.

POEM 33

While tending herd, Kullervo in the afternoon takes the loaf from his rucksack,
begins to cut it, and ruins his knife;
this hurts him more painfully
because the knife is the only memento left from his family (1–98).
He plans to take revenge on the mistress,
drives the cattle into a fen, gathers together a pack of wolves and bears,
which he drives home in the evening (99–184).
While going to milk,
the mistress gets torn to pieces by the wild beasts and is killed (185–296).

Kullervo, son of Kalervo,   put the provisions in his rucksack,
drove the cows along a fen,   trudged up the moor.
He uttered a word as he went along,   kept saying as he was walking:
"Woe is me, poor lad,   woe the unfortunate lad!
Now I have got into something,   have got into the futile occupation
of being herder of a steer's tail,   a tender of calves,
a treader of every fen,   a creeper on bad earth."

He sat down on the ground on a tussock,   reached a sunny slope.
There he said while singing his lays,   spoke thus while singing magic songs:
"Shine, God's sun,   disk of the Lord, shine warm
on the tender of the craftsman's cattle,   on the wretched herdsman,
not in Ilmarinen's buildings,   least of all on his lady!
The mistress lives well,   cuts pieces of wheaten bread,
gobbles up meat pasties,   slices butter and puts it on top;
the wretched herdsman crunches a dry loaf,   a dry crust,
digs into oaten bread,   cuts chaffy bread,
straightens out a piece of straw bread,   gnaws pinebark bread,
gulps down water from a birchbark scoop   from the tip of a wet hummock.
Go, sun, get on, precious thing,   set, God's timepiece!
Go, sun, to the fir grove,   get on, precious thing, to the thicket,
hurry to the juniper grove,   speed to the level of the alders!
Free the herdsman to go home   to take a cut at a dish of butter,
to break off some unleavened bread,   to dig into barley cakes!"

Then, while the herdsman was caroling,   while Kulervo was singing,
Ilmarinen's lady   had now taken a cut at her dish of butter,
had broken off her unleavened bread,   had dug into her barley cakes;
she cooked a watery gruel,   cold cabbage for Kullervo,

from which the mongrel had eaten the fat, Blackie enjoyed a morning meal,
Spots eaten to his heart's content, Brownie bitten off what he wanted.

A bird sang in a grove, a little bird in a hedge:
"Now would be the time for the slave to eat, for the fatherless man to have
  his afternoon meal."
Kullervo, son of Kalervo, looked at the sun high in the sky;
he uttered these words: "Now it is time to eat,
time to start on the food, to look for provisions."
He drove his cows to rest, the cattle to the heath to lie down;
he sat down on a tussock, on the green turf.
He took his rucksack from his back, took the loaf from his rucksack,
looks at it, turns it over; then he uttered these words:
"Many a loaf looks fair on top, the crust very smooth,
inside, on the contrary, it is chaffy bread, under the crust are husks."
He drew his knife from the sheath in order to cut the loaf;
the knife turned on the stone, struck hard on the rock;
the blade came loose from the knife, the blade broke off the sheath knife.
Kullervo, son of Kalervo, looked at his knife,
began to weep, uttered a word, spoke thus:
"The knife was my only brother, the blade my only love,
an object got by my father, obtained by my parent.
I broke it on a stone, struck it hard on a rock,
on the loaf of the bad mistress, on what the bad woman baked.
With what shall I now pay back the woman's mockery, the woman's mockery, the girl's derision,
the wretched woman's food, the baking of the bad whore?"

A crow cawed from a thicket, a crow cawed, a raven croaked:
"O you poor gold buckle, only son of Kalervo!
Why are you depressed of mind, sad of heart?
Take a switch from a thicket, a birch switch from a backwoods dell;
drive the mucky-thighed cattle to the fen, scatter the cows in the mire,
half for big wolves, the other half for backwoods bears.
Round up the wolves, all the bears into a pack.
Change the wolves to a Teenie, transform the bears quickly into a Back-
  stripe;
drive them home in the form of cattle, as brindled cattle to the farmstead.
With that you will pay back the woman's mockery, the bad woman's abuse."
Kullervo, son of Kalervo, uttered these words:
"Wait, wait, demon's whore! If I am bewailing my father's knife,
you yourself, too, may yet bewail, bewail your milchcows."
He took a switch from a thicket, a juniper cattle switch;

he knocked the cows down into the fen,   crowded the steers into a windfall,
half for wolves to eat,   half for backwoods bears.
The wolves he enchanted into cows,   the bears he made into cattle;
one he changed into a Teenie,   the other he fashioned into a Backstripe.
The sun glided toward the southwest,   it turned to late afternoon;
it went to the level of the fir grove,   sped on to milking time.
That poor wretch of a herdsman,   Kullervo, Kalervo's son,
drove the bears home,   the wolf cattle to the farmstead.
He further counseled his bears,   spoke to his wolves:
"Tear off the mistress' thigh,   bite half her calf
when she comes to inspect,   squats down to milk."
He made a horn from the bones of cow,   a clear-toned one from a steer's
horn,
a horn from Chokecherry's leg,   a pipe from Beauty's shankbone.
He gave a blast on his horn,   gave a toot on his horn,
three times outside near the house,   six times at the entrance to the hedge-
lined lanes.

Ilmarinen's lady,   the craftsman's mistress, fine-featured woman
waits a long time without milk,   lolls about without summer butter.
She heard playing from the fen,   a sudden echo from the heath.
She speaks these words,   made this remark:
"Thanks be, O God!   A horn is ringing out, the cattle are coming.
Where did the slave get the horn,   the laborer find a horn
since he comes playing,   tooting along?
He is blasting through my ears,   hurting my head."
Kullervo, son of Kalervo,   uttered a word, spoke thus:
"The slave got the horn from the fen,   brought the horn from the bog.
Now your cattle are already in the lane,   the cows at the head of the cow-
shed field;
get the smudge ready,   go milk the cows."
Craftsman Ilmarinen's lady   ordered an old woman to milk:
"Go, old woman, and milk;   fix up the cattle.
I myself cannot take time   from kneading the dough."
Kullervo, son of Kalervo,   uttered a word, spoke thus:
"Good mistresses,   competent housewives,
formerly always milked the cows themselves,   tended the cattle themselves."
Then Ilmarinen's lady   went to prepare the smudge,
goes then to the milking.   She took one look at her cattle,
eyed the animals,   uttered a word, spoke thus:
"The cattle are fine-looking,   the animals sleek-coated,
all sleek as lynxskin,   like the fluffy down of a forest ewe,
all with heavy udders,   with aching teats."
She stooped to milk,   squatted down to strip a cow;

she gave one pull, then a second, at once tried a third time.
A wolf made a rush at her, a bear hurries to claw her;
a wolf tears her mouth, a bear tugged at her hamstrings,
bit half of her calf, bit off the heel of her shank.

In this way Kullervo, son of Kalervo, took revenge on the girl's ridicule,
the girl's ridicule, the woman's derision, paid the bad wife her wages.

Ilmarinen's stately lady began to weep,
uttered a word, spoke thus: "You acted badly, wretched herdsman!
You drove bears home, wolves to the big farmyard."
To this Kullervo, son of Kalervo, replied:
"I, wretched herdsman, acted badly; you did not act nicely, wretched mis-
tress!
You baked a stony loaf, baked a rock bun;
I struck my knife on the stone, struck it hard on the rock—
the only knife of my father, only sheath knife of my clan!"
Ilmarinen's lady spoke: "O you herdsman, dear herdsman!
Reverse your spell, sing your enchantment backwards;
free me from the wolf's jaws, loose me from the bear's claw!
I will deck you out in shirts, make you fine linen pants,
feed you with butter, with wheaten bread, give you sweet milk to drink,
feed you one year without your laboring, a second without forcing you to
work.
If you do not hurry to free me, not go quickly and release me,
I will soon drop dead, will turn to dust."

Kullervo, son of Kalervo, uttered a word, spoke thus:
"If you happen to die, just die! Vanish if you happen to vanish!
There is a place for the departed in the ground, in the grave for the
deceased,
a place for the mightiest to lie in, for the haughtiest to rest in."

Ilmarinen's lady said: "O Ukko, god on high,
prepare quickly your great crossbow, pick out your best bow;
put a copper bolt in that hard-hitting bow.
Drive a hard-hitting arrow, shoot a copper bolt,
shoot it through his armpits, through his shoulder muscles.
Lay low that son of Kalervo, shoot the wretched fellow dead
with a steel-tipped arrow, with a copper bolt!"
Kullervo, son of Kalervo, uttered these words:
"O Ukko, god on high, don't you shoot me,
shoot Ilmarinen's lady, lay low the base woman
without her stirring from the spot, without her going anywhere else!"

239

Then Ilmarinen's lady,   that wife of the skilled smith,
at once fell over dead,   dropped down like soot from a kettle
in the farmyard of her own home,   in the little yard.
That was the death of the young woman,   of the beautiful mistress,
who long was waited for,   six years asked for
to be a lasting joy for Ilmarinen,   to be an honor to the famed craftsman.

POEM 34

Kullervo flees from Ilmarinen, goes about sadly in the backwoods,
and from the old woman of the thicket learns
that his father, mother, brother, and sister are still alive (1–128).
From the instructions of the old woman of the thicket
he finds them on the frontier of Lapland (129–188).
The mother tells how indeed she had thought
that Kullervo had already long since perished and also how
her elder daughter had vanished on a berrying expedition (189–246).

Kullervo, son of Kalervo,   blue-stockinged son of an old man,
with yellow locks, handsome,   with shoes with fine uppers,
set out to walk   from craftsman's Ilmarinen's
before the master should get word   of his wife's death,
should be weighed down in a gloomy state of mind,   should start a fight.
Playing his pipe he set out from the smith's,   making joyous sounds from the
    lands of Ilma Farm,
tootling on the heath,   making a noise on the clearing.
The fen resounded, the earth shook,   the heath echoed in response
to Kullervo's playing,   to the wicked fellow's music-making.

This was heard as far as the craftsman's smithy.   In the smithy the craftsman
    stopped,
went to the lane to listen,   to the farmyard to see
what the playing in the wilderness was,   the piping on the heath.
Now he saw the real facts,   unequivocal, firm;
he saw that the woman had passed on,   his lovely one had fallen over dead,
had fallen over in the farmyard,   had sunk down on the field.
At that the craftsman stopped short   with heavy heart.
He lay down for a night to weep,   for a week to shed tears.
His spirit was no better than pine tar,   his heart no whiter than charcoal.

Kullervo walked along,   stepped onward toward somewhere or other,
walked by day through dense wildernesses,   over the Demon's timbered
    heaths.
When evening came, when night grew dark,   he dropped to the ground on a
    tussock.
Then the orphan boy sits down,   the unhappy lad reflects:
"I wonder what created me, indeed,   who shaped wretched me,
me forever on the move,   forever under the open sky?
Others go to their homes,   journey to their cottages;

I have my home in the wilderness,   my farmstead on the heath,
my fireplace out in the wind,   the sauna steam out in the rain.
Do not, kind God,   ever, ever at all
create a child as a monster,   not so pitiful a one,
a fatherless one under the open sky,   never at all a motherless one
as you, God, created me,   shaped wretched me,
created me as if among seagulls,   created a seamew on a reef in the sea.
The sun shines on swallows,   gleams on sparrows,
the joy of the sky on birds,   on me never at all;
the sun never comes,   joy never comes at all.
I do not know who made me,   do not know who brought me forth.
Did a goldeneye perhaps make me for a roadside,   a mallard create me for a
   fen?
Did a teal forge me for the shore,   a merganzer for a hole in a rock?
When I was little I was left without a father,   when small without my
   mother.
Father died, mother died,   the rest of my big clan died;
they left me icy shoes,   forgot the slushy stockings,
left me to walk on icy trails,   left me on slippery footbridge logs
to sink into every fen,   to be pressed into the mud.
But I will never now,   never yet end up
as logs of a corduroy road for fens,   as planks for dirty wet places,
I will not sink into a fen   as long as I have two hands,
can stretch five fingers,   raise my ten fingers."

Now it occurred to him,   the thought took root in his mind
to go to Untamo's farm,   to avenge the blows received by his father,
his father's blows, his mother's tears,   his own ill-treatment.
He uttered a word, spoke thus: "Wait, wait, Untamo,
just be patient, death of my clan!   When I come to fight,
see if I do not reduce your buildings to ashes,   your farmstead to embers."
He came upon a woman,   a green-robed maid of the thicket;
she uttered these words,   spoke, said thus:
"Where are you setting out for, Kullervo,   trudging off to, son of Kalervo?
Kullervo, son of Kalervo,   uttered a word, spoke thus:
"It occurred to me,   the thought took root in my mind
to go yonder to another place,   to go to Untamo's farm
to avenge the death of my clan,   the blows suffered by my father, my mother's
   tears,
to burn the buildings to ashes,   to burn them to fluffy ashes."

The woman said in these words,   remarked, spoke thus:
"Your clan has not been killed,   Kalervo not yet fallen over dead.
You have a father alive,   a mother in this world hale and hearty."

"O my gracious woman, speak, my gracious woman!
Where indeed is my father, where the fair one who bore me?"
"Yonder indeed is your father, yonder the fair one who bore you,
on the vast frontier of Lapland beside a fishpond."
"O my gracious woman, say, my gracious woman,
how indeed I may get there, how I will know how to proceed?"
"It will be easy for you to get there, for you a stranger too, to reach the
place,
to go to the corner of a backwoods, to run along the bank of a river.
You walk one day, then a second, you at once walk a third day, too;
you will proceed northwest. You will come upon a hill;
walk along the foot of the hill, go by the left side of the hill.
From there a river will turn up on your right;
go along the side of the river past the foamy part of three rapids.
You will come to the tip of a headland, will get to the end of a long narrow
promontory.
There indeed your father is living, there the fair one who bore you,
there indeed your sisters, too, two beautiful daughters."

Kullervo, son of Kalervo, set out from there to walk.
He walked one day, then a second; he quickly walked a third, too,
he proceeded to the northwest. He came upon a hill;
he walked along the foot of it, along the left side of the hill.
Then he gets to the river; he walks along the side of the river,
the left bank of the river. He walked by three rapids,
came to the tip of the headland, got to the end of the long headland.
There was a house at the tip of the headland, a fishing hut at the end of the
narrow promontory.

Then he went into the house —no one in the house so much as knew him.
"Whence from beyond the water does the stranger come? Where is the
wanderer's home?"
"Do you not know your boy? Do you not know your own child
whom Untamo's men took home with them
when as big as the span of his father's fingers, as tall as his mother's distaff?"
The mother managed to say, the old woman to speak:
"O my poor boy, O wretched gold buckle!
To think that you alive have been traveling over these regions
while I was already lamenting you as dead, as already long since vanished!
I had two sons, two lovely daughters;
of them unfortunately the two eldest vanished,
a boy in a great war, a girl into the unknown.
My boy came back, the girl will probably not come at all."
Kullervo, son of Kalervo, managed to ask:

"Where did your daughter disappear to,   where did my sister go?"
The mother uttered these words,   spoke, said thus:
"My daughter disappeared over yonder,   your sister went yonder.
She set out to the forest for berries,   for raspberries at the foot of the hill;
the chick indeed vanished in that direction,   the bird died an unnatural death,
an unmentioned death   of name unknown.
Who missed the girl?   Who else if not her mother?
The mother was the first to search,   the mother to search, the mother to pine for her.
I set out, miserable mother,   to search for my girl.
I ran through the backwoods as a brown bear,   roamed the wilderness as an otter.
I searched one day, then a second,   searched a third day, too.
At the end of the third day,   at the very end of a week
I went up onto a big hill,   onto a high ridge;
there I cried out for my girl,   sorely grieved for the vanished one:
'Where are you, my little girl?   Come home now, my girl!'
That is how I shouted for my girl,   grieved for the vanished one.
The hills spoke in answer,   the heaths rang out:
'Do not cry out for your girl,   do not shout, do not halloo.
She can never, never,   never in her life return
to the farm of her mother of yore,   to her old father's landing place.' "

POEM 35

At his parents' Kullervo tries to do some jobs,
but when no help is to be got from him in these,
the father sends him to deliver the taxes (1–68).
On the return trip he meets, unknown to him, his sister, who has
lost her way when berrying, and he deceives and seduces her (69–188).
Later when it becomes quite clear who they are,
the sister runs and jumps into a river;
Kullervo hurries home, reports to his mother
the dreadful circumstance of his violation of his sister,
and then considers killing himself (189–344).
His mother forbids him and urges him
to calm his distress of mind in some hiding place.
Thereupon the idea enters Kullervo's head
before all else of going and taking vengeance on Untamo (345–372).

Kullervo, son of Kalervo,   blue-stockinged son of an old man,
was then able to live   sheltered by his parents;
he could not grasp things,   not acquire the mind of a man,
since he had been reared all wrong,   as a child rocked stupidly
in the home of an unkind upbringer,   of a stupid rocker.

The boy is put to work,   is got going on a job;
he trudged off to fish,   to row a big seine.
There he speaks thus,   oar in hand reflects:
"Shall I pull according to my strength,   row according to my energy,
or shall I pull according to the equipment,   row according to the need?"
The steersman from the stern spoke,   uttered a word, spoke thus:
"Even if you pull according to your strength,   row according to your energy,
you will probably not pull the vessel apart   nor the tholepins to pieces."
Kullervo, son of Kalervo,   pulled according to his strength,
rowed according to his energy;   he rowed the wooden tholepins apart,
broke the juniper ribs,   broke the aspenwood boat to pieces.

Kalervo went to look,   uttered a word, spoke thus:
"There is no rower to be got out of you!   You rowed the wooden tholepins
    apart,
broke the juniper ribs,   broke the whole craft.
Go beat fish into the seine;   perhaps you will be a better beater."
Kullervo, son of Kalervo,   went to beat fish into the seine.

There by the beating pole   he uttered a word, spoke thus:
"Shall I beat according to my strength,   strike according to my manly strength,
or strike according to the equipment,   beat according to the need?"
The man who was dragging the seine uttered a word: "What kind of beating is it then
if one does not beat according to one's strength,   strike according to one's manly strength?"
Kullervo, son of Kalervo,   beat according to his strength,
struck according to his manly strength;   he blended the water to gruel,
beat the seines to tow,   pounded the fish to pulp.

Kalervo came to look;   he uttered a word, spoke thus:
"There is no beater to be got out of you!   You beat the seine to tow,
smashed the net floats to rubbish,   broke the float cords to bits.
Set out to deliver the taxes,   to pay the ground rents.
Perhaps you will be better when traveling,   more competent on the road."
Kullervo, son of Kalervo,   blue-stockinged son of an old man,
with yellow locks, handsome,   with shoes with fine uppers,
set out to pay the taxes,   to pay the grain levy.
After he had delivered his tax assessment,   paid the grain levy,
he flings himself into his sled,   sits up in his basket sleigh.
He started to go home,   to travel to his own parts.
He rattles along,   covers ground
on those heaths of Väinämöinen,   on land cleared in days gone by.
He comes upon a girl;   the girl with golden hair is skiing along
on those heaths of Väinämöinen,   on land cleared in days gone by.
Kullervo, son of Kalervo,   now reins in the horse;
he began to address the girl,   to address her, to entice her:
"Get up into my sleigh, girl;   lie down on my fur robes in the back!"
There on her skis the girl says,   on her skis rejects him:
"Death to you in your sleigh,   a plague on your fur robes in behind!"

Kullervo, son of Kalervo,   blue-stockinged son of an old man,
hit the spirited steed with the whip,   made a ringing sound with the beaded lash.
The spirited steed raced, the journey sped on,   the road wound, the sled rattled along.
He rattled along,   covers ground
on the clear surface of the sea,   on the open expanse of the water.
He comes upon a girl;   the girl in shoes with fine uppers is walking along
on the clear surface of the sea,   on the open expanse of the water.
Kullervo, son of Kalervo,   reins in the horse,
gets ready to talk,   plans his speech:

"Come, pretty one, into the sleigh,   best girl in the land, come with me on
  my travels."
In reply the girl says,   the girl in shoes with fine uppers shouts out:
"Death to you in your sleigh!   May the man of the Abode of the Dead be
  with you on your travels!"

Kullervo, son of Kalervo,   blue-stockinged son of an old man,
hit the spirited steed with the whip,   made a ringing sound with the beaded
  lash.
The spirited steed raced, the journey sped on,   the sled rattled along, the way
  grew shorter.
He rumbles along,   covers ground
on those northern heaths,   on the broad marches of Lapland.
He comes upon a girl;   the girl with a tin ornament on her breast was speed-
  ing along
on those northern heaths,   on the broad marches of Lapland.
Kullervo, son of Kalervo,   reins in his horse,
gets ready to talk,   plans his speech:
"Come, girl, into my sled;   come, dear one, in under my woolen sleigh robe
to eat my apples,   to bite my hazelnuts."
In reply the girl says,   she with a tin ornament on her breast snaps out:
"I spit, wretch, on your little sled,   on your sled, good-for-nothing!
It is chill to be under the robe,   dismal to be in the sleigh."
Kullervo, son of Kalervo,   blue-stockinged son of an old man,
dragged the girl into his sleigh,   snatched her up into his sled,
put her in his fur robes,   threw her under the cover.
Then the girl speaks thus,   she with a tin ornament on her breast scolds:
"Let me out of here,   release the child to her own devices
so that I will not hear an evil person,   not serve a villain.
Otherwise I will kick out the bottom,   splinter your slats
splinter your sled to pieces,   your short-runnered work sled to bits."
Kullervo, son of Kalervo,   blue-stockinged son of an old man,
opened his treasure chest,   flung open the lid of many colors,
displayed his silver,   spread out articles of clothing,
gold-edged stockings,   silver-tipped belts.
The fabrics took the girl's fancy,   the money brought about a change in the
  girl,
the silver leads her astray,   the gold entices her.
Kullervo, son of Kalervo,   blue-stockinged son of an old man,
then flattered the girl,   charmed her, cajoled her
with one hand on the stallion's reins,   the other on the girl's nipples.
Then he sported with the girl,   gradually wore out the girl with a tin ornament
under the cover with copper filigree,   on the spotted fur.

Now God brought the morning,   God brought the next day.
Then the girl spoke these words,   questioned, gave utterance:
"From what clan do you come,   from what stock, brave man?
You are probably of a great clan,   of a race great on your father's side."
Kullervo, son of Kalervo,   uttered a word, spoke thus:
"I am not of a great clan,   neither great nor small;
I am just in between,   humble son of Kalervo,
stupid dull boy,   good-for-nothing humble child.
But tell me your own clan,   your own brave stock,
whether you are of a great clan,   of a race great on your father's side."

The girl answers indeed,   uttered a word spoke thus:
"I am not of a great clan,   neither great nor small;
I am just in between,   humble daughter of Kalervo,
stupid dull maiden,   good-for-nothing humble child.
Formerly when I was a child   in my adoring mother's home,
I set out to the forest for berries,   raspberries at the foot of a hill.
I picked strawberries on the ground,   raspberries at the foot of the hill.
I picked by day, I rested by night;   I picked one day, picked a second;
on the third day indeed   I did not know the way home;
the path led into the forest,   the trail into the wilderness.
Then I sat down and wept.   I wept for one day, then a second;
on the third day   I went up onto a big hill,
onto a high ridge.   There I cried out, I kept shouting.
The wilderness spoke in reply,   the heaths resounded:
'Do not cry out, wretched girl!   Do not make a noise, foolish one!
No one at all will hear,   the cry will not be heard as far as home.'
After three days, four,   five, finally six,
I got ready to die,   cast myself down to perish.
However, I did not die at all,   did not perish.
Would that I had died, poor wretch,   that I had been cut off, miserable me,
right in my second year,   might right in my third summer
have shimmered in the form of hay,   frolicked as a flower,
as a nice berry on the ground,   as a red whortleberry,
without hearing these terrible things,   without witnessing the grievous
    things!"

However, she managed to speak,   just managed to say her say.
Immediately she flung herself out of the sleigh,   then rushed into the river,
into the heavy foam of the rapids,   into a raging whirlpool.
There she prepared for her death,   met her end.
She found protection in Death's Domain,   mercy amidst the waves.

Kullervo, son of Kalervo,   rushed from his sleigh,
began to weep violently,   to lament greatly:

"Woe, poor wretch, are my days,   woe, miserable me, my strange evil deeds
when I embraced my sister,   ruined my mother's offspring!
Woe is my father, woe my mother,   woe my esteemed parent!
To what end indeed did you beget me,   for what purpose did you conceive
   the wretched man?
I would have been better   unborn, never to have grown up,
not born into the world,   not come of age on this earth.
Death did not indeed do it properly,   disease not rightly know how
when it did not kill me,   not destroy me when two days old."
With a knife he cut the hames to pieces,   with a blade he cut off the traces;
he jumped on the back of the good animal,   on the flanks of the good horse
   with a blaze.
He rides over a bit of country,   races over a little bit,
comes to his father's farmyard,   his own father's field.
His mother comes out to the farmyard: "O mother, you who bore me!
If you, my poor mother,   when you were bearing me,
had made a smudge in the sauna,   had only shot the bolt of the sauna,
had suffocated me in the smudge,   destroyed me when two days old,
carried me to the water in the streets,   drowned me in the mosquito net,
thrown the swinging cradle into the fire,   thrust the cradle into the hearth.
What if the neighborhood asked: 'Where has the cradle gone from the
   house?
Why is the bolt to in the sauna?'   You might have answered:
'I burned the cradle in the fire,   the swinging cradle in the fire on the hearth.
I was sprouting barley in the sauna,   was sweetening the malt.'"

His mother managed to ask,   his parent to inquire:
"What, my son,   what strange thing have you been hearing?
It is as if you had come from Death's Domain,   had come on a journey from
   the Abode of the Dead!"
Kullervo, son of Kalervo,   uttered a word, spoke thus:
"I have now heard strange tidings,   grievous things have happened
in that I embraced my own sister,   ruined my mother's offspring.
I was coming from delivering the taxes,   paying the land rents;
I came upon a girl,   I sported with her;
she was my sister,   my own mother's child.
She has already dived to her death,   met her end
in the heavy foam of a rapids,   in a raging whirlpool.
I now have no idea,   cannot judge, imagine
where I shall dive to my death,   where I, poor wretch, will kill myself,
whether in the mouth of a howling wolf,   in the jaws of a roaring bear
or in the belly of a whale,   in the teeth of a pike of the sea."

His mother uttered these words: "Do not go, my son,
into the mouth of a howling wolf,   into the jaws of a roaring bear,

not into the belly of a whale   nor the teeth of a terrible pike.
The Finnish peninsula is big,   the marches of Savo are vast enough
for a man to hide his wicked deeds,   to atone for his evil acts,
to hide five, six years,   nine years in all
until time brings pardon,   the years ease distress."
Kullervo, son of Kalervo,   uttered a word, spoke thus:
"I will not set out to go into hiding,   not, evil man that I am, take flight.
I will set out toward the jaws of death,   to the gates of the Grave Spirit's
    farmstead,
to great battlefields,   to the battlefields of men.
Untamo is still alive,   the base man not yet slain;
the blows my father received are unavenged,   my mother's tears unatoned for,
not to mention other troubles, too   —and my own fine behavior!"

POEM 36

Kullervo gets ready to go to war and says farewell to his family,
of whom his mother alone says she cares about him,
cares where he goes, whether he dies or stays alive (1–154).
He comes to Untamo's farm,
lays everybody low, and sets the buildings on fire (155–250).
He returns home and finds the house empty with no other living creature
on the whole place but an old black dog, with which he sets out to live
on what he shoots for himself in the forest (251–296).
In the course of his forest journey he reaches the place
where he seduced his sister and in anguish of conscience
ends his days with a sword (297–360).

Kullervo, son of Kalervo, blue-stockinged son of an old man,
then sets forth to battle, gets ready for the warpath.
One moment he was sharpening his sword, another whetting his spear point.
His mother uttered these words: "Do not, my poor boy,
go to a great war, go to a clash of swords.
One who goes into battle without cause, willingly to a fight,
will be slain in battle, be killed in the fight,
be done in by swords, be laid low by sword blades.
You are setting out to war on a billy goat, to battle on a nanny goat;
the billy goat will soon be defeated, the nanny goat be laid low in the mire.
You will come home on a dog, reach the farmyard on a mere toad."
Kullervo, son of Kalervo, uttered a word, spoke thus:
"I will not fall into a fen then nor drop dead on a heath,
in ravens' dwelling places, on crows' fields
when I fall on battlefields, fall on the fields of battle.
It is fine indeed to die in battle, lovely to die in the clash of swords!
War disease is lovely; a lad goes away suddenly,
goes away without being ill, falls without wasting away."
His mother uttered these words: "If you die in battle,
what will be left for your father against his old age?"
Kullervo, son of Kalervo, uttered a word, spoke thus:
"Let him die on the dunghill in the cattle shed, let him fall dead on the
    farmstead!"
"What will be left for your mother against her old age?"
"Let her die with a sheaf of dry straw in her arms, let her suffocate in the
    cowshed!"
"What will be left for your brother against his future days?"
"Let him perish in the forest, fall down dead on a field!"

"What will be left for your sister   against her future days?"
"Let her fall dead on the path to the well,   fall dead on the path to where
   the laundry is done!"

Kullervo, son of Kalervo,   soon sets out from home.
He speaks a word to his father: "Farewell, kind father!
Will you grieve for me   when you hear I have died,
have vanished from among the people,   gone from the clan?"
His father uttered these words: "I will not grieve for you
when I hear you have died;   another son will be produced,
a son far better,   much cleverer."
Kullervo, son of Kalervo,   uttered a word, spoke thus:
"I will not grieve for you either   should I hear you have died.
I will get me another sort of father,   one with a mouth of clay, a head of
   stone,
eyes of bog cranberries,   a beard of withered grass,
legs from the fork of a water willow,   other flesh from rotten wood."

Then he spoke to his brother: "Farewell, my brother!
Will you grieve for me   when you hear I have died,
have vanished from among the people,   gone from the clan?"
His brother uttered these words: "I will not grieve for you
should I hear you have died;   another brother will be got,
a much better brother,   twice as handsome."
Kullervo, son of Kalervo,   uttered a word, spoke thus:
"I will not grieve for you either   should I hear you have died.
I will get me this sort of brother: one with a head of stone, mouth of clay,
eyes of bog cranberries,   hair of withered grass,
legs from the fork of a water willow,   other flesh from rotten wood."

Then he said to his sister: "Farewell, my sister!
Will you grieve for me   when you hear I have died,
have vanished from among the people,   gone from the clan?"
The sister spoke thus: "I will not grieve for you
when I hear you have died;   another brother will be got,
a much better brother,   much cleverer."
Kullervo, son of Kalervo,   uttered a word, spoke thus:
"I will not grieve for you either   should I hear you have died.
I will get me this kind of sister: one with a head of stone, mouth of clay,
eyes of bog cranberries,   hair of withered grass,
ears of water lilies from a pond,   a trunk from a maple shoot."

Then he said to his mother: "Mother mine, my beloved,
lovely one who bore me,   golden one who carried me in her womb!
Will you grieve for me   when you hear I have died,

have vanished from among the people,   gone from the clan?"
His mother uttered these words,   spoke, said thus:
"You do not understand a mother's mind,   do not know a mother's heart.
I will indeed grieve for you   should I hear you have died,
have been taken away from among the people,   gone from the clan.
I will flood our house with tears,   the floorboards with billows,
flood all the lanes with body bent,   the cattle sheds with stooped back;
I will weep the snow to glare ice,   the glare ice to bare ground,
the bare ground till tinged with green,   the green places till they are
    withered.
What I cannot stand to weep about,   what I cannot bear to bewail,
to weep about in a crowd of people,   that I will weep about secretly in the
    sauna,
weep the benches with floods of water,   sauna platforms with billowing
    waves."

Kullervo, son of Kalervo,   blue-stockinged son of an old man,
set out to battle playing,   to the fight making music.
He played on the fen, played on the land,   he made a noise on the heath,
banged along on the grass,   rumbled along on the withered grass.
A message followed him,   the news reached his ears:
"Now your father at home died,   your esteemed parent dropped dead;
go look at that,   how they are burying the dead man."
Kullervo, son of Kalervo,   he indeed answered:
"If he has died, let him be dead.   At home we have a gelding
with which let him be taken to his place in the earth,   be covered in the
    grave."

He played as he went along the fen,   made a noise on the clearing.
A message followed him,   the news reached his ears:
"Now your brother at home died,   your parent's child dropped dead;
go look at that,   how they are burying the dead man."
Kullervo, son of Kalervo,   he indeed answered:
"If he has died, let him be dead.   At home we have a stallion
with which let him be taken to his place in the earth,   be covered in the
    grave."

He played as he walked along the fen,   tooted in a fir grove.
A message followed him,   the news reached his ears:
"Now your sister at home died,   your parent's child dropped dead;
go look at that,   how they are burying the dead girl."
Kullervo, son of Kalervo,   he indeed answered:
"If she has died, let her be dead.   At home we have a mare
with which let her be taken to her place in the earth,   be covered in the
    grave."

Singing he proceeded on the withered grass, went noisily on the greensward.
A message followed him, the news reached his ears:
"Your lovely mother died, your charming mother dropped dead;
go look at that, how strangers are burying her."
Kullervo, son of Kalervo, uttered a word, spoke thus:
"Woe is me, wretched lad, since my mother has died,
the maker of my mosquito net grown weary, has dropped dead,
the embroiderer of a cloak passed away, spinner of a long thread, wielder
  of a big distaff.
I was not there when she passed away, not present when her spirit departed.
Perhaps she died of severe cold or perhaps from lack of bread.
Let the deceased be washed at home with soap imported from Germany
  and with water,
let her be shrouded in silk, be placed in linen cloths.
Then let her be taken to her place in the earth, be covered in a grave;
let her be taken away with lamentations, be lowered into the grave with
  song.
I cannot go home yet; Untamo has not yet been paid back,
the base man not been laid low, the evil man not got rid of."

Playing he went to war, to Untamo's farm making joyful music.
He uttered a word, spoke thus: "O Ukko, god on high!
If now you would get me a sword and the loveliest blade
that would be effective against a troop, would do against a hundred men!"
He got the sword he desired, the very best blade
with which he laid low the whole group, did away with Untamo's troop.
He burned the buildings to ashes, burned them to fluffy ashes;
he left the stones of the stove, left the tall rowan in the farmyard.

From there Kullervo, son of Kalervo, now turned home
to the dwellings of his late father, to the fields of his parent.
When he came, the house was empty, was desolate when he opened the
  door;
no one comes to hug him, comes to hold out a hand.
He put his hand in the embers; the coals in the embers were cold.
From this he knew when he got there that his mother was not alive.
He thrusts his hand into the hearth; the stones of the stove were cold.
From this he knew when he got there that his father was not alive.
His eyes lit on the floor; the floor had not been cleaned at all.
From this he knew when he got there that his sister was not alive.
He went to the landing place by the water; there was no boat at the landing
  place.
From that he knew when he got there that his brother was not alive.
Then he began to weep; he wept one day, wept a second.
He uttered these words: "O my kind mother!

What did you leave for me here   while you were living on this earth?
Do you not hear me, mother,   as I murmur over where your eyes are,
over where your brows are,   speaking above the crown of your head?"
His mother awakened in the grave,   from under the ground she remarks:
"I left the dog Blackie behind   for you to go hunting with.
Take your dog along,   go yonder to the forest lands,
go up into the backwoods,   to the maidens of the forest,
to the farmyard of the girls in green,   to the edge of Tapio's fir-bough
    stronghold
to search for provisions,   to sue for game."

Kullervo, son of Kalervo,   took his dog with him,
set out to tread the path,   to go up into the backwoods.
He went a little distance,   walked a little way;
he came to that tract in the forest,   got to that place
where he had ravished the maiden,   ruined his mother's offspring.
There the lovely grass was weeping,   the loveliest clearing lamenting,
the young herbs grieving,   the heather blooms complaining
the rape of the girl,   the ruining of the mother's offspring.
Nor had young grass sprung up,   no heather bloom come out,
grown up in that spot,   in that evil place
where he had ravished the girl,   ruined his mother's offspring.
Kullervo, son of Kalervo,   drew his sharp sword;
he looks at it, turns it over,   questions it, inquires of it.
He asked the sword its wish,   whether it wanted
to eat guilty flesh,   drink sinful blood.
The sword knew the man's mind,   understood what the warrior said:
it answered with these words: "Why should I not eat as I want,
eat guilty flesh,   drink sinful blood?
I eat the flesh of an innocent person,   drink the blood of a sinless one, too."
Kullervo, son of Kalervo,   blue-stockinged son of an old man,
pushed the hilt into the field,   pressed the butt into the heath,
turned the point against his breast,   struck himself onto the point.
On that he contrived his death,   met his end.

That was the death of the young fellow,   the death of the man Kullervo,
at long last the end of the man,   the death of the luckless one.

When old Väinämöinen   heard that he had died,
that Kullervo had departed,   he uttered a word, spoke thus:
"Do not, future people,   bring up a child the wrong way,
in the home of one who rocks foolishly,   of a strange luller to sleep.
A child reared the wrong way,   a boy rocked stupidly,
will not grasp things,   not acquire the mind of a man,
even though he should live to grow up,   should become strong of body."

POEM 37

For a long time Ilmarinen weeps over his dead wife;
then out of gold and silver he forges himself a new wife,
which he prepares with great work and pains
but without the breath of life (1–162).
At night he lies beside his golden bride
and when he wakes up in the morning he realizes that that side
with which he has lain against the image was very cold (163–196).
He offers his golden bride to Väinämöinen
who does not, however, care for it,
on the contrary orders Ilmarinen to pound it up for other purposes
or to bring it as it is to other countries for suitors wishing gold (197–250).

Craftsman Ilmarinen   wept for his wife every evening,
sleepless he wept nights,   fasting he wept days;
in the early hours of the morning he lamented,   mornings he sighed
after his young wife had died,   the lovely one been covered in the grave.
Nor did the copper shaft of his hammer   turn in his hand
nor was any pounding heard in his smithy   for one month.
Craftsman Ilmarinen said: "I do not know, wretched lad,
how to exist, how to live.   Whether I sit at night or lie down,
the night is long, the time sad;   troubles there are, low is my strength.
Long drawn out are my evenings,   grievous are my mornings;
then at night it is more unpleasant,   while I am awake more grievous.
It is not long drawn out because of the evenings,   not grievous because of the mornings,
not an affliction merely because of other times;   it is long drawn out because of my lovely one,
grievous because of my beloved,   an affliction because of my dark-browed one.
Just now in this life,   often in the midnight dreams
of sorrowing me   my hand touches something unreal,
my hand touches the illusion   of strange loins, too."
The craftsman lives on without a wife,   grows older without a spouse.
He wept two months, three.   Then indeed in the fourth month
he gathered gold from the sea,   silver from the billows;
he collected a pile of logs,   thirty sled loads;
he burned his wood to charcoal,   forced the coals into the forge.
He took those gold pieces of his,   picked out his silver pieces
the size of a ewe an autumn old,   a hare one winter old.
He thrust the pieces of gold into the furnace,   forced the pieces of silver into the forge,

set slaves to working the bellows,   the hired men to pumping.
The slaves worked the bellows,   the hired men pumped
with unmittened hands,   stripped to the waist.
Craftsman Ilmarinen himself   stirs up the forge,
tried to produce a gold image,   a silver bride.

The slaves do not work the bellows well   nor do the hired men pump them
   well.
Craftsman Ilmarinen started   to work the bellows.
He puffed away once, twice;   the third time
he looked into the depths of the forge,   at the side of his bellows
to see what is being driven out of the forge,   being forced out of the hearth.
A ewe is being driven out of the forge,   sent out from the bellows;
one hair is gold, the other copper,   the third is a silver hair.
The others are delighted with that,   Ilmarinen is not delighted.
Craftsman Ilmarinen said: "The wolf was hoping for the likes of you;
I am hoping for a golden sweetheart,   a silver spouse."

Then craftsman Ilmarinen   thrusts the ewe into the fire.
He added some gold to eke out with,   some silver to fill out with;
he puts the slaves to working the bellows,   the hired men to pumping.
The slaves worked the bellows,   the hired men pumped
with unmittened hands,   stripped to the waist.
Craftsman Ilmarinen himself   stirs up the forge,
tried to produce a gold image,   a silver bride.

The slaves do not work the bellows well   nor do the hired men pump them
   well.
Craftsman Ilmarinen himself   began to work the bellows.
He pumped the bellows once, twice;   then the third time
he looked into the depths of his forge,   at the side of his bellows
to see what is being driven out of the forge,   sent out from the bellows.
A colt is being driven out of the forge,   sent out from the bellows,
the mane of gold, the head of silver,   the whole body of copper.
The others were greatly delighted with that,   Ilmarinen was not delighted.
Craftsman Ilmarinen said: "The wolf was hoping for the likes of you;
I am hoping for a gold sweetheart,   a silver spouse."

Then craftsman Ilmarinen   thrusts the colt into the fire.
He added some gold to eke out with,   some silver to fill out,
set the slaves to working the bellows,   the hired men to pumping.
The slaves worked the bellows,   the hired men pumped
with unmittened hands,   stripped to the waist.
Craftsman Ilmarinen himself   stirs up the forge,
tried to produce a gold image,   a silver bride.

The slaves do not work the bellows well   nor do the hired men pump them well.
Craftsman Ilmarinen himself   began to work the bellows.
He pumped away once, twice;   then the third time
he looked into the depths of the forge,   at the side of the bellows
to see what is being driven out of the forge,   sent out from the bellows.
A girl is being driven out of the forge,   one with gold braids from the bellows,
with a head of silver, hair of gold,   a whole beautiful trunk.
The others were greatly afraid of that,   Ilmarinen was not afraid.

Then craftsman Ilmarinen   hammered away at the gold image,
hammered during the night without letup,   during the day without stopping.
He made legs for the girl,   made legs, shaped hands,
but the legs just do not get up,   the hands not turn to embrace him.
He forged ears for his girl   and the ears hear nothing.
Then he fashioned a pretty mouth,   a pretty mouth, keen eyes.
It could not speak with its mouth   or look meltingly with its eyes.
Craftsman Ilmarinen said: "That would be a pretty girl
if it had the power of speech,   had a mind, a tongue."

Then he brought his girl   under a gauzy mosquito-net,
on soft pillows, on a silky bed.
Then craftsman Ilmarinen   warmed up a vapory bath,
made a soapy sauna;   he prepared twig whisks,
three buckets of water   with which the chaffinch is washed,
the snow bunting cleansed   of that gold slag.
The craftsman bathed himself to his satisfaction,   washed to his heart's desire.
He threw himself at length beside the girl   under the gauzy mosquito net,
under the tent,   the iron mosquito net.
Then right off the first night   craftsman Ilmarinen
calls for plenty of covers,   provides bedcovers,
two, three bearskins,   five, six woolen blankets
to lie on with his spouse,   with that gold image of his.
That side was quite warm   that was against his covers,
the one which was against the young girl,   against the gold image,
that got chilled through,   was frozen to rime,
frozen to sea ice,   hardened to rock.
Craftsman Ilmarinen said: "This is no good to me.
I will take the girl to Väinämöinen's farm   as an eternal spouse
to provide for Väinämöinen,   as a chick by his side."

He takes the girl to Väinämöinen's farm.   Then after he had got there,
he uttered a word, spoke thus: "O you old Väinämöinen,

here is a girl for you,   a maiden beautiful to look at;
she is not, to be sure, much at singing   nor is she very talkative."
Steadfast old Väinämöinen   took a look at that image,
cast his eyes on the gold.   He uttered a word, spoke thus:
"Why did you bring me that,   that curious piece of gold?"
Craftsman Ilmarinen said: "What else but for your benefit!
As an eternal spouse,   a chick by your side."
Old Väinämöinen said: "O craftsman, my boon companion!
Thrust your girl into the fire,   forge her into all sorts of things
or take her to Russia;   take your image to Germany
for rich men to fight to marry,   for noblemen to wage war to woo.
It is not fitting for my clan   nor for me myself
to woo a gold woman,   to try to please one of silver."

Then Väinämöinen forbade,   the bachelor of Slack Water Farm prohibited,
forbade the rising generation,   prohibited those growing up,
to bow down to gold,   to truckle to silver.
He speaks these words,   made this utterance:
"Wretched lads,   especially men growing up,
be you prosperous   or be you poor,
never, never at all,   not while the moon shines gold-bright,
do not woo a gold woman,   try to please one of silver.
'Gold gleams cold,   silver glistens chill.' "

POEM 38

Ilmarinen sets out to North Farm to woo the younger sister of his former wife;
there he gets bad abusive words in reply; at that he becomes angry,
abducts the daughter, and sets out straight for home (1–124).
On the journey the girl reviles Ilmarinen and so offends him
that in his rage Ilmarinen at last sings her into a sea gull (125–286).
Then he comes home and tells Väinämöinen of North Farm's carefree life
thanks to the Sampo, likewise how his trip as a suitor has gone (287–328).

Craftsman Ilmarinen,   eternal smith,
threw away his gold image,   his silver girl.
He put the colt in harness,   the brown horse before the sled,
sits down in the sled,   gets into his sleigh.
He vowed to set out   and contemplated going
to beg at North Farm   for North Farm's second daughter.

He had driven one day,   then gone on a second,
on the third day   he came to the yard of North Farm.
Louhi, mistress of North Farm,   came out into the yard;
she then got to speaking,   turned to inquire
about the state of her own child,   of her dear one's residing
as a daughter-in-law in her husband's home,   as a wife in her mother-in-law's
   home.
Craftsman Ilmarinen   downcast, low in mind,
high-peaked hat all askew,   uttered a word, spoke thus:
"Do not now, my mother-in-law,   do not ask about that,
about your daughter's life,   your dear one's residing.
Death has already taken her with its jaws,   a grievous end came suddenly.
My berry is now in the earth,   my beautiful one in the heath,
my dark-browed one in the withered grass,   my silver one in the greensward.
I set out for your second daughter,   for your younger girl.
Give me, my mother-in-law,   send your second daughter
to the dwelling place of my late wife,   to her sister's place."

Louhi, mistress of North Farm,   uttered a word, spoke thus:
"I did ill, wretched me,   ill indeed, miserable creature,
when I pledged my child,   sent you even the other one
to pass away as a young girl,   as a pink-cheeked lass to drop dead.
I gave her, as it were, into the mouth of a wolf,   into the jaws of a roaring
   bear.

Indeed I will not give you a second at all,   will not send my girl
to wipe the soot off you,   to scrape off bits of caked soot.
Sooner will I send my daughter,   thrust my steadygoing child
into a roaring rapids,   a fierce whirlpool,
into the mouth of a cusk of the Abode of the Dead,   the teeth of Death's
   pike."

Then craftsman Ilmarinen   screwed up his mouth, twisted his head around,
clawed at his black beard,   turned his curly head.
He forced his way into the house,   pressed on in under the roof.
He uttered a word, spoke thus: "Now come to me, girl,
to your sister's place,   to the dwellings of my late wife,
to bake honeybread,   to brew beer."
A child was singing on the floor,   both singing and speaking:
"Away, useless fellow, from our fine house,   strange man, from these doors!
You ruined a lot of fine houses,   you damaged a bit of the house
when you visited once before,   after knocking on the door.
Maiden, you sister!   Do not get infatuated with the suitor,
not with the music of the suitor's mouth   nor with his fine legs.
The suitor has the gums of a wolf,   the wiles of a fox in his pocket,
the claws of a bear under his arm,   a blood-drinking knife in his belt
with which he cuts a head,   slashes away at a back!"

The girl spoke thus   to craftsman Ilmarinen:
"I will not set out to you   nor do I care about triflers.
You killed your late wedded wife,   you murdered my sister;
you would even kill me,   murder me myself, too.
This girl is indeed   worth a better husband,
is a good match for a handsome body,   worthy to fill a finer sleigh,
worthy of better places,   bigger residences,
not for a smith's charcoal bins,   a stupid man's fires."

Craftsman Ilmarinen,   eternal smith,
screwed up his mouth, twisted his head around,   clawed at his black beard.
At the same moment he seized the girl,   embraces her in his arms,
set out from the house like a blizzard,   rushed to his sled;
he pushed the girl into the sled,   flung her into his sleigh
He set out at once to go,   got ready to go,
with one hand on the stallion's reins,   the other on the girl's nipples.
The girl wept and whimpered,   uttered a word, spoke thus:
"Now I have got to a fen for cranberries,   to bogs for water-arum roots;
there I, a chick, will perish,   I, a bird, will die no natural death!
Listen, craftsman Ilmarinen!   Unless you release me,

I will kick your sleigh to pieces,   will break your sled to bits,
kick it apart with my knees,   break it with my feet."
Craftsman Ilmarinen   uttered these words:
"For this reason the sides   of the craftsman's sled are ironclad,
so as to stand the kicking,   the writhing of a nice virgin."
The girl laments,   she with a copper belt complains,
twists her fingers,   wrings her hands.
She uttered a word, spoke thus: "Unless you release me,
I will sing myself into a fish of the sea,   into a whitefish of the deep waves."
Craftsman Ilmarinen   uttered these words:
"You will not get there;   I will be after you in the form of a pike."
The girl laments,   she with a copper belt complains,
twists her fingers,   wrings her hands.
She uttered a word, spoke thus: "Unless you release me,
I will lose myself in the forest,   turn myself into a weasel in a hole in a rock."
Craftsman Ilmarinen   uttered these words:
"You will not get there;   I will be after you in the form of an otter."
The girl laments,   she with a copper belt complains,
twists her fingers,   wrings her hands.
She uttered a word, spoke thus: "Unless you release me,
I will fly warbling off in the form of a meadow lark   to hide behind a cloud."
Craftsman Ilmarinen   uttered these words:
"You will not get there;   I will be after you in the form of an eagle."

He went a short distance,   drove a little way.
Now the horse pricks up its ears,   flop-ears is frightened.
The girl raised her head,   saw tracks in the snow;
she inquired, she spoke: "What has run across here?"
Craftsman Ilmarinen said: "A hare has run across here."
The poor girl sighs deeply,   sighs deeply, gasps;
she uttered a word, spoke thus: "Woe is me, poor wretch!
It would be better for me,   would be better
to be running in the hair's track,   on bandy-legs' trail
than in this suitor's sleigh,   under the wrinkled-faced man's woolen sleigh
     robe.
A hare's fur is finer,   a hare's mouth nicer."

Craftsman Ilmarinen   bit his lip, twisted his head around;
he drives along at an easy pace.   He drove a short distance;
again the horse pricks up its ears,   flop-ears is frightened.
The girl raised her head,   saw tracks in the snow;
she inquired, she spoke: "What has run across here?"
Craftsman Ilmarinen said: "A fox has run across here."
The poor girl sighs deeply,   sighs, gasps;

she uttered a word, spoke thus: "Woe is me, poor wretch!
It would be better for me, would be better
to be rumbling along in a fox's sled, ever riding in a wretched sled
than in this suitor's sleigh, under the wrinkled-faced man's woolen sleigh
  robe.
A fox's coat is finer, a fox's mouth is nicer."

Craftsman Ilmarinen bit his lip, twisted his head around;
he drives along at an easy pace. He drove a short distance;
again the horse pricks up its ears, flop-ears is frightened.
The girl raised her head, saw tracks in the snow;
she inquired, she spoke: "What has run across here?"
Craftsman Ilmarinen said: "A wolf has run across there."
The poor girl sighs deeply, sighs deeply, gasps;
she uttered a word, spoke thus: "Woe is me, poor wretch!
It would be better for me, would be better
to be running in the track of an angry wolf, in the footsteps of a wolf with
  lowered snout,
than in this suitor's sleigh, under the wrinkled-faced man's woolen sleigh
  robe.
A wolf's hair is finer, a wolf's mouth is nicer."

Craftsman Ilmarinen bit his lip, twisted his head around;
he drives along at an easy pace into a new farm for the night.
Wearied by the journey the craftsman sleeps soundly;
someone other than the drowsy man makes the woman laugh.
Then when he woke up in the morning craftsman Ilmarinen
screwed up his mouth, twisted his head around, clawed at his black beard.
Craftsman Ilmarinen said, reflected, spoke thus:
"Shall I now begin to sing, sing such a bride
into the forest as the forest's own or into water as the water's own?
I will not sing her to be the forest's own; the whole forest would be
  depressed;
nor will I indeed sing her to be the water's own; the fishes in the water
  would think it abominable.
Rather will I kill her with my blade, slay her with my sword."
The sword understood the man's utterance, guessed the sense of the warrior's talk.
It uttered a word, spoke thus: "I have probably not been created to kill
  women,
to slay wretched girls." Craftsman Ilmarinen now indeed began to sing,
got angry to the point of singing magically. He sang his wife into a seagull
to scream on a little island, to echo out on reefs in the water,
to whimper on the tips of headlands, to rock on headwinds.

Then craftsman Ilmarinen   flings himself into his sled.
He drives along at an easy pace   downcast, low in mind;
he journeyed to his own parts,   came to familiar lands.
Steadfast old Väinämöinen   comes to meet him on the road;
then he began to speak.   "Good friend, craftsman Ilmarinen,
why are you low in mind,   your high-peaked hat twice as askew
as you come from North Farm?   How are they living at North Farm?"
Craftsman Ilmarinen spoke: "They are living high at North Farm!
There the Sampo is milling away,   the lid of many colors is going round and
      round;
one day it was grinding things to eat,   the next day things to barter,
the third day things to store at home.   I say and I say it,
still again reporting: they are living high at North Farm
because the Sampo is at North Farm!   There is plowing there, sowing there,
there are all sorts of increase there,   everlasting good fortune there."
Old Väinämöinen said: "Good friend craftsman Ilmarinen,
where did you leave the young woman?   Where is the fine bride
since you come empty-handed,   are rattling along still without a woman?"
Craftsman Ilmarinen   uttered a word, spoke thus:
"I sang that kind of woman   into a sea gull on a little island in the sea.
Now that sea gull is crying out,   is cackling like a gull,
screaming on reefs in the water,   shrieking on the rocks."

POEM 39

Väinämöinen urges Ilmarinen to set out with him to get the Sampo
from North Farm, to which plan Ilmarinen agrees,
and the men set out on the journey by boat (1–330).
On the way Lemminkäinen catches sight of them and,
when he hears where they are going, volunteers to be the third man.
They gladly take him on as a third (331–426).

Steadfast old Väinämöinen   uttered these words:
"O craftsman Ilmarinen!   Let us set out for North Farm
to get the fine Sampo,   to look at the lid of many colors."
That craftsman Ilmarinen   uttered a word, spoke thus:
"The Sampo cannot be got,   the lid of many colors not brought
from gloomy North Farm, from dark Sedgy Farm.   The Sampo has been
    taken there,
the lid of many colors carried   to North Farm's hill of rock, to inside the
    copper mountain
behind nine locks;   there its roots have struck
to the depth of nine fathoms,   one root into solid ground,
the second into the shore,   the third into ground near the house."

Old Väinämöinen said: "Good friend smith, my boon companion,
let us set out for North Farm   to get that Sampo.
Let us build a big ship   in which to transport the Sampo,
to carry the lid of many colors   from North Farm's hill of rock,
from inside the copper mountain,   from behind the nine locks."
Craftsman Ilmarinen said: "A journey by land is steadier.
Let the Devil go by sea,   Death go on the broad expanse of the water!
There the wind would shake us,   there a hurricane would toss us about;
our fingers would become rowing oars,   our palms steering oars."
Old Väinämöinen said: "A journey by land is steadier,
steadier, more laborious,   still more roundabout besides.
It is fun for a boat on the water,   for a vessel to rock along,
to make the sparkling water gleam,   to go along on the broad expanse of the
    sea.
The wind rocks the vessel,   a wave drives the ship,
the west wind makes it roll,   the south wind takes it forward.
Be that, however, as it may,   if you are not disposed to go by sea,
then let us travel by land,   rattle along the shore.
Forge me now a new sword,   make me a sharp blade

with which I will thrash the dirty dogs,   drive off the people of North Farm
while I am seizing the Sampo   yonder in that cold community,
at gloomy North Farm,   at dark Sedgy Farm."

That craftsman Ilmarinen,   eternal smith,
thrust pieces of iron into the fire,   pieces of steel into the embers,
a whole handful of gold pieces,   a fistful of silver pieces.
He made the slaves work the bellows,   the hired men pump.
The slaves worked the bellows,   the hired men pumped very hard.
The iron got soft like gruel,   the steel got yielding like dough,
the silver gleamed like water,   the gold sparkled like a wave.
Then craftsman Ilmarinen,   eternal smith,
looked into the depths of his forge,   at the side of his bellows;
he saw a sword being born,   a hilt of gold taking shape.
He took the materials from the fire,   whisked the good smithwork
from the forge to the anvil,   to the hammers, to the sledges.
He pounded the sword as he wished,   a very best blade
which he decorated with gold,   adorned with silver.
Steadfast old Väinämöinen   came to look at that.
He took the sharp sword   in his right hand;
he looks, turns it over,   uttered a word, spoke thus:
"Is the sword right for the man,   the blade suitable for the bearer?"
The sword was right for the man,   the blade suitable for the bearer.
A moon shone on its tip,   a sun shone on its side,
stars gleamed on its hilt;   a horse was neighing on the blade,
a cat mewing on the boss of the hilt,   a dog growling on the sheath.
He swung his sword   in a crack in an iron hill.
He uttered a word, spoke thus: "Now with this sword
I might cleave even mountains,   divide crags in two."

Craftsman Ilmarinen   uttered a word, spoke thus:
"With what will I, poor me,   with what, wretched me, defend myself,
hird myself, gird myself   against the land, against the sea?
Shall I now outfit myself with greaves,   put on iron byrnies,
enclose myself in steel belts?   A man is more secure in armor,
better in iron byrnies,   more effective in a steel belt."

The time comes to set out,   the time agreed on to go arrives.
Old Väinämöinen as one,   craftsman Ilmarinen as the second
set out in search of a horse,   to look for the one with a flaxen mane;
the yearling's bridle was on the belt,   the colt's harness on the shoulder.
The two of them search for the horse,   look for its head through the trees;
they look closely   around about in the hazy-blue wilderness,
find the horse's copse,   flaxen-mane's fir grove.

Steadfast old Väinämöinen,   craftsman Ilmarinen as the second,
pushed its head into the golden bridle,   the bit into the yearling's mouth.
They proceed laboriously   along the two men's shore.
From the shore a plaintive weeping is heard,   lamentation from a landing
  place.

Steadfast old Väinämöinen   uttered a word, spoke thus:
"A maiden is weeping there,   a chick whimpering.
Shall we now go look,   explore from near at hand?"
He steps nearer,   went there to look.
It is not a maiden weeping   nor a chick whimpering;
a vessel was weeping,   a boat lamenting.
Once he reached the vessel   old Väinämöinen spoke:
"Why are you weeping, wooden vessel,   why are you lamenting, boat with
  big tholepins?
Are you bewailing your being of wood,   are you thinking of your being fur-
  nished with tholepins?"
The wooden vessel answers,   the boat with big tholepins says:
"'A boat's desire is for the water,   the tarred planking's desire to be off the
  rollers;
a girl's desire is to marry,   to get away from her stately home.'
This I am weeping for, poor wretch of a vessel,   this I, sorry boat, am lamenting,
weeping for people to take me to the water,   to let me down onto the billows.
While I was being built they said,   while being made they sang
that a warship was being made,   a battleship being worked on,
that I would bring my fill of things,   treasures in my hold.
I have not gone into battle,   not at all on journeys to get valuable things.
Other vessels, even bad vessels,   they are always waging war,
lumbering along to battle.   Three times a summer
they bring their fill of money,   treasures in their hold.
I, a well-built ship   made of a hundred planks,
am rotting here on the chips cut off me,   resting on the place where I was
  shaped.
The worst reptiles in the world   are living under my ribs,
the most dreadful birds of the air   have their nests in my mast,
all the frogs of the backwoods, too,   are hopping about on my bows.
It would be twice as fine,   twice, three times better
to be a pinetree on a hill,   a pine on a heath
for a squirrel to run on the branches,   a puppy to be circling around below."

Steadfast old Väinämöinen   then uttered these words:
"Do not weep, wooden vessel,   do not mourn, boat with big tholepins.
You will soon be able to wage war,   to lumber along to battle.

You will, boat, the Creator's creation, the Creator's creation, product of
  Him Who produced you,
probably plunge straight into the water, speed into the waves of the shore
without a hand's touching you, without a hand's being used on you,
without a shoulder's guiding you, without an arm's directing you."
The wooden vessel replies, the boat with big tholepins says:
"The rest of my big clan, my brother-boats, do not set out to the water
  without a push,
to the billows without being sent down unless they are touched by a hand,
turned about by an arm." Old Väinämöinen said: "If I push you to the
  water,
will you run along without being rowed, unaided by oars,
not steered by a steering oar, without a gust of wind blowing in your sail?"
The wooden vessel answers, the boat with big tholepins says:
"No other of my big clan, no one else of my group
runs along unless rowed by fingers, aided by oars,
steered by a steering oar, unless there is a gust of wind in the sail."
Steadfast old Väinämöinen then uttered these words:
"Will you run along if rowed, if aided by oars,
steered with a steering oar, with a gust of wind in your sail?"
The wooden vessel replies, the boat with big tholepins says:
"Indeed the rest of my clan, all my brothers, boats,
run along if rowed by fingers, aided by oars,
steered with a steering oar, with a gust of wind in the sail."

Then old Väinämöinen left the horse on the sand,
fastened the halter to a tree, hung the reins on a branch,
shoved the boat to the water, sang the vessel to the billows.
He inquired of the wooden vessel, uttered a word, spoke thus:
"O you firm-ribbed boat, wooden vessel fitted with tholepins,
are you as fine for transport as you are fine to look at?"
The wooden vessel answers, the boat with big tholepins says:
"I am fine for transport, also with a bottom spacious enough
for a hundred men to row in, a thousand to sit in besides."
Then old Väinämöinen quietly sings.
First he sang one side full of sleek-haired youths,
sleek-haired, with powerful hands, with finely shod feet.
He sang the other side full of maidens with tin head ornaments,
tin head ornaments, copper belts, with lovely gold rings on their fingers.
Väinämöinen further sang the rowers' benches full of people;
those are old people who have been sitting all their lives
where there was little room available, especially because of young people.
He sits down aft, in the hull of the birchwood stern,

gets his ship going forward.   He uttered a word, spoke thus:
"Run along, vessel, through treeless tracts,   run along, boat, over bright
　　waters.
Proceed like bubbles on the sea,   like pond lilies on the billows."
He set the youths to rowing,   the maidens just to sitting.
The youths rowed, the oars bent;   the journey did not advance at all.
He set the maidens to rowing,   the youths just to sitting.
The girls rowed, their fingers bent;   the journey did not advance at all.
He shifted the old people to rowing,   the youth to looking on from the side.
The old people rowed, their heads shook;   the journey did not advance at all.
Then craftsman Ilmarinen   himself sat down to row;
now the wooden vessel ran along,   the vessel ran along, the journey pro-
　　ceeded.

The splash of oars was heard far off,   far away the murmur of tholepins.
He ripples along.   The rowers' benches shook, the planking bent,
the rowan oars clattered,   the handles of the oars shrilled like ruffed grouse,
the blades cooed like black grouse,   the bow whooped like a swan,
the stern croaked like a raven,   the tholepins hissed like geese.
Old Väinämöinen   sails along easily,
in the stern of the red vessel   with a sturdy steering oar.

On the journey a headland comes into sight,   a miserable settlement looms
　　up.
Ahti lives on the headland,   the man with a far-roving mind in a cove in the
　　headland.
The man with a far-roving mind was weeping over a lack of fish,   Lem-
　　minkäinen over a lack of bread,
Ahti was weeping over the smallness of his storehouse,   the rascal over his
　　lack of good luck.
He was shaping the planks of a boat,   the keel of a new vessel
at the end of long Starvation Headland,   by the mean settlement.
He was keen of ear,   his eye even keener.
He fixes his gaze toward the northwest,   turned his head south;
from afar he sees a rainbow,   farther off a little cloud patch.
It was not a rainbow at all   nor a little cloud patch;
it was a vessel moving along,   a boat making its way
on the broad expanse of the sea,   on the open deep;
a handsome man was in the stern of the vessel,   a fine-looking man at the
　　oars.
Reckless Lemminkäinen said: "I do not recognize that vessel,
do not identify the fine boat;   rowing along it comes from Finland,
stroking the oar from the east,   directing the steering oar toward the west."

Now he uttered a long loud cry,   hallooed, bellowed;
the man shouted from the tip of the headland,   the ruddy-cheeked fellow
   across the water:
"Whose is the boat in the water,   whose is the ship on the billows?"
The men speak from the boat,   the women answer, too:
"Who are you, man, forest-dweller,   you fellow, beater of the backwoods,
not to recognize this vessel,   not identify a boat from Väinämöinen's district,
not recognize the man in the stern   or the man at the oars?"
Reckless Lemminkäinen said: "Now I recognize the occupant of the stern
and I identify the oarsman;   steadfast old Väinämöinen
is guiding the helm,   Ilmarinen the oarsman.
Where are you going, men?   Where are you setting out for, people?"
Old Väinämöinen said: "We are proceeding north
toward the heavy foam,   toward the whitecapped billows
to find the Sampo,   to look at the lid of many colors
in North Farm's hill of rock,   inside the copper mountain."
Reckless Lemminkäinen said: "O old Väinämöinen,
take me on, man,   as a third man
if you are going to lift up the Sampo,   carry off the lid of many colors.
I, too, will make good as a man   should it be necessary to fight;
I will give an order with my hand,   instruction with my shoulders."
Steadfast old Väinämöinen   took on the man for his expedition,
took the rascal into his boat.   Reckless Lemminkäinen
now comes quickly,   moves speedily.
As he comes he brings planking   to Väinämöinen's boat.
Old Väinämöinen said: "There is lumber in my vessel,
planking in my boat;   there is load enough.
Why are you bringing planking,   adding lumber to the vessel?
Reckless Lemminkäinen said: "Precaution does not upset a boat,
a rick does not scatter a pile of hay.   Often on the sea of North Farm
the wind calls for a sideboard,   a headwind for extra freeboard."
Old Väinämöinen said: "For that reason the warship's
side is ironclad   and made with a steel prow
so as not to be altogether carried away by the wind   nor tossed by a sudden
   gust."

POEM 40

The voyagers going after the Sampo come to a rapid and at the bottom
of the rapid the boat gets stuck on the back of a big pike (1–94).
They kill the pike, get the main part into the boat,
cook it, and have lunch (95–204).
From the pike's jawbone Väinämöinen makes a harp
which many have a try at but not a single one can play (205–342).

Steadfast old Väinämöinen   steers easily
from the tip of that long headland,   from out of earshot of the miserable
    settlement.
Singing he steered over the water,   over the billows striking up joyous music.
The girls on the tips of headlands   look about, listen:
"What may be that joyous music on the sea?   What is the song on the
    billows,
each better than the last,   each more fitting than the others?"

Old Väinämöinen steered,   steered on one day over inland waters,
a second day through the waters of a fen,   the third along the waters of a
    rapid.
Then when near the fiery rapid,   by the whirlpool of the sacred stream
reckless Lemminkäinen   remembered a certain charm of his.
He speaks this charm,   utters this enchantment:

RAPIDS CHARMS, LINES 23–82

"Stop, rapid, foaming,   stop, mighty water, surging.
Maid of the rapids, girl of the foam,   sit down on a rock in the seething
    water,
place yourself on a boulder in the seething water;   with your embrace calm
    the waves,
wrap the eddies in your hands,   quiet the foam with your grasp
so that it will not spatter on our chests   nor splash on our heads.
Woman living under the waves,   woman living by the foam,
with the help of your hands rise up onto the foam,   with the help of your
    embrace rise onto a wave
to gather the foam together,   to guide the foamy billows
so that they may not buffet an innocent person,   not thrust a guiltless one
    hither and yon.

"Rocks in the middle of the river,   boulders on the crest of the foam,

let their heads be lowered,   their peaks be pressed down
away from the course of the red vessel,   from the path of the tarred boat.
If this is not enough,   Dread Rock Spirit, son of the Dread one,
bore a hole with an auger,   drill with your bit a hole
in the stone in the middle of the rapids,   in the side of the bad boulder,
so that the vessel may run on without stopping,   the boat without being
   damaged.

"If this is not enough,   master of the water, dweller under the stream,
turn the rocks into moss,   the boat into a pike's air bladder
while it is passing through the foam,   while it is going over the highest waves.

"Maiden by the rapid,   virgin of the riverside,
spin a filmy thread   from a bunch of filmy flax.
Bring your thread to the water,   your bluish thread to the billows,
a thread along which the vessel is to run,   the tarry-sided boat to proceed
   apace,
for a feeble man, too, to go,   for a quite inexperienced man to keep on
   course.

"Steering Oar Spirit, kindly woman,   take your gracious steering oar
with which you keep a helm on course,   with which you speed over enchanted streams
past a magician's Lappish tent,   under a wizard's window.

"If this is not enough,   Ukko, god of heaven,
guide the helm with your sword,   steer skillfully with your unsheathed blade,
so that the wooden vessel may run on,   the pinewood boat proceed."

Old Väinämöinen   steers easily.
He steered between the boulders   over those heavy swells;
the wooden vessel did not stop,   the sage's boat did not get stuck.
As soon as he got there   to those broad waters
the vessel stopped running on,   the boat stopped flying along.
The vessel stops on something solid,   the boat lay to there without moving.
Craftsman Ilmarinen,   reckless Lemminkäinen as the second,
stuck the steering oar into the sea,   the firwood oar into the billows;
they try to pry that vessel loose   from what it was stuck on;
the boat cannot run on   nor does the wooden vessel get free.

Steadfast old Väinämöinen   uttered a word, spoke thus:
"O you reckless son of Lempi!   Bend over and see
what the vessel is stuck on,   the boat fast on

in these broad waters,   quiet lower reaches,
whether on a rock or on a rotten tree trunk   or some other obstacle."
Reckless Lemminkäinen   turned to look;
he looks under the boat,   uttered a word, spoke thus:
"The boat is not on a rock,   not on a rock, not on a rotten tree trunk;
the boat is on a pike's shoulders,   on the shoulder blades of a dog of the
    water."
Steadfast old Väinämöinen   uttered a word, spoke thus:
"This and that is in a river,   rotten tree trunks, pikes, too;
if it is on a pike's shoulders,   on the shoulder blades of a dog of the water,
sweep the water with your sword,   cut the fish in two."
Reckless Lemminkäinen   the lad, ruddy-cheeked rascal,
draws a sword from his belt,   a bone-biter from his side;
he swept the sea with his sword,   pressed down under the side,
went quickly into the water,   tumbled straight into the waves.

Then craftsman Ilmarinen   grabbed the fellow by the hair,
lifted the man out of the sea;   he spoke these words:
"Everyone really is somehow created to be a man,   made to wear a beard,
if merely to round out the number of one hundred,   to fill out the number
    of one thousand!"
He draws a sword from his belt,   from its sheath a sharp blade
with which he struck the fish,   slashed at it under the side of the ship.
The sword broke to bits,   the pike did not even notice it.

Steadfast old Väinämöinen   then spoke these words:
"There are not the makings of half a man in you,   not the third of a person!
Whenever the need arises,   whenever a man's spirit is called for,
then your spirit is just so-so,   your whole activity diverted elsewhere."
He drew his sword,   whipped out his sharp blade.
He thrust his sword into the sea,   dug into the pike's shoulders
under the ship's side,   into the shoulder blades of the dog of the water.
The sword was driven into solid flesh,   was fixed in the gills.
Then old Väinämöinen   hove that fish up,
pulled the pike out of the water;   the pike broke in two,
the tail fell to the bottom,   the main part into the skiff.

Now the boat started to run on,   the vessel got free of the obstruction.
Steadfast old Väinämöinen   brought the boat to a little island,
put it quickly ashore,   He looks about, turns over
that main part of the pike,   uttered these words:
"Whoever is the oldest of the youths,   he indeed is the one to cut up the pike,
to cut the fish into slices,   chop the main part into pieces."

The men speak from the vessel, from the sides the women said:
"The fisherman's hands are indeed the fittest, the catcher's fingers the best."
Steadfast old Väinämöinen drew a knife from his sheath,
a cold blade from his side with which he cuts up the pike,
chops the fish into pieces. He spoke these words:
"Whoever is the youngest of the maidens, she is the one to boil the pike
for midmorning snacks, for fish dinners."

The maidens went to cook, ten indeed competed.
Then the pike is cooked as midmorning snacks.
The bones remained on the little island, the fishbones on the skerry.
Steadfast old Väinämöinen looks at them there,
looks, turns them over. He uttered a word, spoke thus:
"What might come of that, of those teeth of the pike,
of the broad jawbone if they were in a craftsman's workshop,
at a skillful smith's, in the hands of a capable man?"
Craftsman Ilmarinen spoke: "Nothing comes of nothing,
no work tool from a fishbone, not even in a craftsman's workshop,
at a skilled smith's, in the hands of a capable man."

Steadfast old Väinämöinen said these words:
"Nevertheless, from these indeed might come a fishbone harp
were there a competent person, a maker of a bone instrument."
When no one else at all came, when there was no competent person,
no maker of a bone instrument, steadfast old Väinämöinen
turned himself into a constructer, made himself a maker.
He made a pikebone instrument, produced an instrument of eternal joy.
From what was the harp's frame? From the great pike's jawbone.
From what are the harp's pegs? They are from the pike's teeth.
From what are the harp's strings? From the hairs of the Demon's gelding.
Now the instrument was produced, the harp got ready,
the great pikebone instrument, the fishbone harp.

Young fellows came there, married men came,
half-grown boys came, also little girls,
young girls, old women, middle-aged women, too,
to look at the harp, to inspect the instrument.
Steadfast old Väinämöinen ordered a young person, ordered an old person,
ordered a middle-aged person, too, to play with their fingers
that resonant fishbone object, the fishbone harp.
The young played, the old played, the middle-aged, too, played.
The young played, their fingers flexed; the old played, their hands trembled;
the music did not rise to the point of joyous music, the playing not reach the
   heights of playing.

Reckless Lemminkäinen said: "O you half-witted lads,
you silly girls, too, and other no-good people!
There is nothing of a player in you, no skilled performer really!
Bring me the instrument, carry the harp
right to my two knees, to under the tips of my ten fingers."
Then reckless Lemminkäinen got the harp in his hands,
the source of joyous music nearer to himself, the instrument to under his
    fingers.
He tunes the instrument, he turns the harp about;
no music at all sounds forth, no joyous sound echoes.
Old Väinämöinen said: "Neither in this body of young people,
in this people growing up, nor among the old people
is there anyone to play the instrument, anyone to evoke joyful music.
Would North Farm now be able to play the instrument better,
evoke that joyous music if I sent it to North Farm?"
He sent the instrument to North Farm, brought it to Sedgy Farm.
At North Farm the boys played the boys played, also the girls,
the married men played, also the married women.
Even the mistress played, turned it around, turned it about,
tuned it with her fingers, manipulated it with ten fingernails.
At North Farm the boys played, all sorts of people played.
The instrument of joyous music does not produce music, the instrument
    no music.
The strings kinked up, the horsehairs squeaked badly,
the tone reverberated harshly, the instrument sounded terrible.

A blind man was sleeping in a corner, an old man on top of the stove.
The old man on the stove awakened, screeched from the stove stones,
snarled from his sleeping place, growled from his corner:
"Stop, cease, leave off, end it!
It is piercing my ears, hurting my head;
it is making me shudder, it will deprive me of sleep for a long time.
If the instrument of the Finnish people will in the future not produce
    joyful music
or lull one to sleep, induce rest,
then fling it in the water, sink it in the waves
or take it back! Bring the instrument over there
to the hands of the man who made it, to the fingers of the tuner."
The music is spread abroad by the strings, the harp rang out with words:
"I will not yet go into the water, not be placed under the waves!
Rather will I resound in the hands of the player, clang out for him who
    took the trouble to make me."
Now they carried it carefully, bore it nicely
to the hand of the man who made it, to the knees of him who procured it.

POEM 41

Väinämöinen plays the harp and all living creatures,
even denizens of the air, the earth, and the sea,
hurry and assemble to listen to the music (1–168).
Everyone's heart is so moved by the music
that tears well up in their eyes;
great drops trickle from Väinämöinen's own eyes,
fall on the ground, and flow into the water,
where they are changed into beautiful bluish pearls (169–266).

Steadfast old Väinämöinen,   eternal singer,
arranges his fingers,   lightly rubs his thumbs together.
He seats himself on a music stone,   places himself on a song boulder,
on a silver hill,   on a golden knoll.
He took the instrument in his fingers,   on his knees turned the instrument
    with a tapering frame,
the harp under his hand.   He uttered a word, spoke thus:
"Let him come to hear   who previously may·not have heard
the joyous music of eternal lays,   the resonance of the harp."
Thus old Väinämöinen   began delicately to play
the pikebone sounding board,   the fishbone harp.
His fingers rose quickly,   his thumb moved lightly above.

Now joyous music resulted in joyous music,   rapture after rapture burst forth,
the music seemed like music,   the song was like a proper song.
The pike's tooth rang out,   the fish's tail gave forth sound,
the stallion's hairs resounded,   the steed's hairs sang out clearly.
Old Väinämöinen played   nor was there that thing in the forest
running about on four feet,   leaping with its legs,
that did not come to hear,   to marvel at the joyous music.
The squirrels reached out   from spray to spray,
the weasels betook themselves there,   settled themselves on fences.
The elk sprang on the heaths,   the lynxes jumped about joyfully.
In the fen the wolf, too, awoke,   the bear on the heath got up
from its den in the pines,   from out of the scrub firs.
The wolf ran great distances,   the bear roamed the heaths;
at last it settled down on a fence,   flung itself onto a gate.
The fence collapsed onto a rock,   the gate toppled over onto a clearing.
Then it jumped up into a fir,   turned suddenly up into a pinetree
to listen to the playing,   to marvel at the joyous music.

The keen-eyed old man of Tapio's Domain,   the master himself of Woodland
and all Tapio's people,   both girls and boys,
went to the top of a hill   to take in the music.
The mistress of the forest herself, too,   keen-eyed lady of Tapio's Domain,
decks herself out in blue stockings,   put on red laces;
she went to the knee of a birch branch,   moved quickly to the bend in an
    alder branch
to listen to the harp,   to take in the music.
Whatever birds of the air, too,   were soaring on two wings;
they come whirling about,   hurrying they hastened
to listen to the glorious playing,   to marvel at the joyous sound.
When the eagle back home heard   that pretty Finnish instrument,
it left its young in the nest,   began to fly
to the playing of the delightful man,   to Väinämöinen's modulations.
The eagle flew from on high,   the bird of prey through the clouds,
old squaws from deep waters,   swans from watery fens.
Little chaffinches, too,   songbirds,
buntings by the hundred,   nearly a thousand larks
in the air were charmed,   chattered on his shoulders
while the patriarch was making joyous music,   while Väinämöinen was
    playing away.

The very geniuses of the air,   lovely virgins of the air,
marveled at the joyous music,   listened to the harp;
some were radiant on the shaft-bow of the sky,   on the rainbow,
others were magnificent   on the rosy-edged tip of a little cloud.
That Moon Spirit, lovely virgin,   Sun Spirit, competent maid,
were holding their weaver's battens,   lifting up their heddles,
weaving cloth of gold,   thumping off cloth of silver
on the edge of a red cloud,   on the side of a long rainbow.
When indeed they got to hear   the sound of that charming instrument,
the batten now escaped from their grasp,   the shuttle slipped from their
    hands,
the gold threads broke,   the silver heddles sounded softly.

There was not that creature,   not indeed a single six-finned creature
moving in the water,   not the finest school of fish
that did not come to listen,   to marvel at the joyous music.
Pike swam along stiffly,   dogs of the water thrashed about,
salmon wandered in from the little islands,   whitefish from the deep places.
The little carp, perch, too,   whitefish, also, other fish as well
went straight on into the sedge grass,   took their places by the shore
to listen to Väinämöinen's song,   to take in the music.
Ahto, king of the waves,   old man of the water with a sedgy beard,

hauls himself onto the surface of the water,   slips onto a water lily;
there he listened to the joyous music.   He uttered these words:
"Never before have I heard   anything of this sort,
Väinämöinen's playing,   the joyous music of the eternal bard."
The sisters, Spirits of Goldeneye,   the sisters-in-law clad in shore sedge,
were smoothing down their tresses,   brushing their locks
with a silver-tipped brush,   with a gold brush.
They got to hear the unusual sound,   that pretty playing;
the brush slipped into the water,   the brush fell into the billows.
Their hair remained unsmoothed,   the locks only half arranged.
The mistress of the water herself, too,   the old woman with a sedgy breast,
now rises out of the sea   and gradually hauls herself out of the billows;
she went quickly up to the sedge,   betook herself to a reef in the water
to hear that sound,   Väinämöinen's playing,
for the sound was wonderful,   the playing exceedingly lovely.
There she slept soundly,   sank down and lay on her stomach
on top of a rock of many colors,   to the side of a big boulder.

Then old Väinämöinen   played one day, played a second.
There was not that person   or brave man,
not man or woman   or girl with luxuriant hair
who did not start to weep,   whose heart did not melt.
The young wept, the old wept,   the unmarried fellows wept,
the married men wept,   half-grown boys wept,
both boys and girls   and little girls, too,
for the sound was wonderful,   the old man's playing delightful.
Even Väinämöinen's   own tears flowed fast.
Teardrops trickled from his eyes,   drops of water flowed
bigger than cranberries,   plumper than peas,
rounder than the eggs of ruffed grouse,   bigger than swallows' heads.
Tears poured from his eyes,   one quietly flows after another.
They fell onto his cheekbones,   onto his handsome face,
from his handsome face   to his broad jowl,
from his broad jowl   to his splendid chest,
from his splendid chest   to his strong knees,
from his strong knees   to the fine soles of his feet,
from the fine soles of his feet   to the ground under his feet
through five woolen cloaks,   through six gold belts,
seven blue underjackets,   eight homespun kaftans.
The teardrops flowed   from beside old Väinämöinen
to the shore of the blue sea,   from the shore of the blue sea
to under the clear waters   onto the black ooze.

Then old Väinämöinen   uttered these words:
"Is there among these young people,   these handsome youths,

in this great clan,   in the tribe great on the father's side,
anyone to gather up my tears   from under the clear waters?"
Then the young speak thus   and the old answer:
"There is not among these young people,   these handsome youths,
in this great clan,   in the tribe great on the father's side,
anyone to gather up your tears   from under the clear waters."
Old Väinämöinen said,   remarked, spoke thus:
"If someone would bring my tears,   would gather the teardrops
from under the clear waters,   he would receive from me a birdskin-lined fur
   coat."

A raven came flapping clumsily along.   Old Väinämöinen said:
"Bring my tears, raven,   from under the clear waters;
I will give you a birdskin-lined fur coat."   The raven did not get it at all.
A blue goldeneye heard that,   so the blue goldeneye came.
Old Väinämöinen said: "Often, blue goldeneye,
you dive straight in,   go like a flash into the water;
go gather my tears   from under the clear waters.
You will get the best reward;   I will give you a birdskin-lined fur coat."
The goldeneye went to gather   Väinämöinen's tears
from under the clear waters,   from on top of the black ooze.
It gathered the tears from the sea,   brought them to Väinämöinen's hand.
They had already been changed to other things,   grown into beautiful things,
swelled up into pearls,   turned into bluish fresh-water pearls,
as an honor for kings,   as an everlasting joy for rulers.

POEM 42

The men come to North Farm and Väinämöinen says
they have come for a sharing of the Sampo; if they do not get
their half amicably they will take the whole of it by force (1–58).
The mistress of North Farm does not wish to give it up
and she assembles the people of North Farm to offer resistance (59–64).
Väinämöinen takes the harp, begins to play,
and by his playing puts the whole company at North Farm to sleep;
then he goes with his companions to look at the Sampo;
they get it out of the hill of rock and take it to their boat (65–164).
With the Sampo in the boat
they set out from North Farm and proceed happily toward home (165–308).
On the third day the mistress of North Farm awakens and, seeing
that the Sampo has been taken, creates a dense fog, a big gale,
and other obstacles to delay the abductors of the Sampo
until she has time to go after them;
in the storm Väinämöinen's harp disappears into the sea (309–562).

Steadfast old Väinämöinen,   craftsman Ilmarinen the second,
the third Lempi's reckless son,   that handsome man with a far-roving mind,
set out on the clear sea,   on the open billows,
to that cold community,   to dark North Farm,
to the place where a man meets his end,   a person is destroyed.
Who is going to row there?   One is craftsman Ilmarinen.
That is who is going to row there   at the forward oars;
the second is reckless Lemminkäinen   to row at the oars aft;
steadfast old Väinämöinen   himself sat down in the stern.
He steers the boat in easy fashion,   steered through the billows,
through those heavy seas,   through the whitecaps
toward the landing places at North Farm,   to in front of the familiar rollers.
After they arrived there,   reached the end of the journey,
they dragged the boat ashore,   pulled the tarry-prowed vessel
onto the steel rollers,   the copper rollers.

From there they came to the house,   quickly made their way inside.
The mistress of North Farm asked,   inquired of the new arrivals:
"What news do you men have,   what message, you people?"
Steadfast old Väinämöinen   replies to this:
"The men's news is about the Sampo,   the people's about the lid of many
colors.
We have come for a sharing of the Sampo,   for a look at the lid of many
colors."

The mistress of North Farm   uttered a word, spoke thus:
" 'There are not two portions in a ruffed grouse   nor three men's in a
   squirrel.'
It is fine for the Sampo to whir,   for the lid of many colors to rumble
in the hill of rock at North Farm,   inside the copper mountain.
It is fine for me myself to be   the possessor of the big Sampo."
Steadfast old Väinämöinen   uttered a word, spoke thus:
"If you will not give us a share,   that one half of the Sampo,
then we will probably take it all,   transport it to our boat."

Louhi, mistress of North Farm,   took this very, very badly.
She summoned North Farm together,   young men with swords,
men with weapons   destined for Väinämöinen's head.
Steadfast old Väinämöinen   got his harp,
sat down to play,   began to play beautifully.
Everybody starts to listen to that,   to marvel at the joyous music,
the men in a good mood,   the women with laughing mouths,
men with tears in their eyes,   boys on their knees on the ground.
The people grew weary,   the country folk get worn out;
all the listeners fell asleep   and the onlookers sank down;
the young slept, the old slept   to Väinämöinen's music.
Then wise Väinämöinen,   eternal sage,
groped in his pouch,   felt in his wallet.
He takes sleep-inducing thorns,   anointed their eyes with sleep,
crosses their eyelashes,   locked the eyelids
of the weary people,   of the drowsy men.
The whole household of North Farm   and all the people of the community
he put into a long sleep,   put to sleep for quite a long time.

He went to get the Sampo,   to look at the lid of many colors
in North Farm's hill of rock,   inside the copper mountain
behind nine locks,   ten interior bolts.
Then old Väinämöinen   sings softly
on the doors of the copper mountain,   on the sides of the stone stronghold.
Now indeed the gates of the stronghold were moving,   the iron hinges
   starting.
Craftsman Ilmarinen,   he indeed is there as the second man;
he greased the locks with fat,   the hinges with lard
so that the doors would not creak   or the hinges squeak.
He worked the locks loose with his fingers,   raised the bolts with a grub hoe;
now he wiggled the locks to pieces,   worked the solid doors open.

Then old Väinämöinen   uttered these words:
"O you reckless son of Lempi,   my best friend!

Go take the Sampo,   rip off the lid of many colors."
Reckless Lemminkäinen,   handsome man with a far-roving mind,
quick even if not ordered,   spry even if not urged,
went to get the Sampo,   to rip off the lid of many colors.
As he was walking there he said,   as he was going he boasted:
"Whatever there may be of a fellow in me,   of a man of Ukko in the boy,
let it budge that Sampo,   turn the lid of many colors
with the help of my right foot,   with a touch of the heel of my boot."
Lemminkäinen tried to budge it,   budge it, turn it;
he hugged the Sampo with his arms,   kneeling on the ground he worked
   away,
but the Sampo does not move at all,   its lid of many colors not budge;
its roots were rooted   nine fathoms deep.
At North Farm there is a fine steer   which is sturdy of body
with very solid flanks,   with very fine sinews;
its horns are a fathom long,   its muzzle one and a half fathoms thick.
He took the steer from the pasture,   a plow from the edge of the field;
with that he plowed up the roots of the Sampo,   the fastenings of the lid of
   many colors.
The Sampo got to moving,   the lid of many colors came loose.

Then old Väinämöinen,   craftsman Ilmarinen the second,
reckless Lemminkäinen the third,   conveyed the big Sampo
from the hill of rock at North Farm,   from inside the copper mountain.
They take it into their boat,   stowed it in their ship.
They got the Sampo into their vessel,   the lid of many colors into their
   ribbed ship;
they pushed the boat to the water,   the ship of a hundred planks to the
   billows.
The boat plunged into the water,   went straight out onto the billows.
Craftsman Ilmarinen asked,   uttered a word, spoke thus:
"Where shall we take the Sampo,   where transport it
from these wretched parts,   from miserable North Farm?"
Steadfast old Väinämöinen   spoke, said this:
"We will take the Sampo,   transport the lid of many colors
to the tip of the misty headland,   to the end of the foggy island,
for good fortune to stay there,   to reside forever.
There is a little space there,   actually a bit of room,
unplundered, unconquered,   unvisited by the sword of man."

Then old Väinämöinen   set out from North Farm,
set out in a happy state of mind,   rejoicing to his own lands.
Then he spoke thus: "Turn, vessel, away from North Farm,
turn toward home,   stern toward alien lands.

A ROWER'S CHARM, LINES 197-216

"Wind, rock the vessel;   water, row the boat,
give help to the oars,   relief to the steering oar
on these broad waters,   wide open seas.
Should the oars be small,   the rowers feeble,
the helmsmen quite small,   the ship's masters be children,
give us, Ahto, your oars,   your boat, master of the water,
new oars and better,   a steering oar different and stronger;
set yourself at the oars,   apply yourself to rowing.
Let the wooden vessel run on,   the boat with iron tholepins cut
through heavy seas,   whitecapped billows."

Then old Väinämöinen   steers in easy fashion.
Craftsman Ilmarinen,   reckless Lemminkäinen the second,
they are rowing there,   rowing, rowing slowly
over the expanse of the open waters,   the boundless billows.
Reckless Lemminkäinen said: "In days gone by
a rower had water and a singer a song   but nowadays no one ever hears
such chanting in a boat,   such singing on the billows."
Steadfast old Väinämöinen   uttered a word, spoke thus:
"No chanting on the water,   no singing on the billows!
Singing makes one lazy,   songs hold up rowing.
The golden day would pass away,   in the middle of work night surprise us
on these vast waters,   boundless billows."
Reckless Lemminkäinen   uttered a word, spoke thus:
"Time passes anyhow,   the lovely day speeds on,
night comes quickly,   dusk hastens on
even if you never sing,   if you never intone."

Old Väinämöinen steered   over the surface of the blue sea,
went on for one day, went on a second.   On the third day indeed
reckless Lemminkäinen   for the second time repeated:
"Why do you not sing, Väinämöinen,   not intone, good man of good Slack
    Water Farm
now that you have got the good Sampo,   are on the right course?"
Steadfast old Väinämöinen   he indeed answers:
"It is early for singing,   too soon to make joyous music.
Singing would be suitable,   songmaking fitting,
should our own doors appear,   our own doors cry out."
Reckless Lemminkäinen said: "Were I myself in the stern,
I would sing as best I could,   would intone as I was able;
perhaps we will not be able another time,   not do it adequately.
If you will not agree to sing,   I will begin a song."

Then reckless Lemminkäinen,   that handsome man with a far-roving mind,
arranges his mouth,   adjusts his voice.
He began to intone,   began, poor man, to sing
with his harsh voice,   with his raspy throat.
Reckless Lemminkäinen sang,   the man with a far-roving mind kept roaring;
the mouth moved, the beard shook,   the jaws were askew.
The song could be heard quite far off,   the quavering voice across the water;
it was heard as far off as six,   seven settlements across the surface of the water.
A crane was sitting on a stump   on top of a wet hummock;
it is looking at its claws,   lifing up its feet.
It really got terribly frightened   at Lemminkäinen's singing.
The crane stopped its strange doings,   was frightened by the bad voice;
at once it began to fly,   flew off to North Farm.
Then after it had got there,   had reached the fen at North Farm,
it was still shrieking crossly,   screaming angrily.
With that it wakened North Farm,   aroused the evil domain.
The mistress of North Farm got up   after having lain in a long sleep.
She went to the cattle yard,   ran to the granary,
looks at her cattle,   reflects on her things;
no cattle were missing,   her grain supply had not been removed.
Now she went to the hill of rock,   to the door of the copper mountain.
When she got there she said: "Woe is my day, poor wretch!
Some stranger has already come here,   has removed all the bolts,
has moved the gates of the stronghold,   has damaged the iron hinges.
Has the Sampo perhaps been got from here,   taken high-handedly?"
The Sampo had already been got from there,   its lid of many colors taken
    forcibly
from North Farm's hill of rock,   from inside the copper mountain,
from behind nine bolts,   ten interior bolts.

Louhi, mistress of North Farm,   grew very angry at that;
she observed her diminishing power,   her declining prestige.
She prays to the Mist Spirit: "Mist Girl, Fog Maiden!
Sift out mist with your sieve,   hang out some fog,
send down mist from the sky,   let down a light haze from the air
onto the clear surface of the sea,   the expanse of open water
so that Väinämöinen will not get away,   the man of Slack Water Farm not
    be able to.
If not enough comes of this,   eternal Turso, son of the Old Man,
raise your head from the sea,   the top of your head from the billows!
Lay low the Kaleva men,   drown the men of Slack Water Farm,
destroy the wicked people   under the deep waves.
Get the Sampo to North Farm   without its falling out of the boat.
If not enough comes of this,   O Ukko, god on high,

golden king of the air,   silver ruler,
create a violent wind,   raise a great and mighty storm.
Create a wind, send a wave   right against the boat
so that Väinämöinen will not get away,   the man of Slack Water Farm not
  proceed."

The Mist Girl, the Fog Maiden,   breathes forth mist onto the sea,
produced fog in the air;   it held up old Väinämöinen
for three whole nights   out on the blue sea
so that he does not get to his destination,   nor proceed anywhere at all.
After he had stayed for three nights   out on the blue sea,
old Väinämöinen spoke,   remarked, said this:
"A really rather inferior man, indeed,   even a really less enterprising person
must not be downed by mist,   defeated by fog."
He scored the water with his blade,   slashed the sea with the sword.
Mead spattered from the track of the blade,   honey from the spray from the
  sword;
the mist ascended to the heavens,   the fog rose up to the sky.
The sea got clear of haze,   the waves of the sea clear of mist;
the sea opened up large,   the world got big.

It was just a little while,   a short time passed quickly.
Now a loud noise was heard   beside their red boat;
a swell rose high   against Väinämöinen's vessel.
Then craftsman Ilmarinen   got very frightened;
the blood went from his face,   the color left his cheeks.
He pulled a woolen blanket over his head,   adjusted it over his ears;
he covered his face in fine fashion,   his eyes even better.

Old Väinämöinen   looked at the water at the side,
cast his eyes to the side of the vessel,   He saw a funny little creature;
beside the red boat   eternal Turso, son of the Old Man,
raised his head from the sea,   the top of his head from the billows.
Steadfast old Väinämöinen   took a grip on his ears,
lifted him up by the ears,   inquired, spoke,
uttered a word, spoke thus: "Eternal Turso, son of the Old Man,
why did you rise up from the sea,   come up from the waves
into the presence of men,   still more, of a Kaleva descendant?"
Eternal Turso, son of the Old Man,   was not pleased with that
nor was he very frightened,   he does not even answer.
Steadfast old Väinämöinen   just asked a second time,
inquired emphatically a third time: "Eternal Turso, son of the Old Man,
why did you rise up from the sea,   come up from the waves?"
Eternal Turso, son of the Old Man,   now on the third time

speaks a word in reply: "I rose up from the sea,
came up from the waves   because I had in mind
to kill the Kaleva clan,   to get the Sampo to North Farm.
If you will now let me down into the billows,   furthermore grant the good-
for-nothing his life,
I will not come again   into the presence of men."
Then old Väinämöinen   threw the wretch into the billows.
He uttered these words: "Eternal Turso, son of the Old Man,
may you not rise up from the sea,   not come up from the waves
into the presence of men   from this day on."
From that day on   Turso does not rise up from the sea
into the presence of men   as long as the moon, the sun,
the lovely light of day,   the delightful sky exist.

Then old Väinämöinen   sent his ship forward.
It was just a little while,   the short time passed quickly.
Now Ukko, god on high,   the lord of the air himself,
told the winds to blow,   violent storms to rage.
The winds started to blow,   violent storms to rage.
The westwind blew in hard gusts,   the southwest wind wailed,
the southwind blew still more so.   The eastwind whistled dreadfully,
the southwest wind roared horribly,   the northwind howled loudly.
It blew the trees leafless,   the evergreen boughs needleless,
the heather flowerless,   the grass sheathless.
Black ooze rose up   to the surface of the clear waters.
Then the winds blew very hard,   waves pounded the craft.
They carried away the pikebone harp,   the fish-fin instrument
for the benefit of Vellamo's people,   as an eternal joy for Ahto's Realm.
In the waves Ahto noticed this,   Ahto's children in the billows;
they took the lovely instrument,   removed it to their home.
Then tears came   to old Väinämöinen's eyes;
he uttered these words: "There has gone my creation,
gone my lovely instrument,   vanished my eternal source of joy!
I will never get one better than that,   never, never at all,
an instrument of pike teeth,   a clear-toned fishbone one."
Craftsman Ilmarinen,   he really got quite angry;
he uttered a word, spoke thus: "Wretched me, woe was my day
when I set out on these waters,   on the open expanses of the sea,
when I stepped into the rolling boat,   onto the shivering timbers.
Now my hair has suffered the wind,   my hair the dreadful storm;
my beard has suffered   evil days on these waters.
Seldom before has one been able   to perceive a wind like this,
such heavy seas,   whitecapped billows.
Now the wind is my refuge,   the waves of the sea my source of favor!"

Steadfast old Väinämöinen   then reflects on this:
"In a boat there must be no lamenting,   in a vessel no whimpering.
'Weeping does not rid one of distress   nor howling of evil days.'"
Then he uttered these words,   spoke, remarked thus:

[A CHARM TO CALM WAVES, LINES 529-534]

"Water, forbid your son;   billow, check your child!
Ahto, quiet the waves,   Vellamo, quiet the genius of the water
so that it will not splash on the gunwales,   not reach the ribs of my ship."

[A CHARM TO CALM WINDS AND STORMS, LINES 535-542]

"Rise, wind, to heaven,   betake yourself up to the clouds,
to your tribe, to your family,   to your clan, to your family.
Do not overturn the wooden vessel,   tip over the boat of evergreen wood.
Overturn rather trees on a clearing,   topple the firs on knolls."

Reckless Lemminkäinen,   the handsome man with a far-roving mind,
uttered a word, spoke thus: "Come, eagle of Finnmark,
bring three of your feathers,   eagle, three, raven, two,
as a protection for the little boat,   as a gunwale for the poor vessel."
He increased the freeboard,   prepared sideboards;
to these he joined extra boards,   making the whole a fathom high
above the course of waves so   that they would not splash on beards.
Now there was freeboard enough,   sideboards enough on the boat
for the severe wind to blow against in gusts,   for a powerful sea to push against
while passing through the surf,   going over the highest waves.

POEM 43

The mistress of North Farm prepares a warship
and sets out to pursue the abductors of the Sampo (1–22).
Then when she surprises them, a sea battle develops,
in which the Kaleva people gain the victory (23–258).
However, the mistress of North Farm
succeeds in getting the Sampo out of the boat into the sea,
where it breaks up and goes to pieces (259–266).
The larger pieces sink into the water as the property of the sea;
the smaller ones a wave drives ashore.
Väinämöinen rejoices in this and hopes now to get from these
the beginning of new good fortune (267–304).
The mistress of North Farm threatens to destroy
the whole well-being of the Kaleva District,
a threat of which Väinämöinen says he is not afraid (305–368).
In a sorry state of mind over the loss of her power,
the mistress of North Farm goes back,
nor from the whole Sampo does she get anything for North Farm
but the now worthless lid (369–384).
Väinämöinen carefully gathers up fragments of the Sampo on the shore,
gets them to grow, and hopes for good fortune for all time (385–434).

Louhi, mistress of North Farm,   called the men of North Farm together.
She provided the crowd with the crossbows,   fitted the men out with swords;
she outfitted the vessel of North Farm,   put the warship in order.
She lined the men up on her ship,   organized the warriors
as a goldeneye does its young,   as a teal orders its chicks:
a hundred swordsmen,   a thousand crossbowmen.
She stepped the masts,   attended to the yardarms,
hoisted the sails on the mast,   canvas on the mainmast
like a big cloud patch,   a patch of cloud in the sky.
Then she set out to go,   both set out and hurried
to try to get the Sampo   from Väinämöinen's boat.

Steadfast old Väinämöinen   is going ahead on the blue sea.
He uttered these words,   spoke from the stern of his vessel:
"O you reckless son of Lempi,   my very best friend!
Climb to the masthead,   bound up the mainmast.
Take a look at the sky ahead,   scan closely the sky behind
to see whether the horizons are clear,   whether they are clear or not clear.

Reckless Lemminkäinen   the lad, the ruddy-cheeked rascal,
quick without being ordered,   spry without being urged,
climbed to the top of the mast,   went quickly up the mainmast.
He looked east, looked west,   looked southwest, south,
looked across the shore of North Farm.   Then he uttered these words:
"The sky ahead is clear,   the heavens behind hazy;
there is a little cloud in the north,   a cloud patch in the southwest."
Old Väinämöinen said: "Now you are just lying!
That is no cloud at all,   is not possibly a cloud patch;
it is a sailing vessel.   Look a second time more closely."
He looked a second time, looked closely;   he speaks these words:
"From afar an island is visible,   is looming up from a great distance;
the aspens are full of hawks,   the birches full of speckled capercaillie hens."
Old Väinämöinen said: "Now you are just lying!
There are not possibly any hawks,   any speckled grouse;
those are lads from North Farm.   Look closely a third time."
Reckless Lemminkäinen   looked a third time.
He speaks these words,   made this utterance:
"Now the vessel of North Farm is coming,   the boat with a hundred thole-
pins is whipping along.
There are a hundred men at the oars,   a thousand besides sitting down."

Then old Väinämöinen   now recognized the whole truth.
He uttered a word, spoke thus: "Row, craftsman Ilmarinen,
row, reckless Lemminkäinen,   row, you whole company,
that the boat may race on,   the vessel speed ahead."
Craftsman Ilmarinen rowed,   reckless Lemminkäinen rowed,
the whole company rowed.   The hard pine oars jumped,
the rowan tholepins clicked,   the boat of evergreen wood shivered;
the boat made a noise like a seal,   the stern hissed like a rapids,
the water bubbled up,   foam flew by in blobs.
The men are rowing as in a race,   the fellows pulling on the oars as if on a
bet;
the journey does not progress,   the wooden vessel does not speed
ahead of the sailing vessel,   that boat of North Farm.

Then old Väinämöinen   now realized that disaster was coming,
a fateful day falling upon them.   He ponders, reflects
on how to exist, how to live.   He uttered these words:
"I still remember a trick for this,   I will devise a little surprise."
He groped among his pieces of magic tinder,   poked around in his tinderbox.
He took a little flint,   quite a small amount of tinder fungus;
these he drops over his left shoulder   into the sea.

He speaks these words,   made this utterance:
"From that let come a reef,   let sunken rocks grow
for the vessel of North Farm to run onto,   for the boat with a hundred
   tholepins to break up on
in a seething eddy of the stormy sea,   in the surge of the surf!"
From this it turned into a reef,   became a rock in the sea
longwise running east,   crosswise north.
The vessel of North Farm came on swiftly,   whips through the waves;
now it lands on the reef,   stuck fast on the skerry.
The wooden vessel flew apart,   the hundred-ribbed ship broke up.
The masts fell into the sea,   the sails dropped in shreds
to be carried away by the wind,   swept off by the cold spring wind.

Louhi, mistress of North Farm,   jumps straight into the water,
set about raising the vessel,   getting the ship up.
She could not get the boat up   or move the vessel;
all the ribs were broken,   all the tholepins scattered.
She ponders, reflects: "What comes by way of counsel?
What does anyone propose?"   Now indeed she changed herself into something else,
dared to try to become something different.   She took five scythes,
the remains of six battered grub hoes;   these indeed she made into talons,
fashioned them to be her hands;   half the vessel was wrecked:
that she put beneath her;   the planking she knocked into wings,
the steering oar into a tail for herself;   a hundred men are under her wings,
a thousand under the tip of her tail,   a hundred swordsmen, a thousand
   bowmen.
She spreads her wings to fly,   raises herself aloft like an eagle.
She flies swiftly along   seeking out Väinämöinen;
one wing brushed the clouds,   the other grazed the water.

The mother of water, beautiful woman,   she was the one who uttered these
   words:
"O old Väinämöinen!   Turn your head from the south,
cast your eyes to the southwest,   look a little behind you!"
Steadfast old Väinämöinen   turned his head from the south,
cast his gaze to the southwest,   looked a little behind him;
now the old woman of North Farm is coming,   a remarkable bird is moving
   along,
like a hawk to judge from the shoulders,   a griffin to judge from the trunk.
She takes Väinämöinen by surprise.   She flew onto the masthead,
moved quickly down onto the mainmast,   stands on the masthead.
The vessel was about to sink straight down,   the ship to keel over on its side.

Then craftsman Ilmarinen throws himself on his God's mercy,
entrusts himself to his Creator. He speaks these words:

A WARRIOR'S CHARM, LINES 191-206

"Protect me, mighty Creator! Guard me, fair God,
that the lad may not be lost, the mother's child not fall in battle
from among the number created by the Creator, formed by God.
Ukko, renowned god, heavenly father!
Bring me a fiery cloak, a flaming shirt to put on,
in the protection of which I may wage war and behind which I may fight
that my head may not come to grief, my hair not be ruined
in the play of bright blades, on the point of a sharp sword."

Old Väinämöinen uttered a word, spoke thus:
"O mistress of North Farm! Will you now share the Sampo
on the tip of the misty headland, at the end of the foggy island?"
The mistress of North Farm said: "I will not start to share the Sampo
with you, wretch, with you, Väinämöinen."
She tried to seize the Sampo from Väinämöinen's boat.
Then reckless Lemminkäinen drew a sword from his belt,
pulled the steel blade from his left side;
he aims at the eagle's grip, lashes at its feet.
Reckless Lemminkäinen dealt a blow, both dealt a blow and spoke:
"Down, men! Down, swords! Down sluggish people,
a hundred men from under the wings, tens from the tip of the feathers!"
Then the old woman of North Farm spoke, spoke from the top of the mast:
"O you reckless son of Lempi, wretch with a far-roving mind, base man!
You deceived your own mother, you lied to your parent;
you said you would not wage war for six, ten summers
from a craving for gold, a desire for silver."

Steadfast old Väinämöinen, eternal sage,
thought his time was up, felt his hour had probably come.
Now he pulled in the steering oar from the sea, the oaken splint from the
  billows;
with that he dealt the woman a blow, struck some claws from the eagle;
the other claws went to pieces, one little finger was left.
The lads dropped from the wings, the men splashed into the sea,
a hundred men from under the wings, a thousand from the tail.
The eagle itself plopped down, flopped down into the ribbed ship
like a wood grouse from a tree, like a squirrel from a fir branch.
Then she tried to seize the Sampo with her ring finger.
She thrust the Sampo into the water, dropped the whole lid of many colors

from the side of the red vessel   into the middle of the blue sea.
Then the Sampo broke to pieces,   the lid of many colors to bits.

Thus those bits,   big pieces of the Sampo went
under the gentle waters   onto the black ooze;
they remained as a possession of the water,   as treasures for the people of
     Ahto's realm.
Thus never, never at all,   not while the moon shines gold-bright,
will the water lack possessions,   Ahto of the water lack treasures.
Other bits remained, to be sure,   rather small pieces
on the surface of the blue sea,   on the billows of the wide sea,
for the wind to rock,   the waves to drive about.
These the winds rocked,   the billows of the sea sent billowing
along the surface of the blue sea,   on the waves of the wide sea.
The wind thrust them toward land,   the waves drove them ashore.
Steadfast old Väinämöinen   saw the surf thrusting them,
the swell casting them onto the land,   a wave driving them to the shore,
those bits of the Sampo,   pieces of the lid of many colors toward shore.
He rejoiced greatly at that,   uttered a word, spoke thus:
"From that is the germ of a seed,   the beginning of good fortune for all time,
from that a plowing, from that a sowing,   from that all sorts of crops.
From that the moon will get to gleaming palely,   the sun of good fortune
     to shining
on the great farms of Finland,   in Finland's lovely districts."

Louhi, mistress of North Farm,   uttered a word, spoke thus:
"I still remember a trick for that,   remember a trick, will devise a means
to counter your plowing, your sowing,   your cattle, your plants,
your palely gleaming moons,   your shining suns.
I will thrust the moon into a rock,   hide the sun in a crag;
I will let the frost freeze,   further let cold weather hold back
your plowings, your sowings,   your grain, your crops.
I will bring hailstones hard as iron,   I will keep hammering ones like steel
on your good planted clearings,   on your best fields.
I will raise up a bear from the heath,   one with sparse teeth from the
     evergreens
to mangle your geldings,   to kill your mares,
to lay low your cattle,   to scatter your cows.
I will kill the nation by plagues,   slay your whole clan,
so that it will never, never   in the world be mentioned."

Then old Väinämöinen   uttered these words:
"No Lapp will enchant me,   no Finnmark Lapp exert pressure on me.
'God has control of the weather,   the Creator holds the keys of good fortune;

they are not under the arm of a wizard,   not on the fingertip of a malefic
   person.'
If I seek protection in my Creator,   trust in my God,
He will keep grubs from my crops,   enemies from my grain,
keep them from rooting up my crops,   from killing my plants,
from taking my young shoots,   from showing hostility to my grain.
You, mistress of North Farm,   thrust your disasters into a rock,
press your evil things into a crag,   sort your trouble out into a mountain,
never the moon,   never the sun.
Let the frost freeze,   further let cold weather hold back
your own young shoots,   seeds sown by yourself.
Bring hail as hard as iron,   let hail as hard as steel fall on furrows
turned by your own plow   at the end of the fields of North Farm.
Raise up a bear from a heath,   an angry wildcat from a thicket,
a bear with curved claws from the backwoods,   a sparse-toothed one from
   under an evergreen
for the lane of North Farm,   the trails of North Farm's cattle."

Then the mistress of North Farm   uttered a word, spoke thus:
"Now my power has declined,   my prestige has already diminished;
my wealth went into the sea,   the Sampo was smashed in the billows."
Weeping she set out for home,   lamenting her misery she set out north.
Of the whole Sampo she brought home   nothing worth mentioning;
she brought, however, a small bit   on her ring finger;
she carried the lid to North Farm,   got the handle to Sedgy Farm.
For this reason there is poverty at North Farm,   a breadless life in Lapland.
After steadfast old Väinämöinen   had gone ashore,
he found bits of the Sampo,   pieces of the lid of many colors
on the seashore,   on the soft sandy beach.
He brought the bits of the Sampo,   pieces of the lid of many colors
to the tip of the misty headland,   to the end of the foggy island
to grow, to increase,   to yield, to flourish,
as barley beer,   as rye-bread loaves.
Then old Väinämöinen   uttered these words:

A CHARM TO GAIN GOD'S SUPPORT, LINES 401–434

"Let, O Creator, grant, O God,   grant us to be fortunate,
always to live well,   to die with honor
in lovely Finland,   in beautiful Karelia.
Protect us, steadfast Creator,   guard us, gracious God,
from the designs of men,   the plots of women.
Lay low earthly ill-disposed persons,   vanquish water wizards.
Side with your sons,   always be a help to your children,
always a prop by night,   a guardian by day,

so that the sun does not blaze malefically upon us,   the moon not gleam
    palely,
the wind not blow fiercely,   the rain not fall fiercely,
frost not freeze us,   severe weather not touch us.
Build an iron fence,   put together a stone rampart
around my dwelling place,   around both sides of my people,
reaching from earth to heaven,   from heaven to earth,
as my dwelling, as my good dwelling,   as my prop, as my defence,
that no malefic creature may devour me either,   no adversary ever destroy
    my grain,
never, never at all   while the moon shines gold-bright."

POEM 44

Väinämöinen sets out to look in the sea for his lost harp,
which he does not, however, get his hands on again (1–76).
He then makes a lovely new birchwood harp with which
he again plays and delights everything found in nature (77–334).

Steadfast old Väinämöinen   reflects in his mind:
"Now indeed playing would be appropriate,   making joyous music would be
     good
under these new conditions,   in these lovely farmsteads.
But the harp has vanished,   my source of joyous music has gone forever
into the farmstead of the fish,   into the salmon's reefs,
to the rulers of the depths of the sea,   to the eternal power of Vellamo.
No one is likely to fetch it from there,   Ahto not likely to give it back.
O craftsman Ilmarinen,   of yore you forged, yesterday you forged,
forge indeed today, too!   Forge an iron rake,
with close-set teeth in the rake,   close set teeth, a long handle,
with which I will rake the billows,   get the waves into little piles,
the patches of sea sedge into ricks,   all the shores into windrows
in order to get my instrument back,   to find my harp
in the fishes' crannies,   among the salmons' reefs."

That craftsman Ilmarinen,   eternal smith,
forged an iron rake   with a copper handle.
He forged teeth a hundred fathoms long,   made a handle five hundred long.
Then old Väinämöinen   took the iron rake;
he walked a little way,   went a short distance
to the steel rollers,   to the copper rollers.
There was a vessel there, two vessels,   two boats ready
on the steel rollers,   on the copper landing place;
one vessel was a new vessel,   the other vessel an old vessel.
Old Väinämöinen said,   spoke to the new boat:
"Set out, boat, for the water,   vessel, betake yourself to the waves
without an arm turning you,   a thumb guiding you."
The boat went to the water,   the vessel betook itself to the waves.
Steadfast old Väinämöinen   sat down in the stern;
he set out to brush the sea,   to sweep the billows.
He brings water lilies into a pile,   rakes up shore rubbish,
he raked up bits of sedge,   bits of sedge, a litter of rushes;
he raked every deep spot, too,   raked all the reefs into windrows;

he did not get, did not find   his pikebone harp,
the forever-lost source of joyous music,   the vanished harp.

Steadfast old Väinämöinen   walks toward home
downcast, low in mind,   high-peaked hat all askew.
He said these words: "There is probably nothing left
of the pike-tooth source of joyous music,   of the clear-toned fishbone in-
    strument."
As he was walking over a clearing,   going along the edge of the wilderness,
he heard a birch tree weeping,   a curly-grained tree shedding tears.
Now he approached it,   went nearer.
He inquired, he spoke: "Why are you weeping, lovely birch?
Why are you crying, green tree?   Why are you lamenting, white-girdled one?
No one is taking you to war,   no one wants you for combat."

The birch answered skillfully,   the green tree spoke:
"Indeed some say,   certain people think
that I am living in a state of joy,   rejoicing in my happiness;
I, slender tree, am rejoicing   in my anxieties, in my distress,
am crying out in my days of agony,   complaining in my grief.
I, futile one, am bewailing my stupidity,   am lamenting my defects,
for I am unlucky, poor wretch,   quite defenseless, miserable me,
in these wretched places,   vast pasture lands.
Lucky ones, fortunate ones   are always hoping
that the lovely summer will come,   the delightful summer get warm.
Differently indeed with stupid me;   I, anguished one, am fearful
lest my bark be peeled off,   my leafy branches pulled off.
Often in the quick-passing spring   children come near
to luckless me,   often to me, luckless wretch;
with five knives they slash   through my sap-filled belly.
In the summer bad herdsmen   take my white girdle,
one for a water scoop, one for a knife sheath,   one, indeed, for a berry
    basket.
Often girls spend time   beneath luckless me,
often beneath me, luckless wretch,   tumble about beside me,
cut leafy branches off me,   bind the twigs into bath whisks.
Often people fell luckless me,   often me, luckless wretch,
to be slash on clearings,   to split me for firewood.
Three times this summer,   this lovely summer,
men spent time beneath me,   sharpened their axes
to be the death of poor me,   to be the end of my feeble life.
That was the summer's joy,   the lovely summer's delight.
Winter is no better,   snow time no nicer.
Grief always   changes my appearance early,

weighs heavily upon me; my face turns pale
when I recall the dark days, reflect on the evil times.
Then the wind brings agony, the night chill most grievous cares;
the wind takes my green coat, the night chill my beautiful gown.
Thus I, possessing little, I, poor wretched birch,
am left quite naked, really without clothes
to shiver in the cold, to shriek in the frost."

Old Väinämöinen said: "Do not weep, green tree!
Do not keep crying, leafy sapling! Do not lament, white-girdled one!
You will get abundant good fortune, get a pleasanter new life;
soon you will be weeping for joy, rejoicing in your happiness."
Then old Väinämöinen fashioned the birch into an instrument.
Of a summer's day he carved it, carved out a harp
at the tip of the misty headland, at the end of the foggy island.
He carved the body of the harp, the frame of the new source of joyous music,
the body from tough birch, the frame from curly birch.

Old Väinämöinen said, remarked, spoke thus:
"There is the body of the harp, the frame of the eternal source of joy.
Where may pegs be got, whence screws fetched?"
An oak was growing in the cattle yard, a tall tree at the back of the yard;
the oak has sturdy branches, each branch has an acorn,
the acorn a golden ball, the golden ball a cuckoo.
When the cuckoo calls out, keeps uttering its five notes,
gold wells from its mouth, silver trickles
onto the golden hillock, onto the silver hill.
Thence are the harp's pegs, the curly birch frame's screws.
Old Väinämöinen spoke, said, spoke thus:
"I got the pegs for the harp, screws for the curly birch frame.
It is still lacking a little something, the harp lacking five strings.
Where might I get strings for it, how adjust the pitch?"
He set out to look for strings. He walks along a clearing;
a virgin was sitting in the clearing, a young girl in a swale.
That virgin was not weeping nor was she very happy either;
she was just singing to herself, singing to while away her afternoon
in the hope her suitor was coming, thinking about her beloved.

Steadfast old Väinämöinen quickly and lightly walked there unshod,
strode without rags on his feet. Then once he got there,
he began to beg for hairs. He uttered these words:
"Give me, virgin, some of your hair, some of your tresses, charming maiden,
to be strings for a harp, to be the voice of immortal music."
The virgin gave him some of her hair, her fine tresses;

she gave him five, six hairs,   a seventh tress, too;
from these come the strings on the harp,   the strings on the immortal instrument.

The instrument is got ready.   Then old Väinämöinen
seats himself on a solid rock,   on a stone step.
He took the harp in his hands,   source of joyous music closer to himself.
The tapering neck he turned upward,   the tail he supported on his knees;
he adjusts the strings,   regulates the tones.
He got the tones adjusted,   his instrument tuned;
then he put it crosswise   down on his knees.
He lowered some ten fingernails,   stretched five fingers
to fly about on the strings,   to skip about on the resounding strings.
Then when old Väinämöinen   played the harp
with his small hands, with his slender fingers,   with thumbs flexed back,
then indeed the curly birchwood spoke out,   the leafy sapling resounded,
the cuckoo's gold called out,   the virgin's hair rang out.

Väinämöinen played with his fingers,   the harp resounded with its strings.
Mountains echoed, boulders crashed,   all the crags shook,
rocks splashed into the billows,   gravel boiled in the water;
pine trees rejoiced,   tree stumps jumped about on the heath.
The sisters-in-law, the Kaleva women   in the midst of doing embroidery
ran there like a river,   all rushed there like a stream,
young women with laughing mouths,   housewives in joyful spirits,
to hear the playing,   to marvel at the joyous music.
Whatever men were nearby,   they all stood cap in hand;
whatever old women were nearby,   they all stood with their cheeks on their hands.
Daughters with tears in their eyes,   sons on their knees on the ground
listened on to the harp,   marveled at the joyful music.
With one voice they said,   with one tongue they repeated:
"Before now such lovely playing   has never been heard,
never, never at all   while the moon has been gold-bright."
The pretty music is heard,   is heard six settlements away.

There was not indeed a wild animal   that did not come to listen
to the lovely instrument,   to the resonance of the harp.
Whatever forest animals there were,   they squatted on their claws
to hear the harp,   to marvel at the joyous music.
Birds flying about in the air   settled down on twigs;
all sorts of fish of the water   betook themselves to the shore.
Grubs in the ground, too,   moved up to the surface of the soil;

they turned about, they listen   to that lovely playing,
to the ever-joyous music of the harp,   to Väinämöinen's instrument.

Then old Väinämöinen   indeed played prettily,
made the music resound beautifully.   He played one day, played a second
at one stretch   with a single morning meal,
only once putting his belt on,   only once putting his shirt on.
When he played at home   in his cabin of evergreen logs,
then the roof echoed,   the floors thudded,
the ceilings sang, the doors roared,   all the windows rejoiced,
the stove stones stirred,   the birchwood scantling broke into song.
When he went about in a stand of fir,   wandered among the pine groves,
the firs marveled,   the pines on the hill turned about,
the pine cones rolled onto the meadow,   the evergreen needles were scattered
    about at the roots.
When he moved about in a copse   or took a step on a clearing,
the copses frolicked,   the clearings were in perpetual delight,
the flowers became sportively joyful,   the young saplings bent over.

POEM 45

The mistress of North Farm
prepares unusual diseases for the Kaleva District (1–190).
Väinämöinen cures the people
with powerful charms and ointments (191–362).

Louhi, mistress of North Farm,   got to hear the news
that Väinämöinen's district was living,   the Kaleva District prospering
from the fragments of the Sampo they had got,   from bits of the lid of many
   colors.
She greatly begrudged that.   She always keeps reflecting
how she might contrive death,   how she might bring death
to that people of Väinämöinen's district,   to the people of the Kaleva
   District.
She prays Ukko,   beseeches the Thunderer:
"O Ukko, god on high!   Lay low the Kaleva people
with hailstones hard as iron,   with needles like steel,
or kill them by pestilences,   kill the base clan,
the men on the big farmyards,   the women on the floors of cattle sheds."

THE ORIGIN OF PESTILENCES, LINES 23–176

The girl of Death's Domain was blind,   Loviatar, an old woman,
Death's worst daughter,   the wickedest daughter of the Abode of the Dead,
source of all evils,   of thousands of disasters.
She had very dark coloring,   a vile-colored skin.
That dark girl of Death,   the half-blind one of Waste Land,
made her bed on a pathway,   laid her pallet on bad ground.
She lay down back to the wind,   aslant to the severe wind,
back to the blasting cold,   facing the dawn.
A great blast of wind came,   a big gust from the east;
it blew the bad creature heavy with child,   wet her pregnant
in a treeless clearing,   on land bare of tussocks.
She carried a heavy womb,   a stiff bellyfull;
she carried it two moons, three,   a fourth, too, a fifth, too,
seven moons, eight,   around about nine moons,
according to a woman's old reckoning   halfway into the tenth.
At the end of the ninth moon,   at the beginning of the tenth moon,
her womb gets stiff,   gets painful
but the fetus is not born,   the fetuses to be born are not delivered.
She quickly shifted to another place,   chose another locality.

The whore went to bear young,   the whore fit for burning to bear her child
between two crags,   in a crevice among five mountains.
Yet the fetus was not born there,   the fetus to be born not delivered.
She searches for a place to give birth in,   for a place to relieve her belly
by shaking quagmires,   by plashing springs;
she did not get a place there,   relief for her belly.
She was slow at bearing her young,   eased her belly only slowly
in the foam of a fierce rapids,   in the eddy of a mighty stream,
under the cascade of three rapids,   in the lee of nine riverbanks.
But the fetus is not yet born,   the fetus of the bad woman will not get relieved.
The repulsive creature began to weep,   the horrible evil monster to scream.
She does not know where to go,   where to proceed
to ease her belly,   to bear her young.

God spoke from a cloud,   the Creator gave utterance from heaven:
"Over there on the fen is a three-cornered hovel   by the shore of the sea
at gloomy North Farm,   at powerful Sedgy Farm.
Go there to bear young,   to relieve your womb;
you are needed there,   your people are waiting."
That dark girl of Death,   horrible virgin of the Abode of the Dead,
came to the dwellings at North Farm,   near the sauna of Sedgy Farm,
to bear her children,   to get rid of her fetuses.
Louhi, mistress of North Farm,   gat-toothed hag of North Farm,
took her secretly to the sauna,   secretly to the bathing room
without the neighborhood's hearing of it,   without word's getting to the community.
She warmed the sauna secretly,   hurried there quickly;
she smeared the doors with beer,   wet the hinges with table beer,
so that the doors did not creak,   the hinges not squeak.

A CHARM FOR A WOMAN IN LABOR, LINES 115-146

Then she uttered these words,   remarked, spoke thus:
"Maidenly old woman, Nature's girl,   golden woman, fair one,
you who are the oldest of women,   first mother among humans!
Run into the sea up to your knees,   into the billows up to your belt buckle;
take some slaver from a ruff,   some slime from a cusk,
with which to anoint the space between the bones,   to stroke along the sides,
to get rid of the maiden's torments,   the woman's belly cramps,
rid of this severe pain,   of the hard labor pains.
If this is not enough,   O Ukko, god on high,
come here when you are needed,   come when you are summoned.
Here is a maiden in torment,   a woman with labor pains
in the midst of the smoke in a sauna,   in a community bathing house.

Take a golden club   in your right hand;
then smash the barriers,   break any doorjambs,
twist open the Creator's locks,   break off the interior bolts
for a big one to go through, a small one to go through,   for a feeble one to
    pass through."
Then that wicked evil one,   Death's blind girl,
now eased her belly,   bore her hateful children
under a cloak decorated with copper wire,   under a gauzy mosquito net.
During the time one can make one batch of vapor,   prepare one sauna,
she produced nine sons   in one summer's night
from the occupants of one belly,   from a heavy wombful.
She gave her boys names,   ordered her children
just as everyone does his offspring,   his own creations.
One she changed to Sudden Stitch,   another she forced to be Bellyache,
one she formed into Gout,   another she made into Rickets;
one she forced to be Boils,   another she made get to be Scabby,
one she forced to be Cancer,   another she flung away to be the Plague.
One remained nameless,   the youngest brat in the litter.
Him she then ordered yonder,   pushed him into the water to become sor-
    cerers,
into the swales to become wizards,   everywhere to become magicians.

Louhi, mistress of North Farm,   ordered the others to go yonder
to the tip of the misty headland,   to the end of the foggy island.
She got angry at the cross-grained creatures,   sent the unusual diseases
against the people of Väinämöinen's district,   as death to the Kaleva clan.
The boys make Väinämöinen's district ill,   the Kaleva people ailing
with unusual diseases   unknown by name.
The floors under them rot,   the bedclothes over them decay.
Then old Väinämöinen,   eternal sage,
set out to rescue lives,   to save lives.
He set out to war against Death,   to fight against Disease.

A HEALER'S CHARMS, LINES 197–354 PASSIM

He got a sauna good and hot,   the stones producing vapor
heated with pieces of clean wood,   with wood drifted in by the sea.
He brought water under his cloak,   carried the bath whisks warily;
he got whisks scalding hot,   softened the bushy ones.
Then he produced honeyed vapor,   raised honeyed vapor
through the hot stones,   the glowing flat stones.
He speaks with these words,   made this utterance:

A SAUNA-BATH CHARM, LINES 211–228

"Come now, God, into the vapor,   father of the sky, into the warmth
so as to bring about health,   to establish peace.

Wipe away the sacred sparks,   extinguish the sacred infections;
have bad vapor struck to the ground,   send away evil vapor
so that it will not burn your sons,   harm your offspring.
Whatever water I keep throwing   on those hot stones,
may it be changed to honey,   ooze out like honey.
Let a river of honey flow,   let a pond of honey surge
through the pile of stones,   through the moss-caulked sauna.

"We will not be destroyed without cause   nor killed except by natural
    diseases,
not without the permission of the great Creator,   only by a death sent by
    God.
Whoever may destroy us without cause,   may his own magic words go into
    his mouth,
his evil designs into his head,   his intentions redound upon himself.
If I am not the man,   Ukko's lad not the person
to deliver one from wizards' malice,   to free one of injuries,
there is indeed Ukko himself   who rules the clouds,
lives in a fair-weather cloud,   governs the cloud patches.
O Ukko, god on high,   got above the clouds!
Come here when you are needed,   betake yourself here when summoned
to identify these agonies,   to ward off the days of distress,
to deliver us from wizards' malice,   to do away with the infections.
Bring me a fiery sword,   bring a flashing blade
with which I will restrain the evil ones,   suppress the malevolent ones forever,
dispatch our agonies along the path of the wind,   our pains to open clear-
    ings."

CHARMS AGAINST PAIN, LINES 259–312

"I will order pains to over yonder,   exorcise agonies to over yonder,
into stone cellars,   into piles of iron,
to hurt the stones,   to shatter the boulders.
A stone does not bewail its pains,   a boulder not lament its agonies
even though one should strike it a lot,   hit it beyond measure.

"Pain Girl, Death's maid,   you who are sitting on the stone of pain
at the meeting of three rivers,   in the fork of three streams
grinding the stone of pain,   cranking Pain Mountain!
Go gather the pains   into the maw of the blue stone
or roll them into the water,   throw them into the depths of the sea,
unknown by the wind,   unlighted by the sun.

"If this is not enough,   Pain Spirit, good lady,
Spirit of Injuries, fine woman   come along, go along
to bring about health,   to establish peace.

Make the pains painless,   keep the injured places from throbbing
that a sick person may lie down,   a weak one rest quietly,
a person in pain be conscious,   an injured person be able to move.
Put the pains into a pail,   aches into a copper bushel
for you to take the pains yonder,   to sink the injuries
in the middle of Pain Hill,   the summit of Pain Mountain.
There boil the pains   in a little kettle
into which one finger will go,   a thumb fit.
There is a stone in the middle of the hill,   a hole in the middle of the stone,
drilled by an auger,   bored by a bit.
Into that let us thrust the pains,   force the bad injuries,
push the severe aches,   press down the days of distress
to be inactive by night,   unable to escape by day."

Then old Väinämöinen,   eternal sage,
kept anointing the bad places,   laving those injuries
with nine ointments,   with eight magic nostrums.
He speaks these words,   made this remark:
"O Ukko, god on high,   old man of the heavens!
Make a cloud spring up in the east,   raise a cloud patch in the southwest,
send a piece of cloud from the west.   Rain down honey, rain down water
as ointments for sore spots,   as linaments for injuries.
I am capable of nothing at all   unless my Creator grants it.
May the Creator grant me aid,   may God bring me aid
after I have seen with my eyes,   reached with my hands,
spoken with a pleasing mouth,   breathed with my breath.
What my hands may not reach,   may God's hands reach;
where my fingers may not fit,   may the Creator's fingers fit.
The Creator's fingers are more graceful,   the Creator's hands defter.
Come now, Creator, to exorcise!   Come, God, to speak,
Almighty One, to tend us!   Make us healthy at night,
well by day   so that no agony is felt,
no pain felt from the middle of the stones,   no ache enter our hearts,
not the very least little thing be felt,   not the very slightest agony
never, never at all   while the moon shines gold-bright."

Steadfast old Väinämöinen,   eternal sage,
thus undid the harms caused by magic,   got rid of the infections.
He did away with the unnatural diseases,   cured the bad enchantments,
delivered the people from death,   the Kaleva descendants from perishing.

POEM 46

The mistress of North Farm conjures up a bear
to destroy the cattle of the Kaleva District (1–20).
Väinämöinen lays low the bear, from which a traditional ceremonial banquet
is then given in the Kaleva District (21–606).
Väinämöinen sings, plays his harp, and wishes for the Kaleva District
the same joyous life in times to come (607–644).

The news got to North Farm,   the report to the cold settlement
that Väinämöinen's district had recovered,   the Kaleva District freed
of those magically induced plagues,   of those unusual diseases.

Louhi, mistress of North Farm,   gat-toothed dame of North Farm,
she got very angry at that.   She uttered a word, spoke thus:
"I still remember another trick,   indeed know another way.
I will conjure up a bear from the heath,   one with curved claws from the
    backwoods
to attack the livestock in Väinämöinen's district,   the cattle in the Kaleva
    District."
She conjured up a bear from the heath,   a bear from desolate parts
to attack those clearings of Väinämöinen's district,   the cattle lands of the
    Kaleva District.

Steadfast old Väinämöinen   uttered these words:
"Good friend, craftsman Ilmarinen,   forge me a new spear,
forge a spear with a three-cornered point,   with a copper shaft.
There is a bear to be taken,   a bear with a valuable pelt to be laid low
to stop it from harming my geldings,   wanting my mares,
laying low my cattle,   scattering my cows."
The craftsman forges a spear,   neither long nor short;
he forged a middle-sized one: a wolf was standing on the blade,
bruin on the steel tip,   an elk was shuffling along on the ferrule,
a colt was wandering along on the shaft,   a wild reindeer was kicking on the
    grip.
New snow was then falling,   a little fine fresh snow
as much as a ewe born in the autumn,   a hare born in the winter.

A BEAR HUNTER'S CHARMS, LINES 47–144

Old Väinämöinen said,   uttered a word, spoke thus:
"It is my desire,   my desire to go to Woodland,
to the forest's girls,   to the hazy-blue maidens' farmyards.

I am setting out to the forest away from men,   away from people for outdoor
    work.
Take me on, forest, as one of your men,   as one of your people, Tapio.
Help me to have good luck,   to lay low the fine fellow of the forest.

"Darling, mistress of the forest,   Tellervo, Tapio's wife,
fasten up your dogs,   keep your curs
in a woodbine shanty,   in an oakwood shed.

"Bear, apple of the forest,   chunky honey-paws!
When you hear me coming,   hear the splendid man stepping along,
make fast your claws in your fur,   your teeth in your gums
so that they will never touch me,   never stir when you are on the move.
My bear, my darling,   honey-paws, my beauty,
throw yourself flat on a tussock,   on a lovely crag
while the tall evergreens are swaying above,   firs being heard above.
Then bear, turn around,   honey-paws, turn yourself about,
as does a ruffed grouse on her nest,   a wild goose about to brood."

Then old Väinämöinen   heard the dog barking,
the hound baying loudly   in tiny-eye's farmyard,
in stub-nose's cattle yard.   He uttered a word, spoke thus:
"I thought a cuckoo was calling,   the lovely bird singing;
no cuckoo is calling,   no lovely bird singing at all.
Here my dog is doing finely,   my animal excellently
at the door of the bear's house,   in the farmstead of the distinguished man."
Steadfast old Väinämöinen   then encountered the bear;
he upset the satiny beds,   overturned the lovely couches.
He says these words,   made this remark:
"Thanks be, God,   be praised, sole Creator,
for having given me the bear as my share,   the gold of the wilderness as my
    booty."

He looks at his gold.   He uttered a word, spoke thus:
"My bear, my darling,   honey-paws, my beauty,
do not get angry without any reason.   It was not I who killed you;
you slipped from a shaft-bow,   you misstepped from an evergreen branch,
your wooden pants torn through,   your evergreen coat ripped across.
'Autumn weather is slippery,   the cloudy days dark.'
Golden cuckoo of the forest,   lovely shaggy-haired one,
now leave your home deserted,   leave your dwelling place empty,
your birch-branch home,   your cottage of willow withes.
Start, splendid one, to go,   glory of the forest, to step along,
light-shod one to go,   blue-stockings, to trip along

away from this little farmyard,   from these narrow trails
to a crowd of people,   a group of men.
There no one will ill-treat you,   you will not live in poor style;
there one is fed honey,   fresh mead is given to drink
to a stranger who arrives,   to one who wants to be invited.
Set out now from here as if you were really setting out   from this little nest
to under a splendid rooftree,   to under a beautiful roof.
Slide along quietly on the snow   like a water lily on a pond,
float along lightly on the evergreen branch drag   like a squirrel on a branch."

Then old Väinämöinen,   eternal singer,
walked over the clearings playing,   over the heaths singing loudly
with his splendid guest,   with his furry fellow.
The music is already heard as far as the house,   the noise clear to under the
   roof.
The people in the house suddenly said,   the handsome group spoke up:
"Hear this noise,   the words of the musician of the wilderness,
the warbling of a crossbill,   the sound of the pipe of a forest maid."
Steadfast old Väinämöinen   got to the farmyard.
The people came tumbling out of the house,   the handsome group remarked:
"Now the gold is coming,   the silver wandering along,
a lovely piece of money stepping along,   a coin stepping along the trail.
Did the forest give up a honey-eater,   the master of the wilderness yield up a
   lynx
since you come singing,   shuffling along caroling on skis?"

Steadfast old Väinämöinen   then said these words:
"The otter has been charmed,   God's game enchanted;
for that reason we come singing,   shuffling along caroling on skis.
But it will not be an otter,   neither an otter nor a lynx;
the splendid fellow himself is coming along,   the glory of the wilderness
   stepping along,
the old man wandering along,   the broadcloth coat moving along.
If our guest happens to be wanted,   fling open the doors;
but if the guest is hated,   slam them to."

In answer the people say,   the handsome crowd speaks:
"Hail, bear, your arrival,   hail, honey-paws, your paying a visit
to this clean farmyard,   this lovely farmstead!
I always hoped for that,   ever since I have been grown up
I have looked forward to Tapio's ringing out,   to the forest's pipe shrilly
   sounding,
to the gold of the woodland coming along,   the silver of the wilderness coming

to this little farmyard,   to these narrow trails.
I have been hoping for this as for a good year,   been looking forward as to
   the coming of summer
just as a ski to new-fallen snow,   a left ski to good smooth skiing,
a maiden to a young suitor,   a pink-cheeked girl to a mate.
Evenings I used to sit by the windows,   mornings on the storehouse steps,
for weeks by the gates,   for months at the entrance to the lanes,
winters in the cattle yards.   I stood on the snow so that it got hard-packed,
till the hard-packed snow got to be wet ground,   till the wet ground got to be
   gravelly places,
the gravelly places to be loamy places,   the loamy places to be verdant.
I reflected every morning,   every day reflected
as to where the bear was lingering so long,   the lovely fellow of the wilderness spending his time,
whether he might have gone to Estonia,   run away from Finnish soil."

Then old Väinämöinen   uttered these words:
"Where shall I take my guest,   lead my golden one?
Shall I perhaps take him to the shed,   put him in the hay barn?"
In answer the people say,   the handsome group spoke up:
"You will take our guest yonder,   lead our golden one
under the splendid ridgepole,   under the lovely roof.
There food has been prepared,   drinks got ready,
all the floorboards cleaned,   the floors swept;
all the women are dressed   in fresh clothes
with pretty head ornaments,   in white clothes."

Then old Väinämöinen   uttered a word, spoke thus:
"My bear, my bird,   honey-paws, my bundle,
you still have ground to cover,   heath to clamber upon.
Set out, now, gold, to get going   dear one, to step along the ground,
black-stockings, to go along boldly,   cloth pants, to go ahead,
to walk along the chickadee's path,   the sparrow's course
to under five rafters,   to under six rooftrees.

"Look out, wretched women,   lest the cattle be frightened,
the small livestock scared,   the mistress's livestock suffer harm
while the bear is coming into the dwellings,   hairy-muzzle pushing his way in.
Away, lads, from the porch,   girls, away from the doorjambs
while the fellow is coming into the house,   the splendid man stepping along.

"Bear of the forest, apple,   handsome chubby fellow of the forest,
do not fear the maidens   or be afraid of the girls with luxuriant hair;
do not fear the women,   do not feel sorry for those with stockings down at
   the heels.

Whatever women are in the house,   they will all retire to the inglenook
when the man comes into the house,   when the big boy walks in."

Old Väinämöinen said: "Welcome here, God,
under the splendid rooftree,   under the lovely ceiling!
Where shall I now take my darling,   lead my furry fellow?"
In reply the people say: "Welcome, welcome on your arrival!
Put your bird over there,   lead your golden one
to the end of the deal bench,   to the tip of the iron bench
for the pelt to be examined,   the fur to be looked over.
Do not worry about that, bear,   do not take it amiss
when the hour comes to feel your fur,   the time comes to view your coat.
No one will damage your fur   nor by looking change your coat
into the rags of miserable people,   into the clothes of poor wretches."

Then old Väinämöinen   took the pelt off the bear,
laid it away up in the storehouse loft;   he put pieces of the meat in a cauldron,
into a gilded copper kettle,   a copper-bottomed pot.
The pots were already on the fire,   the copper-sided vessels on the flame,
brimful, crammed full   of pieces of meat;
in with them lumps of salt   which had been imported from rather far away,
lumps of salt got from Germany,   from the headwaters of Dvina river,
brought by rowing through the Öresund,   unloaded from a ship.
When the stew had been cooked,   the kettles taken off the fire,
then indeed the booty is brought,   the crossbill carried
to the end of the long deal table   to golden bowls
to drink mead in long draughts,   to partake of beer.
The table was made of pine,   the dishes cast of copper,
the spoons of silver,   the knives fashioned of gold.
All the bowls were brimful,   the dishes full to overflowing
with pieces of the lovely gift of the forest,   of the booty of the wilderness
   gold.
Then old Väinämöinen   uttered these words:
"Old man of the knoll with your golden chest,   master of Tapio's farm,
Woodland's honeyed wife,   lovely mistress of the forest,
handsome man, Tapio's son,   handsome man with a red-peaked hat,
Tellervo, Tapio's maid,   together with the rest of Tapio's people!
Come now to your steer's wedding party,   to your shaggy one's feast!
Now there is plenty ready to eat,   plenty to eat, plenty to drink,
plenty for yourself to keep,   plenty to give a neighbor."

Thereupon the people speak thus,   the fair company said:
"Where was the bear born,   where did the valuable pelt grow up?
Do you think it was born on straw,   grew up in the inglenook of a sauna?"

THE ORIGIN OF BEARS, LINES 353-458

Then old Väinämöinen   uttered these words:
"The bear was not born on straw   nor on the chaff of a kiln.
The bear was born,   honey-paws given birth to
at the Moon's, in the womb of the Sun,   on the shoulders of the Great Bear,
at the virgin's of the air,   at Nature's daughters.
A virgin was treading the border of the sky,   a maiden the heavenly pole;
she was walking along the edge of a cloud,   along the border of the heavens
in blue stockings,   in particolored shoes with heels
with a basket of wool in her hand,   a basket of down under her arm.
She threw a tuft of wool onto the waters,   dropped the down onto the
    billows.
That the wind rocked,   the turbulent air moved,
the spirit of the water swayed,   a wave drove ashore,
to the shore of a honeyed wilderness,   to the tip of a honeyed headland.
Darling, mistress of the forest,   keen-eyed wife of Tapio's Domain,
seized the tuft of wool from the waters,   the soft bits of wool from the bil-
    lows.
Then she placed it cunningly,   swaddled it nicely
in a maplewood box,   in a fine swinging cradle.
She picked up the diaper strings,   carried the golden straps
to the bushiest bough,   to the broadest leafy branch.
After she got there, she swung,   rocked her darling
under a luxuriant crown of a fir,   under a flourishing pine tree.
Then she brought forth the bear,   brought up the fine-coated one
on the edge of a honeyed copse,   inside a honeyed wilderness.
The bear grew to be handsome,   grew up to be very fine looking
with short legs, with bandy legs,   with a soft stubby muzzle,
a broad head, a snub nose,   a fine shaggy coat.

"Not yet had either teeth   or claws been fashioned.
Darling, mistress of the forest,   uttered these words:
'I would form claws for it,   try to find teeth, too,
if it would not get into wrongdoings,   not take to evil deeds.'
Accordingly the bear swore an oath   on the knees of the mistress of the forest,
in the presence of illustrious God,   looking up at the face of the Almighty,
to do no evil,   begin no bad deeds.
Darling, mistress of the forest,   keen-eyed wife of Tapio's Domain,
set out to search for a tooth,   to inquire about claws
from firmly rooted rowans,   from rough junipers,
from matted roots,   from hard resinous pine stumps.
Not a claw did she get there,   not a tooth did she find.
An evergreen was growing on a heath,   a fir rising on a knoll;

on the evergreen was a silver branch,   a gold branch on the fir.
These the maiden seized with her hands,   from them made claws,
attached them to the jawbone,   set them in the gums.
Then she let her furry fellow go,   sent her darling forth;
she put him to rove a fen,   to run over a copse,
to walk on the edge of a clearing,   to clamber on the heath.
She bade him walk nicely,   to run along gracefully,
to live joyous times,   to spend splendid days
on the expanses of the fen, in the farthest parts of the world   beyond the
    playing fields,
to go without shoes in summer,   without short socks on in the autumn,
to survive the worser times,   to take it easy in winter cold spells
inside a chokecherry house,   on the side of an evergreen stronghold,
at the foot of a lovely fir,   in the corner of a juniper grove,
under five woolly mantles,   under eight cloaks.
From there I just now got my booty,   brought this quarry of mine."

The young people speak thus,   the old people keep saying:
"Why was the forest favorably disposed,   the forest favorably disposed, the
    wilderness amenable,
the master of the wilderness delighted,   lovely Tapio obliging
that he gave his precious one,   lost his honey darling?
Was it obtained by a spear   or fetched by an arrow?"
Steadfast old Väinämöinen   uttered these words:
"The forest was very favorably disposed toward us,   the forest favorably
    disposed, the backwoods amenable,
the master of the wilderness delighted,   lovely Tapio obliging.
Darling, mistress of the forest,   Tellervo, Tapio's maid,
maiden of the forest, fair of form,   little maiden of the forest
set out to show the way,   to make blazes,
to point out the sides of the trail,   to direct the journey.
She cut blazes along on the trees,   made marks on the hills
to the doors of the splendid bear,   to the edge of its preserve.
Then after I had got there,   reached my destination,
there was no obtaining by spear,   no going about shooting;
it fell from a shaft-bow,   stumbled from an evergreen branch;
dead branches broke its breastbone,   twigs split open its belly."

Then he uttered these words,   remarked, spoke thus:
"My bear, my pet,   my bird, my darling!
Now leave your head ornament here,   stick out your teeth,
thrust out your sparse teeth,   open your jaws wide!
Do not take offense   if something should happen to us,
a crash of bones, a cracking of skulls,   a loud rattling of teeth.

I will now take the nose from the bear   as a help to my present nose;
I am not taking it as something unlucky   nor will it be all by itself.
I will take an ear from the bear   as a help to my present ear;
I am not taking it as something unlucky   nor will it be all by itself.
I will take an eye from the bear   as a help to my present eye;
I am not taking it as something unlucky   nor will it be all by itself.
I will take the forehead from the bear   as a help to my own forehead;
I am not taking it as something unlucky   nor will it be all by itself.
I will take the muzzle from the bear   as a help to my own muzzle;
I am not taking it as something unlucky   nor will it be all by itself.
I will take the tongue from the bear   as a help to my own tongue;
I am not taking it as something unlucky   nor will it be all by itself.

"Him I would now call a man,   rate as a lucky person
who would enchant the tight-locked teeth loose,   get the set of teeth
from the steely jaw   with an iron grip."
No one else came,   there was no such man.
He himself enchants the tight-locked teeth,   exorcises the set of teeth loose,
kneeling on it with his bony knees,   holding it with his iron grip.
He took the teeth from the bear,   he uttered a word, spoke thus:
"Bear of the forest, apple,   handsome chubby fellow of the forest!
Now you have a journey to make,   a trip to make boldly
from this little nest,   from a lowly cottage
to a finer home,   a roomier dwelling.
Set out now, gold, to go,   lovely in your fur, to step along
the side of pigs' trails,   across the tracks of young pigs
toward the scrub-grown hill,   to the high hill,
to the bushy pine,   to the hundred-branched evergreen.
It will be nice for you to live there,   lovely to pass your time
within hearing of a cowbell,   near the tinkling of a little bell."

Steadfast old Väinämöinen   now came home from there.
The young people speak thus,   the handsome crowd remarked:
"Where did you take your booty,   where did you bring your prey?
Perhaps you left it on the ice,   sank it in the slush,
knocked it down into the ooze of the fen,   buried it in the heath."
Steadfast old Väinämöinen   uttered a word, spoke thus:
"Indeed I did not leave it on the ice,   sink it in the slush;
there dogs would keep disturbing it,   bad birds would be all over it.
Nor did I knock it down into the fen,   bury it in the heath;
there grubs would destroy it,   black ants devour it.
I took my booty,   brought my trifling prey
to the top of a golden knoll,   to the shoulder of a copper ridge.
I put the skull in a fine tree,   in a hundred-branched evergreen,

on the bushiest bough,   on the leafiest spray
as a joy to men,   as an honor to passers-by.
I laid it with the gums to the east,   I left it with the eyes to the southwest.
I did not put it right in the crown;   had I put it in the crown,
there the wind would damage it,   the cold spring wind treat it badly.
Nor did I put it on the ground;   had I put it on the ground,
pigs would have shifted it,   the creatures with lowered snouts would have
    turned it over."

Then old Väinämöinen   burst out singing
in honor of the splendid evening,   as a source of joy for the closing day.
Old Väinämöinen said,   remarked, spoke thus:
"Stay now, torch holder, alight   so that I may see to sing.
My turn to sing is coming,   my mouth desires to ring out."
Then he sang so that it resounded,   sang joyfully throughout the evening.
At last he said his say,   finally said:
"Grant us another time, God,   in the future, steadfast Creator,
to rejoice at such festivities,   to do it another time
at the festivities of a chubby lad,   at the feast of a long-haired one.
In any event allow, God,   another time, true Creator,
blazes to be made,   trees to be marked
among the manly folk,   the manly bands.
In any event allow, God,   another time, true Creator,
Tapio's horn to sound,   the woodland pipe to sound out shrilly
in this little farmyard,   in this confined farmstead.
By day I would it might be sung,   by night that joyous music be made
in these parts, in these districts,   in these great farms of Finland,
among the rising generation,   among the people growing up."

POEM 47

The sun and the moon come down to hear Väinämöinen's playing;
the mistress of North Farm gets her hands on them,
hides them inside a hill, and steals the fire, too,
from the houses of the Kaleva District (1–40).
Ukko, god on high, finds the darkness in the heavens strange
and strikes fire to become a new sun and moon (41–82).
The fire drops to earth
and Väinämöinen sets out with Ilmarinen to look for it (83–126).
A virgin of the air tells them that the fire has got into Lake Alue
and that there a fish has swallowed it (127–312).
Väinämöinen and Ilmarinen set out with a bast net to catch the fish;
they do not get it with that (313–364).

Steadfast old Väinämöinen   played the harp a long time,
both played and sang   so that it was joyful, indeed.
The music was heard as far as the moon's dwellings,   the joyous sound heard
    up to the sun's windows.
The moon comes from its house,   steps onto a bend in a birch branch;
The sun came out from its fine house,   took its place on the crown of a pine
to listen to the harp,   to marvel at the joyous music.

Louhi, mistress of North Farm,   gat-toothed dame of North Farm,
then seizes hold of the sun,   caught the moon with her hands,
the moon from the bend on the birch branch,   the sun from the crown of
    the pine.
She brought them home at once   to gloomy North Farm.
She ordered the moon into a rock with mottled sides   so that it did not
    gleam,
she enchanted the sun into a steel hill   so that it did not shine.
She then spoke thus: "May you not get free from here,
not rise, moon, to gleam palely,   not to get, sun, to glow
unless I come to free you,   I myself come to fetch you
together with nine stallions,   with the get of one mare."
When she had removed the moon   and carried off the sun
into North Farm's hill of rock,   into the iron crag,
indeed she even stole light,   fire from the houses of Väinämöinen's district;
she caused the houses to be without fire,   the cabins without light.
Now night was perpetual,   long, dark as pitch.
It was night in the Kaleva District,   in those houses of Väinämöinen's dis-
    trict,

also there in the firmament,   in Ukko's abodes in the sky.
It is grievous to be without fire,   a great distress to be without light,
tiresome for men,   tiresome for Ukko himself, too.
Ukko, god on high,   great creator of the sky,
began to find it strange.   He ponders, he reflects
over what peculiar thing is in front of the moon,   what kind of mist in the
    path of the sun
since the moon does not gleam at all   nor the sun shine at all.
He walked along the edge of a cloud,   along the boundary of the heavens
in blue stockings,   in his ornamented shoes with heels;
he went to look for the moon,   to encounter the sun.
He does not find the moon   or encounter the sun.

THE ORIGIN OF FIRE, LINES 67-364

Ukko of the sky struck fire,   made flame flash
with his very sharp sword,   with his sparkling blade;
he struck fire on his fingernail,   made it flash on a finger joint
up in the heavens,   on a level with the constellations.
He got fire by striking.   He hides the spark
in a golden pouch,   in a silver setting.
He let a maiden rock it,   a virgin of the air swing it
in order to fashion a new moon,   to be the beginning of a new sun.
The maiden on a long cloud,   the virgin on the edge of the sky
rocked that fire,   swung the light
in a golden cradle,   on silver cords.
The silver straps swayed,   the golden cradle rattled,
the clouds moved, the heavens cried shrilly,   the vault of heaven bent
as the fire was being rocked,   the light being swung.
The virgin of the air rocked the fire,   swung the flame,
guarded the fire with her fingers,   tended the flame with her hands.
The fire fell from the foolish girl's hands,   the flame from the careless one's,
from the hand of her who was turning it about,   from the fingers of her who
    was jiggling it.
Holes were rent in the heavens,   windows in the whole sky.
The spark fell,   a red spark was sent flying,
slid through the heavens,   dropped through the clouds,
through the nine heavenly spheres,   through the six vaults of many colors.

Old Väinämöinen said: "Good friend, craftsman Ilmarinen,
let us set out to look,   let us go to learn
what kind of fire that fire was,   what kind of strange flame dropped
from the heavens above   to the earth beneath,
if it might be the disk of the moon   or the sphere of the sun.
The two men set out.   They stepped along, they pondered

how they might get there and how find their way
to where the fire had gone, to where the flame had fallen.
A river is running in front of them like a biggish sea.
Then old Väinämöinen began to fashion a boat,
to knock one together on the edge of the backwoods. As second craftsman
  Ilmarinen
made paddles from a fir, thick oars from a pine.
The boat is got ready with its tholepins, with its oars;
thus they bring the boat to the water.
                            They keep rowing aimlessly
around in the Neva river, they skirt a headland of the Neva.
Air Spirit, lovely virgin, eldest of Nature's daughters,
she comes toward them speaking, talking:
"What manner of men are you, what are your names?"
Old Väinämöinen said: "We are seamen,
I old Väinämöinen, the other craftsman Ilmarinen.
But name your own clan; what is your name?"
The woman uttered these words: "I am the oldest of women,
oldest of the virgins of the air, first mother among human beings,
I who have the stateliness of five women, the beauty of six brides.
Where are you going, men? Where are you setting out for, fellows?"
Old Väinämöinen said, uttered a word, spoke thus:
"Our fire has been put out, our light been lost.
Long we have been without fire, been hidden in darkness.
Now we have in mind to go to find out about some fire
that came from heaven, dropped from the clouds."

The woman uttered these words, remarked, spoke thus:
"That fire is terrible to find out about, the flame dangerous to get.
The fire has already played tricks, the flame caused damage.
The spark slid down, the red disk fell
from spaces created by the Creator, by the blows of Ukko of the sky,
through the smooth firmament, through that marvelous sky,
through a sooty smoke hole, through a dry rooftree
into Tuuri's new house, into the Worshipful One's roofless house.
Then after it came there to Tuuri's new house,
it applied itself to evil deeds, gave itself over to outrageous acts.
It crushed the daughters' breasts, grabbed the girls' nipples,
destroyed the boy's knees, burned the master's beard.
The mother was nursing her baby in a wretched cradle.
After the fire got into that, then it did its worst work:
it burned the baby in the cradle, burned the mother's breasts.
The baby went to the Abode of the Dead, the boy actually to Death's Domain,
the boy who was created to die, destined to perish

in the agonies of the red fire, in the pains of the flame.
But the mother knew better, the mother did not go to the Abode of the
 Dead;
she knew how to exorcise fire, to make flame
sink through the little eye of a needle, through the slot of an axhead,
through the ferrule of a hot ice pick, along the edge of a field."

Steadfast old Väinämöinen managed to ask:
"Where did the fire set out for from there, where did the spark fly
from the edge of Tuuri's field? To the forest or to the sea?"
In reply the woman says, uttered a word, spoke thus:
"While the fire was going from there, the flame hastening,
it first burned over a lot of land, a lot of land, a lot of fen;
finally it went into the water, into the waves of Lake Alue.
It was about to blaze up into fire, to flash like sparks.
Three times of a summer's night, nine times of an autumn night
the lake surged up to the level of the firs, spurted onto the banks
in the control of that fierce fire, in the power of the hot flame.
Its fish surged up onto dry land, its perch onto solid ground.
The fish look about there, the perch reflect
on how to exist, how to live; a perch was bewailing its provision sheds,
the fish their farmsteads, a ruff its stronghold in the rocks.
A curved necked perch set out; it encountered the spark
but the perch did not get it at all. Then a blue whitefish went there;
it swallowed the spark, downed the flame.
Now Lake Alue got filled again, got its shores back
to their former place during one summer's night.

"A little time passed. Agony came to the one who swallowed it,
pain to the one who devoured it, great anguish to the one who ate it.
It swam about, wam about; it swims for one day, it swims a second
along the side of whitefish islands, among salmon skerries,
past the tips of a thousand headlands, along the coves of a hundred islands.
Every headland gave advice, every island had a message:
'There is not in the tranquil water, in agonized Lake Alue
anyone to swallow the miserable fish, to down the wretched one
burning in the agony of the fire, in the torments of the flame.'

"This is a silvery lake trout; it swallowed that bluish whitefish.
A little time passed. Agony came to the one who swallowed it,
pain to the one who devoured it, great anguish to the one who ate it.
It swam about, wam about; it swims for one day, swims a second
among the salmon skerries, the farmsteads of the pike,
past the tips of a thousand headlands, along the coves of a hundred islands.
Every headland gave advice, every island had a message:

'There is not in the tranquil water,   in agonized Lake Alue
anyone to swallow the miserable fish,   to down the wretched one
burning in the agony of the fire,   in the torments of the flame.'

"Then a grayish pike came along,   swallowed the silvery lake trout.
A little time passed.   Agony came to the one who swallowed it,
pain to the one who devoured it,   great anguish to the one who ate it,
It swam about, wam about;   it swims for one day, it swims a second
among the sea-gull skerries,   along the rocky crags of the sea mew,
past the tips of a thousand headlands,   along the coves of a hundred islands.
Every headland gave advice,   every island had a message:
'There is not in the tranquil water,   in agonized Lake Alue
anyone to swallow the miserable fish,   to down the wretched one
burning in the agony of fire,   in the torments of the flame.' "

Steadfast old Väinämöinen,   craftsman Ilmarinen the second,
weave a bast net,   noisily weave one of juniper;
they dyed it in a willow decoction,   did this with water-willow bark.
Steadfast old Väinämöinen   pressed women to the net.
The women set out to the net,   the sisters set out to drag it.
They row about, they glide about   from headland to headland, from island
    to island,
among salmon skerries,   along the side of whitefish islands
to the brown watergrass,   to the lovely beds of rushes.
They try, they fish,   they pull, they swish the net about;
they lower the net into the water wrongside up,   drag the net in wrong
    directions.
They do not get that fish,   trap nothing for all their efforts.
The boon companions set out to the water,   the men go to the net.
They rinse the net, swish it about,   pull it, seine
the openings of the bay, the ends of the skerries,   the stony Kaleva crags;
they do not get that fish   which was so needed.
The gray pike did not come   from the quiet waters of the bay
nor from the great expanse of the waters.   The fish are little, the nets are few.

Now the fish there complained,   pike speaks to pike,
the whitefish asks of the ide,   one salmon of another salmon:
"Have the illustrious men already died,   the Kaleva descendants perished,
the casters of flax-cord nets,   the makers of cord nets,
the guiders of the big beating pole,   the movers of the long staff?"

Old Väinämöinen heard this.   He spoke these words:
"The men have not died,   the Kaleva people not perished.
One died, two were born   who have better poles,
staffs a foot longer,   nets twice as big."

POEM 48

They make a flax-cord net and with it set out to catch the fish
that swallowed the fire, and they get that fish (1–192).
They find the fire in the fish's belly, but it suddenly again breaks loose
and badly burns Ilmarinen's cheeks and hands (193–248).
The fire goes up into the forest, burns over a lot of land,
and keeps going on until it is finally caught and brought
to the darkened dwellings of the Kaleva District (249–290).
Ilmarinen recovers from the ravages of the fire (291–372).

Steadfast old Väinämöinen,   eternal sage,
then comes upon a plan,   hits on a design
to weave a flax-cord net,   to try to make one with a hundred meshes.
Now he said these words,   remarked, spoke thus:
"Is there a sower of flax,   a sower, a plowman
to make a net,   to get one with a hundred meshes
to kill the dreadful fish,   to lay low the base creature?"

They found a bit of land,   a place not burned over
on the biggest ridge in the fen,   in a space between two stumps.
They dig up the root of the stump;   there a flaxseed was found
from the store of Death's grub,   from the supplies of a maggot of the earth.
There was indeed a pile of ashes,   a heap of fluffy ashes
from the burning of a wooden vessel,   from the consuming of a boat.
In that they sowed the flax,   plowed it into the soft ashes
on the shore of Lake Alue,   into a clayey field.
From that a sprout then came up,   a splendid flax plant spread out,
a sturdy flax plant grew up   in a single summer's night.
That night the flax was sown,   was plowed by moonlight,
cleaned, carded,   plucked, rippled,
pulled smartly,   the knots flicked out vigorously.
The flax was taken to be retted;   it soon got soft.
They lifted it up quickly,   speedily dried it.
It was brought into the house at once,   was soon cleaned of shives,
cleaned clatteringly with a brake,   cleaned deftly with a swingle.
It was combed vigorously,   brushed quickly in the dusk;
it soon got to be a tuft of flax,   quite quickly ready for the distaff
in one summer's night,   in the time between two days.

The sisters spin it,   the sisters-in-law thread the netting needle,
the brothers weave it into a net,   the spouses attach the drag ropes.
Then didn't the netting needle move,   the roller go back and forth
when the seine was being made ready,   the cord being made

during one summer's night,   indeed in half of it!
The net was got ready,   the rope net prepared,
the bag a hundred fathoms long,   the wings seven hundred.
They weighted it properly with sinker stones,   provided it suitably with floats.
The young people go to the seine,   the old at home reflect:
will that fish really be got   that is being fished for with a will?
They pull, they drag with difficulty,   they fish, they struggle;
they pull it down stream,   drag it across stream.
They get a few fish: wretched fish fry,
bony perch,   carp bitter as gall;
they did not get that fish   for which the seine was made.

Old Väinämöinen said: "O craftsman Ilmarinen,
let us ourselves set out yonder,   with seines to the water."
The two men set out;   they drag their nets to the water.
They cast one wing   onto an island out in the water,
the other wing they cast   onto the headland of a strip of meadow.
A hauling-in place is set up there   at old Väinämöinen's landing place.
They cast, throw it,   pull, drag with difficulty.
They get plenty of fish: lerch, perch,
sea trout, rea trout,   bream, salmon,
all fish of the water;   they do not get that fish
for which the seine was made,   the rope net prepared.
Then old Väinämöinen   added still more nets,
extended the wings on the side   by five hundred fathoms,
the rope-net by seven hundred.   He uttered a word, spoke thus:
"Let us take the nets to the deep places,   transport them farther off;
let us again drag the water   a second time."
They take the nets to the deep places,   quickly transport them farther off;
they again dragged the water   a second time with the net.

A FISHERMAN'S CHARM, LINES 123–150

Then old Väinämöinen   uttered these words:
"Vellamo, mistress of the water,   old woman of the water with a sedgy
   breast!
Come for a change of shirt,   a change of clothes.
You have a sedgy shirt on,   a tunic of sea foam
made by a daughter of the wind,   gift of Wave Spirit.
I will give you a flaxen shirt,   get you one of pure flax;
it was woven by Moon Spirit,   spun by Sun Spirit.
Ahto, master of the waves,   ruler of sea with its hundred deep spots!
Take a sapling five fathoms long,   grasp a pole seven fathoms long
with which you will move over the open waters,   stir up the bottom of the
   sea,
raise up a pile of fish bones,   drive a school of fish

to where this seine is being pulled up, the one with a hundred floats being
  hauled in,
from fishes' deep recesses, from salmons' caverns,
from the great expanses of the deep, from the gloomy depths
unlighted by the sun, from places unsoiled by sand."

A little man rose up out of the sea, a fellow came up out of the waves;
he stands on the surface of the sea. Then he uttered these words:
"Is there need for a beater, for a plier of a long pole?"
Steadfast old Väinämöinen uttered these words:
"Indeed there is need for a beater, for a plier of a long pole."
The little man, the tiny fellow grabbed a tall evergreen from the shore,
a long tree trunk from a pine grove, attached a boulder as a weight.
He inquires, he speaks: "Shall I beat according to my strength,
really according to my strength, or shall I beat according to the equipment?"
Wise old Väinämöinen uttered a word, spoke thus:
"If you beat according to the equipment, there will be plenty of beating
  there!"

The little man, the tiny fellow now gives a sudden blow there,
beats the water according to the equipment; he drove a lot of fish
to where that seine was being pulled up, the one with a hundred floats
  being hauled in.
The craftsman is at the oars, steadfast old Väinämöinen
is the one who hauls up the seine, pulls in the one with a hundred floats.
Old Väinämöinen said: "Now there is a school of fish
where the seine is being pulled up, the one with a hundred floats being
  hauled in."
Then they take up the seine, empty it out, shake it out
into Väinämöinen's boat; they get the school of fish
for which the seine was made, the cord net prepared.

Steadfast old Väinämöinen steered the boat to land,
to the side of the blue pier, to the end of the red landing stage.
He cleaned the school of fish, took out a pile of fish bones.
There they got the gray pike which had long been fished for.
Then old Väinämöinen ponders there:
"Do I dare touch it with my hands without iron gauntlets,
without stone mittens, without copper gloves?"
Sun's son heard that. He uttered a word, spoke thus:
"I might split the pike open, might dare take it in my hands
if I had my father's sheath knife, my esteemed parent's knife."
The knife fell from the heavens, the sheath knife dropped from the clouds
with its gold pommel, its silver blade, fell onto the belt of Sun's son.
Then Sun's competent son seized the knife with his hands;

with that he splits open the pike,   opens the fish with a wide mouth.
In the gray pike's belly   they find the silvery lake trout;
in the belly of the silvery lake trout   there was the smooth whitefish.

He split the smooth whitefish open;   from there he got a blue clew
from a bend in the pike's gut,   from the third coil.
He unwound the blue clew;   from inside the blue clew
a red clew fell out.   He loosened that red clew;
in the middle of the red clew   he found the drop of fire
which had come from the heavens,   fallen through the clouds
down from eight heavenly spheres,   from the ninth heaven.
While Väinämöinen was pondering   in what one might take that
to the fireless houses,   to the dark cabins,
the spark gave a bounce,   got out of the hand of Sun's son.
It burned Väinämöinen's beard,   the fire burned the craftsman's
cheekbones even worse,   scorched his hands.
Going from there   it went over the waves of Lake Alue.
It sped to a juniper grove,   then burned a juniper-grown heath;
it hurled itself into a stand of fir,   burned the lovely stand of fir.
It went still farther,   burned over half of the north country,
the frontier of the tip of Savo,   two thirds of Karelia.

Steadfast old Väinämöinen   set out to walk.
He went up into the backwoods   on the track of the fierce fire.
There he ran into the fire   under the root of two stumps,
inside the trunk of a dead alder,   in the bend of a rotten stump.
Then old Väinämöinen   uttered these words:
"Fire, creation of God,   flame, the Creator's creation!
Without reason you went into the depths of the lake,   went very far without
  cause.
You will do better if you burn   in a stone stove,
confine yourself to soft ashes,   lie hidden dead in the embers,
by day to be kept   in a pile of birch firewood,
by night to be hidden   in the curved back part of a golden-glowing hearth."
He yanked the spark   into burning tinder fungus,
into solid birch fungus,   into a copper kettle.
He carried the fire in the kettle,   transported it on a piece of birchbark
to the tip of the misty headland,   to the end of the foggy island.
The houses got fire,   the cabins light.

Craftsman Ilmarinen   rushed straight into the sea,
drags himself to a rock in the water,   goes to a boulder by the shore,
agonized by the burning fire,   tortured by the flame.
There he subdued the fire,   tamed the flame.
He says these words,   made this remark:

CHARMS AGAINST BURNS, LINES 301–366

"Fire, creation of God,   flame, Sun's son!
What made you bad   so that you burned my cheeks,
scorched my loins,   got cross at my sides?
With what shall I now subdue the fire,   tame the flame,
make the fire impotent,   the flame powerless
so that it will not smart for a long time,   not cause pain for a very long time?
Come, girl, from Finnmark,   maiden, set out from Lapland
with slush on your stocking, ice on your shoe,   with rime on the beads of
   your jacket,
with a rimy kettle in your hand,   an icy dipper in the kettle.
Throw cold water,   sprinkle sleety water
on the burned spots,   on the ugly ravages of the fire.

"If that is not enough,   come, boy, from North Farm,
child, come from the heart of Lapland,   tall man, from Gloomy Farm,
one the size of backwoods firs,   as big as a bog pine,
with slushy mittens on your hands,   slushy boots on your foot,
a slushy cap on your head,   a slushy belt girded on your waist.
Bring slush from North Farm,   ice from the cold community.
There is a lot of slush at North Farm,   ice in the cold community.
The streams are slushy, the lakes are iced over,   the very air is glare ice.
Slush-coated hares hop about,   ice-coated bears dance
halfway up the snow-covered hill,   on the lower slope of the snow-covered
   mountain.
Slush-coated swans glide about,   ice-coated mallards paddle about
in the middle of the snowy river,   on the edge of the icy rapids.
Bring slush on a little sled,   haul ice on the sled
from the top of the grim bald mountain,   from the lower slope of the
   mighty hill.
With that slush congeal,   with that ice cool off
the ravages caused by the fire,   the places badly seared by the flame.

"If that is not enough,   O Ukko, god on high,
Ukko, guardian of the clouds,   ruler of the cloud patches,
create a cloud in the east,   send a cloud bank from the west,
thrust them together side by side,   bang them together edge to edge.
Let it pour slush, let it sleet,   let it drop good ointment
on the burned places,   right on the injured places."

With that Ilmarinen   quenched the fire,
put out the flame.   The craftsman got better,
attained his former health   after the fierce ravages of the fire.

POEM 49

Ilmarinen forges a new moon and sun but does not get them to shine (1–74).
By divination Väinämöinen learns
that the moon and sun are inside the hill at North Farm;
he sets out for North Farm,
fights with the people of North Farm, and gains the victory (75–230).
He goes to see the moon and the sun in the hill but does not get inside (231–278).
He returns home to forge tools with which to tear the hill open.
While Ilmarinen is forging these, the mistress of North Farm fears
that things are going badly for herself
and releases the moon and the sun from the hill (279–362).
When Väinämöinen sees the moon and the sun in the heavens,
he salutes them and expresses the hope that they will always make
their fair rounds and bring good fortune to the region (363–422).

Still the sun does not shine,   the golden moon not gleam palely
on those dwellings in Väinämöinen's district,   on the heaths of the Kaleva
    District.
The cold gets into the crops,   a state of affairs dreadful for the cattle,
strange for birds of the air,   disagreeable for humans
when never does the sun shine   nor the moon gleam palely.

The pike knew the deep places,   the eagle knew the course of the birds,
the wind knew the day's journey of a ship;   the sons of men do not know
when the morning will begin,   when it will be about to be night
on the tip of the misty headland,   at the end of the foggy island.
The young take council,   the middle-aged ponder
on how one may exist without the moon,   live without the sun
in those wretched regions,   in those miserable northern lands.
The maidens take council,   the young girls reflect;
they come to the craftsman's smithy,   they utter these words:
"Craftsman, get up from by the wall,   smith, from behind the stone stove,
to forge a new moon,   a new disk of a sun.
It is bad when the moon does not gleam palely,   strange when the sun does
    not shine."

The craftsman got up from by the wall,   the smith got up from behind the
    stone stove
to forge a new moon,   a new disk of a sun.
He fashioned a moon of gold,   made a sun of silver.
Old Väinämöinen came,   takes up a position by the door;

he uttered a word, spoke thus: "O craftsman, my boon companion,
what are you banging away at in your smithy, what are you pounding away
    at all the time?"
That craftsman Ilmarinen uttered a word, spoke thus:
"I am fashioning a gold moon, a silver sun
for up there in the heavens, above the many-colored vaults of heaven."
Then old Väinämöinen uttered these words:
"O craftsman Ilmarinen, now you are doing useless things!
Gold will not gleam like a moon, silver not shine like a sun."
The craftsman fashioned a moon, prepared a sun.
He lifted them up eagerly, propped them up nicely,
the moon on the crown of a fir, the sun on the top of a tall pine.
Sweat poured off the man carrying them, moisture from the bearer's brows
during the laborious work, the difficult lifting up.
He got the moon lifted up, the sun put in place,
the moon on the crown of the fir, the sun on the top of the pine.
The moon does not gleam at all nor does the sun shine either.

Then old Väinämöinen uttered these words:
"Now it is time to turn a divining lot over, to ask of a man's mark
where the sun got away from us, where the moon vanished from us."
Old Väinämöinen, eternal sage,
cut divining chips from an alder, arranged the chips correctly,
set to turning the lots over, with his fingers to getting the lots ready.
He said these words, made this utterance:

A LOT-CASTING CHARM, LINES 89–104

"I ask leave of the Creator, indeed demand an answer:
tell the truth, Creator's mark, say, God's divining lot,
where the sun got away from us, where the moon vanished from us,
since one never, never at all sees them in the sky.
Speak, lot, according to the true state of affairs, not according to a man's
    wish;
bring here a true report, report things positively predestined.
If the lot should lie, then its value will go down,
the lot will be thrown into the fire, the mark of men will be burned."

The lot made a true report, the mark of men answers.
It said the sun had set out yonder, the moon had disappeared yonder
into the hill of rock at North Farm, into the copper mountain.
Steadfast old Väinämöinen then uttered these words:
"If I now set out for North Farm, to the paths of the lads of North Farm,
I will get the moon to gleam palely, the golden sun to shine."
He both set out for, and got to, gloomy North Farm.

He walked one day, walked a second;   on the third day indeed
the main gate of North Farm appears,   the rocky knolls loom up.
First he shouted long and loud   by that river of North Farm:
"Bring a boat here   so that I may get across the river."
When no one heard the shout   or brought a boat,
he gathered a pile of wood,   the needled branches of a dry fir.
He made a fire on the riverbank,   produced a dense smoke.
The fire rose to heaven,   the smoke grew dense in the sky.

Louhi, mistress of North Farm,   went to the window.
She looked over toward the entrance to the sound,   uttered a word, spoke
   thus:
"What kind of fire is burning over there,   there at the entrance to the sound
   of the island?
It is small for a fire to warn of war,   big for a seiner's campfire."
A lad of North Farm   soon dashed into the farmyard
to look, to hear,   to give careful heed:
"There on the other side of the river   a distinguished man is walking along."
Then old Väinämöinen   now shouted a second time:
"Bring a boat, lad of North Farm,   a boat for Väinämöinen."
Then the lad of North Farm says,   spoke, answered:
"No boat is to be got from here.   Come with your fingers as oars,
your palms as steering oars   across North Farm's river."
Then old Väinämöinen   ponders, reflects:
"He who turns back   is not really a man."
He went into the sea as a pike,   into the placid river as a whitefish;
he soon swims across the sound,   meanwhile goes over without delay.
He took one step, took a second,   quickly reached the shore of North Farm.

Then the lads of North Farm say,   the evil crew shouts:
"Just you go to the yard of North Farm!"   He went to the yard of North
   Farm.
The lads of North Farm say,   the evil crew shouts:
"Just you come into the house of North Farm!"   He went into the house
   of North Farm,
tramped into the entryway,   put his hand on the door handle,
then pressed on into the house,   went in under the roof.
There the men were drinking mead,   drinking deep of mead,
all the men with swords in their belts,   people in battle dress,
ready for Väinämöinen's head,   for the death of the man of Slack Water
   Farm.
They asked the newcomer,   said these words:
"What news has the wretched man brought,   what is the plan of the person
   who has been swimming?"

Steadfast old Väinämöinen   uttered a word, spoke thus:
"The news about the moon is strange,   about the sun very remarkable.
Where did the sun get away from us,   where did the moon vanish from us?"
The lads of North Farm speak,   the evil crew gives utterance:
"The sun got away from you,   the sun got away, the moon vanished
into the mottled rock,   the iron crag.
They will not get free from there unless released,   not escape unless let go."

Then old Väinämöinen   uttered these words:
"If the moon does not get free from the rock,   the sun not get free from the
    crag,
let us fight hand to hand,   make trial of it with swords."
He drew his sword, pulled out the blade,   jerked from its sheath the sharp
    sword
on whose point a moon shone,   on whose hilt a sun flashed,
on whose back a steed is standing,   on whose stud a cat was sleeping.
They measured their swords,   tested their short swords.
Old Väinämöinen's sword   was a little longer,
longer by one barleycorn,   longer by a straw's breadth.
They went out into the farmyard,   stood face to face in the yard.
Then old Väinämöinen   struck like a flash once,
struck once, struck twice;   he lopped off the heads of the lads of North Farm
like turnip roots,   knocks them off like heads of flax.

Then old Väinämöinen   goes to look at the moon,
to collect the sun   from the mottled rock,
from the steel mountain,   from the iron crag.
He stepped along a little way,   proceeded a short distance
till he saw a verdant copse.   In the copse is a lovely birch,
under the birch a big boulder,   under the boulder a rock
with nine doors in front,   with a hundred bolts on the doors.
He discovered a streak in the rock,   a secret line in the stone.
He drew his sword from the sheath,   drew a design in the stone
with his fire-sharp sword,   with his sparkling blade.
The stone split in two;   the boulder burst into three pieces.
Steadfast old Väinämöinen   looks through a chink in the rock.
There adders are drinking beer,   reptiles sipping maltwort
inside the mottled rock,   in a crevice of the liver-colored rock.
Old Väinämöinen said,   uttered a word, spoke thus:
"Bad housewives get less beer
because adders are drinking the beer,   reptiles sipping the wort."
He cut the head off a reptile,   broke the neck of a snake.
He speaks these words,   made this remark:
"Never, never at all   from this day forth

may adders drink our beer,   reptiles our malt drinks."
Then old Väinämöinen,   eternal sage,
tried the doors with his grip,   the bolts with the power of a charm.
The doors do not open to his hand,   the bolts pay no attention to his magic
　words.
Then old Väinämöinen   uttered these words:
"A man unarmed is just a woman,   a miserable creature without at least a
　grub hoe."
He sets out at once for home   downcast, low in mind
for he had not yet got the moon   nor come upon the sun.
Reckless Lemminkäinen said: "O old Väinämöinen,
why did you not take me   along with you as a magician?
The locks would have slipped loose,   the inner bars broken off;
the moon got free to gleam palely,   the sun have risen to shine."
Steadfast old Väinämöinen   uttered these words:
"One does not break bolts by charms,   crush locks by enchantment
or by touching them with the hands,   by twisting them with the arms."
He went to his craftsman's smithy.   He uttered a word, spoke thus:
"O craftsman Ilmarinen!   Forge a three-tined cultivator hoe,
forge a dozen ice picks,   a great bunch of keys
with which I will free the moon from the stone,   free the sun from the rock."
That craftsman Ilmarinen,   eternal smith,
forged what the man needed,   forged a dozen icepicks,
a great bunch of keys,   a considerable bunch of spear points,
neither large nor small,   he forged them just in between.

Louhi, mistress of North Farm,   gat-toothed dame of North Farm,
made wings together with their feathers,   flitted off.
She flew around near the dwellings,   thence she flung herself farther off
across the sea of North Farm   to craftsman Ilmarinen's smithy.
The craftsman opened his window,   looked to see whether a gale was coming
　up.
No gale was coming up;   it was a gray hawk.
Craftsman Ilmarinen   uttered a word, spoke thus:
"What are you hunting for, you creature?   Why are you sitting beneath my
　window?"
The bird begins to speak,   the hawk talks:
"O craftsman Ilmarinen,   eternal smith!
How very competent you are,   indeed a skilled smith!"
Craftsman Ilmarinen said,   uttered a word, spoke thus:
"It is probably not in the least remarkable   if I am an able smith
since I forged the heavens,   pounded out the vault of the sky."

The bird began to speak,   the hawk talks:

"What, craftsman, are you preparing there? What, blacksmith, are you making?"
Craftsman Ilmarinen says in reply:
"I am forging a neck ring for that dame of North Farm
with which she will be made fast to the lower slope of a great mountain."
Louhi, mistress of North Farm, gat-toothed dame of North Farm,
now sensed disaster coming, a day of trouble coming upon her.
At once she started to fly, got away to North Farm.
She set the moon free from the stone, let the sun loose from the rock.
She changed herself into something different, made herself into a pigeon;
she flaps along to craftsman Ilmarinen's smithy.
She flew to the door as a bird, to the threshold as a pigeon.
Craftsman Ilmarinen uttered a word, spoke thus:
"Why, bird, did you fly here come, pigeon, to the threshold?"
The creature answered from the doorway, the pigeon spoke from the
    threshold:
"That news I happen to be bringing on the threshold:
the moon has already risen from the stone, the sun got free from the rock."

Craftsman Ilmarinen went to see for himself.
He steps to the door of the smithy, looked carefully to the heavens.
He saw the moon gleaming palely, saw the sun shining.
He went to Väinämöinen's, uttered a word, spoke thus:
"O old Väinämöinen, eternal singer!
Do go look at the moon, examine the sun!
They are now already in the heavens in their places of old."
Steadfast old Väinämöinen went quickly out to the farmyard,
indeed raised his head, took a look at the heavens.
The moon had risen, the sun got free, the sun had reached the heavens.

Then old Väinämöinen got to talking.
He says these words, made this remark:
"Hail to you, moon, for gleaming palely! Hail, beautiful one, for showing
    your face!
Hail, lovely sun, for dawning! Hail, sun, for rising!
Lovely moon, you got free from the stone, beautiful sun, from the rock;
you rose like a golden cuckoo, like a silver dove
to your former state, to your rounds of old.
Always rise mornings from this day forth.
Give us health, make the game accessible to us,
bring the prey within reach of our thumb, good luck to the tip of our fish-
    hook.
Go now your way in good health, go on your rounds in fine shape;
complete finely your daily round, in the evening attain to joy."

POEM 50

From a whortleberry a boy is born to the virgin Marjatta (1–350).
When little, the boy disappears and is finally found in a fen (351–424).
An old, old man is fetched to christen him, but the old man
will not christen a boy without a father before someone investigates
and decides whether the boy should be left alive (425–440).
Väinämöinen comes to investigate the matter and decides
that the strange boy should be put to death, but the half-month-old boy
upbraids him for handing down a wrong verdict (441–474).
The old man christens the boy King of Karelia,
at which Väinämöinen gets angry and departs forever,
prophesying that he will be needed once again to make
a new Sampo, harp, and light for the people; he departs in a copper boat
to between heaven and earth where he presumably still is, but he bequeaths
the harp and his great songs as a heritage for the people (475–512).
Epilogue (513–620).

Marjatta, man-shy youngest child,   she long grew up at home,
in the home of her esteemed father,   in the house of her loving mother.
She wore through five key-ring chains,   wore out six rings
with her father's keys,   with the shining keys on her skirt.
She wore out half the threshold   with her showy skirts,
half a lintel   with the smooth silk hair ribbons on her head,
half the doorjambs   with the soft ends of her sleeves,
the floorboards   with the heels of her shoes with ornamented uppers.

Marjatta, man-shy youngest child,   that little maid,
long kept her virtue,   ever her modesty.
She eats fine fish,   soft pine-bark bread;
she did not eat the eggs of a hen   defiled by a cock
nor the flesh of a sheep   which rams had had.
Her mother ordered her to go milk;   she did not go milk.
She uttered these words: "No girl like me
will touch the teat of that cow   which has been mounted by bulls,
only if something trickles from heifers,   drips from calves."
Her father ordered the stallion to be hitched to the sled;   she does not hitch
   the stallion to the sled.
Her brother brought a mare.   The girl spoke these words:
"I will not hitch to the sled a horse   which stallions may have had,
only if foals pull it,   month-old ones draw it."

Marjatta, man-shy youngest child,   ever living as a maiden,
lissome like a maid,   living modestly as a girl with luxuriant hair,
became a shepherdess,   set out with the sheep.
The sheep went about on a hill,   the lambs on the ridge of the hill;
the maiden stepped lightly over a clearing,   moved lightly through an alder
   grove
while a golden cuckoo was calling,   a silver one singing loudly.
Marjatta, man-shy youngest child,   looks about, listens.
She sat down on a berry-grown tussock,   settled down on the slope of a hill.
There she uttered these words,   remarked, spoke thus:
"Call out, golden cuckoo!   Silver one, sing loud!
Sing out in song, clear-voiced bird!   Say, German strawberry,
whether I shall long go about as one with flowing hair,   long as a shepherdess
on these open clearings,   in these extensive leafy groves.
One summer, two,   five, six
or even ten summers?   Or not fully that?"

Marjatta, man-shy youngest child,   spent a long time as a shepherdess.
It is hard being a shepherdess,   especially, too, for a young girl.
A serpent is crawling in the grass,   lizards are wriggling there.
But the serpent really did not crawl,   nor the lizard wriggle.
A berry cried out from a rise,   a whortleberry from the heath:
"Come, maiden, to pluck me,   rosy-cheeked girl, to pick me,
clear-voiced girl, to pluck me,   girl with a copper belt, to choose me
before a slug eats me,   a black reptile suddenly puts me in its mouth.
A hundred have come to look at me,   a thousand furthermore to sit beside
   me,
a hundred girls, a thousand women,   countless children,
but none would touch me,   pick poor me."

Marjatta, man-shy youngest child,   went a little way,
went to look at the berry,   to pick the red whortleberry
with her fine finger tips,   with her fair hands.
She found the berry on the rise,   the whortleberry on the heath.
It looks like a berry,   like a whortleberry from its shape,
rather high from the ground to eat,   rather low to climb after.
She snatched a club from the heath   with which she knocked the berry to the
   ground.
Then indeed the berry rose from the ground   to the fine leather uppers,
from the fine leather uppers   to the lovely knees,
from the lovely knees   to the fine apron.
Then it went up to the belt buckle,   from the belt buckle to her breasts,
from her breasts to her chin,   from her chin to her lips;

then it slipped into her mouth,   made a quick turn onto her tongue,
went from her tongue into her throat,   from there slipped into her belly.

Marjatta, man-shy youngest child,   swelled from that, got full from that,
got fat from that,   put on flesh.
She began to spend time without a waistband,   to loll about without a belt,
to visit the sauna secretly,   to sneak about in the dark.
Her mother keeps pondering,   her mother keeps reflecting:
"What is the matter with our Marjatta?   What is wrong with our chick
that she should be spending time without a waistband,   always lolling about
   without a belt,
visiting the sauna secretly,   sneaking about in the dark?"
A child is able to say,   a little child to remark:
"This is the matter with our Marjatta,   this indeed the matter with poor
   Marjatta:
she was long a-herding,   wandered long tending cattle."

She carried a hard womb,   a heavy bellyful
for seven moons, eight,   nine moons in all,
according to woman's old reckoning   half way into the tenth.
So in the tenth moon   the virgin begins to suffer pain;
her womb contracts severely,   becomes urgent.
She asked her mother for a sauna bath: "O mother mine, my beloved,
prepare a warm place,   a warm room
as a maiden's little hiding place,   a room for a woman's labor."
Her mother says,   her own parent gets to answering:
"Woe is you, demon's whore!   Whose bedfellow are you?
Are you an unmarried man's   or a married man's?"
Marjatta, man-shy youngest child,   replies to this:
"I am neither an unmarried man's   nor a married man's.
I went to the rise for a berry,   to pick a red whortleberry;
I took the berry with pleasure,   next put it on my tongue.
It went into my throat,   then slipped into my belly.
From that I swelled up, from that I got full,   from that I got pregnant."
She asked her father for a bath: "O father mine, my beloved,
give me a warm place,   a warm room
where a poor girl might get relief,   a maiden endure her pain."
Her father says,   her father answers:
"Go, whore, farther away,   go off yonder, whore fit for burning,
to bruin's stone-piles,   to the bear's dens in a rock,
there, whore, to bear your child,   whore fit for burning, to give birth to a
   child."
Marjatta, man-shy youngest child,   answered shrewdly:

"I am, I think, by no means a whore,   no whore for burning.
I am about to give birth to the Great Man,   to bear the Great Birth
Who will have rule over rulers,   power even over Väinämöinen."

Now the maiden was in a quandary   as to where to go, where to proceed,
where to ask for a bath.   She uttered a word, spoke thus:
"Lassie, smallest of my maids,   best of my paid servants,
go beg a bath in the community,   a sauna in Saraja
where a poor girl might get relief,   a maiden endure her pain.
Go quickly, make great haste;   you will need to hurry even more!"
Lassie, the little maid,   uttered a word, spoke thus:
"From whom shall I ask for a sauna,   from whom beg for help?"
Our Marjatta said,   uttered a word, spoke thus:
"Ask for Ruotus' sauna bath,   a sauna on the outskirts of Saraja."
Lassie, the little maid,   was meekly obedient,
quick without ordering,   spry without urging,
goes out like so much mist,   gets to the farmyard like so much smoke.
She gathered up her skirt in her hand,   twisted her clothes in her grip,
ran and got   quickly to Ruotus' home.
The hills rang out as she went,   the mountains shook as she went up them,
the pine cones on the heath swayed,   the gravel in the fen was scattered
     about.
She came to Ruotus' house,   got inside the log building.

Loathsome Ruotus in a shirt   is eating, drinking in the manner of the great
at the head of his table in his shirt,   right in his linen shirt.
Ruotus spoke from over his food,   barked out from behind his dish:
"What are you saying, base creature?   Why, wretch, are you hopping about?"
Lassie, the little maid,   uttered a word, spoke thus:
"I set out to get a bath in the community,   a sauna in Saraja
where a poor girl might get relief;   a girl in agony needs help."
Ruotus' loathsome lady   came in, hands on hips,
fluttered about where the floorboards meet,   shuffled down the middle of the
     floor.
She managed to ask,   uttered a word, spoke thus:
"For whom are you requesting a bath,   for whom are you asking help?"
Lassie, the little maid, said: "I am asking for our Marjatta."
Ruotus' loathsome lady   uttered these words:
"There are no bathhouses available for a stranger,   no saunas at the entrance
     to Saraja.
There is a bathhouse on the burned land,   a horse shed in the evergreen grove
for the whore fit for burning to bear sons in,   for a loose woman to give birth
     to her child.

When the horse puffs,   then may you bathe!"

Lassie, the little maid,   quickly took her way back,
ran and got there.   When she got back, she said:
"There is no bathhouse in the community,   no sauna at Saraja.
Ruotus' loathsome lady   uttered a word, spoke thus:
'There are no bathhouses available for a stranger,   no saunas at the entrance
   to Saraja.
There is a bathhouse on the burned land,   a horse shed in the evergreen-
   grove
for a whore fit for burning to bear sons in,   for a loose woman to give birth to
   her child.
When the horse puffs,   then let one bathe there.'
So it is, so she said,   just so did she answer."

At that Marjatta, lowly girl,   burst out crying.
She uttered these words: "I will have to set out
just as a hired hand of yore   or at least as a paid slave,
set out to the burned land,   have to go to the evergreen grove."
She twisted up her clothing in her hands,   gathered up her skirt in her
   grip.
She took a bath whisk to cover her,   a lovely spray of leaves to shelter her.
She steps along quickly   in severe labor pains
to the shed in the evergreen grove,   to the stable on Tapio Rise.
She says these words,   made this remark:
"Come, Nature, to protect me,   to help me, merciful one,
in these severe labors,   in these very difficult times.
Free the maid from her torment,   the woman from her labor pains
so that she may not lapse into agony   nor pine away in agony."

Then, after she got to her destination,   she uttered these words:
"Breathe, good horse,   puff, draft colt,
puff bath vapor,   send warm sauna steam
that I, poor wretch, may get relief.   I, anguished one, need help."
The good horse breathed,   the draft colt gave deep puffs
on the belly of the anguished girl.   By as much as the horse breathes,
by so much was sauna vapor produced,   water thrown and vapor produced.
Marjatta, lowly maiden,   pure little maid,
bathed all she wanted in the bathhouse,   all she cared to in the steam.
There she produced a little boy,   bore an innocent child
on the hay by the horse,   in the shaggy one's manger.
She washed her little son,   wrapped him in his swaddling clothes,
took the boy on her knees,   fixed up the child on her lap.
She kept her son out of sight,   cared for her beauty,

her golden apple, her silver staff.
She nursed him in her arms, turned him over in her hands.
She set the boy on her knees, the child on her lap,
began to groom his head, to comb his hair.

The boy disappeared from her knees, the child from her lap.

Marjatta, lowly maid, becomes greatly distressed at that.
She rushed off to search for him. She searched for her little boy,
her golden apple, her silver staff
under the grindstone, under the sled runner,
under the sieve for sifting, under the bucket for carrying things,
shaking trees, tedding hay, pulling fine blades of grass apart.
For a long time she searched for her boy, her boy, her little one.
She searched hills, pine groves, stumps, heaths,
surveying every heath, searching through every bit of scrub growth,
digging in juniper roots, straightening out the branches of trees.

She walks pensively, goes along lightly.
She comes upon Star. She bows to Star:
"O Star, creation of God, do you not know about my boy,
not know where my little boy is, my golden apple?"
Star was able to answer: "If I did know, I would not tell.
It was he who created me for these evil times,
to shine in cold places, to twinkle in dark places."

She walks pensively, goes along lightly.
She comes upon Moon, then she bows to Moon:
"O Moon, creation of God, do you not know about my boy,
not know where my little boy is, my golden apple?"
Moon was able to answer: "If I did know, I would not tell.
It was he who created me for these evil times,
to lie on watch alone by night, to go to bed by day."

She walks pensively, goes along lightly.
She came upon Sun, she bows to Sun:
"O Sun, creation of God, do you not know about my boy,
not know where my little boy is, my golden apple?"
Sun answered knowingly: "Of course I know about your boy.
He created me for these fine times,
for me to jingle in gold, to tinkle in silver.
Indeed I know about your boy, alas, poor wretch, about your boy!
There is where your little boy is, your golden apple:
he is up to his waist in the fen, up to his armpits on the heath."

Marjatta, lowly maid,   searched for her boy in the fen.
The boy was found in the fen,   from there was brought home.
Then a fine-looking boy   grew up for our Marjatta.
No one knows a name for him,   knows by what name to call him.
His mother called him "Little Flower,"   outsiders "Lazybones."
They search for a christener,   look for a baptizer.
An old man came to christen him,   Virokannas to baptize him.
The old man uttered these words,   remarked, spoke thus:
"I will not christen one possessed,   in no wise baptize the miserable one
unless he is first examined,   examined, judged."

Who is to be his examiner,   his examiner, his judge?
Steadfast old Väinämöinen,   eternal sage,
he is the one to be his examiner,   his examiner, his judge.
Steadfast old Väinämöinen   judges him there:
"If the boy was got from a fen,   begotten of a berry from the ground,
let the boy be put on the ground   beside a berry-grown tussock
or taken to a fen,   hit on the head with a club."
The half-month-old boy spoke,   the two-week-old child cried out:
"O you, wretched old man,   wretched old man, stupid man,
how foolishly you have judged,   how wrongly you have laid down the law.
For greater reasons,   for even worse deeds,
you yourself were not taken to a fen   or hit on the head with a club
when as a rather young man   you gave away your mother's child
to free your own head,   to ransom yourself.
Neither then nor since   has anyone taken you to a fen,
when as a rather young man   you drowned young girls
under deep waves,   in the dark ooze."

The old man christened him quickly,   speedily baptized the child
King of Karelia,   guardian of the whole realm.
Then Väinämöinen got angry,   indeed got angry and was put to shame.
He set out to walk   to the shore of the sea.
There he began to sing.   He sang magically for his last time,
sang up a copper boat,   a copper-decked vessel.
He sits down in the stern,   set out for the clear expanse of the sea.
He was still speaking as he was going,   remarking as he went along:
"Let time pass,   one day go, another come;
they will need me again,   be looking, waiting for me
to fetch a new Sampo,   to prepare a new instrument,
fetch a new moon,   free a new sun
when there is no moon, no sun   nor any worldly joy."
Then old Väinämöinen   sets out quickly

in the copper boat,   in the flat-bottomed copper craft
toward the upper reaches of the world,   to the lower reaches of the heavens.
There he stopped with his vessel,   out of weariness stopped with his boat.
He left the harp behind,   the fine instrument for Finland,
the eternal source of joyous music for the people,   the great songs for his
    children.

[EPILOGUE, LINES 513-620]

"Now one should shut one's mouth,   bind fast one's tongue,
end the singing of the song,   stop the resonant voice.
'A horse puffs   after it has gone a long way,
an iron scythe tires   after it has been cutting summer hay,
water slows down   after it has run through the bends of a river,
a fire dies out   after it has burned all night long.'
Why, therefore, should not a song get tired,   delicate songs not slow down
from a long evening of joyous music,   from singing at sunset?

"So I heard it said,   viewed in another way:
'Even a streaming rapids does not   send down all its water
nor does a good singer   sing everything he knows.
It is a better idea for one to stop   than to be cut off in the middle.'
Accordingly I will leave off, end it,   stop, cease.
I will wind my verses up in a clew,   form them into a tangled mass,
put them up in the loft of the cattle shed   behind locks of bone
from which they will never get free,   never, never at all
escape without moving the bones from their place,   prizing the jaws apart,
scattering the teeth,   moving the tongue quickly.

"What of it if I sing,   if I put much, too, into verse,
if I sing in every valley,   sing plaintively in every fir grove!
My mother is not alive,   my own parent not awake
nor is the loved one listening,   my own dear one teaching me.
The firs are listening to me,   the evergreen boughs teaching me,
the leafy birch sprays loving me,   the rowans caring for me tenderly.
As a little boy I was left without a mother,   as a poor little thing without my
    mother.
I was left like a lark on a stone,   like a thrush on a rock pile,
to warble like a lark,   to sing plaintively like a thrush
in the care of a strange woman,   at the mercy of a stepmother.
She turned me out, poor me,   drove the orphan child
from the house to a windy quarter,   from home to northern parts
for the wind to carry the defenseless child away,   the cold spring wind the
    orphan.

337

"I, skylark, got to wandering,   I, poor bird, to going about,
I, delicate one, to traversing lands,   wretched one, to roving about,
to feeling every wind,   to experiencing the roaring gale,
to shivering in the cold,   to screaming out in the severe frost.

"Now there is many a one,   is many a one
who speaks to me with angry voice,   who snaps at me with an unkind voice.
Such a one harshly blamed my tongue,   such a one roared at my voice
slanderously charged that I sang discordantly,   said I sang too much,
sang badly,   turned my verses wrong.

"Do not, good people,   regard that as odd
if I, a child, sang too much,   a little one, sang feebly and badly.
I was not instructed,   did not visit the land of seers,
did not get words from outside,   phrases from farther off.
All others were taught;   I did not get away from home
from the help of my mother alone,   from around that lonely one.
I had to learn about it at home   under the rooftree of my own storehouse,
by my own mother's distaff,   by the chips my brother whittled,
even that as a small boy, a little boy,   a little boy in a ragged shirt.

"But be that as it may,   I blazed a trail for singers,
blazed a trail, broke off tree tops,   broke branches, showed the way.
Thence the way goes now,   a new course stretches out
for more versatile singers,   for ampler songs
in the rising younger generation,   among the people growing up."

THE END

APPENDICES

I. MATERIALS FOR THE STUDY OF THE *KALEVALA*

A. ELIAS LÖNNROT[1]

Elias Lönnrot was born 9 April 1802 in the parish of Sammatti (province of Uusimaa, Swedish Nyland) on Lake Haarjärvi, in a cottage which later became Paikkari Farm, state-owned for the benefit of veterans [now a little museum], and died 19 November 1884 at Lampi Farm in the same village. He was a physician and discoverer of our traditional poetry. His father, Fredrik Juhana Lönnrot, was a tailor, his mother, Ulriika Wahlberg, a peasant's daughter.

Life was hard in Lönnrot's childhood. Elias, the fourth of seven children, was in the first instances put by his father to learning tailoring, but his overwhelming desire to read drew him to books. In 1814 his eldest brother got the boy into an elementary school at Tammisaari [Swedish Ekenäs], where he studied for three terms. From 1816 to 1818 Lönnrot attended the cathedral school at Turku [Swedish Åbo], and after learning Swedish, which at first caused him very great difficulties, he worked his way in spite of this to the top of his class. Finally lack of means seemed to be an insurmountable obstacle. The curate at Sammatti, Juhana Lönnqvist, then began to give private instruction to the boy who was so eager for knowledge, advised him to get the necessary means by soliciting in his parish scholarship-money for high school, and in the spring of 1820 took him to the high school at Porvoo [Swedish Borgå]. For lack of means he moved after a few weeks to Hämeenlinna [Swedish Tavastehus], where L. J. Bjugg needed in his pharmacy an apprentice competent in Latin, a post to which he was bound for five years. Besides working for his living, Lönnrot, helped by both the district doctor J. E. Sabell and the school principal H. Langström, continued his studies and in October 1822 became a student at the University of Turku.

Study at the University of Turku threatened to become an unbearable struggle against poverty. Happily, on the recommendation of Professor Johan Agapetus Törngren, M.D., Lönnrot got the position of private tutor in the parish of Eura on Lake Pyhäjärvi in Satakunta and in 1824

[1] By Aarne A. Anttila, in *Iso Tietosanakirja* [The Big Encyclopedia], 2d ed., vol. VII (Helsinki, 1935), coll. 277–84, with a few minor omissions.

in Törngren's own family. Under the circumstances Lönnrot spent his winters in Turku, later in Helsinki [Swedish Helsingfors], his summers on the Törngren family estate "Laukko" in the parish of Vesilahti [Swedish Vesilax], which in his adult years he visited as a family friend. This fine and hospitable home counted greatly in Lönnrot's development.

Five years later, in June 1827, Lönnrot passed the examination for the master's degree at Turku after defending a thesis "De Vainamoine, priscorum fennorum numine" [Väinämöinen, a Divinity of the Ancient Finns], done under the guidance of Associate Professor Reinhold von Becker. This pamphlet aimed, on the basis of the then-known songs, to explore the time and place of the origin of their main hero, matters of family relationship, characteristics, and so forth. Of the actual conclusion nothing is known, for the end of the thesis was destroyed in the 1827 fire of Turku.

Using to his advantage an opportune period of free time, Lönnrot set out in April 1828 on a song-collecting trip to Häme [Swedish Tavastland], Savo [Swedish Savolax], and through Finnish Karelia. On the trip Lönnrot got a clear idea of eastern Finland's wealth of song, and met at least one man especially expert in the old songs, Juhana Kainulainen, in the parish of Kesälahti (province of Kuopio), and at Rautalampi (province of Kuopio) a couple of composers of newer songs, Paavo Korhonen and Pentti Lyytinen. Already while on the trip Lönnrot had arranged his collection for the press, and he published it in 1829–1831 in four fascicles as *Kantele* [The Harp]. There would have been material enough for two more fascicles, but in the meanwhile his plans had changed.

In October 1828 Lönnrot began to continue his studies at the medical school of Helsinki University. After he had got his first medical degree, he was assigned as an intern at the cholera hospital at Hietälahti near Helsinki and then as an inspector with a roving commission to the eastern part of the province of Uusimaa and the southern part of the province of Häme. On one such trip of inspection he noted down spring-festival songs at Ritvala in the parish of Sääksmäki (province of Häme). After defending his final thesis, "Om Finnarnes magiska Medicin" [The Magical Medicine of the Finns], later published in *Finska Läkaresällskapets Handlingar* [Transactions of the Finnish Medical Society], I (1842), 199–244, Lönnrot got his M.D. at the first graduation exercises of Helsinki University in 1832. Thus the materials of both the M.A. and M.D. theses were the old poetry and lore of the Finnish people which the Finnish Literature Society (Suomen, later Suomalaisen Kirjallisuuden Seura), founded in 1831 and of which Lönnrot was the first secretary, aimed to bring to light. In the latter half of 1832 Lönnrot was assigned as an assistant circuit physician in

"A single man, by scurrying about, has created a heritage for us"
(Inscription adapted from Ennius' *Annals*, xii, fr. 1. v. 1)

A. W. Linsén's cartoon, 1847, of Lönnrot on a field trip

Elias Lönnrot at age 43

Elias Lönnrot in his later years

Lönnrot's birthplace, Paikkari cottage, at Sammatti

the province of Oulu, which had been afflicted with epidemics, and in January 1833 first as a temporary, a few months later as permanent, doctor for the Kajaani [Swedish Kajana] area, town and castle. In this district, about sixty miles in extent, there were hundreds of sick people who lacked food and the most rudimentary knowledge of the treatment of epidemics and of contagion. Lönnrot began at once to take energetic measures, until in February 1833 he came down with typhus and for a month hovered on the brink of death, so that a report of his death spread to southern Finland. To mitigate the distress of future crop-failure years, Lönnrot adapted and translated into Finnish Gustafva Schartau's pamphlet *Hyväntahtoisia neuvoja katovuosina* [Well-intentioned Advice in Crop-Failure Years] (1834), and, adapting Carl Nordblad's *Sundhets-lärobok för menige Man* [Health-Manual for the Common People], drew up a set of instructions for the treatment of common diseases, *Suomalaisen talonpojan koti-lääkäri* [The Finnish Peasant's Home Doctor] (1839, 3d ed. 1867).

In the summer of 1833 Lönnrot got the idea of collecting and arranging in groups everything sung about Väinämöinen, Ilmarinen, and Lemminkäinen. On the trips planned to carry this out and on the compilation of the *Kalevala* see the article "The *Kalevala*" below.

Evidence of the fact that Lönnrot's side-activities were gaining recognition among the authorities was a year's leave of absence from his medical work. The Finnish Literature Society gave him 1000 roubles [about $500] traveling money. From September 1836 to October 1837 Lönnrot traveled about, first in the Archangel part of Karelia, eventually farther on right up to the Arctic coast and back through Petsamo (formerly province of Lapland), Lake Inari [Swedish Enare] (province of Lapland), and Sodankylä (province of Lapland), and immediately after that he wandered back and forth across Finnish Karelia. The spoils were unexpectedly rich and included all kinds of traditional poetry. Lönnrot undertook to arrange the lyrical songs for the press and for this purpose made a few more short collecting trips in Finnish Karelia. As new additions continued to increase the manuscript had to be recopied four times. The songs finally amounted to 650. On his thirty-eighth birthday, in 1840, Lönnrot signed the preface of the *Kanteletar* [The Spirit of the Harp], in which the author's aesthetic views are best reflected. At about two-year intervals there appeared the two remaining cornerstones of our traditional poetry, *Sananlaskut* [Proverbs] and *Arvoitukset* [Riddles]; the former contains 7077 proverbs, the latter 1679 Finnish and 135 Estonian riddles.

On his long trips Lönnrot had become familiar with Lappish and Karelian, and from these languages had begun to collect materials for a comparative Finnish grammar and a vocabulary of the eastern dialect.

In 1840 the Finnish Literature Society asked Lönnrot to complete the big Finnish-Swedish dictionary which after Kaarle Niklas Keckman's death had remained unfinished. For this work the Cabinet granted him a two-year leave from his official medical duties. In January 1841 Lönnrot set out for the Olónetz area of southern Karelia, always intending to go clear to Archangel, but on account of a defective passport he had to return from Petrozavodsk [Finnish Petroskoi] (Karelian SSR) with almost nothing accomplished. In the autumn of the same year he set out again with M. A. Castrén on a roundabout course by a northern route through Inari, Norway, and Russian Lapland and came back alone from Archangel via the Veps country in the Olónetz area. In 1844 Lönnrot made a final exploratory trip to Estonia lasting half a year . . . On his return journey through Ingria in the rectory of Kattila Lönnrot noted down Vote songs from an excellent woman singer, Anna Ivanovna.

Apart from the above-mentioned publications of traditional poetry, Lönnrot's correspondence in the thirties and forties absolutely teemed with literary projects: a Finnish-language lawbook, a medical guide, geography, history, and arithmetic aimed at the enlightenment of the peasantry in all fields of knowledge. To this end Lönnrot founded in 1835 the first Finnish-language periodical, *Mehiläinen* [The Bee], in order to publish specimens of different kinds of traditional poetry and articles in a rustic style in the above-mentioned fields of knowledge. As an appendix were serialized von Becker's Finnish translation of a history of antiquity, Juhana Fredrik Cajan's history of Finland, and a history of Russia adapted by the author himself and Gustav Ticklén. *The Bee* appeared in 1836–37 and 1839–40. In 1840 Lönnrot was busy establishing the scholarly and patriotic periodical *Suomi* [Finland]. During the first, most difficult years Lönnrot's share was noteworthy on the side of both quality and quantity. Among the newspapers of the capital Lönnrot enthusiastically supported *Helsingfors Morgonblad* [Helsingfors Morning Journal] during those years when Runeberg and Fabian Collan were its editors. When in 1844 Snellman began to issue in Kuopio *Maamiehen ystävä* [The Farmer's Friend] and the Swedish language *Saima*, Lönnrot was associated as a contributor to both. Of the articles sent in by Lönnrot to the former the most significant is a serialized and popularly written account of the vicissitudes of Finland, of those sent to the latter a presentation of the fundamentals of the metrics of Finnish traditional poetry. Here Lönnrot insisted firmly in the quantitative basis of the meter of the classical languages and of the ancient *Kalevala*-type verse. When *Saima* was suppressed in 1846, Lönnrot edited with Snellman *Litteraturblad för allmän medborgerlig Bildning* [Literary Journal for General Civic Culture] from 1847 to

1849. His articles touched on popular education, temperance, native literature, and the preparation of the New Kalevala ("Anmärkningar till den nya Kalevala-upplagen," 1 Jan. 1849, pp. 15–21).

At the beginning of 1844 Lönnrot got a five-year leave for the preparation of the big Finnish-Swedish dictionary, but his many side-activities got in the way of the main work. He was forced in 1847 to undertake the task of preparing Ruotsin, suomen ja saksan tulkki [A Swedish, Finnish and German Interpreter] and the Finnish part of Chief-of-Protocol Agathon Meurman's Russian-Swedish dictionary. From the first-mentioned there grew a work containing nearly 10,000 words and some 2000 idioms. Other tasks during the period of leave were the posthumous publication of Paavo Korhonen's collected poems and the editing of the New Kalevala, whose preface he finished on 17 April 1849.

The second edition of the Kalevala was not received with nearly the same enthusiasm as the first—such great expectations had had time to develop. Many persons expressed the hope that Lönnrot himself or someone else would edit another new revised edition. The more years that passed the less did anybody want this, apart from abridgments for school instruction like the one that Lönnrot himself got out in 1862. The Kalevala is the great creation of our period of national romanticism and is an integral part of it; its second (1849) edition in particular has attained an unrivaled and dominant position in our literature and spiritual life.

In 1849, when the five-year leave was coming to an end, Lönnrot petitioned for an extension of it, or for a discharge from his medical post, in order to prepare the dictionary. Revolutionary movements abroad had, however, made Governor-General Alexander Sergevitch Mcnshikov extremely suspicious, and both requests were denied. Accordingly, in the summer of 1849 Lönnrot again began to attend to his medical practice and married Maria Piponius, the energetic, practical, pious daughter of a dyer in Oulu [Swedish Uleåborg]. As a sideline he edited in 1852–53 the Oulu Wiikko-Sanomat [The Weekly News] without complaining about the restriction of the very worst and most rigid censorship.

When a professorship for the Finnish language and literature was established at Helsinki University, no amount of persuasion changed Lönnrot's opinion that M. A. Castrén was best qualified for it. When on Castrén's death in 1852 the chair again fell vacant, Lönnrot was persuaded at the last moment to accept it. After the defense of his inaugural thesis "Om det Nord-Tschudiska språket" [The North Tschud Language], Lönnrot was named professor of the Finnish language and literature in October 1853. His scholarly publications of this period are, apart from one, *Ueber den Enare-lappischen Dialekt* [The Inari-Lapp Dialect], fairly short articles.

Much greater than as a theoretical investigator is Lönnrot's significance as a practical linguist who, from out of the confusion of the struggle of the Finnish dialects, efficiently guided the standard literary language that was gradually being accepted—and this regardless of the fact that his own style, particularly during his early years, is characterized by long sentences, is very stiff, and would be quite tiresome to read but for a playful turn that now and then brightens it up. His chief aim was to write in language that as many people as possible might understand easily. In all main points he kept the West Finnish morphological system, already to some extent established in earlier literature, but as the need arose he enriched it with additions borrowed from East Finnish dialects, for example, with the reflexive verb forms and above all with a rich stock of words. As a many-sided expert in Finnish dialects Lönnrot was an incomparable coiner of neologisms . . . Most of Lönnrot's word formations are in the fields of history, linguistics, medicine, arithmetic, botany, and law. Basic and exemplary in this connection are his *Flora Fennica: Suomen kasvisto* [The Flora of Finland] (1860, 2d ed. 1866), and Johan Philip Palmén's *La'in opillinen käsikirja yhteiseksi sivistykseksi* [Juridical Handbook for General Enlightenment], done into Finnish by Lönnrot in 1863.

Lönnrot was charged with reacting coolly to the political movement of pro-Finnicism, apparently because the greater part of his scholarly production was in Swedish and because as a known man of peace he presumably did not try to fight for recognition of the Finnish language. He often openly expressed his appreciation of the Swedish language and Swedish culture, but in the annual main addresses which he delivered as head of the Finnish Literature Society he pointed out again and again that in both educational institutions and government offices Finnish must become the equal of Swedish. In the spring of 1862 Lönnrot was invited to be a member of a committee which was to deliberate the abolishment of the bad practice whereby the majority of the people got their official documents in Swedish, a language incomprehensible to them. Because of the attitude of the majority of the committee, the committee's report contained only cautious hopes. In Lönnrot's opinion newly appointed judges and officials ought to be obliged to use Finnish as well as Swedish. In order not to be left alone Lönnrot associated himself with a rather firm demurrer in which a five-year respite was prescribed.

In the summer of 1857, when crop failure threatened northern Finland, the government sent Lönnrot there to direct the preparation of food substitutes. At that time he published in Finnish and Swedish *Neuvoja erästen jäkäläin käyttämisestä ruuaksi* [Advice on Using Certain Lichens as Food] (2d ed., 1867). To check infant mortality Lönnrot wrote in 1859 a pamphlet *Minkätähden cuolee Suomessa niin paljon lapsia ensimmäisellä ikävuodellansa?* [Why Do So Many Children in Finland Die in Their First Year?]. Lönnrot adapted to Finnish several books of popular instruction to promote temperance and a decent life.

In the spring of 1862 Lönnrot retired from his professorship. From a neighbor near Paikkari Farm, the home of his birth, he bought Niku Farm, put it into first-class shape, and few years later got Lampi, a backwoods farm in the middle of the forests of northern Sammatti, situated back at the end of inconvenient roads, so as to be able in peace and quiet to devote the powers of even his old age to the Finnish language and literature.

In 1863 Lönnrot was invited to join a committee whose task was the publication of a radically modernized Finnish hymnal. He was the most active member of the committee. Leaving out of account the hundreds of hymns left more or less ready in manuscript and those published in the newspaper *Tähti* [The Star], Lönnrot has to his credit about ten hymn publications. Of these the most important is *Suomalainen virsikirja väliaikaiseksi tarpeeksi* [A Finnish Hymnal for Temporary Use] (1872), of which there appeared in 1883 an edition emended and notated for four voices. The greater part of the contents of these publications is old material linguistically revised. Lönnrot's own hymns are not especially poetical nor at all smooth as to rhythm, but they are devout, simple, and easy to understand.

Another work, which Lönnrot had started on from time to time since 1840 but did not really get going on until he retired, is the big *Suomalais-ruotsalainen sanakirja* [Finnish-Swedish Dictionary], which appeared in fourteen parts between 1866 and 1880 (2d printing, 1930; 3d printing, 1958). It aimed to include the whole Finnish vocabulary. The collecting of this was, however, carried out unevenly, casually and with too little help; it is unreliable especially in the derivatives, material made according to a pattern which had never appeared in living Finnish. Regardless of its shortcomings, it was, while appearing, an indispensable aid, and indeed even now is incomparably the largest Finnish vocabulary, containing more than 200,000 words.[2]

During the last years of his life Lönnrot returned to the traditional poetry. In 1880 he published *Suomen kansan muinaisia loitsorunoja* [Old Metrical Charms of the Finnish People], and on J. V. Snellman's seventy-fifth birthday in 1881 a poem *Turo, kuun ja auringon pelastaja. Inkerin kansarunoista kokoon sovittanut Elias Lönnrot* [Turo, Savior of the Sun and the Moon. From Ingrian Songs concatenated by Elias Lönnrot]. As a very last work Lönnrot made a new arrangement of the

---

[2] Now in many, though not all, respects surpassed by the monolingual *Nykysuomen sanakirja*, 6 vols. (Porvoo-Helsinki, 1951–1961).

Kanteletar [The Spirit of the Harp], of which he managed to reorganize and greatly enlarge the third volume. Julius Krohn published the manuscript in 1887 in the third printing of the *Kanteletar*.

Already during his lifetime Lönnrot received public recognition and marks of distinction in abundance, but these seem to have brought him less pleasure than distress. Lönnrot was in his proper milieu at home at a work-desk that he had ingeniously made, in well-worn peasant clothes with a pipe in his mouth and all his manuscripts and equipment in fine order. When taking time off from work, as his relaxation he sang traditional songs and lays, accompanying himself on a harp, and took regular walks, swam, and skied up to the last years of his life.

In his old age Lönnrot, like a great patriarch surrounded by his family, was the all-in-all of his local chapel. There having been for years no clergyman, he conducted divine services every third Sunday in the church at Sammatti; sick people went to him for treatment without charge, often getting at the same time their medicines, which were decocted from native herbs. As a memorial to his nearest relatives, many of whom died before him, he at one time paid for an addition to the district school; at other times he had the church repaired, presented it with an altarpiece painted by Adolf von Becker, out of his own means established a lending library, and finally assigned in his will the largest part of his estate to found a school of home economics at Sammatti. Lönnrot left the Finnish Literature Society his literary remains with all rights.

Without being a writer in the proper sense of the word, as a publisher of the traditional poetry, compiler of our national epic, "second founder of our written language"—the first being Michael Agricola (ca. 1510–1557)—Lönnrot created the basis on which one could and can build. As a human being Lönnrot is the epitome of a Finn, and, even if one tries, it is hard to find in him any objectionable traits; indefatigable assiduity and power of concentration, a quiet firmness and a kindly sense of humor under all circumstances, reasonableness and tolerance, extreme unpretentiousness, and truly Christian humility were characteristic of him.

Of Lönnrot's writings preserved in the archives of the Finnish Literature Society there have been published (in Helsinki), among others, *Kalevalan esityöt* [Work Preliminary to the *Kalevala*], 3 vols. (1891, 1895); *Elias Lönnrotin matkat* [Elias Lönnrot's Trips], 2 vols. (1902); *Elias Lönnrot's svenska Skrifter* [Elias Lönnrot's Swedish Writings], 2 vols. (1908–1911); *Alku-Kalevala* [The Proto-Kalevala] (1929); *Alku-Kanteletar* [The Proto–Spirit of the Harp] with addenda (1929); *Loihtoja* [Charms] (1930), facsimile of the first edition.

Bibliography. Emil Fredrik Nervander, *Elias Lönnrotin nuoruuden ajoilta Laukon kartanossa* [From the Times of Elias Lönnrot's Youth on the Laukko Estate] (Helsinki, 1893); Aukusti Robert Niemi, "Elias Lönnrotin lapsuus" [Elias Lönnrot's Childhood], *Valvoja* [The Guardian], XV (1895), 455–471; Eemil Nestor Setälä, *Elias Lönnrot ja suomenmielisyys* [Elias Lönnrot and Pro-Finnicism] (Helsinki, 1898); Oskar Albin Kallio, *Elias Lönnrot* (Helsinki, 1902), reprinted in *Suurmiestemme elämäkertoja* [Biographies of Our Great Men] (Helsinki, 1929); Aarne A. Anttila, *Elias Lönnrotin elämä ja toiminta* [Elias Lönnrot's Life and Works], 2 vols. (Helsinki, 1931–1935), abridged ed. 1945.

B. THE KALEVALA[1]

The idea of concatenating Karelo-Finnish traditional songs into an epiclike whole was first advanced by Kaarle Akseli Gottlund in 1817: ". . . if one should desire to collect the old traditional songs [National-sångerna] and from these make a systematic whole, there might come from them an epic, a drama, or whatever, so that from this a new Homer, Ossian, or *Nibelungenlied* might come into being" (*Svensk Literatur-tidning* [Swedish Literary News], No. 25, 21 June 1817, p. 394). In 1820 Reinhold von Becker published in three installments in his *Turku Weekly News* an article of his own, "Concerning Väinä-möinen,"[2] which in its consequences was important for the birth of the epic. In this article von Becker reports where the old songs are still being sung, and urges that they be recovered. He regards the songs that tell of Väinämöinen as the most remarkable. He presents in prose form what the songs know about Väinämöinen, and at the end gives a 265-line compilation which contains "Väinämöinen's Courtship," "The Wound in the Knee," "The Origin of the Harp [*kantele*]," a fragment of "The Boatbuilding," "The Visit to Antero Vipunen," and the "Contention" song. Soon afterwards Zachris Topelius, Sr., published a notable collection of songs; his last song notes were from the year 1803 and the resulting collection was published between 1822 and 1831 in five parts as *Suomen kansan wanhoja runoja ynnä myös nykysempiä lauluja* [Old Songs of the Finnish People together with Songs of Later Date]. He was the first to deal with the rich store of songs in the Archangel Government, and he showed that the heyday of the songs had not yet passed, as it had ever since Porthan's time been customary to bemoan.

Von Becker's influence on Elias Lönnrot appears *inter alia* in the fact that the latter chose a subject for his master's thesis from the field of traditional poetry, completing in 1827 his investigation "De Vaina-

[1] By Väinö W. Salminen and Viljo Tarkiainen, in *Iso Tietosanakirja* [The Big Encyclopedia], 2d ed., vol. V (Helsinki, 1933), coll. 1141–55; material of secondary interest for the English-speaking reader has been omitted.

[2] "Väinämöisestä," in *Turun Wiikko-Sanomat*, No. 10 (11 March), pp. 2–4, No. 11 (18 March), pp. 1–4, No. 20 (20 May), pp. 2–3.

moine, priscorum fennorum numine [Väinämöinen, a Divinity of the Ancient Finns]. This influenced the history of the genesis of the *Kalevala* to the extent that Lönnrot there became acquainted with what had been collected and investigated up to then and learned to combine verses taken from different songs. Lönnrot regarded the songs as pieces of historical evidence which shed light on the way of life, religion, and customs of the Finns. Like von Becker, Lönnrot did not in this investigation conceive of Väinämöinen as a divinity, but on the contrary as a hero who attained immortality only by singing. When because of the 1827 fire of Turku the university was closed, Lönnrot set out in the spring of 1828 to collect traditional songs. In the province of Häme [Swedish Tavastland] his notes were not increased, and the spoils were likewise poor in the province of Savo [Swedish Savolax], but in Finnish Karelia the finds were unexpectedly abundant. The trip had not yet been extended to the Archangel Government. After he returned from the trip Lönnrot started to edit the songs for press. In 1829–1831 four fascicles of these appeared, *Kantele taikka Suomen kansan sekä wanhoja että nykyisempiä runoja ja lauluja* [The Harp, or Old and Later Poems and Songs of the Finnish People], in which there are in all ninety old and twenty later songs. Many of the songs were pieced together from five or even six different variants.

After he had visited Repola behind the Russian border in 1832 and gone all the way to Akonlahti, Lönnrot intended to publish a continuation, *Kantele* [The Harp], in fascicles. Then a new idea flashed in his mind and he wrote about it to the secretary of the Finnish Literature Society: "How would it be if the Society were to reprint all the Finnish songs which have merited its esteem and assemble them in order, so that what is to be found in different places about Väinämöinen, Ilmarinen, Lemminkäinen, and others were joined together or combined and variant readings put at the bottom of every passage?" At the same time he reported that he had tried "to join the songs about Lemminkäinen together in that way" and had come to the conviction that variants of the same song should be woven into one song and not published separately. In the same way one ought to combine all variants that were connected with the name of the same person. That first work, "Lemminkäinen," merely a trial compilation preserved in manuscript, is relatively unpretentious, the outline of an epic 825 lines long and arranged in two parts. In the first part is told of "The Origin of Beer," "The Invitations to the Wedding," "Lemminkäinen's Journey to the Sun's Domain [*Päivölä*]," "The Duel," and "The Flight to The Island"; in the second part is told how Lemminkäinen went wooing at the Demon's [*Hiisi*] and how he was killed. Lönnrot intended to combine the narrative songs about Väinämöinen and Ilmarinen in the same way. But before he started on that he made a new expedition of discovery to the Archangel Government which was rich in results. In the village of Vuokkiniemi Lönnrot met two such skilled singers that he got a totally new idea about the homogeneity of the songs. Vaasila Kielevänen sang as a single song the heroic deeds of Väinämöinen, of Ilmarinen, and to an extent of Kullervo. Antrei Malinen in turn had recalled that the Sampo cycle and the "Courtship Journey" belong together, for the maiden wooed is to be given to him who forges the Sampo as a task to earn her. It now began to become clear to Lönnrot that it would be possible to create out of the songs a single epic, since the singers of songs used to sing them as a long series. When he got back from the trip he combined into a single whole of 1867 lines the variants telling of Väinämöinen and Ilmarinen, using for this the title "Väinämöinen." Into this are admitted Väinämöinen's unsuccessful attempts to woo first Vellamo's maiden, then the virgin of North Farm (Pohjola), and finally Joukahainen's sister. Even after he had become interested in fitting songs together, Lönnrot at the same time arranged as a one-part experiment the wedding lays into a song cycle 499 lines long. Meanwhile he noticed that Ilmarinen gets a bride from North Farm and that the wedding is then celebrated. He joined the wedding lays to "Väinämöinen," and thus came into being at the end of 1833 the "Proto-Kalevala," a manuscript containing 5052 lines comprising sixteen poems which is customarily entitled "Collected Songs about Väinämöinen" [Runokokous Väinämöisestä], published in 1929 under the title Proto-Kalevala [Alku-Kalevala]. In this Lönnrot was thus able to include his compilations made up to that time: the songs about Lemminkäinen, Väinämöinen, and the wedding party. He sent the manuscript to Helsinki, but even while sending it he questioned whether this "Collected Songs" was as yet a work which "future generations will possibly hold in as great esteem as the Germanic nations esteem the Poetic Edda and Greeks and Romans esteem, if not precisely Homer, at least Hesiod." He proposed that the printing not be begun until he had once more visited eastern Karelia, in the Archangel Government. On the journey of April 1834 new materials accumulated to such an extent that in the spring Lönnrot set out for Helsinki in order to combine them with the "Collected Songs." To this there came such really notable additions as "The Birth of Väinämöinen," "The Death of Aino," and "Kullervo's Farewell"; these fitted into the framework of the "Collected Songs," so that there was no need, as before, to take the whole thing apart at the seams. Magical charms, too, were represented. The manuscript was got ready in the winter of 1835; the preface bore the date of 28 February, since 1920 unofficially celebrated as Kalevala Day. Volume I appeared before Christmas 1835, Volume II in February 1836. The title of the work was Kalewala taikka wanhoja Karjalan runoja Suomen kansan muinosista ajoista [The Kalevala, or Old Karelian

Songs from the Ancient Times of the Finnish People]. The epic, which is now usually called *Vanha Kalevala* [The Old Kalevala], is divided into thirty-two poems, in which there are in all 12,078 lines.

Before *The Old Kalevala* appeared Lönnrot made in the spring of 1835 a fruitful trip to the vicinity of Repola and Uhtua, and in September 1836 he set out on his longest collecting trip, with the university student Juhana Fredrik Cajan as his companion at the start. For two months he moved about in far corners up north right to the Kola Peninsula and clear to Lake Inari [Swedish Enare]. After he had rested in Kajaani he again set out by way of Vuokkiniemi, Repola, Eno, Liperi, and Kide to wander through Sortavala and back through southern Savo. On both trips he gathered songs in abundance. In Finnish Karelia there were above all lyrical songs. Lönnrot started arranging the new materials just as soon as he got back from the trips. From the lyrical songs he edited the collection *Kanteletar* [The Spirit of the Harp], which appeared in 1840.

David E. D. Europaeus, engaged by Lönnrot in 1845 to make a clean copy of his dictionary materials, collected folktales and songs between the White Sea and Lake Ladóga between 1845 and 1847, and brought songs from such altogether new areas as Salmi, the Karelian Isthmus, and Ingria. Nearly half of all the additions gathered into the 1849 *Kalevala* are from notes taken by Europaeus. Several scholarship men of the Finnish Literature Society also collected additional material: August Engelbrekt Ahlqvist in 1846 in the districts of Ilomantsi, Korpiselkä, and Taakkima; the university students Zacharias E. Sirelius and Rietrikki Polén in 1847 in southern Savo and Finnish Karelia; Henrik A. Reinholm in 1847 along with Europaeus in Ingria, and at the end of the same year with the university student Carl M. Forsberg in the Karelian Isthmus.

At the beginning of 1847 Lönnrot started to prepare a new edition of the *Kalevala*. Beside the collections already mentioned he was able to make use of the collections of Anders Johan Sjögren and Matias Aleksanteri Castrén. First Lönnrot picked out all the variants dealing with the same matter and wrote them down in their appropriate places. A whole year elapsed before he could start combining the texts of the new edition into a unit. As editor he used the same procedure as before. The main aim was a connected presentation in which through its songs the Finnish people itself pictures its former way of life, its thoughts and customs. The narrative thread maintaining the homogeneity of the epic in the *Old* and *New Kalevala* is the Sampo and the struggle between the Kaleva District (*Kalevala*) and North Farm (*Pohjola*). Lönnrot viewed the *Kalevala*-type songs as having first been composed immediately after the events. As times changed supplementary features were invented; the homogeneity of the songs and the order in which they were sung gradually got confused. In "Anmärkningar til den nya Kalevala upplagan" [Notes on the New *Kalevala* Edition], *Litteraturblad för allmän medborgerlig Bildning* [Literary Journal for General Civic Culture], No. 1 (January 1849), pp. 15–21, Lönnrot himself explained his view about the songs: "I cannot regard the order used by one singer as more authentic than another's; on the contrary, I explain both as born of that desire which everyone has to put his knowledge into some sort of order, which then according to the singer's individual way of presentation has created differences. Finally, since not a single one of the singers could vie with me in wealth of songs, I thought that I myself also had the same right as most singers, namely, the right to arrange the songs as they best fitted into one another—or, to speak in the words of a song [cf. Poem 12, lines 167–168], 'I began to practice magic, started to become a sorcerer'—that is, I regarded myself as a singer of songs as good as even they."

In 1849 the new edition of the *Kalevala* appeared. It was divided into fifty poems comprising 22,795 lines. The arrangement of the poems was changed to the extent that the shooting of Väinämöinen took place after the creation of the world, and the "Sowing of the World" and the "Aino Poem" were fitted in between. The narrative materials grew, especially the Kullervo and Lemminkäinen poems; lyrical songs and magic charms were generously added, so that in its final form it reflects all the poetical genres composed in the old traditional meter.[3]

There has been some debate as to whether the Finnish people or Lönnrot is to be regarded as the maker of the *Kalevala*. Although Lönnrot conscientiously preserved the manuscripts and rough drafts which he used, the issue is sometimes viewed as not a little obscure. The homogeneous epic is the work of Lönnrot. But Lönnrot put the *Kalevala* together not as a real scholar or literary artist but as a singer of traditional songs. He departed from the singers only in that he used writing as an aid to his memory so that it was possible for him to command a great number of song variants. But he subsequently read and reread the notes until he knew a great part by heart and could, while composing from memory, let supplementary verses ring out just like a real singer of songs. Lönnrot to be sure normalized the language of the variants and corrected metrical defects, but the singers, too, used their own dialects. Lönnrot took from the variants the best features to be used, and connected verses, even whole descriptive passages, from quite other contexts. The singers did the same; they, too, could expand their songs with magic charms, lyrical materials, proverbs, and so on. Thus the whole plot, indeed, of a song could be appreciably changed by different singers. Lönnrot did not wish to add to the

---

[3] I have appended to this article two concordances which indicate rather graphically the extent of the shifts and expansions alluded to here. See page 362.

Kalevala anything at all out of his own head. As far as possible he used the verses of a traditional song—a few hundred linking verses are all that he really added of his own. The verses composed by Lönnrot in the "Collected Songs about Väinämöinen" are only five per cent of the whole, and they are adaptations. Lönnrot was ahead of the singers in that he had more developed taste in selecting the materials; he also had the advantage of literacy and models, especially the Homeric epics . . .

Epical songs of the *Kalevala* type are best preserved among the folk of Karelia; the *Kalevala* poems are for the most part based on variants got from the latter. Songs of this type were still being sung in the last century throughout all Estonia, Ingria, and the Karelian Isthmus, on the western and northern shores of Lake Ladóga, in Finnish Karelia, northern Olónetz, and the western part of the Archangel Government.[4] But the farther south we go from that basic singing area of narrative songs, from west of the White Sea, the shorter the heroic songs become.

Lyrical material is most abundantly represented in Estonia, Ingria, and southern Karelia. The reason is that in the southern districts singing is just the occupation of women. As a result the songs are rather short game, joke, and courtship songs and sentimental songs and ballads. These areas have been a battleground for Germans, Swedes, Lithuanians, Poles, and Russians. Only in Finnish Karelia and in the Archangel Government have men had the peace and quiet to meditate on long hero-songs while at their domestic occupations and when on hunting and fishing trips. There foreign cultural trends have not done away with calm meditation, so that the rich old-time song singing was preserved there last . . .

As to the age of the songs, Kaarle Krohn was at first of the opinion that in general they originated in the Christian era, only a few in the "semi-darkness" of the time of the transition from paganism to Christianity, and were brought to the Archangel Government only in later times. In his later studies, *Kalevalastudien* (6 pts., 1924–1929) Krohn almost completely reverses his earlier position, and holds that most of the hero songs of the *Kalevala* were historical in their basic character, the personages heroes who lived in the Viking Age. Furthermore, he sees in the *Kalevala*-type songs a considerable number of elements based on Biblical themes and saints' legends. The scene of action and place of origin would have been almost exclusively western Finland; the

---

[4] Four such *Kalevala*-type songs or "variants" by two distinguished woman singers from northern Russian Karelia, followed by five lyrical pieces, including cradle songs, are finely recorded on a 24 cm. or 9¾" LP record, "Runonlaulua Kalevalan Syntysijoista," *Otavan kirjallinen äänilevy* 8 ["Song-singing from the Birthplaces of the *Kalevala*," Otava's Literary Record 8] (Helsinki, 1960); there are accompanying transcripts of the texts, references to corresponding portions of the *Kalevala*, and biographical data on the singers.

Island (*Saari*) of the songs, the site of the theft of the Sampo, was the Swedish island of Gotland. The Karelians are claimed to be merely preservers of the songs. The latter were composed in western Finland and "traveled" across Finland as integral units, in later times reaching Karelia, where they were longest preserved. The similarity of the songs of Estonia and the Archangel Government is explained by the fact that contact between Estonia and western Finland had not yet been interrupted in the pagan period when the hero songs came into being, also to some extent because in both regions the same song plots were invented separately. The oldest songs are supposed to have originated between A.D. 700 and 1000. The composers were chiefly aristocratic persons, the disseminators toward the east being mainly junior clergy. The names, too, of the *Kalevala*-type heroes are derived in great measure from Germanic originals.

Eemil Nestor Setälä does not regard a Germanic origin of the *Kalevala* hero names as credible. In his work *Sammon arvoitus* [The Riddle of the Sampo] (1932) he takes a negative position also as to a late migration of the songs from western Finland to Karelia and Ingria, and assumes that in the Karelian area and in Estonia the poetry was preserved as an inheritance from one generation to another. Setälä claims that in the very ancient songs there are different strata and that even the Karelians composed additions to them; he thinks it is possible that some songs are of their own composition, even though the material might have been got from elsewhere.

If these songs have only in recent times become the subject of extensive and many-sided scholarly study and discussion, there have not been many facts from which scholars might draw positive conclusions. Unanimity has been reached on the point that the plots of the hero songs originated near the sea, namely the Baltic and its gulfs of Finland and Bothnia, and that the oldest are from before the twelfth century, possibly many centuries earlier. No movement of songs with *Kalevala*-type material from Estonia or western Finland took place before the seventeenth century, since no old hero songs have been got from the Savakko and Äyrämö peoples, originally of the Karelian Isthmus, who were relocated in Ingria after the 1617 Treaty of Stolbóva; only Ingrians of Karelian origin preserved them.

Kalevala variants and the ancient Finnish songs have been published as follows: Aksel Borenius (later Lähteenkorva) and Julius Krohn, *Kalevalan toisinnot* [*Kalevala* Variants], 2 vols. (1888–1895), and *Kalevalan esityöt* [Work Preliminary to the *Kalevala*], 2 vols. (1891–1895); Aukusti Robert Niemi, *Vanhan Kalevalan eepilliset ainekset* [The Epical Materials in the *Old Kalevala*] (1895); and A. R. Niemi, Väinö W. Salminen, et al., edd., the series *Suomen Kansan vanhat runot* [Old Songs of the Finnish People], 14 vols. in 33 parts (Helsinki, 1908–1948).

Kalevala translations . . . In English the first information about the *Kalevala* was furnished by the botanist Professor Thomas Conrad Porter of Marshall College, later of Lafayette College, who wrote on the connection between the *Kalevala* and Longfellow's *Song of Hiawatha* in *"Kalevala* and *Hiawatha," Mercersburg Quarterly Review,* VIII (1856), 255–275, and to demonstrate the relationship published in English the opening words of the *Kalevala* from Anton Schiefner's 1852 German verse translation of the 1849 *Kalevala.* The chemist Professor John Addison Porter of the Yale Sheffield Scientific School posthumously published *Selections from the Kalevala, Translated from a German Version* (New Haven, Conn., 1868, 2d printing 1873), including Poems 3–4 and parts of Poem 2 together with an analysis, all based on the 1849 edition. In *Stray Leaves from Strange Literatures* (Boston, 1884), pp. 137–165, Lafcadio Hearn likewise translated a few prose excerpts based on Louis A. Léouzon le Duc's complete French prose translation of the 1835 *Kalevala,* included in his *La Finlande; son histoire primitive, sa mythologie, sa poésie épique, avec la traduction complète de sa grande épopée le Kalevala* (Paris, 1845), Vol. I, pp. 1–130 (Poems 1–16), Vol. II, pp. 1–133 (Poems 17–32). Professor John Martin Crawford of Pulte Medical College got out the first complete *Kalevala* translation, *The Kalevala: The Epic Poem of Finland* (New York, 1888); based on Crawford's verse translation was a rather complete prose adaptation for young people with illustrations, mostly of Lappish scenes, by R. Eivind, *Finnish Legends for Children* The Children's Library (London, 1893; New York, 1894). In 1907 (with many later printings) there appeared in Everyman's Library a two-volume verse translation by the English entomologist William Forsell Kirby, made directly from the Finnish. There is also an abridged prose translation by Aili Kolehmainen Johnson (Hancock, Michigan, 1950), and an adapted verse translation of part of Poem 50 ("Marjatta") in *Flower of Finland from the Kalevala* (Helsinki, 1954) by Margaret Sperry. For a survey of the American translations see Ernest J. Moyne (formerly Möykkynen), *"Kalevalan* käännökset Amerikassa" [Translations of the *Kalevala* in America], *Kalevalanseuran vuosikirja,* XXIX (1949), 121–140.

Aesthetic studies. Many foreigners have studied and interpreted the *Kalevala* from an aesthetic point of view, as for instance Jakob Grimm (1785–1863), Johann Karl F. Rosenkranz (1805–1879), Heymann Steinthal (1823–1899), Wilhelm J. A. von Tettau (1804–1894), Domenico Comparetti (1835–1927), Karl B. Wiklund (1868–1934), and Ferdinand Ohrt (1873–1938). Among Finnish students of the subject are Matias Aleksanteri Castrén, (1813–1852), Johan Robert Tengström (1823–1847), Fredrik Cygnaeus (1807–1888) (*Om det tragiska Elementet i Kalevala* [The Tragic Element in the *Kalevala*], 1853), Frithjof Perander 1838–1885), August Engelbrekt Ahlqvist, (1826–1889), Julius

Krohn (*Kaunotieteellinen katsaus Kalevalaan* [An Aesthetic Look at the *Kalevala*], 1855), Bernhard Fredrik Godenhjelm (1840–1912), Eliel Aspelin-Haapkylä (1847–1917), Kaarle Krohn (1863–1933), Viljo Tarkiainen (1879–1951), Rafael Zacharias Engelberg (1882—) (*Kalevalan sisällys ja rakenne* [The Content and Structure of the *Kalevala*], 1914), Franz Akseli Hästesko [in Finnish, Heporauta] (*Kalevalan kauneuksia* [The Beauties of the *Kalevala*], 2 vols., 1920, 1927), and Augusti Robert Niemi (1869–1931) ("Kalevalan esteettisesta arvioimisesta" [An Aesthetic Appraisal of the *Kalevala*], *Kalevalanseuran vuosikirja* IV, 1924, 110–134.

The aesthetic interpretation and appraisal of the *Kalevala* depends in great measure on the position taken in an investigation of the history of the origin of our old epical poetical corpus, whether mythological or historical. One arrives, of course, at one aesthetic result if one interprets the basic material of the corpus as mythological—if, for example, one interprets Väinämöinen as the tutelary genius of water, Joukahainen as the genius of snow, and the "Contention" poem [Poem 3], accordingly, as a contest between summer and winter, or if one interprets Pohjola (North Farm) as the vicinity of the North Star in the heavens, the maiden of North Farm as the glow of light in the heavens, the Sampo as the pillar of the world, and the Sampo expedition as a sailing trip through blue space taking place in an imaginary vessel, or as a horseback rider on an imaginary colt, as Setälä has interpreted it. One arrives at quite another result if in the manner of Kaarle Krohn one views our old poetic corpus as from the beginning fundamentally historical, its personages as heroes of the Finnish Viking Age, the Sampo directly as a costly tangible object, a decorated pillar, for example, and the Sampo expedition as a Viking expedition from the original Suomi area in southwest Finland overseas to Gotland, called "the land of Vuojo" (*Vuojonmaa*). Up to now aesthetic study of the *Kalevala* has, generally speaking, set out from the historical point of view which Lönnrot represented and has viewed its epical events and its personal portraits as based on historical reality, even though styled by the imagination and here and there fancifully colored. Starting from this basis, the relations between two tribes and the contest over the Sampo have been viewed as the narrative framework. The *Kalevala's* narrative structure is not, to be sure, as close-knit as the Homeric poems, for instance, nor was its action ever really developed into an exciting physical conflict; witness the entire peaceful character of the Aino and Kullervo episodes, also the lyrical wedding lays and the magic charms. But coherence is given to the poetical narrative by the consistency of the personal characterizations, which remain unchanged through the whole work, the animistic-magic underlying tone of the view of nature, and above all the epical verse form, with its alliterative runs and variations or parallelisms. One can say that certain typical fundamentals of the Finnish national character are outlined in the *Kalevala's* great personal characterizations. For example, in Väinämöinen one sees meditative stability and wisdom, in Ilmarinen workaday industry, in Lemminkäinen sportive recklessness, in Kullervo dark defiance, in Aino a tender dreaminess, and in many of the mothers loving affection. Domestic conditions and everyday tasks are pictured in the wedding lays (Poems 21–25) in the greatest detail and with the greatest clarity. Manly heroism and resourcefulness occasionally flash out for a moment on the military expeditions, while the Finnish landscape nature is a singularly living and richly nuanced backdrop and has a part in every description of an action, not least in the numerous lyrically sentimental bits. But fancy and feeling every now and then transform and enhance in dimension—to a remarkable degree embellish and extend—the descriptions both of nature and of persons, and often give a story a very free-soaring and glowing fantasy, just as is the case in certain folk epics of India. Taken from this point of view the *Kalevala* has sometimes been called a folktale or sorcery epic, even though some sort of historical fact might have been the starting point of its stories. In certain respects it represents a more primitive stage of spiritual development than the old epics of the Western peoples. For this reason an aesthetic appraisal of its poetry entails special difficulties . . .

The influence of the Kalevala on literature and art. The *Kalevala* has influenced Finnish literature and art in a most fructifying fashion. The Finnish-language lyric derives one of its main sources of inspiration from the traditional poetry. Already in Kallio (pen name of Samuel K. Berg, 1803–1852), Oksanen (pen name of Aukusti Engelbrekt Ahlqvist, 1826–1889) and Suomio (pen name of Julius Krohn, 1835–1888) one finds echoes of the traditional poetry. Juhana Heikki Erkko (1849–1906), also Kasimir Leino (originally Lönnbohm) (1866–1919) and Eino Leino (1876–1926) often took material from it: one need only mention Eino Leino's *Tarina suuresta tammesta* [Story of the Big Oak], *Tuonelan joutsen* [The Swan of Death's Domain], and *Helkavirsiä* [Spring Festival Songs]. From the literature of the drama, note the play by Aleksis Kivi (originally Stenvall, 1834–1872), *Kullervo* (1864); Erkko's play of the same title (1895), also his *Aino* (1893) and *Pohjolan häät* [The Wedding at North Farm] (1902); Eino Leino's *Sota valosta* [The War for Light] and *Karjalan kuningas* [The King of Karelia]; the *Lemminkäinen* (1907) of Larin Kyösti (Kyösti Larsson, 1873–1948), and the *Lemmin poika* [Lempi's Son] (1922) of Lauri Haarala (1890–1944). Among novels in which *Kalevala* figures appear, the most noteworthy is *Panu* (1897), by Juhani Aho (1861–1921).

Among sculptors who have fashioned works of art based on *Kalevala* subjects one should mention Erik Cainberg (originally Kaino) (1771–

1816), Carl Eneas Sjöstrand (1826–1906), Johannes Takanen (1849–1885), Robert Stigell (1852–1907), Emil Wikström (1864–1942) and Eemil Halonen (1875–1950). Among artists the foremost is Akseli Gallen-Kallela (1895–1931), who became especially absorbed in the *Kalevala* and from it created many notable works, such as the National Museum frescoes "Sammon puolustajat" [The Defenders of the Sampo], "Lemminkäisen äiti" [Lemminkäinen's Mother], "Joukahaisen Kosto" [Joukahainen's Revenge], "Kullervon kirous" [Kullervo's Curse], and "Kullervon sotaanlähtö" [Kullervo's Setting out to War]. In 1922 appeared Gallen-Kallela's *Koru-Kalevala* [The Decorated *Kalevala*], in which the songs are embellished with illustrations at the beginning and end of each. Gallen-Kallela only lived to prepare the illustrations for the first few poems of a large scale "Suur-Kalevala" [Great *Kalevala*]. Among the numerous other artists who have treated the *Kalevala* one may mention further the Swedish artist Johan Zacharias Blackstadius (1816–1898), Robert Vilhelm Ekman (1808–1873), Berndt Abraham Godenhjelm (1799–1880), Sigfrid August Keinänen (1841–1914), Pekka Halonen, (1865–1933), and Joseph Alanen (1885–1920).

In our music *Kalevala* subjects have a distinguished place. One may cite, for example, among operas Oskar Merikanto's (1868–1924) *Pohjan neiti* [The Maiden of North Farm] (1899), Erkki Melartin's (1875–1937) *Aino* (1909), Armas Launis' (1884–) *Kullervo* (1917), also *Die Kalewainen in Pohjola* [The Men of the Kaleva District at North Farm] (1891) by the German composer Karl Muller-Berghaus (1829–1907), who worked in Turku in 1886–1895; among symphonies Robert Kajanus' (1856–1933) *Aino* (first performance 28 February 1885); among symphonic poems Johan Julius (known as Jean) Sibelius' (1865–1956) "Kullervo" (1892), "Lemminkäisen paluu" [Lemminkäinen's Homecoming] (1899), and "Tuonelan joutsen" [The Swan of Death's Domain] (1895), Leevi Madetoja's (1887–1947) "Kullervo" (1913), and Johan Filip van Schantz's (1835–1865) orchestral prelude "Kullervo"; among vocal works with orchestral accompaniment Sibelius' "Tulen synty" [The Origin of Fire], Madetoja's "Väinämöisen kylvö" [Väinämöinen's Sowing] and "Sammon ryöstö" [The Theft of the Sampo]; and among choral works Sibelius' "Venematka" [The Boat Journey] and "Terve, kuu!" [Hail, Moon!], among others.

The *Kalevala* brought into being two other poems in which use is made of materials from this traditional poetry: in 1853 the Estonian *Kalevipoeg* [Kalev's Son] by Friedrich Reinhold Kreutzwald, and in 1855 *The Song of Hiawatha* by the American poet Henry Wadsworth Longfellow [on which see E. J. Moyne and T. F. Mustanoja, "Longfellow's *Song of Hiawatha* and *Kalevala*," *American Literature*, XXV (1953), 87–89].

Bibliography. (In this selective list, the place of publication, unless otherwise noted, is Helsinki.) C. J. Billson, *The Popular Poetry of the Finns*, Popular Studies in Mythology, No. 5 (London, 1900); Kaarle Krohn, *Kalevalan runojen historiaa* [The History of the *Kalevala Songs*], 7 pts. (1903–1909); Kaarle Krohn, *Kalevalastudien*, 6 pts. (1924–1928); Laina Hänninen, *Luettelo ennen vuotta 1927 painetusta Kalevalaa koskevasta kirjallisuudesta* [A Catalogue of the Literature Touching the *Kalevala* Published Before the Year 1927] (1928); Väinö W. Salminen, *Kertovien runojen historiaa* [The History of the Narrative Songs], vol. I: *Ingria* (1929); Kaarle Krohn, *Kalevalan opas* [A Guide to the *Kalevala*] (1931); Eemil Nestor Setälä, *Sammon arvoitus* [The Riddle of the Sampo] (1932); Väinö W. Salminen, *Suomen muinaisrunojen historiaa* [The History of the Ancient Finnish Songs] (1933); Onni Okkonen, A. *Gallen-Kallelan Kalevala-taidetta* [*Kalevala* Art] (1935); Väinö Kaukonen, *Vanhan Kalevalan kokoonpano* [The Compilation of the *Old Kalevala*] (1939–1946); August Annist (born Anni), *Kalevala taideteoksena* [The *Kalevala* as a Work of Art] (1944); Väinö W. Salminen, *Kalevala-kirja* [A *Kalevala* Book], 2d ed. (1947); Björn Collinder, *Det finska nationaleposet Kalevala* (Stockholm, 1951); Martti Haavio, *Väinämöinen, Eternal Sage*, Folklore Fellows Communications, No. 144 (1952); Jalmari Jaakkola, *Suomen Varhaishistoria: Heimokausi ja "Kalevala-Kultturi"* [The Early History of Finland: The Tribal Period and "*Kalevala* Culture"], 2d ed. (1956), esp. pp. 381–430, 459–462; V. Tarkiainen and Eino Kauppinen, *Suomalaisen Kirjallisuuden Historia* [History of Finnish Literature], 2d ed. (n.d. [1961?]), pp. 15–75 ("Kansanrunous" [The Traditional Poetry]), and pp. 385–386 (bibliography); Matti Kuusi et al., edd., *Suomen kirjallisuus* [Finnish Literature], vol. I: *Kirjoittamaton kirjallisuus* [The Unwritten Literature] (Helsinki, 1963), esp. pp. 129–417 (on *Kalevala*-type poetry of various periods), and pp. 624–630 (bibliography).

C. CONCORDANCES

Old Kalevala—New Kalevala

Old Kal. Poem	(lines)	New Kal. Poem	(lines)	Old Kal. Poem	(lines)	New Kal. Poem	(lines)
1	(315)	1 & 6	(578)	17	(706)	26–27	(1196)
2	(213)	7	(368)	18	(593)	28–30	(1396)
3	(200)	8	(282)	19	(534)	31–33	(1218)
4	(424)	9	(586)	20	(224)	37–38	(578)
5	(350)	10	(510)	21	(344)	39	(426)
6	(275)	12	(504)	22	(392)	40–41	(608)
7	(641)	13–14	(730)	23	(422)	42–43	(996)
8	(289)	15	(650)	24	(329)	2	(378)
9	(231)	16	(412)	25	(310)	45	(362)
10	(489)	17	(628)	26	(533)	47–48	(736)
11	(391)	18	(706)	27	(277)	49	(422)
12	(281)	19	(518)	28	(607)	46	(644)
13	(420)	20	(614)	29	(248)	44	(334)
14	(384)	21	(438)	30	(243)	3	(580)
15	(471)	22–24	(1900)	31	(348)	4–5	(759)
16	(314)	25	(738)	32	(280)	50	(620)

New Kalevala—Old Kalevala

New Kal. Poem	Old Kal. Poem	New Kal. Poem	Old Kal. Poem	New Kal. Poem	Old Kal. Poem	New Kal. Poem	Old Kal. Poem
1	1	14	7	27	17	39	21
2	24	15	8	28	18	40	22
3	30	16	9	29	18	41	22
4	31	17	10	30	18	42	23
5	31	18	11	31	19	43	23
6	1	19	12	32	19	44	29
7	2	20	13	33	19	45	25
8	3	21	14	34	—	46	28
9	4	22	15	35	—	47	26
10	5	23	15	36	—	48	26
11	—	24	15	37	20	49	27
12	6	25	16	38	20	50	32
13	7	26	17				

The first concordance shows the extent to which the poems in the *Old Kalevala* were expanded and rearranged in the *New Kalevala*. The second concordance indicates which *Old Kalevala* poem (in whole or in part) each of the *New Kalevala* poems was based upon.

D. LÖNNROT'S PREFACES
TO THE KALEVALA

I. FOREWORD (1834) TO THE *Proto-Kalevala*[1]

The following essay might perhaps do as a foreword:

"The following collection of songs about Väinämöinen is presented not with the idea or hope that it is in any degree complete but with the thought and hope through this of better filling out what is lacking. Of course it is easier to improve a road once it has been constructed than to construct a new one from nothing, and from this collection everybody can now better see what has already been collected concerning Väinämöinen and what is now lacking. If anyone who has songs about him which have previously been collected, or who might happen to obtain such, would kindly send these to the Finnish Literature Society (*Suomen* [later *Suomalaisen*] *Kirjallisuuden Seura*), this would be the best way to complete the collection of songs. It goes without saying that no one will have taken such trouble in vain or be unmentioned.

"There is not a great deal to say about the labors and activities of collecting the songs presented here to be read, though a few words are in order. Most of these have been previously read in the collection of the late provincial physician-in-chief and knight Zachris Topelius, Sr., *Old Songs of the Finnish People together with Songs of More Recent Times* (*Suomen kansan wanhoja runoja ynnä myös nykyisempiä lauluja*), 5 pts., Turku-Helsinki, 1822–1831, others in the books of Christfrid Ganander, *Finnish Mythology, or an Elucidation of Gods and Goddesses, Notable Personages of Antiquity . . . collected and interpreted from Old Songs* (*Mythologia Fennica, eller Förklaring öfver Afgudar och Afgudinnor, Forntidens märkelige Personer . . . af gamla Runor samlad och uttydd*), Abo, 1789, and Christian E. Lencqvist, *de Supersti-*

---

[1] This foreword to "A Collection of Songs about Väinämöinen" (*Runokokous Väinämöisestä*) is an extract from a letter of Lönnrot's to Kaarle Niklas Keckman, Secretary of the Finnish Literature Society, as published by Eemil Nestor Setälä et al., edd., *Suomen Kansalliskirjallisuus* (Finnish National Literature), II (Helsinki, 1935), 231–34. Pending the collection of new material, publication of this work was suspended, and in its place there appeared in 1835 The [Old] *Kalevala*, whose preface is translated below. The manuscript remained unpublished until 1892. It was brought out as The *Proto-Kalevala* (*Alku-Kalevala*) by the Finnish Literature Society in 1929.

tione veterum Fennorum theoretica et practica [On the Theoretical and Practical Superstitions of the Ancient Finns] 2 vols., Åbo, 1782. What is not found in these works was collected quite independently during the last three sumers [1831–1833] and the summer of 1828, mostly from the Archangel and Olónetz Governments in Russia, from which areas came at the same time many additions to, and improvements in, previously known songs. One can scarcely read a single one of the following Väinä-möinen poems which one might not put together from songs got from at least five or six different singers. Sometimes it was really hard to choose the best of these, and the work is perhaps not always quite successful. It would be appropriate to put these variants either at the foot of the page or afterward by way of example or commentary, but we have not done this because we feared that the book would become too big. Some other time, when we edit the Väinämöinen songs more completely and with greater financial resources, we will not fail to print these, too.

"Not everybody will presumably view as good and suitable the order in which we have arranged these songs. Here we have followed what, from the reports of old people, we have heard about Väinämöinen's ac-tivities, and at the same time have arranged the songs as we thought the nature of the song materials demanded. The least complete is a song in which one reads about Väinämöinen's and Ilmarinen's plans to attach a new moon, sun, and stars to the heavens after the previous ones had been hidden by the dame of North Farm (*Pohjola*). In places it has been necessary to fill it out with our own words, though not, however, in such a way as to be diverted from the basic matter, which both in talking and in singing was shaped by the people . . ."

You may also deal with the foreword as you like, whether you wish to print it as is or with improvements or to disregard it entirely and write a new one. I am in a quandary as to the title of the book. If one called it *Väinämöinen* it would have a namesake in Karl A. Brakel's *Väinä-möinen. Ett lyriskt Försök* (Stockholm, 1828), as a result of which buyers and sellers would make mistakes; a similar confusion would at once arise with Kaarle A. Gotlund's *Väinämöiset* (Helsinki, 1828). One cannot call it *Ilmarinen* or *Lemminkäinen, nam omnis denominatio, non nisi a potiori* ("for no title except from the name of the more im-portant person"). What if one should include all three heroes and call the book *Väinämöinen, Ilmarinen, and Lemminkäinen,* or *A Finnish Mythology compiled from Old Songs* (*Suomen Mythologia vanhoilla runoilla toimitettu*), or *Väinämöinen's District and North Farm* (*Väinölä ja Pohjola*), namely, from the places where most of the events in the book take place, or *Väinämöinen's Harp* (*Väinämöisen Kan-tele*) or whatever one views as good—not a single one of these titles would be altogether acceptable.

Kajaani, 14 March 1834

II. PREFACE (1835) TO THE *Old Kalevala*[1]

Even after these songs have finally been got ready for publication, they are indeed still woefully incomplete. At all events, in the hope of adding to them by collecting new ones, I would by no means let them out of my hands prematurely if, thinking along other lines, I did not fear that they might remain forever uncompleted by me. Better plans and undertakings by many others have before now come to nothing in this way.

Above all I regard it as my duty to explain how these songs were got. A few of them have been previously included, perhaps even more inadequately, in the works of the late Christian E. Lencqvist, of Christfrid Ganander, of Henrik Gabriel Porthan [*Dissertatio de Poesi Fennica* (in 4 pts., 1766–1778), pt. 3, Turku, 1778], and of Zachris Topelius, but much the greater part is previously unknown. I myself have in the course of time collected these in Finnish and Russian Karelia and a few from the Kajaani area [now province of Oulu]. There are also several sent me which were written down elsewhere. The localities in which these songs were mostly collected are the parishes of Kite, Kesälahti, Tohmajärvi, Ilomantsi, and Pielinen in Finnish Karelia (province of Oulu), the parishes of Vuokkiniemi (Russian Voknavolotskaia), Paanajärvi, and Repola (Russian Rebola) in Russian Karelia (Olónetz Government) [now the Karelian SSR], and the communities of Kuhmo and Kianta in the Kajaani area. From many places which I visited for this purpose I got nothing worth mentioning. In 1828 I collected songs in the above-mentioned places in Finnish Karelia, in 1831 and the following years in Kuhmo and Kianta, in 1832 in Repola; and after I was transferred to Kajaani I visited the Russian parishes four times, each time for a good many weeks.

Perhaps songs such as these are still to be found to some extent in popular memory; similarly it is possible that in times past they were much more numerous. At Vuokkiniemi on Latvajärvi an old peasant Arhippa, then eighty years old, from whom I wrote uninterruptedly what I could for two days running, spoke of the matter as follows: "My," he said, "when as a child I used to go seining at Lapukka with my father! We had as a hired man a certain man from Lapukka, indeed a fine singer but not my father's equal. Every night they used to sing continuously and never the same words twice. In those days there was story-telling! Just a tall slim boy, I used to sit by the campfire listening and learning what every now and then I began to remember. But much escaped my mind. Were my father now living, you would not

---

[1] *The Kalevala, or Old Karelian Songs from the Ancient Times of the Finnish People* (*Kalewala taikka Wanhoja Karjalan Runoja Suomen Kansan muinaisista Aijoista*), 2 vols. (Helsinki, 1835); facsimile ed., 2 vols. in 1 (Helsinki, 1930); reprinted in Eemil Nestor Setälä et al., edd., *Suomen Kansalliskirjallisuus* II (Helsinki, 1935); for Lönnrot's foreword see pp. 242–258.

write down his songs in two weeks. Singers like that are no longer born on earth, and all the old songs are disappearing from among the people. The people of today are already giving up those old beautiful songs and compose their own, mostly about jokes between boys and girls with which I would not insult my mouth."[2]

I have tried to put these songs into some sort of order, a task of which I should give some account. Since to my knowledge no one has previously tried to order them or so much as mentioned doing so, I will first report on how I came upon this idea. Already while reading the songs previously collected, particularly those collected by Ganander, I at least wondered whether one might not possibly find songs about Väinämöinen, Ilmarinen, and Lemminkäinen and other memorable forebears of ours until from these had been got longer accounts, too, just as we see that the Greeks [in the Homeric poems] and the Icelanders [in the *Poetic* or *Elder Edda*] and others got songs of their forebears. This idea was just getting a firm place in my mind when in 1826 with the help of Reinhold von Becker, associate professor of history at Turku (Swedish Åbo), I got to writing a B.A. thesis on Väinämöinen, and while preparing it I saw that there was no lack of tales about him. I also wondered why Ganander had not already done this, but I soon came to understand that he did not have the songs necessary for the task. He published the best passages in the songs he collected in his *Mythologia Fennica* (Turku, 1798), but he had scarcely any of these in very ample form. An early death had taken off Zachris Topelius, Sr.; otherwise he would in the course of time have been able to devote himself to this work.

If I knew now that the order in which these songs have been planned here would be pleasing to others, I would stop and say no more about it, but the matter is such that what one person thinks suitable another views as inappropriate. In my opinion the songs run along fairly well in the order in which they are arranged, but they might perhaps go better in some other. While organizing them I paid attention to two things: first, I followed what I observed the best singers paid attention to in matters of arrangement; and second, when no help was forthcoming from that quarter, I sought a basis for arrangement in the songs themselves and arranged them accordingly.

The reader may ask whether our ancestors sang these songs in any sequence or sang them singly. It seems to me that these songs, as it happens, turn up singly. The various songs about Väinämöinen, Ilmarinen, and Lemminkäinen must be the compositions not of one person but of several. One singer memorized one thing, another another, what each individual had observed or heard. But nowadays I scarcely

---

[2] For some discussion of this quotation in the framework of oral literature see *Britannica: Festschrift für Hermann Flasdieck* (Heidelberg, 1960), pp. 188–191.

find a single song which seems to have been preserved down to our time in just its original words.[3] Everybody will see how easily poetic composition eludes many of the peasants if he undertakes to sing completely about any familiar subject whatever, and discovers of course that the very best memory cannot preserve word for word what is heard in long songs sung by another. But he will more easily remember the subject matter, and from passage to passage, if remembering most of them he relates it in verse to someone else, forgetting some passages, improving others. One can gradually distort the basic plot of a song from its original character so that it is told quite differently. This has already happened partly at least in the case of proper names. What formerly may have been told of memorable men and women with their right names might, as Christianity spread in the country [from ca. A.D. 1150], be changed so that in place of the men one often put Jesus Christ, St. Peter, Herod, Judas, and others, in place of the women the Virgin Mother Mary.

That the subjects sung about in the songs were not all without some foundation in fact anybody will easily understand, but what the real truth is—what things may be described in some other way in a song, what ones may be completely invented—is now quite difficult to distinguish. Certain matters, even when one hears especially odd things or somewhat incredible ones, should on careful investigation somehow clear up. None of us should view Väinämöinen's and Ilmarinen's troubles as deriving from the disappearance of the sun and the moon, and how would the dame of North Farm (*Pohja*) have hidden them in the hill? But when one remembers what is said of our forefathers' coming here, that they got here to the far north from very southerly lands, and what we know about the disappearance of the sun in winter in high latitudes, we will realize that had they gone clear up north, this phenomenon could, as something strange to them, even arouse a great fear that the sun had gone forever. If also they had wars with the Lapps who formerly lived in Finnish territory, Lapps from whom there was reason to fear everything bad and who were regarded as superior wizards, then the mistress of North Farm soon got the blame for it. And what in the first instance could come to be told about the disappearance of the sun could later also get to be told of the moon and stars.

Early on in all the songs there appear two peoples who did not live on very good terms with one another. One of these we might call the people of North Farm (*Pohja, Pohjola*), the other Kaleva's people.

[3] For a curious and surely almost meaningless attempt to reduce a considerable number of the narrative songs—not merely those of the *Kalevala* type—to an ur-form see Kaarle Krohn, *Suomen Muinaisrunoja kertovaisia peruspiirteisiinsä palauttaa yrittänyt K. K.* [An Attempt to restore Some Ancient Finnish Narrative Poems to their Basic State] (Helsinki, 1930).

According to the poetry Louhi is often mentioned as the chief personage among the people at North Farm; she is also called "the dame of North Farm" (*Pohjolan akka*), and seems to take principal charge of their doings. Among Kaleva's people were many champions, the greatest being Väinämöinen, Ilmarinen, and Lemminkäinen. Concerning Lemminkäinen let it be duly said, however, that the songs do not give precise information as to whether he was possibly to be counted among the people of North Farm, too. Those song types which I have selected for this book certainly show that he was often a help to Väinämöinen, sometimes waged war at North Farm on his own, paid court at North Farm, and so forth, but in other songs it is related that he paid court at the Sun's Domain (*Päivilä*) or among the Devout Ones (*Jumaliset*), by which names we should rather think that Kaleva's people were indicated. Again, I would regard Joukahainen as a champion of the people of North Farm—who knows whether he is?—who here and there is called a lad of North Farm and a Lapp. A few songs report specifically that he was freed from a fen by Väinämöinen in the same way as is told of a Lapp in Poem 1 of the present [1835] work [now Poem 3] and that he ambushed and shot Väinämöinen by a rapids. It seems, too, that his sister, whom he promised to Väinämöinen, was a daughter of the mistress of North Farm, for the latter previously had hoped for Väinämöinen as her son-in-law.

I said I have called "Kaleva's" that people to which Väinämöinen, Ilmarinen, and Lemminkäinen are assigned in these songs. But lest I be charged with being quite mistaken in this designation—since many regard Kaleva's name as exactly equal to "Demon" (*Hiisi*) and "Devil" (*Lempo*)—let me express my thoughts more clearly. It seems to me that Kaleva was the very oldest Finnish champion, of whom we nowadays know nothing at all. He may be the person who first established himself permanently on the Finnish peninsula and whose clan spread into the hinterland. The places in which Väinämöinen and the others live is often called *Kalevala* ("Kaleva's District"); elsewhere mention is made of Kaleva's heaths, burned-over clearings, wells, dogs, cuckoos, and the like, as in an old Karelian song where a girl asks her suitor who has just arrived: "Did you visit Kaleva's District?" The suitor: "I did visit Kaleva's District." The girl: "Did Kaleva's dogs bark on the heaths of Kaleva's District?" The suitor: "They did indeed bark, etc." The girl: "Did Kaleva's cuckoos call on the path (also burned-over clearings) of Kaleva's District?" The suitor: "They did indeed call, etc." The girl: "Did Kaleva's maidens look out the windows of Kaleva's District?" The suitor: "They did indeed look out, etc." And when such pleasant matters as courtship conversations between boys and girls make mention of Kaleva's District, I should not regard it as equivalent to the "Demon's Domain" (*Hiitola*) or to "the Devil" (*Lempo*). For when does one hear such things of "the Abode of the Dead" (*Manala*) and of "Death's Domain" (*Tuonela*)?

The reason why Kaleva came to be felt to be a bad name may have come from the fact that he was frightful and terrifying to the people of North Farm, who for that reason called him bad, just as we right up to present times have regarded Turks, the cynocephali, and, a little before that, "Red Beard" (*Punaparta*)—the devil—not exactly as human beings but as slightly more powerful evil creatures. But what of these!—in the minds of our ancestors did not the Pope stand directly for God? Why then have his name and good repute now changed? Let us, accordingly, not come to a decision on a much older matter on the basis of modern presuppositions before looking into the question closely. Just as we said, Kaleva's name might have been feared among the people of North Farm, but in the course of time the Lapps partly begin to mingle with the Finns, and, partly as slaves and hired hands, roved the countryside. Then through them Kaleva's name, when Kaleva was no longer well remembered, lost its original good repute even in Finland. And where they may not have had influence, the spread in the land of the new faith did. It is odd that the names Väinämöinen and Ilmarinen have preserved their original good repute. How quickly a change of this sort takes place may be illustrated in another connection. Does not the general notion now prevail in the countryside that the first churches in Finland were built by giants? On my trips I ran into scarcely a single ancient stone church of which some such story was not told locally. What is the reason for this? It seems to me thus. While Christianity was spreading in Finland, there still were in the forests and wilds pagan Lapps who were very hostile to this doctrine. After the Finns had, as a result of Christianity, become more civilized, the Lapps could not appraise this very accurately but thought that the new doctrine received from the Finns had produced some effect, for which there was cause to hate it all the more. While the churches were being built, it could occur to the Lapps that it would be to their advantage to destroy these structures, and they perhaps often at night tore down and destroyed what had been done by the Finns by day. But as this could scarcely succeed and since the Finns were much bigger physically, they viewed the builders as giants and gradually spread these beliefs of theirs throughout Finland. Thus today Finns regard the first church builders as giants, not knowing that they themselves could be spoken of as giants. And when in turn among them, too, because of the nightly depredations, the rumor grew up that giants had destroyed the buildings by night, then such stories originated among the people as we now hear here and there . . .[4]

[4] For more on these curious beliefs see Martin Puhvel, "The Legend of the Church-Building Troll in Northern Europe," *Folklore* LXXII (1961), 567–583.

In the folktales today Kaleva's sons have two kinds of reputation. Some view them as bad giants, others call them Väinämöinen, Ilmarinen, Lemminkäinen, Joukahainen, Kihavanskoinen, Liekkiö, Kullervo, and so on, none being mentioned as especially bad except the last named, Kullervo, who for that reason was even put out of his home. The reason, as we understand it, for the "bad giant" reputation has mentioned, but for the good reputation there may perhaps have been a better basis, though little more can be rightly known about their names. At any rate it is said that they were twelve in number. Now whether Väinämöinen was a first-generation son of Kaleva or was of some succeeding generation we cannot judge. However, I should think that he was of some later generation, for if he were of the first generation he and Ilmarinen would have been brothers; this does not seem to be the case, even if Väinämöinen occasionally calls Ilmarinen his brother and child of his mother. Similarly Lemminkäinen, too, would become Väinämöinen's brother, but the latter never calls him that at all, just mentioning him now and again as his very best friend. Even if they are of a later generation, one can for that reason very well call them "Kaleva's sons"; even now Jews are still called "the children" of Abraham and of Israel. From this it would also be understandable how Kullervo, who is specifically a "son," that is, "descendant," of Kaleva, could be sold to Ilmarinen, another "son" of Kaleva. I may perhaps further mention the fact that I have heard a few people identify Antero Vipunen with Kaleva, as is once said in a song, too.

Though it is not possible to make out anything more about these, I believe that Kaleva is much older than Väinämöinen, Ilmarinen and the other champions named above, perhaps, as I in fact said, thus the person who brought the first Finns to these regions. The localities in which his successors settled seem to have been designated as "Kaleva's District" (*Kalevala*)—this could be the same as those special designations "Väinämöinen's district" (*Väinölä*), "Sky" (*Ilma*), the name of Ilmarinen's home, "Misty Headland" (*Utuniemi*), "Misty Island" (*Terhensaari*), "Finland" (*Suomela*), "Faraway Headland" (*Kaukoniemi*), "Gotland" (*Vuojela*), "Small Island" (*Luotola*), [the place of ?] the Devout Ones (*Jumaliset*), and the rest; accordingly I have also entitled this collection of poems *Kalevala* ("Kaleva's District"). A title had to be given it, and most of the action in these poems did, according to this interpretation, take place in Kaleva's district.

If Finnish mythology might derive any help from these poems—which is, as a matter of fact, unlikely to be the case—then one of my hopes will have been realized; but there are still other matters. I would hope to get some elucidation from these of our forebears' life of old and some benefit for the Finnish language and poetic art. I may well be able to add a word or so about each and all of these points, for they were in my mind at least while I was editing these poems.

Heretofore Finnish mythology has of course already been to some extent investigated by, among others, Lencqvist, Ganander, and Porthan, but without doubt there are still grave errors, mistakes in many places. Apart from what little has been said about Kaleva and his sons, one may ask on what basis did people begin to view Ilmarinen as a god of the wind, sky, and also fire? One can hardly find a single passage in the poems where one would get the very slightest basis for this notion. It seems as if he was made a god of the wind and sky from his name [cf. *ilma* 'sky, air'], and of fire, too, from his smithying; or is the latter attribute from the fact that as a companion of Väinämöinen he once struck fire in the heavens? He is not in the least like that in the songs. For fire they always prayed to Ukko, who, along with other things, was the lord of fire. In the grip of the wind while fleeing from North Farm Ilmarinen got frightened sooner than the others. The fact that, while forging the Sampo, he got to blowing the fires certainly admits of another sort of explanation, and from that circumstance one does not need to make him a fire god. Had he been a god of the sky, Väinämöinen would hardly have forced him to North Farm in the air against his will, and it was Väinämöinen, no less, not Ilmarinen, who bewitched the mistress of North Farm when the latter threatened to cause rain, hailstones, and cold to spoil the fruits of the Sampo. According to the songs Ilmarinen was merely an excellent worker in iron, copper, silver, and gold, in other respects an earnest, truthful, and honest man; at least when one encounters him, industrious in his work, he is rarely wanting in other matters.

Nowadays one can always sing about Väinämöinen what formerly was sung in the name of others, and who can stop that? What is attributed to him concerning the creation of the world, the moon, the sun and stars, one could of old tell of any god, and then, when the names were forgotten, pass them over to Väinämöinen. For what reason was Antero Vipunen, for what reason Kaleva, for what reason the supreme god Ukko, left so soon wholly unsung, although in these oral accounts it is still first and foremost told of Antero Vipunen that "Väinämöinen was a mere child compared to him"?

If in these songs Väinämöinen has here and there been reduced from his former reputation as a god, I can of course do nothing about it. I had to deal with these matters as I myself got them without considering whether Väinämöinen was viewed as a god or not. From time immemorial we have been accustomed to viewing him as a god of our ancestors, a reputation in which they do not seem to have held him, regarding him rather as mighty, as very clever, as a champion. He himself often prays for the help of the supreme god Ukko, and thus with his own lips admits who was a god. Väinämöinen indeed has both fame and honor even without divinity, and it is probably better for anyone to be a high-minded peasant than a bad master, better to be a very wise human being than a wooden idol. Even now if we ask the peasantry of those districts where Väinämöinen's memory is most alive who Väinämöinen was, they answer at once as follows: "He was a memorable champion of our earliest ancestors and famous singer." But if you ask them whom they hold as their god, then in many cases they will answer that they pray to Ukko, who created the heavens and the earth. Nor do I in the least doubt that already before the coming of Christianity our ancestors had knowledge of one single god whom they sometimes served by the present name [jumala 'god'], sometimes by the name Ukko or "creator" [luoja], nor do I charge them with great stupidity if they were not so clever as to get for themselves a pantheon like many another people of antiquity. In these songs Väinämöinen is usually referred to as steadfast, wise, prophetic, as providing what was to the advantage of oncoming generations, as a man of great knowledge, very effective in singing and playing, and as the hero of Finland. Beside that he is all but invariably called "old"; perhaps his mere age did not bother him greatly in his courtings.

Of another sort was Lemminkäinen: light-hearted, young, arrogant, boastful of his strength and knowledge, giving little thought to the future, even if heroic and a champion. The tasks which, while he was a suitor, were assigned him at North Farm cannot rightly be explained, for on another occasion precisely the same tasks were assigned to Ilmarinen. I have chosen songs which set them at least a little apart.

This time I am leaving unmentioned many other names one can find in those songs which help in correcting previous errors or which are to some other advantage for the mythology. Among these errors may be that odd one, namely, that from the word kave is obtained a special or peculiar being, even though by kave one nowhere understands anything other than "created being, human being," or some other creature; similarly odd is the regarding of Ukko and Väinämöinen by some people as a single person.

I do not intend to dwell much upon the evidence from which it might be possible to start out to explain ancient customs. I should certainly be able to get some examples from the Kalevala were there time to reflect. Poem 13, line 116 [New Kalevala, Poem 20, line 435] shows how the people of old did their cooking with hot stones and by pouring water on them. In many other passages we would find that parents were held in honor, even though Lemminkäinen in an outburst of manly zeal went slightly against his mother's wish. In the same way we see that in those days it was customary to assign stipulated tasks to suitors. Many people, however, may think that there is in these songs too much talk about matters of courtship, so that as a result the whole book—and why not?—might be changed into the form of new-style fiction and novels. If it is really that way, so be it; but let us also remember that among our forebears, who did not have the present-day many-sided contacts and things to talk about in their solitary lives, plans of courtship, warfare, and catching fish and forest game were the most memorable activities. Hence these matters are reported on again and again in the songs.

In these poems one meets the Finnish language and Finnish poetics in perhaps a purer form than in any other book. Many words and phrases appear here and there in their original form or in the same form as one hears them in the mouth of the peasantry. Persons learned in other languages, even though they of course command Finnish, often find it hard not to change the basic nature of the language to conform with other languages. For the peasant population, however, which understands nothing but its mother tongue, this danger is nonexistent . . .

Concerning Finnish songs it has probably already been stated that they are certainly of two different kinds: narrative songs and magic songs. It may also have been mentioned that the charms were from the beginning nothing but narrative songs which later, according to the material, began to be changed into something else. The poems in the present book are mostly narrative. What I judged to be the main version among these is not on that account more valuable for the investigation of ancient matters than what one hears told some other way. Both have been got from the same places and are equally old. A few individual songs I got from so many singers and in so many different forms that it is certainly an open question which is the best variant. In other songs the difficulty for me was to get them in a very full form from one singer or another. There are both those persons who hold our old songs indeed in great esteem and those who esteem them very little. I would not want the songs to be disparaged nor to be biasedly regarded on the other hand as very great. These are not by any means on a par with those of the Greeks and Romans, but it is quite all right if they at least show that our forebears were not unenlightened in their intellectual efforts—and the songs at least show that.

This work has not been burdensome to me nor has it demanded any great outlay of money, so that there is nothing special to be said on that score. What one does of one's own free will and not under compulsion must, to say the least, be accounted a pleasure; at no one else's urging it I have collected these songs of my own free will and fitted them together. One added pleasure in this work has been to notice that my efforts have also been acceptable to many others. I have reason to thank these people exceedingly for their encouraging and friendly communications.

The starting point from which many others get encouragement from their activities is quite different, namely, the hope of achieving a complete and beautiful piece of work. In my case this hope is totally lacking. Dubious, to say the least, of my ability to produce something suitable, I have occasionally been plagued with doubt to such an extent that I have been on the verge of throwing the whole thing into the fire. This temptation arose because I did not believe it in my power to edit these songs as I wanted to, nor did I, furthermore, think it proper by my own work and labor to be subjected to criticism on the basis of a half-finished work. Go forth now, however, poems of Kaleva's District, even if not very complete, unless, even after spending time in my hands, fire might make you more complete!

Kajaani, 28 February 1835.[5]

III. PREFACE (1849) TO THE New Kalevala[1]

1. *The Order of the Kalevala Poems.* The present book concerning the activities, life, and ancient condition of our forebears now appears in a much fuller form than what it was in its previous state [1835], and will very likely remain in its present form; for relevant uncollected songs of this type can no longer be found, since all localities where there was even a little hope that songs were being sung have now been criss-crossed and explored many times by many collectors. Remembering well that these poems are coming to be the oldest specific memories surviving for the Finnish people and the Finnish language as long as these exist at all, one is called upon to arrange them with all possible care and diligence and to concentrate them as well as possible and to include in them everything the songs have preserved in the way of information about the life, customs, and vicissitudes of that time. In arranging them a good deal of arbitrary choice has, however, been exercised, for few songs were obtained from even the best singers in a single sequence and those not always in the same way. For this reason it has, of course, often been necessary to make the internal claims of the material the basis and, regardless of the previous edition of the *Kalevala*, to depart from the order adopted there. Presumably this work of arrangement has by no means been successful to the point of pleasing everybody's taste and of never leaving this or that open to objection.

2. *The Proper Names in the Songs.* Not only in the order but often in the personal names also, songs obtained from different singers and from different localities differ from one another. One sings of Väinä-

---

[5] Since 1920 unofficially designated "Kalevala Day," Feb. 28 is celebrated by certain unofficial public demonstrations, including a student parade to Lönnrot's statue by Emil Wikström erected in 1902 in Lönnrotinkatu [Lönnrot Street], facing the rear of Vanha Kirkko [the Old Church], Helsinki. In 1942 a statue by Mauno Oittinen was erected in Kajaani.

[1] See *Kalevala* (*Uuden Kalevalan kahdeskymmeneskolmas painos*), 23d ed. and printing (Helsinki, 1951), pp. i–ix.

Two folk singers with a harp accompanist
in a one-room Finnish farmhouse, 1799

Earliest photograph of Finnish folk singers

Semeika, Onola, and Kuokka, folk singers from Karelia

The singers Olli Kymäläinen and Pietari Makkonen

A sauna with old-fashioned mixed bathing at Kemi, 1799
At the door a visitor checks a thermometer-reading.

möinen what another sings of Ilmarinen, a third of Lemminkäinen; one sings of Lemminkäinen what another sings of Kullervo or Jouka-hainen. In place of Kullervo on his tax-paying trip (Poem 35, lines 63–358) some singers have Tuiretuinen, Tuurikkinen, Lemminkäinen, or a son of old Väinämöinen (vanha Väinön poika).

A similar inconsistency is also troublesome in the case of place-names . . . Such confusion among these as well as among the personal names is quite usual in rather unimportant matters, rarer in major ones. In all such confusion of names there have been, however, two very helpful guides, namely, the source of the material and the songs of the best singing centers.

3. *The Present-day Native Habitat of Kalevala-type Songs.* The best and richest home of the songs is certainly the parish of Vuokkiniemi [Russian Voknavolskaia] in the Dvina or Archangel Government. As one goes from there due east to Lakes Jyskyjärvi and Paanajärvi or due north to Lakes Tuoppajärvi and Pääjärvi the songs get poorer and poorer. They are better preserved to the south, first in Repola and Himola in the Olónetz [Finnish Aunus] Government and then across the border into Finnish territory, coming to Ilomantsi, Suojärvi, Suis-tamo, Impilahti, Sortavala, and along the western shore of Lake Ladóga as far as Ingria, where some *Kalevala*-type songs are still re-membered, though perhaps imperfectly.

4. *The First People to Point out the Native Habitat of Kalevala-type Songs and the Ordering of the Same.* It must be mentioned to the credit of the former physician-in-chief, Dr. Zachris Topelius, Sr., that in his song collection published in five parts in the years 1822–1831, *Old Songs of the Finnish People,* he furnished the first information about the true home of these songs. Before that an associate professor (now full professor) at the Swedish Academy of Turku (Swedish Åbo), Reinhold von Becker, had already collected in Ostrobothnia a few songs about Väinämöinen, and in March and May 1820 had arranged them ("Väinämöisestä" [Concerning Väinämöinen]) in some kind of order in his *Turku Weekly News;* this was the first attempt of that kind. Without these two men the *Kalevala*-type songs would perhaps still be in their former nooks and crannies; for who without Topelius' lead would have dreamed of setting out then to look far in Russian Karelia, and into whose head could suddenly have come the idea of weaving them together if von Becker's attempt had not led the way in that direction?

5. *The Authenticity of the Kalevala Poems.* Many passages in poems found in the *Kalevala* are sung separately, too. Such are "The Origin of Iron" (Poem 9), "A Huntsman's Charms" (Poem 14), "Bear Charms" (Poem 32), "The Origin of Fire" (Poem 47), and other charms, wed-ding lays (Poems 21–25), and "Bear Songs" (Poem 46). Taking my lead

from singers of *Kalevala*-type songs who, when they come to such passages, often leave them unsung, saying: "Here begins the usual course of the Iron Charm," or "Here one must sing wedding lays which one gets from the women," I have assembled these and filled them out with the general help of all songs of this kind, regardless of whether they were sung in one sequence with the *Kalevala*-type songs or separately. Such songs are still used at the present time for their normal purposes throughout all Karelian territory, on the Finnish as well as on the Russian side of the border, also in Ingria and here and there also in Savo (Swedish Savolax) and Ostrobothnia. Into these perhaps, as presumably into other songs, new words and ideas have in the course of time here and there entered as additions in their appropriate places; it is, however, difficult if not impossible to distinguish these from original, early *Kalevala*-type ones. It is better to disregard such rather minute distinctions and rather to regard those original songs as nothing but seeds sown on folktale ground from which the present crop of songs has in the course of hundreds, perhaps thousands, of years sprung up and multiplied.

As for the authenticity of the songs, the matter runs about as follows: At a feast or some other social gathering someone hears a new song and tries to remember it. Then on another occasion when this person himself is now singing it before a new audience, he remembers quite exactly the material proper rather than its narrative word for word in every detail. Those passages which he does not remember in just the original words he tells in his own, in places perhaps better even than they were before. And if some rather insignificant incident among them is left out, another can take its place out of the singer's own head. In the same way, then, second and third persons who hear it proceed to sing it and the song is changed, changed rather in individual words and details than in the material itself. Parallel to this kind of versified story there runs, however, another which keeps closer to the old words and their linking together, namely, a child's learning from its parents from generation to generation. But at the same time that this prevents the other migratory sister-song from deviating too far, it must itself at times follow the other lest it be left far behind.

6. *The Dreaded Extinction of the Old Songs.* From the fact that in Russian Karelia the old songs and their singers have down to the present been held in esteem, one might conclude that the singers have not forgotten their songs but have in numerous variants rather improved and embellished them into their present-day form. A few centuries ago these might not have been found in such abundance, though certainly already at that time all were putting out shoots and burgeoning. From now on they will again begin to dwindle rather than to multiply with new additions, for whoever at any time wants can get hold of them as a complete book and in fuller form than what any single memory might retain. In this way esteem of singing will pass out of memory, and after

the esteem has passed the singing itself, too, will pass from memory. It is just as with the different dialects of any language, once they have got under the control of a standard written language. Before that they have gone their several ways, one dialect departing from another and sometimes new ones turning up. After a written language is established, the dialects all begin to unify around it.

7. *Words of Foreign Origin.* From the above-mentioned way in which songs migrate and are preserved one can easily understand how time after time it was possible to assimilate into them words which presumably only entered the language in later times, words from which one must by no means conclude that the songs themselves are not older. The words and language of the songs are nothing but a story's outer garb created in the course of time. Many words, too, of Swedish and Russian origin found in the old songs could already have been current during the time of the Permian trading community[2] [especially in the ninth and tenth centuries], when according to old traditions the Permians or North Karelians of the Kola Peninsula [Old-Norse *Bjarmar,* the *Béormas* of King Alfred the Great][3] traded with Icelanders and Norwegians as well as with Russians. And trading peoples always get, in addition to trade, new words in their language. A great number of such words of Swedish origin, ordinarily viewed as coming only later from Swedes after Finland and Sweden were united [ca. A.D. 1150], are likewise found behind the Russian border in Karelia and Olónetz. Finding them there is hard to explain by circumstances other than that they were already familiar before the partition of the Finno-Karelians under Swedish and Russian domination by the terms of the 1323 Treaty of Pähkinäsaari [Hazelnut Island].

8. *The Time of the Genesis of the Songs and the Original Home.* There has also been much speculation as to the time and place of the genesis of these songs. More reasonable than others seem to be the theory which views them as having originated during the time of the Permian trading community on the southwest shore of the White Sea or in the region of the great lakes of Voikojärvi, Onéga, and Ladóga, which lie in an arc between the White Sea and Onéga Bay on the one hand and the Gulf of Finland on the other. That segment of the Finns living in Russian Karelia, among whom these songs have been preserved through the centuries, seems to have been a tribe directly descended from the old, rich, powerful, and famous Permian people. For more than

---

[2] My rendering of *Permian vallan aikana,* where *valta* does not refer to a political entity but to what has been described elsewhere as a *kauppavalta* 'mercantile or trading community.' For discussion of all this see Jalmari Jaakkola, *Suomen Varhaishistoria: Heimokausi ja "Kalevalan Kultturi"* [The Early History of Finland: the Tribal Period and *"Kalevala* Culture"], 2d ed. (Helsinki, 1956), pp. 241–259.

[3] On these identifications see Alan S. C. Ross, *The Terfinns and Béormas of Óhthere,* Leeds School of English Language, Texts and Monographs, No. VII (Leeds, 1940).

other Finns these have a certain external culture inherited from olden times, curious traces of communal life, an extraordinary zeal for trade which rejects all rebuffs and obstacles, speed both in bodily movement and in presence of mind in their enterprises, all of which, including at the same time their present dwelling places, their remembrance of songs, the Swedish loan-words encountered in their language, the unique ornaments of the women-folk, and so forth, is best explained by a consideration of old Permian times. In physical agility, quick-witted presence of mind, and a desire to trade, the Finnish Ostrobothnians and the Karelians are nearest akin to them, the latter together with the Ingrians also in remembering songs.

9. *The Inhabitants of North Farm (Pohja, Pohjola)*. One finds plenty of reason for the notion that by the "people of North Farm" one should understand "Lapps" in these songs; it seems more likely, however, that Lapps did not live at North Farm but Finns of a different tribal group [from those of "Kaleva's District"]. To be sure, in instances of parallelism or variation North Farm is sometimes called Lapland, but that seems merely to have been a derogatory name like Gloomy Farm (*Pimentola*), Untamo's Farm (*Untamola*), Cold Community (*Kylmä kylä*), Place of Man-Eaters (*Miesten syöjä sia*), and others. Only in one passage (Poem 12, lines 199–200) is there a indication of a foreign language being spoken at North Farm, and that passage can be explained thus: when Lemminkäinen's mother forbade her son to set out for North Farm and, along with other reasons which should keep him from going said: "You do not understand the language of Finnmark (*Turja*), you cannot sing magically in Lappish," by "language" she did not mean ordinary speech but some magic skill peculiar to North Farm. Furthermore, that passage could have entered the song later on or, originally from somewhere else, it might have got into it from another song; however it may be, it cannot mean much of anything in the face of those numerous other passages which indicate that the inhabitants of North Farm and of Kaleva's District understood one another's language easily. In other respects the whole way of life at North Farm is very different from present-day life in Lapland, as presumably from even the ancient way of life, and in the whole preceding part of the *Kalevala* the people of North Farm stand out as more powerful than anything that would ever at all be true of Lapps. Lemminkäinen recalls (Poem 27, lines 109–114) barleycorns brought both by others and by himself to North Farm, by which of course nothing can be meant but a grain tax and a subjection, which may also be referred to in another passage, too (Poem 35, lines 65–74). But when has any other people been subject to taxation by Lapps? The mistress of North Farm also recalls (Poems 42, lines 335–336, 43, lines 371–374) her former supremacy. Thus it is highly credible that there lived at North Farm some Finnish tribal group to which

earlier a tax was paid from Kaleva's District until Väinämöinen, Ilmarinen, and Lemminkäinen put a stop to this subjection to taxation. The central thread or unity of the *Kalevala*-type songs lies in just this point, namely, that they tell how Kaleva's District gradually achieved a prosperity equal to that of North Farm and finally attained victory over it.

10. *The Language of these Poems* is ordinary Karelian Finnish and does not differ much from the speech of other Finnish provinces. For this reason a Finn from anywhere at all will with a little practice understand them easily . . .[4]

12. *The Collecting of Kalevala-type Songs and the Collectors.* During those fourteen years which have elapsed since the first edition of the *Kalevala* was published in 1835 many new collections of songs have been made, and the collectors of these have been Juhana Fredrik Cajan (also known as Kajaani) [1815–1887], a student at the Swedish Academy in Turku, Matias Aleksander Castrén, M.A. [1813–1853], the university students David E. D. Europaeus [1820–1884], August E. Ahlqvist [1826–1889], Fredrik Polén [1823–1884], Zachrias E. Sirelius [1822–1848], and Henrik A. Reinholm, M.A. [1819–1883], also the editor of the present edition; of these Cajan, the first mentioned above, went about collecting these with his own means, the others with the support of the Finnish Literature Society (Suomen [now Suomalaisen] Kirjallisuuden Seura). Europaeus was especially lucky in managing during the years 1845, 1846, and 1848 to collect many songs both altogether new ones and variants of earlier ones. As a result of these big collections of songs got by him and others, which together with the earlier collections will be preserved in the Finnish Literature Society in Helsinki, the present edition of the *Kalevala* soon grew to be twice as big and extensive as the first. Whether, in the order of the poems and in other internal matters, this one is better than the previous edition is a matter left for each reader to decide for himself.

13. *The Size of the Present Kalevala Edition in relation to the Former.* In the previous edition there were in all thirty-two poems which together contain 12,078 lines; in the present edition, on the other hand, there are fifty poems and in all 22,795 lines.

Elias Lönnrot

Laukko, 17 April 1849.

[4] For Lönnrot, past master of the eastern dialects, "a little practice" no doubt describes the situation, but for the ordinary well-educated native speaker of Standard Finnish the differences between the phonology, morphology, and syntax of his speech and the language of the *Kalevala* may well seem considerable, and differences in vocabulary very considerable indeed. For accounts in English of the language of the *Kalevala* see Charles Norton Edgecombe Eliot, *A Finnish Grammar* (Oxford, 1890), pp. 223–229, and, somewhat more briefly, Björn Collinder, et al., *Survey of the Uralic Languages* (Stockholm, 1957), pp. 54–57. For a complete schematic paradigm of the eastern reflexive conjugation see *Nykysuomen sanakirja* [Dictionary of Contemporary Finnish], vol. I (Helsinki, 1951), p. xviii.

E. PORTHAN ON CEREMONIAL PEASANT SINGING

In his *Dissertatio de Poësi Fennica*, pt. IV (Turku, 1778), pp. 73–79, § XI,[1] Henrik Gabriel Porthan (1734–1804) published what may be viewed as a classic description of the performing techniques of the singers of old on festive or formal occasions, the manner of singing variously referred to as "hand in hand" (*käsi käteen*), *à deux*, or "singing in turn" (*vuorolaulu*), referred to at the start of Poem 1 and elsewhere in the *Kalevala*. This I translate below. This peasant singing *à deux* has been well represented graphically, as in the painting by Budkowski reproduced above.

Our peasant singers, when singing their songs, employ furthermore a quite special manner inherited from their ancestors. They sing, as everybody knows, always *à deux* and in a ceremonious way surrounded by a circle of listeners who stand there attentively. The main singer (*laulaja*) or leader (*päämies*), who either is uniquely able or competent above others in delivering a song or excels in age or esteem (and whose tasks a fine singer always assumes when a song is to be rattled off extemporaneously), associates himself with a companion or aide called in Finnish *puoltaja* 'supporter, supporting singer' or *säistäjä* [now *säestäjä*] 'supporter, second,' with whom the singing is alternately shared in such a way that after the main singer has brought a verse to about the third syllable from the end, or to the last measure, the supporting singer comes in with his voice—for by estimating from the sense itself and from the meter one can easily finish off the rest of the measure—and thus they both produce it. After that the supporting singer repeats the verse alone in a slightly varied tone as if he would give his unqualified approval. Meanwhile the main singer remains silent until the supporting singer again reaches the final measure, which both utter in unison. Then the main singer alone adds the next, similarly to be repeated by the supporting singer, and so on to the end of the song. In order that the whole matter may be more clearly understood, in the following sample those

[1] Also in *Henrici Gabrielis Porthani Opera Selecta*, Suomalaisen Kirjallisuuden Seuran Toimituksia, No. 21, 5 vols. (Helsinki, 1859–1873), III, 362–366.

syllables in which both singers join voices are indicated by a different [italic] type:

> Kansa outoja ano*pi,*
> itäwöitze ilma *kaikki*
> menot kurjat kuult*axensa,*
> saadansa sadat sano*mat.*

("The people are begging for strange items, the whole world is longing to hear of the miserable doings, to receive hundreds of bits of news.")

The interval vouchsafed him while the supporting singer is repeating a previous verse the main singer, composing extemporaneously, uses to think up and compose the coming verse, something which can, however, only be successful in the case of a singer with great experience and gifted with a quick mind and a fertile imagination. The melody which the main singer employs is always one and the same, with scarcely no variation; it is very simple and strongly suggests a very ancient origin . . .

The singers sit either side by side or facing one another, close enough to bring in contact their right hands and also their knees (the right knee, of course, of one, the left of the other), on which they prop their clasped hands. While singing they move their bodies gently as if wanting to touch heads, and they assume a reflective and serious expression. On the rarest occasions they sing standing up, and if they ever happen, as if moved by some poetic afflatus, to start singing in a standing position, they soon go and sit down hand in hand and continue their singing in the usual way. This kind of ceremonious singing is, however, mostly done at feasts, when "Bacchus, giver of joy" [*Aeneid* i, 734] is present and is wont to rouse the emotions. One often sees beside the singers a flagon of beer, from which, when a song has been brought to the end and they are getting ready for a new song, they usually forthwith drink deep and gather their forces. Thus, too, they rarely start singing before their spirits have been aroused by the gifts of Bacchus and their minds rendered more lively. Nor do such singers usually lack songs, and they often continue this entertainment until far into the night. Nor when gathered for a feast do our ancestors seem to have indulged in really any other sort of entertainment. I find no amusements special or native to the people to have been in use; even today [1778] the people of the provinces of Savo [Swedish Savolax] and Karelia know nothing of round dances or lively dances in general; the people of the province of Häme [Swedish Tavastland] and those living along the coast have no doubt learned these dances from Swedes, as attested by the [Swedish loan-] words *tant*zi 'a dance', *tantzan* 'I dance' . . .

Whenever our fellow-countrymen entertain themselves with ceremonial singing, they most usually like to do it to the music of a harp or *kantele*. If a competent player is available, he accompanies the singers on a harp. If only one person is singing, then the harp player assumes the function of a supporting singer and repeats on the harp the melody which ordinarily is the charge of the supporting singer, the main singer meanwhile keeping silent . . .

II. TRANSLATOR'S APPENDIX

A. ON THE TRANSLATION
OF CERTAIN WORDS

There are certain words in the *Kalevala*, which have been variously dealt with by various translators, about which a word of comment is to the point.

1. *kantele*, an ancient Finnish five-stringed instrument, held on the knees and plucked with fingers, is probably most conveniently rendered by "harp," though it might be thought of as an unsophisticated zither. The instrument is described in Poems 40 (a pikebone harp) and 44 (a birchwood harp); both types are discussed by Aimo Turunen, *Kalevalan sanakirja* (Helsinki, 1949), s.v. *kantele*, with illustrations. See further Martti Haavio, *Väinämöinen, Eternal Sage* (Helsinki, 1952), pp. 140–173. The *kantele* is illustrated, under Porthan's comment on it, on the page preceding this.

2. *kylä*, a common word in the *Kalevala*, today means "village," with the normal connotation of a settlement comprising several houses, a street, and at least one store; today one might expect a filling-station. But in the *Kalevala* no such elaborate scene is to be imagined, and the word can probably only refer in a rather general way to a community, settlement, or neighborhood, and has been so rendered. With *kylä* is involved the phrase *käyä kylähän* (Finnish *käydä kylään*), literally "to go to the village," also "to go visiting, go out on the town." None of these equivalents is acceptable in the contexts of the *Kalevala*, and in Poems 11 and 12, in connection with Kyllikki's neighborhood doings, the phrase has been rendered "to gad about," with such overtones as the reader may care to ascribe to it.

3. *runo*, earlier *runoi*, originally meant a singer of magic charms, and is based on Old Germanic *rūnō* 'secret thing, magic charm,' later coming to designate a character of the runic alphabet or, more accurately, futhark. The old meaning of *runo*, "singer," is preserved in the *Kalevala*, but the later meaning, "song, poem," is also represented. Lönnrot used *runo* to describe the fifty main divisions of his compilation, and in this sense it is here translated as "poem," the basic modern meaning. Ordinarily to describe a major division of a long narrative poem one would not use "poem" but rather "canto," but the *Kalevala* is no ordinary long poem composed as a continuum. It is made up of Lönnrot's conflations of the songs of many singers concatenated by him. Were the various divisions merely transcriptions of performances by individual singers, "song" would be the right word. Thus both "canto" and "song" create a false impression, and "poem" seems the best compromise, conveying a certain sense of discontinuity. Lönnrot's *runo* has been retained by some translators, by others slightly adapted to "rune"

or "(Finnish) rune," but these are not really English words and might well strike one as jargon or as exceedingly precious.

4. *sauna* is primarily a bath-hut, but is also commonly understood as referring to the very dry steam bath taken in such a hut, where the dryness of the steam is a primary characteristic. Both the word and the thing are becoming increasingly well known in the western world through various channels. The preparation of sauna baths is described in Poems 18 and 45; in Poems 35, 45, and 50 it is mentioned as a suitable place for a woman to bear a child; in Poems 23, 25, and 35 it is a good place to clean flax and malt grain. For full information on the sauna see Hillari Johannes Viherjuuri, *Sauna: The Finnish Bath*, translated by Wendy Hall (Helsinki, 1952), fully illustrated and including architectural drawings for the construction of a sauna.

5. *sininen salo*, lit. 'blue wilderness,' is here rendered "hazy blue wilderness," since "blue" alone is far too bright and strong a word for the phenomenon obviously observed by the singers. *Sininen* is the ordinary Finnish word for blue, and is often used in the *Kalevala* in connection with the sea (*meri*) and the surface of the sea (*selkä*), but the blueness here implied is really a grayish or hazy blue resulting from a rising ground-haze in extensive forest areas, especially on lowlying ground.

6. *uros* (gen. *uro[ho]n*)—with metathesis Finn. *urho* (gen. *urhon*) 'hero' —has at times proved an awkward word to deal with, for in the *Kalevala* (Karelian) it is a virtual synonym of *mies(i)* 'man,' a word for which English has no real synonym comparable to German *Mann* 'man' and *Mensch* 'human being.' At times "person" is usable and in the plural "people," on occasion "fellow"; and here and there "one, someone" helps out. In any event "hero" or even "champion" seems unusable in connection with the personalities of the *Kalevala*.

7. *vemmel* (stem *vempele-*), today more commonly *luokki, luokka*, and here rendered "shaft bow," is a flexible bow, often a bass or linden sapling, arching like an inverted U above a draught animal's shoulders with the butt ends laced to the inside of each shaft. In Finnish and in the *Kalevala* the word *vemmel* is sometimes used figuratively for a rainbow or a slender tree bent over in a gale. In the Finnish-English dictionaries these words are misleadingly defined as "collar bow," though the thing itself forms no kind of collar nor is it in any contact with the animal's collar; for good representations see A. Turunen, *Kalevalan sanakirja* (Helsinki, 1949), p. 321, s.v. *valjahat* (harness), and *Iso tietosanakirja*, Vol. 14 (Helsinki, 1938), col. 1078, s.v. *valhaat* (harness), cut at top right. The corresponding Italian *sellone*, on gala occasions decorated with flowers, often appears in pictures of Sicilian donkey carts.

8. Diminutives. Finnish is rich in diminutives, and these are freely used by the singers, though mostly in a purely formal way without any accompanying sense of smallness. Thus *päivyt*, formally a diminutive of *päivä* 'sun,' is no smaller than any sun, nor is *Sammut* (gen. *Sampuen*) any smaller than *Sampo* (gen. *Sammon*), of which there is only one. All such forms I have rendered by the simple parent word unless the singer qualifies it with *pieni* 'small, little.'

B. GLOSSARY OF PROPER NAMES

The *Kalevala* includes some 180 proper names: names of persons, place names and other toponymic names, and designations of certain nature spirits and other personifications looking back to an animistic view of the natural world. In earlier translations these names have commonly been left in Finnish, the reader being referred to a glossary in which many of these are translated into English. This system leaves the reader facing a large number of Finnish names, really Finnish words, that have no meaning for him, and almost forces him to learn a bit of Finnish if he is to read the *Kalevala* intelligibly. This has seemed an undesirable arrangement, and consequently I have adopted a different procedure.

Now, there are a certain number of *Kalevala* proper names which have no usable English equivalent and are untranslatable or virtually so, and these I have perforce left in Finnish—chiefly such personal names as Ahti, Ilmarinen, Lemminkäinen, Louhi, Vellamo, and Väinämöinen. Many, however, if not most, lend themselves readily to translation. By way of illustration I will comment briefly on two large categories of names that are readily translatable, personal names in *-tar*, *-tär*, and place-names in *-la*, *-lä*. *-tar* or *-tär* is a common Finnish personal suffix designating a female person or being, often the female counterpart or spouse of some corresponding masculine word; so *kuningas* 'king' has the feminine matrimonial derivative *kuningatar* 'queen.' In the *Kalevala* this suffix is freely combined with various nature words to designate a female spirit that is, so to speak, its essence or tutelar diety, a sort of minor divinity; so from *ilma* 'air' is formed *Ilmatar* 'Air Spirit,' from *kuu* 'moon' *Kuutar* 'Moon Spirit.' All such names have been translated. In the realm of nature names and place names there is a highly productive habitative suffix *-la* or *-lä*, designating a site, often a farm owned or somehow characterized by the word to which it is affixed. Thus from *tuoni* 'death' is formed *Tuonela* 'Death's Domain,' from *pohjo*, variant of *pohja* 'north,' comes *Pohjola* 'North Farm,' the place in question clearly being nothing more than a prosperous farm; on the difficult name *Kalevala* see "Kaleva District" in the glossary below. The rendering of most of these names is obvious.

In addition to the main lexical sources mentioned in the Foreword, I have found help in the late Yrjö H. Toivonen et al., *Suomen kielen etymologinen sanakirja* [Etymological Dictionary of the Finnish Language], Helsinki: Suomalais-ugrilainen Seura (Fenno-Ugric Society), 1955—, now through *roska*, and to a more limited extent in Marti Haavio's *Karjalan jumalat* [The Gods of Karelia], Helsinki: Söderström, 1959, to which I have given a number of references. I was unable to derive any useful information from Pentti Pajunen's eight curious articles, *Sherlock Holmes Sammon ryöstäjien jäljillä* [Sherlock Holmes on the Trail of the Robbers of the Sampo], first published serially in *Helsingin Sanomat* (14 August–9 September 1960) and reissued in the same year as a 59-page pamphlet by the publishers of that distinguished newspaper. Finally I would note that with one or two minor exceptions all identifiable geographical names are given according to *Webster's Geographical Dictionary: Dictionary of Names and Places with Geographical and Historical Information and Pronunciation*, Springfield, Mass.: G. and C. Merriam Co., 1949.

ABODE OF THE DEAD (*Manala*), a mythical place name identified with, and slightly more frequently used than, Death's Domain (*Tuonela*), is pictured as lying in the same plane as the surface of the earth but separated from it by a dark, wild river. It is occasionally spoken of as an "island" (*saari*), which need only imply a discrete area of some sort, like the Finnish *saareke*. There is a hill and there are habitations. It is presided over by Death (*Surma, Tuoni*), also called "the man of the Abode of the Dead" (*manalainen*), who has a dumpy, hideous daughter called "Death's daughter," also Loviatar, q.v. The name occurs in Poems 6, 14–17, 19–20, 23, 26, 32, 35, 38, 45. As a result of folk-etymologizing, *mana* combined with the habitative terminal *-la* may look back to such expressions as *maan ala* 'space under the earth, the underworld,' or the ultimate meaning may have been "the act of vanishing," "the spirit of a departed person haunting its body's grave," hence Abode of the Dead or the like.

AHTI, with the diminutive *Ahtinen*, a by-name of Lemminkäinen, is often used, especially in Poems 20, 27, as a sort of uninflected title before *Saarelainen* 'man of the Island,' the combination *Ahti Saarelainen* here being rendered "Island-Ahti" with reference to his escapades on the Island (*Saari*) told in Poem 11. The name, mentioned in Poems 11–12, 20, 26, 28, 30–31, is perhaps to be associated with the verb *ahtaa* 'to set (snares, *ansoja*),' and is fundamentally a variant of Ahto, below.

AHTO, "king of the waves" (*aaltojen kuningas*), tutelary genius of the sea or water and apparently a variant, formally a diminutive in -o, of Ahti, above, is mentioned in Poems 5, 41–42, 48. His spouse is Vellamo.

AHTO'S REALM (*Ahtola*), based on Ahto with the habitative terminal *-la*, comprises all seas and waters and occurs in Poems 5, 42; the derivative *ahtolaiset* (Poem 42), rendered by "people of Ahto's realm," is based on *Ahto* plus *-lainen*, indicating residence or nationality.

AINIKKI, Lemminkäinen's tattletale sister, is in the singing tradition commonly thought of as Ahti's daughter. The name, mentioned in Poem 12, is formed with the suffix *-kki* suggesting affection (in the *Kalevala* common too in cow-names), from *aino*, poetic for *ainoa* 'peerless, splendid,' thus meaning "peerless one" or the like.

AINO, with the diminutive *Ainonen*, is Joukahainen's sister, pledged to Väinämöinen. The name, identical with the adj. *aino* 'peerless, splendid' (Finnish *ainoa*), is Lönnrot's invention and occurs in Poems 3–5.

AIR SPIRIT (*Ilmatar*), the most important of a number of nature spirits that play various roles in the poems, is Väinämöinen's virgin mother, shaper of many geographical features of this earth, a demiurge of sorts. She is more commonly referred to by such by-names as "maiden, virgin of the air" (*ilman tyttö, impi*), and once she gets down into the primordial sea she becomes "the mother of the water" (*veen emo*). The name, made up from *ilma* 'air' with the feminine suffix *-tar*, occurs in Poems 1, 47.

ALUE, fictional lake in which Ukko's fire gets temporarily lost, occurs in Poems 47–48. The name, made up on a base *al-* 'lower, under' and the formative element *-ue* used to make collectives, seems to mean "low-lying place," specifically "low-lying lake," and is perhaps somehow to be associated with the Dead Sea (1285 feet below sea level) in the Holy Land.

ANNIKKI, Ilmarinen's sister mentioned in Poem 18, whose epithets are "of fair name," "girl working at night, maid working at dawn," is Lönnrot's adaptation of *Anni* with the suffix *-kki* (see *Ainikki*). In the singing tradition her name is *Anni*, which in turn looks back to Anna, St. Anne, virgin mother of the Virgin Mary.

ANTERO, first name of Vipunen, presumably looking back to Andreas, St. Andrew, is mentioned in Poem 17.

APPLE (*Omena*), a cow name, occurs in Poem 32.

BACKSTRIPE (*Kyyttä*), a cow name used in Poem 33, describes a cow with a stripe or a streak on its spine, sometimes also on the flanks and underbelly; the name is a variant of the generic term *kyytö* 'cattle with a streak or stripe on the spine, sometimes also on the flanks and underbelly.'

BLACKIE [1] (*Musti*), a dog name based on *musta* 'black,' occurs in Poems 23, 33, 36.

BLACKIE [2] (*Muurikki*, with the diminutive *Muurikkinen*), a cow name in *-kki* (see *Ainikki*) mentioned in Poems 1, 11, is based on the common noun *muurikki* '(black) cow.'

BRANDLE (*Kirjas*), see Brindle.

BRINDLE (*Kirjos*), a cow name in Poem 32, is based on *kirjo-* 'with patterns, designs' and describes a brindled or streaked cow; in variation is the echoic doublet, *Kirjas*, without meaning and here rendered Brandle.

CLAW RAPIDS (*Kynsikoski*), a fictional rapids said in Poem 32 to be in the river of Death's Domain, is made up of *kynsi* 'claw, talon' and *koski* 'rapids.'

CHOKECHERRY HILL (*Tuomivaara*), a fictional name in Poems 25, 32, is made up of *tuomi* 'chokecherry' (*Prunus padus*) and *vaara* 'wooded height, (arctic) hill, mountain.'

CHOKECHERRY SPIRIT (*Tuometar*), made up of *tuomi* 'chokecherry' and the feminine suffix *-tar*, is mentioned in Poem 32.

CREATOR (*Luoja*), God, sometimes used of the Biblical diety and thus the equivalent of God (*Jumala*) when so used, occurs in Poems 2–3, 8–9, 11,

387

15, 17, 21, 24, 26, 30, 32, 39, 43, 45–47, 49–50; in Poem 14:47 *luoja* describes Ukko. This agent noun in *-ja* is based on the stem of the verb *luoda* 'to create.'

DARLING (*Mielikki*), "mistress of Woodland" (*Metsolan emäntä*), the common noun *mielikki*, formed with the suffix of affection *-kki* and *mieli* in the sense of "feeling, desire" and meaning "favorite, pet, darling," occurs in Poems 14, 32, 46.

DAWN GOD (*Koijumala*), mythological name in Poem 17 made up of *koi* 'dawn, daybreak' and *jumala* 'God,' amounts to a personification of the dawn and is quite like the non-*Kalevala* name *Koitar* 'Dawn Spirit.'

DEATH (mostly rendering *Tuoni*, occasionally *Surma*), personification of death and the designation of the master of Death's Domain, also referred to as the Abode of the Dead (*Manala*), is mentioned in Poems 12–16, 19, 22, 25–26, 35, 38, 45, 48; cf. Grave Spirit. *Tuoni* (older *tooni*), poetical for *kuolema* 'death,' may look back to a strong past participle of some form of the Germanic "die" verb (cf. Old Guthnic *doyia*, Old Swedish *döia*), less likely to the "dead" adjective, Old Swedish *dödher*, Swedish *död*.

DEATH'S DAUGHTER (*Tuonetar; Tuonen tyttö* 'Death's maiden'), often with the epithet *matala* 'dumpy' who challenges Väinämöinen's attempt to cross the river of Death's Domain, is mentioned in Poems 16, 23, 45. She is also known as the 'maiden of the Abode of the Dead" and as Loviatar.

DEATH'S DOMAIN (*Tuonela*), mythical place name formed from *tuoni* 'death' and the habitative terminal *-la*, is identical with the Abode of the Dead, whose description above serves equally well here. The Finnish word *Tuonela*, if not the meaning, is familiar to many concertgoers as the program title of the late Jean Sibelius' tone poem "The Swan of Tuonela" (*Tuonelan joutsen*), better titled "The Swan of Death's Domain"; cf. Poem 14. The region is mentioned in Poems 4, 6, 14–17, 19–20, 23, 25, 32, 35, 45, 47.

DEMON, DEMONS (*Hiisi*, *Kalevala* nom. pl. *hiiet*) offers problems for the translator, and the name might perhaps as well be rendered Evil Spirit as anything else. The word *hiisi* (gen. sg. *hiien*) originally referred to a sacred or sacrificial grove, a sense still partly preserved in Estonian *hiis* 'leafy grove, copse,' and traces of this older sense may occasionally survive in the *Kalevala*, where it might be rendered "dread place" or some such. But *hiisi* developed—and in the *Kalevala* this is altogether the most prominent sense—into the idea of an evil being particularly associated with woods, streams, and hills, here rendered "demon." There is clearly one chief Demon—here capitalized—who is aided and abetted by a number of lesser demons, his henchmen, rendered "demons." The chief Demon figures prominently as the inspirer of a magic elk made up of odd bits of rotten wood, grass, and other plants which Louhi sends Lemminkäinen to capture; cf. Poems 13–14. The name occurs in Poems 6, 8–9, 11–14, 17, 19, 26–27, 30–31, 33–34, 40, 50.

DEMON'S DOMAIN (*Hiitola*), describing the imaginary haunts of the Demon (*Hiisi*) and his henchmen (*hiiet*), is conceived as a dreary region with charred and burned heaths and hills not far from North Farm (*Pohjola*) and in Lapp country. Mentioned in Poem 14 and implicitly described in Poem 13, the name is made up of *hiito*, formally a diminutive of *hiisi* 'demon,' and the habitative terminal *-la*.

DEVIL (*Lempo*, gen. *Lemmon*), Devil or evil being, is mentioned in Poems 6, 8, 12–13, 17, 19, 22–23, 26–27, 29–31, and in meaning is not very different from *hiisi* 'demon.' *Lempo* is unconnected with *lempi* 'erotic love' which forms part of the name Lemminkäinen.

DEVOUT ONES (*jumaliset*), only in Poem 20, line 6, and designating some otherwise unspecified group of prospective banqueters at North Farm, is the plural of *jumalinen* 'god-fearing, devout, faithful,' in turn based on *Jumala* 'God.' In the singing tradition this describes some banqueters in the Sun's Domain (*Päivilä*), who are also on occasion referred to collectively as *jumalisto* 'pantheon, (all) gods.'

DREAD ONE (*Kammo*), in Poem 40 the father of Dread Rock-Spirit, is a mythological specialization of *kammo* 'great fear, dread.'

DREAD ROCK SPIRIT (*Kivi-Kimmo*), personification of danger to vessels from rocks in rapids, and apostrophized in Poem 40, is compounded of *kivi* 'stone' and *kimmo*, a mythological name meaning "dread spirit" or the like and closely related to the Dread One (*Kammo*), above. This *kimmo* is unrelated to the cow name Frisky (*Kimmo*), below.

DRINKER (*Juotikki*), cow name in Poem 32, is based on *juottaa* 'to water (cattle)' with the suffix *-kki* common in cow names, and presumably describes a cow that drinks a lot of water; cf. Eater, below.

DVINA (*Viena*, with characteristic Finnish reduction of the cluster *dv-*), river from whose headwaters in the Valdai Hills, northwest Russia, salt is said in Poem 46 to have been exported, is the Southern or Western Dvina, German Düna, Latvian Dauvaga, and empties into the Gulf of Riga. This is to be kept distinct from the Northern Dvina of the White Sea basin, which empties into the White Sea at Archangel and as *Vienan meri* 'Dvina Sea' is the Finnish designation of the White Sea.

EATER (*Syötikki*), a cow name in Poem 32, is based on *syöttää* 'to give fodder to, to feed' with the suffix *-kki* common in cow names, and presumably describes a cow that eats a lot of fodder; cf. Drinker, above.

ESTONIA (*Viro*), Estonian *Eesti* (also used in Finnish, especially during the period of Estonian independence, 1918–1940), is today an area incorporated in the Soviet Union as the Estonian SSR, south of the Gulf of Finland. Its capital is Tallinn (q.v.), and the region is mentioned in Poems 11, 25, 46, at times somewhat disparagingly. Finnish *Viro* derives from Estonian *Virumaa*, a large province in northeast Estonia; cf. Germany (*Saksa*) and Russia (*Venäe*), below.

EVERGREEN SPIRIT (*Hongatar*), made up of *honka* 'long-boled conifer' and the feminine suffix *-tar*, is mentioned in Poem 32.

EVIL ELF (*Keitolainen*), whose spear is mentioned in Poem 26 as the source of a serpent's tongue, is a specialization of *keitolainen* 'elf, fairy.'

FABRIC SPIRIT (*Kankahatar*), personification of the art of weaving, based on *kangas* (gen. *kankahan*) 'cloth' with the feminine suffix *-tar*, is mentioned in Poem 25 and is a figure much like Moon Spirit and Spirit of the Great Bear, below.

[FARAWAY FARM or the farm of the man with a far-roving mind (*Kaukola*) is not recorded but is implied in the derivative *kaukolainen* 'man of Faraway Farm' or 'person from the farm of the man with a far-roving mind,' which occurs in Poem 12:2 with reference to Lemminkäinen. Cf. Faraway Headland, Man with a far-roving mind.]

FARAWAY HEADLAND (*Kaukoniemi*), site of Lemminkäinen's evidently not very prosperous farm mentioned in Poems 11, 20, 26, appears to be made up of *kauko-* 'far' and *niemi* 'headland.' Since, however, "Kauko" occurs as a truncated form of Lemminkäinen's epithet-name *Kaukomieli* 'man with a far-roving mind' (q.v.), *Kaukoniemi* may have been apprehended as standing for 'Lemminkäinen's Headland.'

FINLAND (*Suomi, Suomenmaa* 'Land of Suomi') may refer to the Finnish peninsula in general and thus more or less correspond to present-day territorial Finland, or it may refer more specifically to a small southwest corner of the country (province of Turku-Pori), the original homeland of the Suomi tribe (*suomalaiset*). The latter, more limited area later came to be designated V*arsinais-Suomi* 'Finland proper,' Swedish *egentliga Finland*, and its original designation *Suomi* came in time to define all present-day Finland. The name occurs in Poems 19–20, 35, 39–41, 43, 46, 50. Cf. Suomela, below. The name Finland is of disputed etymology, but is clearly Germanic and originally meant "land of the Lapps," who were called in Anglo-Saxon *Finnas*, in Old Scandinavian *Finnar*; this original meaning is clearly preserved in the provincial name Fin(n)mark, the "Lappish district" of Arctic Norway and Sweden, a region which the Lapps, retreating before the Finns, began to reach in the ninth century or even earlier and where they are now making their last stand. The corresponding area in Finland is called *Lapinlääni* 'Lapp province'; cf. Lapland, below.

FINNISH (*suomalainen*) occurs in Poem 20; see Finland, above.

FINNMARK (*Rutja, Turja*) refers to the Lapp country of Norway. (1) One name for the region occurs in Poems 12 and 17, in the phrase *Rutjan koski* 'rapids of Finnmark,' conceived as a fiery maelstrom and perhaps somehow associated with the river of Death's Domain. *Rutja* is a distortion of *Ruija* 'Finnmark,' a Norwegian province (*fylke*) whose principal town is Hammerfest; the name *Ruija* is of unknown origin. (2) Another name for Finnmark is *Turja*, synonymous with *Rutja* (*Ruija*), above, and close to *tarjalants*, the Norwegian Lapps' designation of themselves. The name occurs in Poems 12, 20, 48. The corresponding sb.-adj. *turjalainen*, mentioned in Poems 12, 26, 43, is used of certain Lappish wizards and once to describe an eagle. For Finnish Lapland see Lapland, below.

FOG MAIDEN (*Terhen neiti* 'fog maiden'), mentioned in Poem 42 and identical with Fog Spirit, is a tutelary spirit capable of summoning up and dispersing fog and mist.

FOG SPIRIT (*Terhenetär*), mentioned in Poem 19, is based on the stem form *terhene-* 'fog' and the feminine suffix *-tär*, and is identical with Fog Maiden, above.

FRESHNESS (*Tuorikki*), cow name in Poem 32 based on *tuori*, dialectal for *tuore* 'fresh, sweet (of milk)' and the suffix *-kki* common in cow names, describes a cow yielding an abundance of milk.

FRISKY (*Kimmo*), cow name in Poem 1 identical with *kimmo* 'springiness, bounciness,' evidently describes a frisky, lively cow. This *kimmo* is unrelated to (*Kivi-*)*Kimmo* 'Dread Rock-Spirit.'

GERMAN, GERMANY (*Saksa*), is mentioned in various connections, mostly as the source of boots, salt, soap, split logs for benches; it is also a land of mighty warriors. Väinämöinen says falsely that he is going fowling in its unidentified sounds (*Saksan salmet*). The emphasis on trade presumably echoes medieval contacts that Finland enjoyed with the Hanseatic league. Like Old Norse *Saxland* (later *Tyskland*) 'Germany' the Finnish designation is based on the Saxon name (Finnish *Saksi*), whence by extension it came to cover a large part of what one today thinks as of Germany; cf. Estonia (*Viro*). The name occurs in Poems 18, 21, 25, 31–37, 46.

GLOOMY FARM (*Pimentola*), a designation of North Farm (*Pohjola*) and often in variation with it, occurs in Poems 6, 7, 12, 22, 27, 29–30, 48. The name is based on *pimento* 'dark, shady, gloomy spot' with the habitative terminal *-la*; behind this lies *pimeä* 'dark, gloomy.'

GOBLIN'S CRAG (*Hornan kallio*) is mentioned in Poem 3. *Horna* is a word much like *hiisi* 'demon' and *lempo* 'devil' and here defines a crag in which evil spirits dwell. A mountain so designated (*Hornan vuori*) is known on the island of Soisalo, largest island in Finland, in the southeast part of Lake Kallavesi, province of Kuopio.

GOD (*Jumala*), mentioned in Poems 2, 7, 9, 11–19, 21, 28, 30, 32–35, 43, 45, 46, 48–50, seems originally to have meant little more than a "powerful or sacred being," even just a "(wooden) idol," and in the *Kalevala* it ranges from that to the Biblical God. The name is usually equivalent to "Creator" (*Luoja*), while Ukko's stock epithet, an invention of Lönnrot's, is *ylijumala* 'God on high'; see Ukko, below.

GRAVE SPIRIT (*Kalma*), personification of *kalma* 'grave' and thus equivalent to Death, is mentioned in Poems 13, 17, 26, 27, 30, 32, 35.

GREAT BIRTH (*Jalo Synty*), meaning Jesus Christ, whose nativity was viewed among the Greek Orthodox Karelians as the birth par excellence, is mentioned in Poem 50; cf. also Profound Birth.

GREAT MAN (*Suuri Mies*), Jesus Christ, identical with the Great Birth, above, is mentioned in Poem 50.

HÄLLÄ-WHIRLPOOL (*Hälläpyörä*), a legendary whirlpool (*pyörä*) thought of as being in the province of Häme (Swedish Tavastland), occurs in Poem 3; the first element, *hällä*, is of unknown etymology.

HÄME (*Swedish Tavastland*), province of southwest Finland with the capital Hämeenlinna (Swedish Tavastehus) 'stronghold of Häme,' is as a name probably etymologically identical with *sabme* (*gen. säme*), the Lapps' name for themselves, looking back to a base-word **šämä*. The element *Tavast-*, used in Swedish, has a long history and is of uncertain etymology; see Jaakkola, pp. 193ff. and 444, esp. n. 15. The name occurs in Poems 3, 20.

HOARFROSTY (*Kuura* 'hoarfrost'), by-name of Lemminkäinen's brother-in-arms Snowfoot (*Tiera*), q.v., is mentioned in Poem 30. Both by-name and main name clearly somehow reflect an ability to put up with hard going in severe weather, particularly when the snow is likely to form cakes under one's shoes.

HONEY-FRAGRANT ISLAND (*Simasalo*), a fictional name occurring in Poem 18, is made up of *sima* 'honey, mead' and *salo* 'largish wooded island,' with the implication of an island much frequented by bees; it is thought of as lying off North Farm (*Pohjola*) in Lovers' Bay (*Lemmenlahti*).

ILMA, the name of Ilmarinen's farm mentioned in Poems 24, 34, is formally identical with *ilma* 'air, sky' but is obviously likewise involved in the name Ilmarinen, from which it is here presumably a back-formation; it is thought of as being in the Kaleva District (*Kalevala*).

ILMARINEN, with the variant *Ilmari*, along with Väinämöinen, his boon companion, and Lemminkäinen, is one of the Big Three in the narrative poems of the *Kalevala*. Only in the *Kalevala* does he have a sister Annikki. As he appears in the singing tradition, he would seem to be a conflation of two originally distinct personages. First, he is a worker in metals with the stock epithets "craftsman" (*seppo*) and "eternal smith" (*iänkuinen takoja*, 'eternal hammerer, forger'). He is a competent, steadygoing work-man whose chief exploits are the forging of the unique Sampo for North Farm (*Pohjola*), of an unsatisfactory gold and silver bride for himself, and of an ineffective gold moon and silver sun for the Kaleva District. In Poem 49 he claims to have forged the vault of heaven. His name, formed on *ilma* 'sky' and the occupational, agential suffix *-ri*, perhaps originally was apprehended as "maker (of the vault) of the sky"; the longer and most commonly used form of his name is based on *Ilmari* and the diminutive suffix *-nen*. If he was originally a divinity, all trace of this has disappeared in the *Kalevala*; he is certainly not thought of as a sky god or god of the elements, a role filled by Ukko. Secondly, he is a more or less ordinary person who woos and wins the daughter of Louhi of North Farm (*Pohjola*). The name occurs in Poems 1, 7, 9, 10, 15, 17–19, 21, 22, 24, 25, 30, 31, 33, 34, 37–40, 42–44, 46–49.

ILMARINEN'S LADY (*Ilmarisen emäntä*), nameless elder daughter of Louhi of North Farm (*Pohjola*) and wife of Ilmarinen, is the short-lived mistress of his household. Her story is told in Poems 32–33 and she is briefly mentioned as his late wife (*nainen*) in Poems 34, 37, 38. Famous for her beauty and sought after by many, she is before her marriage the equally nameless 'maid of North Farm' (*Pohjolan, Pohjan neiti*).

ILPO'S DAUGHTER (*Ilpotar*), in Poem 27 Louhi's patronymic, is the result of distortion and is really meaningless. Behind it lies a place-name *Ilpola*, in turn distorted from *Ilmola* 'world of men,' based on *ilmo*, diminutive of *ilma* 'air,' and the habitative terminal *-la*.

IMATRA, spectacular rapids in the Vuoksi (q.v.) in the province of Kymi in southeast Finland, with a drop of some 60 feet in about 435 feet. Of unknown etymology, the name occurs in Poems 3, 30.

INGRIA (*Inkeri* or *Inkerinmaa*, Swedish *Ingermanland*) was from early times a district in Russia at the southeast end of the Gulf of Finland. Swedish between 1617 and 1703, its chief stronghold on the Neva (q.v.) was captured in 1703 by Tsar Peter the Great, who there founded St. Petersburg (Finnish *Pietari*), later Petrograd, now Leningrad. Ingria is now part of the Leningrad Region, USSR. Mentioned in Poem 11, the name is of uncertain origin; in Poem 11:56 there occur two nonsense place names, *Penkeri*, *Pänkeri*, invented to form echoic variations on *Inkeri*, here rendered Pengria, Pangria.

ISLAND, THE (*Saari*), legendary home of Kyllikki, who, wooed and abducted by Lemminkäinen, proves an unsatisfactory, gadabout wife; the name, a specialization of *saari* 'island' and occurring in Poem 11, has been variously though indecisively identified with the island of Kotlin (Finnish Retusaari), now the site of Kronstadt in the Gulf of Finland, today part of the Leningrad Region, USSR, also with the Åland Islands (Finnish Ahvenanmaa), or some other island. The adjectival form *saarelainen* 'of or pertining to *Saari*, the Island,' is at times used in connection with Lemminkäinen's by-name Ahti (q.v.).

ISLAND-AHTI, see Ahti and the Island, above; the present combination occurs in Poems 11, 20, 27, 28, 30.

JACK FROST (*Pakkanen*, also a diminutive *Pakko*), is in Poem 30 a personification of *pakkanen* 'severe cold, bitterly freezing weather.'

JOUKAHAINEN, also a truncated diminutive *Jouko*, is a crude, inexperienced youth who unwisely enters into a contest of wisdom with Väinämöinen. Commanding only a series of banal maxims, he is badly defeated and to save his life promises his sister Aino to Väinämöinen as a spouse. Nursing a grudge, he later shoots the horse of Väinämöinen from under him so the latter falls into the water and is carried out to sea. His chief epithet is "scrawny Lappish lad," though there is no likelihood of his ever having been seriously considered a Lapp. The name, mentioned in Poems 1, 3, 4, 5, 6, is of uncertain etymology; on the basis of certain Lappish material an ulterior meaning, "genius of ice and snow," has been suggested.

JOUKAHAINEN'S FARM (*Joukola*) is mentioned in Poem 7; it is made up of the truncated diminutive *Jouko* and the habitative terminal -*la*; this same farm is occasionally referred to as Luotola, q.v.

JUNIPER SPIRIT (*Katajatar*), personification of *kataja* 'juniper' with the feminine suffix -*tar*, occurs in Poem 32.

JUORTANI (*Juortanin joki*), fictional river mentioned in Poem 17, may well look back to the Biblical Jordan in Palestine, but, even if this is right, it is doubtful if latter-day singers felt any such connection. The present Finnish name of the Biblical river is, like the English, *Jordan*.

KALEVA, fictional ancestor or "father" of several personalities, male and female, mostly "Kaleva sons or male descendants" (*Kalevan pojat*), who appear in the *Kalevala*. The origin of the name is disputed. A plausible, though probably not demonstrable, etymology is proto-Baltic *kaləvijas* (cf. Lithuanian *kálvis*, Latvian *kalējs*) 'blacksmith,' whose sons in folk tradition are commonly thought of as mighty, often superstrong boys and men capable of prodigies; of this tradition in the *Kalevala* Kullervo is the sole representative. From the phrase *Kalevan pojat* and the like, perhaps originally 'blacksmith's sons,' there would seem to have been extracted in popular tradition sometime somewhere a person named Kaleva. In some respects Kaleva is close to Osmo (q.v.). The name occurs in Poems 2, 6, 7, 13–15, 20, 21, 42, 44, 45, 47.

KALEVA DISTRICT (*Kalevala*) refers to a fictional and geographically clearly somewhat limited tract inhabited by Kaleva sons and daughters or, better, descendants, notably the Big Three, Väinämöinen, Ilmarinen, and Lemminkäinen. This district is viewed as lying along the sea; it features an often-mentioned misty headland and foggy island, and is once described (Poem 26) as across a bay from, and within earshot of, North Farm (*Pohjola*), though it is usually thought of as a three days' journey from there. The name is based on Kaleva, above, with the habitative terminal -*la*, but since there seems never to have been any Kaleva a noncommittal designation like Kaleva District (Kaleva Community would be just as good) is probably preferable to a more specific-sounding term such as the Land of Kaleva or Kaleva's Domain. Still less satisfactory is Land of Heroes, a formula used in the past, for the *Kalevala* poems do not designate any of their characters as a "hero" (Finnish *sankari, urho*); see the discussion of *uros* in the first section of this appendix. The people of the district are sometimes referred to as *kalevalaiset*, formed from *Kalevala* with the adj. suffix -*inen*, plural -*iset*, as if 'Kalevalians'!

The name Kalevala, adopted by Lönnrot as the title of both versions of his poem (here, too, used as the title), is mentioned in Poems 1, 3, 5–8, 10, 45–47, 49.

KALERVO, father of Kullervo, is probably a mere variant of Kaleva in which the element -*rvo* was perhaps or probably substituted for -*va* under the influence of the name Kullervo, which so often precedes it in the whole-verse formula "Kullervo, son of Kalervo" (*Kullervo Kalervon poika*). The name occurs in Poems 31–36.

KARELIA (*Karjala*), a large region on both sides of the Russo-Finnish border extending from the White Sea (Archangel Region, USSR) to Lake Ladóga, is the area where most of the narrative songs used in compiling the *Kalevala* were collected. On the Russian side of the border this territory was formed into a Karelo-Finnish SSR in 1940. The name is quite possibly, though not certainly, based on *karja* 'cattle' and the habitative suffix -*la*, meaning "cattle-land, cattle-country"; consideration should perhaps be given to the Old Icelandic form *Kirjalir* 'Karelians', also *Kirjala-land* 'land of the Karelians' recorded in the tenth or eleventh century *Egils saga*, chs. 14, 17. The name occurs in Poems 3, 20, 31, 43, 48, 50.

KARELIAN (*karjalainen*) is used in Poem 20 to define Virokannas, would-be butcher or, more precisely, knocker of the big Karelian steer.

KAUPPI, maker of skis, particularly of the skis used by Lemminkäinen in tracking down the Demon's elk (*Hiien hirvi*), is mentioned in Poem 13. His identity is confused; he is simultaneously said to be handsome and Lappish, then wise and a man from *Vuoji (vuojelainen*), a place of quite uncertain identification but certainly not originally Lapland. *Vuoji may in the first instance have meant the Swedish island of Gotland, then Germania, and by extension the land of Northern Europeans in general, and then, by still further extension, perhaps on occasion Lapland. Despite its obvious similarity to *kauppa* 'trade,' *kauppias* 'trader,' the name is probably merely a truncated form of *Jaakoppi* 'Jacob, James' with perhaps some late working of folk etymology. *Vuojelainen* has here been ambiguously rendered "man of northern parts." His by-name is Lyylikki.

KEMI (*Kemijoki*), river in northern Finland flowing some 300 miles into the head of the Gulf of Bothnia, mentioned in Poem 20, is the river (*joki*) on which stands the town of *Kemi* 'dry land by a river.'

KUIPPANA, called "king of the forest" in Poem 32, is a minor tutelary genius whose name is of uncertain origin but is perhaps to be associated with Hubert(us), bishop of Liège (d. 727), patron saint of huntsmen and of the chase.

KULLERVO, also a diminutive *Kullervoinen*, is the powerful and tragic son of Kalervo, mentally disturbed from having been rocked excessively as a baby, mentioned in Poems 31–36. The name, of disputed origin, is possibly based on *kulta* (gen. *kullan*) 'gold, dear one' and thus a formation comparable to *Pellervoinen* 'Spirit of Arable.'

KYLLIKKI, also the truncated diminutive *Kylli*, Lemminkäinen's unsatisfactory wife from the Island (*Saari*), is mentioned in Poems 11–13, 15; her epithets are "maiden," "flower of the Island." This woman's name may be from the same root as *kyllä* 'sufficiency, abundance' or it may be of foreign origin. It is formed with the suffix of affection *-kki* (see Ainikki).

LAPLAND (*Lappi*), in part at least corresponding to the present-day Finnish province of Lapland (*Lapin lääni*) above the Arctic Circle, is mentioned, at times to define various sorts of Lapps, in Poems 5, 7, 10, 12, 13, 17, 18, 20, 25, 26, 32, 35, 43, 48. In Poem 3 the name occurs with the prefixed *taka-* 'behind, back' in the sense of "backcountry, remotest Lapland." The name has been much studied, and a presently favored speculation would make it originally pejoratively jocular, meaning "patch of cloth, rag, tatter," to describe Lappish clothing. The name is first recorded in the twelfth century and gradually replaced "Finn," which was earlier used by Anglo-Saxons and Scandinavians to refer to Lapps. Now the Lappish name for themselves is *sabme*, probably etymologically identical with Häme, above.

LAPP, LAPPISH (*lappalainen*), inhabitant of Lapland, occurs in Poems 3, 6, 10, with reference to Joukahainen, in Poem 13 with reference to the ski-maker Kauppi, and in Poems 12, 15, 26, 30, with reference to Lappish wizards.

LASSIE (*Piltti*), Marjatta's serving maid in Poem 50, is identical with *piltti* 'lad(die), boy,' but here applied to a girl.

LAZYBONES (*vennon joutio* 'mere loafer') occurs in Poem 50 as a disparaging name for Marjatta's son; cf. Little Flower, below.

LEMMINKÄINEN, with Väinämöinen and Ilmarinen one of the Big Three in the *Kalevala*, is presumably based on *lempi* (gen. *lemmen*) 'erotic, passionate love' with the secondary denominative suffix *-(i)nkäinen*—so *pörrinkäinen* 'tousle-head, Slovenly Peter,' based on *pörrö* 'bushy, tousled hair'—and would thus mean 'lover, lover boy,' a name altogether appropriate to Lemminkäinen's character. His father Lempi is as a person presumably a back-formation from the son's name; his sister is Ainikki. His mother plays an important part in his life, including resurrecting him from the dead. With a stock epithet "reckless" (*lieto*) he is also often referred to as the "(handsome) man with a far-roving mind" (*Kaukomieli*), also as Ahti and Island-Ahti. He is very much of a ladies' man and as such gets into no end of trouble. His apparently run-down farm seems to lie somewhat apart from the others in the Kaleva District, and once in Poem 12 he is spoken of as a "man of Faraway Farm" (*kaukolainen*). The name Lemminkäinen is mentioned in Poems 1, 11–15, 20, 26–30, 39, 40, 42, 43, 49.

LEMMINKÄINEN'S MOTHER (*Lemminkäisen äiti*), otherwise unnamed, is characterized by her great devotion to, and solicitude for, her "reckless" son. Her character may, indeed, in some respects have been influenced by the relation of the Virgin Mary to her Son. She is mentioned in Poems 11, 12, 15, 20, 26, 28–30.

LEMPI (gen. *Lemmen*), personification of *lempi* 'erotic love' and father of Lemminkäinen, exists only in the patronymic formula "Lempi's son" (*Lemmen poika*); this name, today a woman's name but until recently a man's name, occurs in Poems 40, 42, 43, and means 'pet, love, favorite.'

LITTLE FLOWER (*kukkalainen*, diminutive of *kukka* 'flower') is Marjatta's endearing name in Poem 50 for her little boy. Cf. Lazybones, above.

LOKKA, Ilmarinen's mother with the epithet "a Kaleva daughter," that is, "a Kaleva female descendant" (*Kalevatar*)—see Kaleva, above—is mentioned in Poem 25; the name is perhaps merely the Karelian form of *lokki* 'seagull.'

LOON RAPIDS (*Kaatrakoski*), fictional rapids said in Poem 3 to be in Karelia, is made up of *kaatra* 'loon, northern diver' and *koski* 'rapids' and would describe a rapids frequented by these birds.

LOUHI, with "mistress of North Farm" (*Pohjolan akka, emäntä*) as her common epithet, is in her way something of a *grande dame* presiding over a prosperous Viking Age type of farm; she is a solicitous hostess, fairly competent witch, and the mother of Ilmarinen's two wives. With a secondary epithet "gat-toothed" (*harvahammas* 'sparse-tooth, microdont,' i.e., 'with small or short teeth'), Louhi appears, like Chaucer's Wife of Bath, to have suffered from microdontia, associated with a longish jaw and smallish teeth. The name Louhi would seem to be some kind of reduction of the name-type represented by Loviatar, below, and occurs in Poems 1, 10, 12–15, 18–22, 27, 30, 38, 40, 42, 43, 45, 46, 49.

LOVERS' BAY (*Lemmenlahti*), fictional bay in Poem 18, thought of as near North Farm, is made up of *lempi* (gen. *lemmen*) 'erotic love' and *lahti* 'bay' and may suggest a bay whose shores afford trysting places for lovers.

LOVIATAR, half-blind daughter of Death's Domain and identical with Death's daughter, above, is mentioned in Poem 45. Among the variant forms in the singing tradition, those of the type *Louhetar* with the feminine suffix *-tar* virtually assure some connection with Louhi, above, and suggest a meaning "daughter of Louhi, Lovi" or the like. Many etymologies have been proposed, none fully convincing, ranging from a derivation based on Laufey, mother of the Old-Norse god Loki, to Finnish *lohi-käärme* 'flying serpent, dragon' as a half-translation loan from Old Norse *flug-dreki*, Old Swedish *flogh-draki* 'flying dragon,' meaning "witch of the wind."

LUOTOLA occurs in Poem 7 in variation with *Joukola* 'Joukahainen's farm,' with which it must be identified. On its face Luotola is based on *luoto* 'little island, skerry' in a lake, river, or the sea, with the habitative terminal *-la*, thus meaning "Island Farm," "farm with some offshore islands or skerries," or the like; but since possible connections with the Old Norse god Lódhurr, even with St. Nicholas, have been proposed, the name has been left untranslated.

LYYLIKKI, by-name of the ski-maker Kauppi, may be a formation with the suffix *-kki* (see Ainikki) and a base *lyyli*, in turn perhaps a variant of *lyly* 'left-hand ski'; but the name may reflect the man's name Lydecke, adapted from German Ludwig, introduced in the Middle Ages through Hanseatic channels. The name occurs in Poem 13.

MAID OF NORTH FARM (*Pohjolan, Pohjan neiti*), Louhi's eldest daughter who marries Ilmarinen and is thereafter referred to as Ilmarinen's lady (*Ilmarisen emäntä*), is mentioned in Poems 8, 10, 18, 19, 22, 24.

MAN OF SLACK WATER FARM (*Suvantolainen*, also distorted to *Uvantolainen*), an epithet-name for Väinämöinen, occurs in Poems 6, 7, 16, 18, 19, 42, 49—the forms without *S-* in Poems 7, 16, 18, 42. The name is an adjectival derivative in *-inen* from *Suvantola* 'Slack Water Farm,' q.v., below.

MAN WITH A FAR-ROVING MIND (*Kaukomieli*, also a truncated diminutive *Kauko* and a diminutive *Kau'ut* [gen. *Kaukuen*]), is an epithet-name for Lemminkäinen with reference to his characteristic wanderlust. The name, made up of *Kauko-* 'far' and *mieli* 'mind, desire,' occurs in Poems 1, 11, 12, 14, 15, 20, 26–30, 42, 43.

MARJATTA, also a diminutive *Marjattainen*, virgin mother and principal figure in Poem 50, with the epithet "man-shy youngest child" (*korea kuopus*), looks back to Maria, the Virgin Mary, but has been influenced by the name *Marjetta, Marjatta*, by-forms of the Margaret-name which occur in the singing tradition. It is also hard not to imagine some influence from *marja* 'berry,' specifically *puolukka* 'whortleberry,' which plays so prominent a part in Marjatta's immaculate conception.

MASTER OF NORTH FARM (*Pojolan isäntä*), mentioned in Poems 18, 21, 27, 28, is, compared to his dynamic wife Louhi, very much a lay figure. His most notable achievement is getting his head cut off in a duel with Lemminkäinen in Poem 27.

MIMERKKI, a pseudomythological name as if formed with the *-kki* suffix, designates in Poem 14 a "mistress of the forest" (*metsän emäntä*), but from such variants elsewhere in the singing tradition as *Himmerkke, Himmerken*, it is commonly viewed as a distortion of the latter, it and the H- names looking back to Swedish *himmelrike* 'Kingdom of Heaven,' as if meaning "lovely, heavenly one." Recently Haavio (p. 217) has suggested an etymology based on the phrase *mi[kä] merkki?* 'what (is) the omen (for a successful hunt)?' but this, attractive as it is, is hardly demonstrable.

MIST GIRL (*Utu-tyttö*), a personification of *utu* (gen. *u'un*) 'haze, mist,' is invoked by Louhi in Poem 42 to drop a blanket of fog on fleeing Väinämöinen's ship, which is carrying the Sampo away from North Farm (*Pohjola*). Cf. Mist Spirit, below.

MIST SPIRIT (*U'utar* 'maiden of the mist'), a personification of *utu* 'mist,' occurs in Poem 42 and is identical with Mist Girl, above.

MOON (*Kuu*, with the diminutive *Kuuhut*), a personification who in vain woos Kyllikki on behalf of its son, is mentioned in Poem 11; in Poem 15 it will give Lemminkäinen's mother no information as to the whereabouts of her son, nor in Poem 50 will it help Marjatta.

MOON'S ABODE (*Kuutola*) in Poem 11 is a fictional region to which Kyllikki is unwilling to go. The name is based on *kuu* 'moon' with the habitative terminal *-la*, but the element *-to-* is meaningless and is the result of some kind of distortion or fancifulness.

MOON SPIRIT (*Kuutar*), personification of *kuu* 'moon' with the feminine suffix *-tar* and especially associated with the art of weaving, is mentioned in Poems 4, 24, 25, 41, 48. She is clearly closely related to Fabric Spirit and to the Spirit of the Great Bear.

NEVA is a navigable river flowing about 40 miles from Lake Ladóga to the Gulf of Finland in the Leningrad Region, USSR, and in whose delta Leningrad, formerly St. Petersburg, then Petrograd, is situated. The name, mentioned in Poem 47, is identical with Karelian *ńeva* 'water, river' (Finnish *neva* 'treeless peat bog'). See also Ingria, above.

NORTH FARM (*Pohjola*, occasionally *Pohja*) is conceived as a prosperous and even splendid Viking Age type of farm presided over by Louhi. It is further thought of as lying north of the Kaleva District (*Kalevala*), at times merely across a bay (Poem 26), mostly, however, as a three days' journey away. In spite of its prosperity, due mainly to possession of Ilmarinen's Sampo, it is presented as a cold, gloomy place not far from Death's Domain (*Tuonela*), the Demon's domain (*Hiitola*), and the Lapp country; it is called a "cold settlement" (*kylmä kylä*), and has the pejorative by-names Gloomy Farm (*Pimentola*) and Sedgy Farm (*Sariola*). The name is based on *pohjo*, a diminutive variant of *pohja* 'north,' with the habitative terminal *-la*. The name occurs in Poems 1, 2, 5–10, 12–15, 17–30, 32, 35, 38–40, 42, 43, 45–49.

NOVGOROD (*Uusilinna*) was a Swedish Viking or Varangian settlement on the Volkhov, established ca. 862 and later a medieval principality (Novgorod Region, USSR); see further Sweden, below. The Russian name, of the Neuburg or Newcastle type and now used in Finnish, is made up of Russian *nov-* 'new' and *gorod* 'enclosed, stockaded place,' later 'town,' rendered in Poem 25 by the equivalent Finnish elements *uusi* 'new' and *linna* 'stronghold.'

NYYRIKKI, Tapio's son, of uncertain origin though formally made up with the suffix *-kki*, occurs in Poems 14, 32. Haavio's attempt (pp. 182–197) to associate him with St. Bartholomew, patron saint of the chase, seems dubious.

OGRESS (*Syöjätär*), personification of ogresses from whose buckles come serpents' mouths, occurs in Poem 26; the word is an agential substantive in -*jä* with the feminine suffix -*tär*, based on *syödä* 'to eat,' and thus means "devourer, vampire" or the like.

OLD MAN (*Äijö*), the Devil, is named in Poem 42 as the father of Turso; the name is a diminutive in -ö of the common substantive *äijä* 'old man.'

ÖRESUND, THE (*Suolasalmi* 'the salt sound'), in English also known as the Sound, designates the strait mentioned in Poem 46 between southern Sweden (Skåne) and the Danish island of Sjælland (Zealand); in Finnish this strait is today known as *Juutin rauma* 'Jutland current,' viewed as a current flowing from the Baltic into the Atlantic via the Kattegat and past the tip of the Jutland peninsula. The Swedish name is made up of *öre*- (Old Swedish gen. plur. *öra*) 'of sandbanks, gravel' and *sund* 'sound, strait.' The *Kalevala* name appears to be ancient and is obviously a partial translation-loan of Old-Norse *Eystrasalt* 'the More Easterly Sea' (Old Norse *salt* 'salt, sea'), that is, the Baltic.

OSMO, with a diminutive *Osmoinen*, a mythical being parallel to Kaleva, is chiefly mentioned in connection with such natural features as 'an Osmo field' (*Osmon pelto*), paralleling similar combinations with Kaleva. The name is formally an epithet for *osma, osmo* 'wolverine, bear,' but the concept of a mythical being is probably the older. The name occurs in Poems 2, 4, 10, 20.

OSMO DISTRICT (*Osmola*), formed from Osmo with the habitative terminal -*la*, is equivalent to the Kaleva District (*Kalevala*) and occurs in Poem 17.

OSMO DESCENDANT (*Osmotar*), parallel to a "Kaleva (female) descendant" (*Kalevatar*), is mentioned in Poems 20, 23, where she is active in connection with the origin of beer, and is based on Osmo, above, with the feminine suffix -*tar*, here in the sense of "daughter, female descendant" of the base-word.

PAIN GIRL (*Kiputyttö*), in Poem 45 a personification of *kipu* (gen. *kivun*) 'pain' and *tyttö* 'girl' with specific reference to the power of alleviating pain, is identical with Pain Spirit and Spirit of Injuries, below.

PAIN HILL (*Kipumäki*), fictional hill in Poems 9, 45, into which pains are exorcized, is made up of *kipu* 'pain' and *mäki* 'hill' and is identical with Pain Mountain, below.

PAIN MOUNTAIN (*Kipuvuori*), fictional mountain in Poems 9, 45, into which pains are exorcized, is made up of *kipu* 'pain' and *vuori* 'mountain, hill,' and is identical with Pain Hill, above.

PAIN SPIRIT (*Kivutar*), in Poem 45 a personification of *kipu* (gen. *kivun*) 'pain' with reference to the power to alleviate pain and the feminine suffix -*tar*, is identical with Pain Girl, above, and Spirit of Injuries, below.

PANGRIA, see Ingria.

PENGRIA, see Ingria.

PISA HILL (*Pisanmäki, Pisanvuori*), of the commune of Nilsiä, northern Save (Swedish Savolax), province of Kuopio, mentioned in old boundary books and occurring in Poem 3, is made up of dialectal *pisa* 'demon, devil' and *mäki, vuori* 'hill.'

PROFOUND BIRTH (*Syvä Synty*), mentioned in Poem 8, refers in Karelian

Greek Orthodox tradition to Jesus Christ, and is identical with Great Birth, Great Man, above.

REMUNEN, a being conceived as father of the hop vine, is a fanciful name apparently based on *remu* 'joyful noise, noisy gaiety,' conceivably with some reference to the humming sound of fermenting beer; it occurs in Poem 20.

ROAD (*Tiehyt*, diminutive of *tie* 'road, way'), a personification unwilling to inform Lemminkäinen's mother as to the whereabouts of her son, occurs in Poem 15.

ROWAN SPIRIT (*Pihlajatar*), from *pihlaja* 'rowan' with the feminine suffix *-tar*, is a personification of that variety of mountain ash (*Sorbus aucuparia*) indigenous to Finland and Karelia, which was there, as in the Old Germanic world, regarded as sacred. It is mentioned in Poem 32.

RUOTUS, presumably a distortion of the Biblical name Herod(us) with particular reference to the tetrarch Herod Antipas before whom Jesus Christ was tried, appears in Poem 50 as a "loathsome" (*ruma*), unfriendly man, mentioned chiefly as his unnamed wife's husband.

RUOTUS' LADY (*Ruotuksen emäntä*), wife of Ruotus, appears in Poem 50 as a "loathsome" (*ruma*) woman who suggests a horseshed as a substitute for a sauna for Marjatta's lying-in.

RUSSIA (*Venäe*, also *Venäjä* [only in Poems 20, 31:9]), especially Russia south of the Gulf of Finland, occurs in Poems 20, 22, 31, 37. Karelian *Venäe* (gen. *Venäehen*) presumably looks back ultimately to a type *Venädheh* based on or adapted from the ethnic name *Venadi* (with variant forms) originally designating the coastal Slavs or Wends, and was gradually applied specifically to Russians; in German and other languages this designation came to be applied to the Sorbs or Wends settled in eastern Saxony. Likewise from a base Venädh-arose a Finnish type *Venät* (gen. *Venään<*Venädhän*), whence presumably with a dialect shift of intervocalic *dh* to *j* arose the present standard form of the word for Russia, *Venäjä*, possibly influenced or encouraged by place names in *-ja* and *-jä*, such as *Lohja* (Swed. *Lojo*). On the word "Russia" see under Sweden, below.

SAMPO, also a diminutive *Sammut* (gen. *Sampuen*), is a magical object forged by Ilmarinen for Louhi of North Farm (*Pohjola*) in part payment for the hand of her daughter, the maid of North Farm. The Sampo is pictured as a three-sided mill, one side or face grinding out grain, one salt, and one money, all in unlimited amounts. Much is made of its lid (*kirjokansi*) which, like Jacob's coat, is "of many colors." Louhi sets up the Sampo in a cave in a hill of rock where it strikes three roots. It is a producer and symbol of prosperity, a quality to some extent shared even by its fragments. There seems to be no question of ever making a duplicate. This mysterious object is in a sense central to much of the action of the *Kalevala*, in that it becomes a bone of contention between the peoples of North Farm and the Kaleva District (*Kalevala*).

The name would seem to be somehow connected with *sammas* (gen.

sampaan) 'pillar, post' in Vote and *sammas* (gen. *samba*) 'prop, mainstay, support' in Estonian. Estonian *sammas* posits a base-word *sampa*, of which *Sampo* would be an *o*-diminutive and thus mean or suggest "prop of life." It is mentioned in Poems 1, 10, 15, 19, 38, 39, 42, 43, 45.

SAMPSA, an agricultural and vegetation divinity with the stock epithet "Spirit of Arable" (*Pellervoinen*), in the singing tradition commonly *Sämpsä*, whose name may well be connected with Ingrian *sämpsäheinä* 'bulrush' (*Scirpus silvaticus*), is mentioned in Poems 2, 16.

SARAJA, also SARAOJA, is in Poem 50 the place on whose outskirts Marjatta bears her son. The source of the name may be, as has been urged, Old Norse *Jórsalaborg, Jórsalir* (plur.) 'Jerusalem,' of which *Saraja* would be an adapted form far from the Old Norse; but it is hard to imagine that the singers did not in time apprehend it as 'ditch in a field of sedge hay' (*sara* 'sedge hay' *oja* 'ditch').

SAVO (Swedish Savolax), a district in east-central Finland, now a part of the province of Kuopio, abutting on Karelia, is mentioned in Poems 35, 48; it is of unknown etymology and is first mentioned as a regional name by the seventeenth-century historian, bishop Petrus Bång. Swedish Savolax looks back to a dialect type *Savon laksi* (Finnish *lahti* 'bay, gulf'), with which compare Kandalax (Finnish *Kantalahti* 'Kandalax Bay') in the Murmansk Region, USSR. The alternation between *lahti* and *laksi* corresponds, for example, to Standard Finnish *lähti* 'set out, set forth,' dialectal *läksi*.

SEDGY FARM (*Sariola, Saran talo*), alternative designation for North Farm (*Pohjola*), often in variation with the latter, would seem to be based on *sara* 'sedge, sedge hay' (*Carex*); in this event *Sariola* with the habitative terminal *-la* would be a derivative in *-io/-iö* used in the formation of such local names as *aukio* 'open, fallow field' (cf. *aukea* 'open') and *Perniö* 'a place characterized by a stand of linden trees' (*pernä* 'linden') and thus mean a "farm with a characteristic growth of sedge." Often with the adj. *summa* 'gloomy, dark,' *sanka* 'mighty,' it is indistinguishable from *Saran talo* 'sedge farm' used only in Poem 28. *Sariola* occurs in Poems 7, 8, 10, 18, 20, 21, 26, 27, 39, 40, 43, 45. Any connection with the Jerusalem name (cf. Saraja, above) seems far-fetched.

SHARP AIR (*Kova Ilma*) is used in Poem 30:182 as a by-name of Jack Frost.

SLACK WATER FARM (*Suvantola*), a tract equivalent to Väinämöinen's farm (*Väinölä*), is formed from *suvanto* 'slow-running, quiet, slack water above or below a rapids or at the mouth of a river' and the habitative terminal *-la*, and occurs in Poem 6; it is also the source of the adjectival form *suvantolainen* 'man of Slack Water Farm,' above.

SNOWFOOT (*Tiera*, also the diminutive *Tieranen*), Lemminkäinen's brother-in-arms, is mentioned in Poem 30 on the occasion of a set-to with Jack Frost (*Pakkanen*). *Tiera* is a Finnish word for snow caked up under a horse's hoof or a person's shoe, for which I know no precise English equivalent. Snowfoot is a compromise suggesting the essential features of Finnish *tiera*. Taken with his by-name Hoarfrosty (*Kuura*), he was clearly thought of as a man able to withstand severe weather and heavy going.

SOPPY HAT (*Märkähattu*), old, partly blind cattle-herder, in Poems 12 and 14 of North Farm, in Poem 15 of one Untamo's farm, is insulted by

Lemminkäinen in Poem 12, in Poem 14 attacks him and causes his death in the river of Death's Domain; in Poem 15 Lemminkäinen, after his resurrection, tells his mother how Soppy Hat plotted his death. This disparaging name, made up of *märkkä* '(sopping) wet' and *hattu* 'hat', would be calculated to picture a bedraggled, slovenly person.

SOUTHWIND SPIRIT (*Etelätär*), personification of *etelä* 'south, southwind' with the feminine suffix -*tär*, occurs in Poem 32.

SPIRIT OF ARABLE (*Pellervoinen*), by-name and fixed epithet of Sampsa, is based on *pelto* (gen. *pellon*) 'arable (land) field,' a loan from Old Germanic **feltha-* 'open country'; cf. the South African Veldt vs. Engl. "field." The name occurs in Poems 2, 16.

SPIRIT OF INJURIES (*Vammatar*), personification of the power to heal a bruise or injury (*vamma*) with the feminine suffix -*tar*. *Vamma* is an Old Germanic loan; cf. Gothic *wamm*, Old-Norse *vamm* 'defect, loss, misfortune.' The name occurs in Poem 45 and is identical with Pain Girl, Pain-Spirit, above.

SPIRIT OF NATURE (*Luonnotar*), based on *luonto* (gen. *luonnon*) 'nature' with the feminine suffix -*tar*, appears in Poems 1 and 2 as a single being, in Poems 32–41 as a group of several, and in Poems 9 and 26 as a triad, the latter perhaps somehow reflecting the three Marys: the Blessed Virgin, Mary Magdalene, and Mary, sister of Lazarus.

SPIRIT OF THE GOLDENEYE (*Sotkotar*), water spirit concerned with the care of goldeneyes (*Fuligula clangula*), is mentioned in Poem 41. The name is based on *sotko*, diminutive of *sotka* 'goldeneye,' with the feminine suffix -*tar*.

SPIRIT OF THE GREAT BEAR (*Otavatar*), personification of *otava* 'Great Bear' with the feminine suffix -*tar*, is mentioned in Poem 24 as helpful in weaving; cf. Fabric Spirit, Moon Spirit.

SPIRIT OF THE STEERING OAR (*Melatar*), personification of *mela* '(steering) oar' with the feminine suffix -*tar*, is helpful in getting a boat through difficult places, such as white-water rapids, and occurs in Poem 40.

SPOTS (*Merkki*), a dog name identical with *merkki* 'mark,' in Poem 23 describes a dog with markings or spots on its coat.

STAR (*Tähti*), a personification who in vain woos Kyllikki on behalf of its son, is mentioned in Poem 11; in Poem 50 it will give Marjatta no information as to the whereabouts of her boy. It is very likely that *Tähti* is to be apprehended as the North Star or (Stella) Polaris (Finnish *pohjantähti*), the star par excellence.

STAR'S ABODE (*Tähtelä*) in Poem 11 is a fictional region to which Kyllikki is unwilling to go; the name is made up of *tähti* 'star' and the habitative terminal -*lä*; see Star, above.

STAR SPIRIT (*Tähetär*, Finnish *Tähdetär*), personification of *tähti* 'star,' presumably the North Star, with the feminine suffix -*tär*, is mentioned in Poem 24.

STARVATION HEADLAND (*Nälkäniemi*), made up of *nälkä* 'hunger, famine' and *niemi* 'headland,' is conceived in Poem 30 as part of a miserable settlement where no food is to be had.

STRAWBERRY (*Mansikki*), cow name based on *mansikka* 'strawberry' adapted to the *-kki* suffix, occurs in Poem 11.

STRINGY (*Hermikki*), cow-name based on *hermo* 'sinew' adapted to the *-kki* suffix common in cow names, in Poem 32 describes a lean cow with sinews showing; as a cow name this recalls the medieval French *Chichevache* 'lean cow' who fed only on patient wives and hence got little to eat.

SUMMER SPIRIT (*Suvetar*), personification of *suvi* 'summer, south' with the feminine suffix *-tar*, is mentioned in Poem 32.

SUN (*Päivä*, with the diminutive *Päivyt*), a personification who woos in vain on behalf of its son, is mentioned in Poem 11; in Poem 15 it will give Lemminkäinen's mother no information as to the whereabouts of her son. In Poem 50 it gladly helps Marjatta to find her son.

SUN'S ABODE (*Päivälä*) in Poem 11 is a fictional region to which Kyllikki is unwilling to go; the name is based on *päivä* 'sun' with the habitative terminal *-lä*.

SUN SPIRIT (*Päivätär; Päivän tytär* 'Sun's daughter'), personification of *päivä* 'sun' with the feminine suffix *-tär*, is mentioned in Poems 4, 24, 25, 41, 48.

SUOMELA, a tract equated in Poem 18 with Väinämöinen's farm (*Väinölä*), has been somehow adapted to the *Suomi* name; see Finland, above.

SUOVAKKO, an old woman in Poem 18 who is good at interpreting omens. The name would seem to be based on the participial adjective *suova* 'ungrudging, willing' (inf. *suoda*) with the suffix *-kko* used to form names of living things, and thus here designates an ungrudging, obliging person.

SWEDEN (*Ruotsi*) is mentioned in Poem 20 and conceivably includes Finland as part of territorial Sweden before 1809; the Karelians of a century and more ago at times referred to Finns as *ruotsit* 'Swedes.' The Finnish name *Ruotsi*, earlier *Rootsi*, is primarily based on the word element occurring in Old Swedish *rōth(r)s* 'rowing,' found in Old Swedish *rōthsmæn, rōthskarlar* 'rowers, seafarers' and in the name of Roslagen, the coastal area of Uppland, Sweden, once an important recruiting center for Viking crews and colonists; from this came the Finnish national name *Rootsi* as if "rowers' district." From non-Finnish quarters this same name became attached to the Swedish Varangian founders of Novgorod (q.v.), who were called *Rus*, whence later latinized Russia 'land of the Rus.'

SWEETIE (*Mairikki*), cow name in Poem 32, is based on *mairea* 'sweet, lovely' adapted to the suffix *-kki* (see Ainikki, above).

TALLINN (*Tanikan linna*, literally 'Tanikka's stronghold'), also formerly known as German, Swedish Revel, Russian Reval, Finnish Rääveli (Swedish *revel* 'sandbank, sandspit'), seaport and capital of Estonia (Estonian *Tallinn*) mentioned in Poem 25, was first founded by Danish vikings in the twelfth century as a stronghold, *Danaborg* 'Danes' stronghold.' The latter name was later partially Estonianized with older Estonian (*Taani*)*linn* 'Denmark's stronghold' for Old Norse *borg*, with *Taani*, assimilated from the gen. pl. *Dana*. So much for the Tallinn name. In the *Tanikan linna* of the *Kalevala*, the element *linna* is clearly the same as *-linn* in Tallinn, but *Tanikka* is not obvious nor can it have anything to do with Finnish *tanikka* in *jalantanikissa* 'on foot' or *tanakka* 'stocky, sturdily built.' One might think of it as a reduction of *Tanimerkki* 'Denmark' of the singing tradition, where this very name gets distorted to *Tasa-Martti* 'smooth, level Martin' (!).

TAPIO, a woodland deity presiding over the forest game, is mentioned in Poems 14, 32, 41, 48. The base of the name is presumably the same as Estonian *taba* 'bolt, lock' with the suffix *-io* used in forming the names of beings, as *rautio* 'worker in iron, blacksmith' from *rauta* 'iron,' and thus originally designating a person occupied with traps or snares for catching game. Were there any reason to suppose that the singers felt such a connection or meaning, it would be tempting to render the name "lord of the chase" or the like.

TAPIO RISE (*Tapiomäki*) is in Poem 50 the site of the horseshed in which Marjatta bears her boy. Here as elsewhere *mäki* 'hill' often implies only a very slight rise in the ground, just enough, say, to provide adequate drainage.

TAPIO'S DOMAIN (*Tapiola*) refers to the forest in general where game is to be had, and is virtually synonymous with Woodland (*Metsola*); it is made up of *Tapio*, above, with the habitative suffix *-la*, and occurs in Poems 14, 15, 20, 32, 41, 46.

TEENIE (*Pienikki*), a cow name based on *pieni* 'little, small' with the suffix *-kki* common in cow names, occurs in Poem 32.

TELLERVO, Tapio's daughter (also known as "Wind Spirit,") and handmaiden and once referred to as his wife, is a forest deity, perhaps deliberately created in imitation of *Pellervo(inen)* 'Spirit of Arable' who in the singing tradition is mentioned as Tapio's son; the name occurs in Poems 14, 32, 46.

THUNDERER (*Pauanne*), by-name of Ukko in Poems 18, 45, is made up of the element *pau(h)a-* found in *pauhua*, *pauhu* 'noise of thunder,' *pauhuta* 'to thunder,' and the suffix *-nne* (gen. *-nteen*), commonly used to form nature names, as *alanne* (*alanteen*) 'low-lying place.' For a different analysis of this name, using Lappish material, see Haavio, pp. 99–100.

TURSAS, friendly water-spirit who helps Väinämöinen in the first sowing of this earth, is mentioned in Poem 2. The name looks back to Old Norse *thurs* (Anglo-Saxon *thyrs*) 'giant, monster' and is a variant of the very different Turso, below.

TURSO, always with the prefixed epithet *Iku-* 'eternal' and usually referred to as "son of the Old Man" (*Äijön poika*), is, in contrast to Tursas, above, a malefic water spirit evoked by Louhi in Poem 42 to retrieve the Sampo from Väinämöinen. The name is etymologically a variant of Tursas, above.

TUURI, based on the name of the Old Norse god Thor, is a divinity casually mentioned in Poems 15, 47, with the epithet "Worshipful One," q.v.

TYRJÄ'S RAPIDS (*Tyrjän koski*), a fictional river, in form perhaps slightly influenced by the Biblical sea, Tiberias, the Sea of Galilee, is mentioned in Poem 9.

UKKO, with Lönnrot's 1849 epithet *ylijumala* 'god on high' for *pilvenpäällinen* 'above the clouds' of the variants, also "Thunderer," is the ancient

Finnish thunder-god and chief and most frequently evoked deity in the *Kalevala;* he is the god of all the elements and answers closely to Thor of Scandinavian mythology. The name is identical with *ukko* 'old man,' while the diminutive *ukkonen* is the common Finnish word for thunder. Ukko is mentioned in Poems 1, 9, 12, 14, 17–19, 26, 28, 32, 33, 36, 40, 42, 43, 45, 47, 48.

UNTAMO: (1) A spirit of sleep in Poem 5 and utilized by Lönnrot in Poem 26 as the name of the owner of some wolves, this is apparently based on some derivative of *uni* 'sleep' with the suffix *-mo* used in forming the name of living beings; (2) with the diminutive *Untamoinen* and the truncated form *Unto* he is Kalervo's brother with whom he feuds and on whom Kullervo, his nephew, ultimately wreaks vengeance, mentioned in Poems 31, 34–36. Neither of these appears to be associated with the Untamo implied in Untamola (1), below.

UNTAMO'S FARM (*Untamola*) is (1) in Poem 15 a farm with which Soppy Hat is exceptionally associated; (2) with the variant *Untola* the farm of Untamo of Poems 31, 36. The farm name is made up of the truncated *Unto* and the habitative terminal *-la.*

VÄINÄMÖINEN, a diminutive of Väinämö (not in the *Kalevala*), also a truncated form Väinö, common today as a man's name, is the chief of the Big Three along with Ilmarinen and Lemminkäinen. His main epithets are "old" (*vanha*) and "steadfast old" (*vaka vanha*), and he is conceived as being old even at birth. He is an "eternal sage" and a supernaturally gifted singer and player of the harp (*kantele*), rather like Orpheus; he is consistently unsuccessful in getting a wife.

The base of the name is *väinä*, a near-synonym of *suvanto* 'slack water' (see Slack Water Farm, above), with the *-mö* suffix (see Untamo, above) and the diminutive ending *-inen*. Väinämöinen means in effect 'man of Slack Water Farm' and might well be so rendered if tradition did not cry out against any tampering with the famous name. He appears in Poems 1–4, 6, 8–10, 16–21, 25, 35–50. For a comprehensive study see Martti Haavio, *Väinämöinen, Eternal Sage*, Helsinki: Finnish Academy of Sciences, 1952 (Folklore Fellows Communications No. 144).

VÄINÄMÖINEN'S DISTRICT, FARM (*Väinölä*), mentioned in Poems 3, 5–8, 10, 18, 37, 39, 45–47, 49, at times seems to mean specifically "Väinämöinen's farm" and thus is much the same as Slack Water Farm (*Suvantola*), at times may be conceived in a more extended way as not very different from the Kaleva District (*Kalevala*).

VEIN SPIRIT (*Suonetar*), personification of *suoni* 'vein, sinew' with the feminine suffix *-tar*, is evoked to help suture ruptured veins in the vein charm of Poem 15.

VELLAMO, female water deity and spouse of Ahto, is based on the verbal root *velloa* 'to splash' with the suffix *-mo* (see Untamo, above) and occurs in Poems 5, 42, 44, 48. The name, if not the significance or identification, is familiar to many visitors to Finland and to countless Finns who have traveled from Stockholm to Turku (Åbo) by a steamer of this name.

VIPUNEN, with a first name Antero and quite likely based on *vipu* 'snare, trap,' is pictured as a mythical giant long since dead but still immensely learned in magic spells; his *Kalevala* epithets are "well-stocked (with charms)" (*varaväkevä*), "of great knowledge of magic" (*mahtipontinen*), and "skilled in (magic) songs" (*virsikäs*), epithets which may to some extent reflect Lönnrot's mishearing of certain formulas; see Turunen s.v. *varaväkevä* ad fin. The name occurs in Poems 1, 17.

VIROKANNAS of Poems 20, 50, is, as Haavio (pp. 249–257) has convincingly shown, originally a Middle Low German name made up of *wî-rôk* 'incense' (German *Weihrauch*) and Hannes, a common reduction from Johannes, and hence meaning "Incense John"; this would be a most suitable rendering were there any likelihood that latter-day singers understood what the name meant. In Poem 50 this sacerdotal name is perhaps to be associated with John the Baptist. In Poem 20 his priestly function is less clear, but his abortive attempt to knock out the big steer may well look back to some sacrificial act.

VUOKSI is the great watercourse in eastern Finland, running from Saimaa to Lake Ladóga, in which are the famous Imatra rapids (q.v.). Formally identical with *vuoksi* 'tide, flood, flow of water,' it means "the flowing one," and occurs in Poems 17, 30.

WASTE LAND (*Ulappala*), in Poem 45 in effect equivalent to Death's Domain, is based on *ulappa* 'open sea,' then here by extension "flat, open, desolate tract" with the habitative terminal *-la*.

WAVE SPIRIT (*Aallotar*), personification of *aalto* (gen. *aallon*) 'wave, billow' with the feminine suffix *-tar*, is mentioned in Poem 48.

WHORTLEBERRY (*Puolukka*), cow name identical with the name of the red whortleberry (*Vaccinium rubus* type), occurs in Poem 11.

WINDBLAST (*Puhuri*), personification of a severe gale and conceived as the father of Jack Frost (*Pakkanen*), is mentioned in Poem 30. The name is formed on the root *puhu-* 'blow' familiar in *puhua* 'to speak' and *puhaltaa* 'to blow' with the agent suffix *-ri*, and means "blower, blaster."

WIND SPIRIT (*Tuulikki*), Tapio's daughter, usually called Tellervo, is mentioned in Poem 14. The name is made up of *tuuli* 'wind' and the suffix *-kki* (see Ainikki).

WOAD SPIRIT (*Sinetär*), personification of *sini* 'blue, the color blue' with the feminine suffix *-tär*, symbolizes the woad plant (*Isatis tinctoria*) whose leaves with the essential indigotin, identical with that in indigo, yield a blue dye. This spirit is mentioned in Poem 27 in connection with dyeing cloth.

WOODLAND (*Metsola*), identical with Tapio's domain (*Tapiola*), is made up of *metso*, diminutive variant of *metsä* 'forest,' and the habitative terminal *-la*, and is mentioned in Poems 14, 15, 20, 32, 41, 46.

WORSHIPFUL ONE (*Palvoinen*), epithet-name of Tuuri (Poems 15, 47) and of Virokannas (Poem 20), is based on *palvoa* 'to adore, worship' with the adjectival suffix *-inen*.

C. REFERENCE LIST
OF FINNISH NAMES

The following is a cross-reference list between all proper names used in Lönnrot's *Kalevala* and their counterparts in the translation and glossary above. Where the Finnish name, e.g., *Ahti*, is retained in the translation, it is merely repeated here; where the name has been translated, the translation follows the Finnish word. That the reader may readily see which *Kalevala*-names are in use as personal names today, I have given in parentheses after each such name the name-day of the official Finnish calendar of personal names according to Kustaa Vilkuna, *Oma nimi ja lapsen nimi* (Helsinki, 1959). Where today only a derivative of a *Kalevala*-name is in use I have given this together with its name-day in brackets. I have put an asterisk before those names which Vilkuna lists (p. 20) as having come into use directly from the *Kalevala*.

Aallotar: Wave Spirit
*Ahti (*June* 21)
Ahti Saarelainen: Island-Ahti
Ahto (*June* 21)
Ahtola: Ahto's realm
Ahtolaiset: *see* Ahto's realm
Ainikki (*May* 10)
Aino (*May* 10), Ainonen
Alue
Annikki (*Dec.* 9)
Antero (*Nov.* 30)

Etelätär: Southwind Spirit

Hermikki: Stringy
Hiisi: Demon
Hiitola: Demon's domain
Hongatar: Evergreen Spirit
Hornan kallio: Goblin's Crag
Hälläpyörä: Hällä-whirlpool
Häme

Iku-Turso: *see* Turso
Ilma: Ilmarinen's farm
Ilmarinen, *Ilmari (*Jan.* 16)
Ilmarisen emäntä: Ilmarinen's lady
Ilmatar (*Aug.* 8): Air Spirit
Ilpotar [cf. Ilpo (*April* 28)]: Ilpo's daughter

Imatra
Inkeri: Ingria

Jalo Synty: Great Birth
Joukahainen, *Jouko (*Dec.* 14)
Joukola: Joukahainen's farm
Jumala: God
Jumaliset: Devout Ones
Juortan
Juotikki: Drinker

Kaatrakoski: Loon Rapids
*Kalervo (*Nov.* 3)
Kaleva (*Oct.* 9)
Kalevala: Kaleva District
Kalevalaiset: *see* Kaleva District
Kalma: Grave Spirit
Kammo: Dread One
Kankahatar: Fabric Spirit
Katajatar: Juniper Spirit
Karjala: Karelia
Karjos: Brandle; *see* Brindle
*Kauko (*March* 3): *see* Man with a far-roving mind
Kaukolainen: Man of Faraway Farm
Kaukomieli, Kau'ut: Man with a far-roving mind
Kaukoniemi: Faraway Headland
Kauppi (*July* 25)

407

Keitolainen: Evil Elf
Kemijoki: Kemi
*Kimmo: Frisky
Kipumäki: Pain Hill
Kiputyttö: Pain Girl
Kipuvuori: Pain Mountain
Kirjas: Brandle; see Brindle
Kirjos: Brindle
Kivi-Kimmo (Kimmo, Aug. 2): Dread
  Rock Spirit
Kivutar: Pain Spirit
Koijumala: Dawn God
Kova Ilma: Sharp Air
Kuippana
Kukkalainen [cf. Kukka (May 13)]:
  Little Flower
*Kullervo, Kullervoinen (Sept. 25)
Kuu: Moon
Kuura: Hoarfrosty
Kuutola: Moon's abode
Kuutar: Moon Spirit
*Kyllikki, Kylli (Dec. 8)
Kynsikoski: Claw Rapids
Kyyttä: Backstripe

Lappalainen: Lapp, Lappish
Lappi: Lapland
Lemmenlahti: Lovers' Bay
Lemminkäinen
Lemminkäisen äiti: Lemminkäinen's
  mother
Lempi (Nov. 24)
Lempo: Devil
Lokka
Louhi
Loviatar
Luoja: Creator
Luonnotar: Spirit of Nature
Luotola
Lyylikki [cf. Lyyli (May 23)]

Maikikki [cf. Maire (Aug. 1)]
Manala: Abode of the Dead
Mansikki: Strawberry
Marjatta, Marjattainen (Aug. 15)
Merkki: Spots
Metsola: Woodland
*Mielikki (Sept. 23): Darling
Musti: Blackie (1)
Muurikki, Muurikkinen: Blackie (2)
Märkähattu: Soppy Hat

Neva
*Nyyrikki (Jan. 15)
Nälkäniemi: Starvation Headland

Omena: Apple
*Osmo (May 11), Osmoinen

Osmola: Osmo District
Osmotar: Osmo's (female) descendant
Otavatar: Spirit of the Great Bear

Pakkanen: Jack Frost
Palvoinen: Worshipful One
Pauanne: Thunderer
Pellervoinen [cf. *Pellervo (Feb. 4)]:
  Spirit of Arable
Penkeri: see Ingria
Pienikki: Teenie
Pihlajatar: Rowan Spirit
Piltti: Lassie
Pisamäki: Pisa Hill
Pohjan, Pohjolan neiti: Maid of North
  Farm
Pohjola, Pohja: North Farm
Pohjolan isäntä: Master of North Farm
Puhuri: Windblast
Puolukka: Whortleberry
Päivä [cf. Päivi (June 16)], Päivyt: Sun
Päivälä: Sun's abode
Päivätär, Päivän tytär: Sun Spirit
Pänkeri: see Ingria

Remunen
Ruotsi: Sweden
Ruotuksen emäntä: Ruotus' lady
Ruotus
Rutja: Finnmark

Saari: The Island
Saksa: German, Germany
*Sampo (April 3), Sammut
*Sampsa (Dec. 7)
Saraja
Sariola, Saran talo: Sedgy Farm
Savo
Simasalo: Honey-fragrant Island
Sinetär: Woad Spirit
Suolasalmi: Öresund
Suomela
Suomi, Suomenmaa: Finland
Suovakko
Surma: Death
Suuri Mies: Great Man
Suvantola: Slack Water Farm
Suvantolainen: Man of Slack Water
  Farm
Suvetar [cf. Suvi (June 7)]: Summer
  Spirit
Synty: see Great, Profound Birth
Syvä Synty: Profound Birth
Syötikki: Eater

Tanikan linna: Tallinn
*Tapio (June 18)
Tapiola: Tapio's domain

Tapiomäki: Tapio Rise
Tellervo (*April* 13)
Terhenetär [cf. *Terhi (*Feb.* 2)]: Fog
    Spirit
Terhen-neiti: Fog Maiden
Tiehyt: Road
Tiera, Tieranen: Snowfoot
Tuometar [cf. Tuomi (*April* 14)]:
    Chokecherry Spirit
Tuomivaara: Chokecherry Hill
Tuonela: Death's Domain
Tuonen tyttö: Death's maiden
Tuonetar: Death's daughter
Tuoni: Death
Tuorikki: Freshness
Turja: Finnmark
Turjalainen: of Finnmark, a Finnmark
    Lapp
Tursas
Turso
Tuulikki (*Feb.* 22): Wind Spirit
Tuuri
Tyrjänkoski: Tyrjä's Rapids
Tähetär: Star Spirit

Tähtelä: Star's abode
Tähti: Star

Ukko (*April* 4)
Ulappa: Waste Land
*Untamo, *Unto (*Aug.* 5)
Untamola: Untamo's farm
Ututyttö: Mist Girl
Uusilinna: Novgorod
U'utar: Mist Spirit

Vammatar: Spirit of Injuries
*Vellamo (*Dec.* 3)
Vennon joutio: Lazybones
Venäe: Russia
Viena: Dvina
Vipunen
Viro: Estonia
Virokannas
Vuoksi
Väinämöinen, *Väinö (*Feb.* 17)
Väinölä: Väinämöinen's district

Äijö: Old Man

D. LIST OF CHARMS, IN ORDER OF OCCURRENCE

E. CORRIGENDA

The emendations listed below are designed to make this translation consistent with my translations in *The Old Kalevala and Certain Antecedents* (Harvard University Press, 1969). They are cited by poem and line number. A few of the alterations are simple corrections of errors. Most are made in order to render recurring Finnish words or groups of words by exactly the same English words, to bring out the frequent repetitions of phraseology on the part of the native singer which are of the very nature of narrative oral poetry. Properly to render these verbal or phraseological echoes within one poem of any considerable length is taxing enough on a translator; to strive for this verbal consistency through three long poems and the scattering of verse in von Becker's essay and Lönnrot's dissertation is as difficult as striving for such consistency in rendering, say, the *Iliad* and the *Odyssey*, and the chances of inconsistencies on the translator's part are very great. It is hoped that the following emendations will serve to bring the earlier translation substantially into agreement with those in the companion volume.

2:28, *for* in *read* on
2:30, *for* flooded *read* boggy
3:184, *for* power *read* measure
3:283, *read* Then Väinämöinen got angry,
3:298, *read* solid boulders split,
3:523, *for* defense *read* protector
4:7, *for* gathered *read* plucked
4:45f, *read* This, father mine, I am weeping about, This I am weeping and complaining about:/The cross dropped from my breast, the ornament dropped from my belt,
5:115, *for* wash *read* wipe
6:30, *for* ornaments *read* decorates
6:145, *for* drew *read* took
6:186, *for* went *read* plunged
8:95, *for* cleave a swan *read* split a horsehair
8:100, *for* cleaves a swan *read* splits the horsehair
9:62, 64, 66, *for* was *read* is
9:72, *for* got *read* grew
9:211, *read* as steel-tempering venoms,
9:233, *for* looked *read* looked down

9:279, *for* tall *read* fine
9:377, *for* just the same *read* then
9:490, *read* from producing salves,
9:527, *read* to hurt stones,
9:548, *for* already *read* now
10:13, *read* He clatters along,
10:34, *for* leaves *read* needles
10:166, *read* cold spring wind, get him
10:200, *delete* these
10:99, 257, *for* payment *read* reward
10:100, 258, *for* work *read* labor
10:412, *for* spiritedly *read* quickly
11:4 *for* reckless *here and elsewhere read* restless
12:193, *for* a *read* the
12:333, *for* rang out *read* made a ringing sound
12:413–414, *read* Farm was moving about where
14:61, *for* Perhaps *read* Probably
14:175, *for* to *read* more to
14:267, *delete* already
14:448–449, *read* Like a flash he cut / the man into
15:104, *for* choice reindeer *read* lions

15:197, *for* craftsman's *read* craftsmen's
15:223–226, *read* That sun, God's creation, sun created by the Creator, / . . . birch branch, winged its way to the bend in an alder branch.
16:115, *read* he lacked three charms
16:143, *delete* whole
17:142, *read* pounds away quickly;
17:150, *delete* are you
17:329, *for* heel *read* heel-cord
17:564, *for* he sang *read* recited
18:75, *for* stony island *read* rocky skerry
18:76, *for* rotten stump *read* branch fallen
18:152, *for* a pup *read* the pups
18:263, *for* bow *read* stern
18:309, 310, *for* the *read* one
18:534, *for* mumbling *read* talking like a fool
19:226, *for* one *read* pike
19:266, *for* bird of prey *read* griffin
19:334, *for* stomach *read* belly
19:336, *for* tasted the stomach *read* tried the taste
20:75–80, *for* from *read* in
20:182, *for* could *read* did
20:206, 276, 340, *for* hands *read* of them
20:230, *for* distance in between *read* intervening distance
20:241, *for* looked for *read* broke off
20:295, *read* It ran a long way quickly,
20:296, *for* quickly roved *read* roved quickly
20:303, 304, *for* in *read* on
21:42, *for* ravenous *read* ravening
21:155, *for* kind *read* kinds
21:162, *for* doorjamb *read* lintel
21:241, *for* stoups *read* a stoup
21:247, *for* stoups *read* stoup
21:366, *for* threw himself into *read* set upon
22:1, *for* had drunk plenty *read* had been celebrated sufficiently
22:2, *for* the *read* that
22:154, *for* joyfully *read* happily
22:159, *for* anxiously *read* with anxiety
22:348, 388, *for* bitter water *read* tears of yearning
22:522, *for* coins *read* pieces
23:92, *for* by *read* on
23:149, *for* shed *read* sheds
23:339–342, *read* rinse out the bowls, remember the lips, the spoons, remember the handles. / Keep count of the spoons, keep . . .
23:395, *for* Brew *read* Boil
24:363–364, *read* . . . from here, so to speak, from this . . .
25:34, *for* prow *read* front

25:101, *read* Now I see this without asking,
25:173, *for* spun right *read* kept spinning
25:222, *read* neither before nor yesterday
25:486, *for* lovely *read* watery
25:568, *delete* engaged
25:617–618, *read* From yonder was got the maid of honor, from yonder the happy choice fetched
25:627–28, *read* Thence was got the maid of honor, thence the happy choice fetched.
25:683, *for* singer's *read* bard's
25:689, *delete* here
26:22, *for* set *read* sets
26:28, *for* put *read* set
26:29, 37, *for* person *read* man
26:30, 38, *for* man *read* one
26:39, *delete* she was
26:40, *for* to get *read* getting
26:137, 208, *for* something *read* a means
26:237, *for* In *read* On
26:281, *for* are *read* will be
26:284, *for* they have drunk *read* drinking
26:358, *delete* him
26:475, *for* ahead *read* on
26:521, 533, *for* northwest *read* southwest
26:529, 541, *for* on *read* for
26:635, *for* dead *read* withered
27:73, *delete* my
27:79, *for* bread is *read* loaves are
27:131, *for* the spoons *read* a spoon
27:132, *for* the wooden ladles *read* a wooden ladle
27:185, *delete* me
27:204, *delete* had
27:308, *for* yours *read* you
27:382, *for* stalk *read* root
28:145–146, 149–150, 153–154, *for* their *read* the
28:171, *for* as you should *read* right
28:172, *for* lived *read* living
28:202, *read* is cropped . . .
28:280, *for* there *read* yonder
29:31, *for* sat *read* sits
29:41, *for* uninhabited *read* unsettled
29:42, *for* unknown *read* uninhabited
29:128, *for* a piece of land *read* space
30:260, *for* there *read* here?
30:282, *for* Demon's *read* Devil's
30:408, *for* Guardian of the Grave *read* Grave Spirit
30:427, *for* will *read* well
31:311f, *read* . . . pines as palings just as they were, / whole tall firs he sets up as posts;

32:60, *for* cattle *read* cows
32:146, *for* their *read* the
32:207, *for* splendid *read* fine
32:226, *for* ever full *read* brimful
32:235, *read* so that the cattle may get fine-looking,
32:236, *read* the mistress' cows flourish
32:315, *for* Bear *read* Bruin
32:323, 491, *read* during this lovely summer,
32:324, *read* warm summer of the Creator.
32:347, *for* tinkle *read* sound
32:415, *for* we make *read* we will make
32:485, *for* the *read* even the
32:544, *for* craftsman *read* smith
33:207, *delete* all
36:292, *for* maidens *read* girls
36:293, *for* green *read* hazy blue
36:294, *for* Tapio's *read* the
37:63–64, *read* That craftsman Ilmarinen started to work the bellows.
37:67, *for* of the *read* of his
38:195, *for* hair's *read* hare's
38:301, *for* spoke *read* said
39:11ff, *read* . . . North Farm, from dark Sedgy Farm. / The Sampo has been taken there, the lid of many colors carried / to North Farm's hill of rock, to . . .
39:34, 42, 43, *for* steadier *read* safer
39:38, *delete* would
39:44, *delete* besides
39:164, *delete* are you
39:195, *read* world, too,
39:198, *for* in my *read* on the
39:252, *read* all my brother boats,
39:253, *for* run *read* ran
39:254, *for* aided *read* if aided
39:417, *for* rick *read* pole
40:235, *for* frame *read* body
40:263, *for* music *read* making of music
40:338, *for* clang *read* ring
41:32, *read* nor in the forest was there that thing
41:33, *delete* about
41:69, *for* listen to *read* hear
41:136, *for* water lily *read* lilypad
41:198, 199, *for* jowl *read* jowls

42:151, *for* took *read* brought
43:111–112, *read* these he drops into the sea   over his left shoulder.
43:254, *read* a thousand fellows from the tail.
43:356, *delete* further
44:27, *for* in *read* among
44:28, *delete* among
44:143–144, *read* always changes   my
44:181, *for* pegs *read* the pegs
44:182, *for* screws *read* the screws
45, *transpose* 153–154 *and* 155–156, *capitalizing* She *instead of* during
45:247, *delete* you are
45:263, *for* hurt *read* torment
45:298, *for* summit *read* peak
46:48, *for* go to *read* go about in
46:49, *for* forest's girls *read* girls of the forest
46:50, *read* to the farmyards of the girls in hazy blue.
46:70, *for* you are *read* I am
46:109, *delete* any
46:110, *for* killed you *read* laid you low
46:111, *for* slipped *read* fell
46:195, *for* Tapio's *read* Tapio's horn
46:345, *for* yourself *read* oneself
46:465, *for* wilderness *read* backwoods
46:534, *for* lucky *read* real
46:591, *for* the skull *read* it
47:203, *for* was *read* had been
47:210, *read* to make flame sink
47:211, *delete* sink
48:163, *for* tree trunk *read* pine bole
48:227, *for* pike's *read* whitefish's
48:368, *for* quenched *read* subdued
49:216, *for* sleeping *read* mewing
49:307, 361, 407, *for* stone *read* rock
49:308, 362, 408, *for* rock *read* crag
49:377, *for* already *read* now
49:391, *delete* already
49:419–420, *read* Make your journey safe and sound,   your trip comfortably;
50:106, *for* climb after *read* go up a tree for
50:294, *delete* at least
50:324, *for* gave deep puffs *read* puffed
50:336, *for* manger *read* stall
50:430, *after* outsiders *add* just plain